Cultural Cognition and Psychopathology

Cultural Cognition
and Psychopathology

Edited by John F. Schumaker and Tony Ward

Westport, Connecticut
London

Library of Congress Cataloging-in-Publication Data

Cultural cognition and psychopathology / edited by John F. Schumaker
  and Tony Ward.
    p. cm.
  Includes bibliographical references and index.
  ISBN 0-275-96604-6 (alk. paper)
  1. Cultural psychiatry. 2. Cognition and culture.
I. Schumaker, John, F., 1949– II. Ward, Tony.
RC455.4.E8 C795 2001
616.89--dc21   00-022888

British Library Cataloguing in Publication Data is available.

Library of Congress Catalog Card Number: 00-022888
ISBN: 0-275-96604-6

First published in 2001

Praeger Publishers, 88 Post Road West, Westport, CT 06881
An imprint of Greenwood Publishing Group, Inc.
www.praeger.com

Printed in the United States of America

The paper used in this book complies with the
Permanent Paper Standard issued by the National
Information Standards Organization (Z39.48-1984).

10 9 8 7 6 5 4 3 2

Copyright Acknowledgment
Portions of chapter 15 previously appeared in T. Ward and T. Keenan (1999),
"Sexual Offenders' Implicit Theories," *Journal of Interpersonal Violence, 14,*
821–838. Copyright © 1999 by Sage Publications, Inc. Reprinted by permission
of Sage Publications, Inc.

To the memory of Jim Chamberlain,
My friend and mentor
JS

To my wife Claire,
With thanks and love
TW

Contents

Introduction   ix

Part I: Theoretical and Historical Perspectives   1

1. Culture, Cognition, and Psychological
    Individualism   3
    Tod Sloan

2. Cultural Cognition and Psychopathology:
    Anthropological Perspectives   17
    Harvey Whitehouse

3. Cultural Sources of Cognition   31
    Charles Nuckolls

Part II: Cultural Cognition and Specific Disorders   51

4. Cultural Cognition and Depression   53
    John F. Schumaker

5. The Cognitive Socialization of Stress and Anxiety   67
    Joseph Westermeyer and Eric Dieperink

6. The Role of Cultural Cognition in Substance
    Abuse and Alcoholism   81
    M. Dawn Terrell

7. Eating Disorders, Culture, and Cognition   95
    Myra Cooper

8.   Cognitive Enculturation and Sexual Abuse   107
     Gordon C. Nagayama Hall and Amber H. Phung

9.   Culture, Cognition, and Trauma: Crosscultural
     Evaluations   119
     Pittu Laungani

10. Cultural Risk Factors in Personality Disorders   145
     Joel Paris

11. Culture, Cognition, and Dissociative Identity
     Disorder   157
     Martin J. Dorahy

12. Culture, Cognition, and Schizophrenia   171
     Richard J. Siegert

Part III: Applications and Implications   191

13. Translating Cultural Observations Into
     Psychotherapy: A Functional Approach   193
     *Junko Tanaka-Matsumi, Douglas Y. Seiden,
     and Ka Nei Lam*

14. Culture and Cognitive Theory: Toward a
     Reformulation   213
     Jo Thakker and Russil Durrant

15. Toward a New Model of Symptom Formation:
     Implicit Theories and Sexual Offending   233
     Tony Ward and Thomas Keenan

16. Cultural Assumptions, Social Justice, and Mental
     Health: Challenging the Status Quo   251
     Isaac Prilleltensky

     Index   267

     About the Editors and Contributors   275

Introduction

John F. Schumaker

This book is an attempt to bring together the concepts of culture and cognition within the wider context of psychopathology. While it may seem obvious to some people that culture and cognition are important factors in the etiology of many forms of psychopathology, it is quite surprising how little has been done in terms of integrating these three areas into useful theoretical and treatment models. An analysis of the history of psychology explains in part why the field of psychology has been very slow to recognize and acknowledge the role of culture in normal as well as abnormal behavior.

The early history of psychology is full of mesmerizing psychoanalytic case studies that read like detective stories, and seem to reveal that individual psychodynamics, as they combine with primitive instinct, can provide a sufficient explanation for psychopathological patterns. As it would turn out, many of these case histories were contrived and embellished, giving a false impression of the power of intrapsychic and local situational factors. Freud himself viewed society in large part as a moral force that competed with, and demanded repression of, the instinctual drives of the individual. An overemphasis on instinctual motivation prevented him from realizing that the individual is shaped in many ways by culture, and that culture is far more than an obstacle with which the personal psyche must contend. Nonetheless, psychoanalytic models left a lasting impression that invited psychologists to limit their theoretical and treatment formulations to that of the individual. Even the so-called neo-Freudians, who began to speak of the "social being," did not really come to terms with the concept of culture.

The most obvious exception was Erich Fromm who understood that human behavior was primarily a cultural product, and that psychopathology could not be separated from cultural structures, and even cultural health. But by the 1950s, when Fromm's cultural models were being published, psychology became overtaken by behavioral psychology, which again located psychopathology at the level of the individual. The growing popularity of behaviorism saw psychopathology framed as behavior patterns that are shaped and maintained as individuals respond to reinforcement contingencies. Social learning theory was embraced by growing numbers of psychologists who realized that radical behaviorism was not a useful explanatory mechanism for most types of disorders. But here too, the social emphasis was not broad enough to include macroscopic cultural forces that impinge on members and create the wider foundation for mental disturbance.

The recent cognitive revolution in psychology has unfolded within the lengthy history of individualism. For the most part, specific cognitive models of psychopathology perpetuate the notion of human beings as isolated from an overarching cultural context. The cognitions that are deemed to underlie mental disturbance tend to be described as ones that are self-delivered by autonomous and socially disconnected individuals. It is not uncommon to find textbooks on the subject of cognitive clinical psychology that make no reference whatsoever to the concept of culture. The same is true of introductory textbooks in psychology. Research shows that only 3 percent of the material contained in these texts deals with culture or related issues (Bernal & Castro, 1994).

A recent survey of 106 accredited clinical psychology programs in the United States concluded that current training approaches fail to educate students on the topic of culture, and do not equip them to work in diverse cultural groups (Bernal & Castro, 1994). A different study revealed that a scant 6 percent of clinical psychology programs in the United States were involved in crosscultural research, with only a slightly higher percentage being involved with research related to minority mental health (Sayette & Mayne, 1990). It was also found that only 5 percent of student research projects contained variables related to cultural issues. Very few of the clinical graduates surveyed felt that their training was adequate to prepare them for work in a crosscultural context. Thus it is not surprising that the present structure of clinical psychology has led to criticisms of its being ethnocentric and monocultural. Kazarian and Evans (1998) observe that the prevailing orientation of clinical psychology encourages psychologists to employ psychotherapeutic strategies that foster "individual self-containment" (p. 18), which allows little room for cultural considerations. It is also the case that those who define themselves as cognitive psychologists often pay little or no attention to the cultural sources of cognition.

Sloan (1996) remarked that most psychologists today "view individuals as disconnected from their social, cultural, and economic contexts and seek solutions to human problems through scientistic schemes" (pp. 39–40). In this volume (chap. 1), Sloan observes that some contemporary cognitive psychologists are beginning to wake up to the sociocultural realities that are important determinants of all dimensions of human behavior. For the first time, writes Sloan, they are asking about the nature of culture, as well as the ways in which it mediates thoughts, beliefs, and consciousness patterns. He adds that, as the field of psychology begins to embrace the concept of culture, many individualistic theories and practices are presenting themselves as impediments to the advancement of our knowledge. Furthermore, they have come to operate like ideologies that have a life of their own, and that cannot be easily dismantled through critical analysis. Yet they will need to undergo considerable revision as we seek to come to terms with the concept of culture. Sloan makes the important point that a culturally informed psychology has the additional advantage of expanding our theoretical and treatment horizons in order that we can begin to address large-scale social problems that have been sorely neglected. Among these are poverty, racism, ethnic conflict, terrorism, world peace, sexism, overpopulation, migrant and refugee experiences, environmental preservation, and the mental health consequences of modernization.

The continuing challenge for psychology is to liberate itself from what Sarason (1981) called a misdirected asocial psychology of the individual organism. In Sarason's opinion, clinical psychology still battles to see beyond the "mammoth distraction" of the disturbed individual, a factor that has prevented psychotherapy strategies from maturing beyond their current fixation on individual cases. Sarason called on clinical psychologists to confront their crippling parochial perspectives, and to begin thinking in terms of wider cultural frameworks and circumstances. Among other things, this would allow the mental health profession to exert influence on social orders for the well-being of all people.

Recently, Marsella (1998) wrote about the need for psychologists to extend their horizons in order to recognize that much of human reality is culturally constructed.[1] While acknowledging that the cultural construction of reality does not exclude the input from a host of other determinants, Marsella makes it clear that culture is an essential and indispensable determinant of human behavior, one that cannot be ignored by those concerned with biological, psychological, or environmental variables, but rather must be integrated into all behavioral equations. He goes on to explain that the combined influence of culturally constituted representations and symbols yields shared bodies of cognition and affect which, in turn, produce cultural continuity across time. Cultural input into all levels of the cognition process means that cultural constructions play a key role in ontogenies, epistemologies, praxologies, cosmologies, ethoses, values, and behavior patterns. This bears considerable resemblance to Spiro's (1984) assessment of the role of culture in the formation of thought, belief, and emotion:

Thinking and feeling are often determined by culture. That is, we most often think by means of concepts comprising cultural propositions, and our emotions are often aroused by them; in short, many of our thoughts and emotions are culturally constituted. (p. 324)

In Spiro's analysis, culture is, first and foremost, a cognitive system that determines normative as well as descriptive propositions about the social and physical world. D'Andrade (1984) emphasizes the meaning systems that are generated by culture when he writes that "culture consists of learned systems of meaning, communicated by means of natural language and other symbol systems, having representational, directive, and affective functions, and capable of creating cultural entities and particular senses of reality" (p. 112). One could easily conceive of these "learned cultural entities" as the basic building blocks of cultural cognition, as well as the central blueprint for so-called individual cognition.

THE CULTURAL CONSTRUCTION OF COGNITION

Al-Issa (1995) made the provocative observation that twentieth-century psychologists "have been engaged in a futile search for disturbance originating *within* the individual, or *within* an abstraction called 'mind' or 'psyche,' or 'personality' " (p. 368). This failure can be traced once again to the fact that twentieth-century psychologists have been unable to locate culture as a central determinant of psychopathology. The ability of culture to elude psychologists, of course, is owing in part to the slippery nature of this concept, and the many ways in which it can be defined. Marsella (1998) defines culture in the following way:

Shared behavior that is socially transmitted. . . . Culture is represented externally in artifacts, roles, institutions, symbols, and activity contexts. Internally, culture is represented in beliefs, values, attitudes, consciousness patterns, and meanings. (p. 1282)

The definition provided by Lumsden and Wilson (1981) conveys some of the same aspects:

The sum total of mental constructs and behaviors, including the construction and employment of artifacts, transmitted from one generation to the next by social learning. (p. 47)

Both of the above definitions are correct in depicting culture as a *mental* process that is transmitted through social means. The learning of culture is the strongest of all human motivations (Hall, 1976). As members act upon this fundamental motivation they absorb the mental constructs and consciousness patterns that we can just as easily refer to as cognitions. In this regard, Spiro (1994) writes that culture generates a set of cognitions that serve to enculturate novice members. As part of this, they acquire cognitively salient personal beliefs. Thus Spiro is able to forge a conceptual link between personal cognition and the broader process of cognitive socialization. This approach paves the way for understanding individual cognition as derivations and interpretations of cultural cognition.

In their essay "Cultural Dimensions of Cognition," Serpell and Boykin (1994) give an excellent analysis and overview of the cultural origins of cognition. They argue that culture needs to be understood as a dynamic cognitive system that exerts a powerful shaping influence at all levels of behavior. Furthermore, they demonstrate that individual cognition tends to mirror very closely the wider patterns of cultural cognition. In their words, "the development of individual cognition can be construed as a process of appropriating the resources of the culture for the purpose of socially meaningful action" (p. 371).

Serpell and Boykin then specify some of the specific dimensions of cognition that are shaped by culture. One of these is the knowledge base employed by members to solve problems and deal with a variety of situations. This is a culturally transmitted pool of information and knowledge that enables members to order their thoughts and perception of both the world and themselves. Often this knowledge base is experienced by members as having universal veracity, but in actuality it has a strong degree of cultural bias.

Culture influences the structural organization of cognition. As Serpell and Boykin note, culture plays an active role in the construction of the cognitive architecture that leads to different patterns of cognition. This does not mean that culture generates an entirely predictable cognitive style, but rather that culture patterns the routines, meanings, possibilities, and constraints in which its members are invited to operate.

Culturally constituted value systems also operate to establish the design and content of cognition. Sometimes these are functional values that contribute to the productive capabilities of the culture. Alternatively, these can be broad overarching values that underlie belief systems and forge the directions in which reality is translated and coded.

The influence of culture on cognition can result in a wide range of orientations and conceptual schemes. Serpell and Boykin cite the example of contemporary Western culture wherein cognitive socialization inclines members to code reality in terms of materialism and the manipulation of objects. This contrasts with cognitive socialization strategies in other cultures that cause members to organize reality in nonmaterial ways that emphasize spiritual elements. Differences in cognitive enculturation bring about widely varying structures of the self as they emerge in different cultural contexts.

According to Shore (1991), enculturation is a conservative process that makes the human mind resistant to alternatives. In this regard, he views cultural cognition as the interface of the mind and the texts that exist in cultural space. The close association of culture and cognition dictate a high probability that conventional forms of cultural life will be incorporated by individual members. However, Shore qualifies this in saying that cultural cognition is not monolithic since cultural texts are vulnerable to a certain amount of subjective interpretation; some degree of variation will be apparent in terms of the method and content of these translations. Thus a variety of intrapersonal factors must be taken into account when addressing the issues of cultural learning and cultural cognition (Handwerker, 1991).

The concept of cultural cognition is foreign to most psychologists, even though for some time it has been part of the vocabulary of cognitive anthropologists.

Within psychology, research and theory that deal with the interface of culture and cognition have focused mostly on differences in cognitive abilities across cultures. Very little has been done in terms of comprehending psychopathology in relation to cognition that arises at the level of culture. D'Andrade's (1995) *The Development of Cognitive Anthropology* chronicles the history of the concept of cognition in the field of anthropology. A reading of his book reveals that, as with psychology, a good deal of emphasis in cognitive anthropology has been on cognitive abilities (e.g., memory, judgment, etc.). D'Andrade also chronicles the anthropological work, however, that has employed cultural cognition in order to understand personality, emotion, motivation, and relationships.

Some of this study has led cognitive anthropologists to explore phenomena directly or indirectly related to psychopathology. For instance, Levy (1984) developed the theory that culture can function to hypocognize emotion. This occurs when an emotion is underschematized, and only weakly represented in cultural patterns and models. Levy's work in Tahiti demonstrates that sadness is hypocognized in that culture, reflected in the absence of a clear word there to indicate sadness. Without an obvious cultural foundation for sadness, the result is that expressions of this emotion tend to be far less salient than in many other cultures. For example, in Tahitian culture, the loss of significant others has a relatively small emotional impact, and this loss is usually rectified quickly as the person finds a replacement partner.

This type of cognitive anthropology research has important implications for our understanding of mood disorders, as well as other forms of psychopathology that involve the emotions. It points out new directions for psychological research in a variety of areas. For instance, D'Andrade describes the secondary appraisal systems that enable culture to be an important mediator of emotion. Depending on the nature of secondary cultural appraisal, members might never become fully conscious of an emotion. D'Andrade gives the example of the Utka Eskimos who do not have the conscious experience of anger due to cognitive socialization patterns that leave unspecified this particular emotion. The Utka do not even have a word in their language to indicate anger, other than words that refer to immature behavior, or the behavior of foreigners. The absence of the conscious experience of anger among the Utka is reinforced by cultural cognitions that cause members to actively devalue actions that approximate anger.

Alternatively, cultural cognition can be organized in such a way that an emotion is given a great deal of cultural elaboration, and brought forward as an element of conscious experience. As an example, D'Andrade cites the Samoan hypercognized cultural complex known as *alofa,* which means *love,* but has extended cultural meanings that incorporate generous, forgiving, tranquil, empathetic, other-oriented, and rich in pity and compassion. Alofa differs in many ways from the Western cognitive cluster of *love,* which is experienced in relation to themes of possessiveness, arousal, idealization, intensity, and bodily expression.

Researchers and scholars in the field of cognitive anthropology have studied other processes that have implications for our eventual understanding of psychopathology. For instance, the cultural molding of emotion has been studied in relation to the concept of *internalization,* which refers to the mechanisms by which cultural representations are absorbed and incorporated by individual members. Spiro's (1987) work is especially interesting in that he specifies a number of levels of internalization, each one of which reflecting different degrees to which cultural beliefs and values are adopted by individuals. At the weakest level of internalization, members are acquainted with aspects of cultural representation, but are not necessarily inclined to embrace them. In some instances, factors may even intervene so that the individual rejects part or all of a cultural claim. Using the modern Western cultural ideal of beauty, for example, one could try to imagine a situation wherein a member does not internalize to any extent the cultural claim that one must be thin in order to be physically attractive. Logic would tell us that this low level of internalization would have implications for psychopathologies that relate to disordered eating.

Spiro writes that, at the other end of the internalization continuum, members internalize cultural claims and representations such that they become highly salient features of cognition. Additionally, members build on these representations by initiating relevant activity patterns and imbuing the representations with emotion. In terms of the above example, we could envisage a member who internalizes the "be thin" cultural suggestion to such an extent that it becomes a core element of her belief system, and she becomes charged with sufficient emotion to shift motivation toward the goal of becoming thin. Mental health professionals could increase their knowledge of eating disorders by looking more closely at the variables that determine differential levels of internalization of predisposing cultural claims. This is also true of many other types of psychopathology, which speaks once again to the need to bridge the knowledge that exists in different academic disciplines. An interdisciplinary venture, such as this multiauthored book, represents one of the best ways to take our formulations of psychopathology to a higher and more productive level. This is especially true if it can be accomplished in relation to a greater awareness of the cultural construction of the cognitions that establish the foundation for mental disturbance.

Although sociology has been largely overlooked by cognitive sciences that are monopolized by assumptions of cognitive individualism, recent years have seen a rejuvenated interest in the sociology of thinking. A useful history and overview of the development of cognitive sociology can be found in Eviatar Zerubavel's (1997) book *Social Mindscapes: An Invitation to Cognitive Sociology.* As a field, cognitive sociology is critical of radical cognitive individualism and the notion of solitary thinkers since these fail to convey that we are products of conventional *thought communities* that socialize the broader structures of cognition. Cognitive sociology is also critical of cognitive universalism, which is viewed as excessively focused on the search for the universal foundations of human cognition. Instead, the field strives toward an integrative model that views us as individuals whose cognitive worlds are shaped within particular social environments.

While not disregarding input from individuals, cognitive sociology stresses the importance of looking beyond the private experiences and idiosyncratic interpretations that can explain part of the cognition process. It is especially interested in the nonpersonal foundations of thought, and in the identification of commonalities that stem from shared patterns of cognitive socialization. In other words, it seeks to account for similarities in thought that are at least as important as the differences that can be observed between individuals. An effort is made to transcend subjectivity as the basis for understanding cognition, and to embrace methods that explain cognitive development in relation to the social construction of intersubjectivity. Ultimately, the exploration of cognitive cultures and subcultures can go further in explaining cognitive diversity than approaches that are restricted to individuals who are deemed to operate in isolation from surrounding cognitive traditions.

DiMaggio's (1997) essay "Culture and Cognition" spells out the ways in which sociology and psychology are converging toward the goal of a more accurate and comprehensive understanding of culture and cognition. He posits that sociologists are beginning to endorse more complex views of culture, in which culture has some degree of interaction with the individual. These new models, he claims, recognize that choice can play a strategic role in determining the extent to which members embrace and absorb cultural claims.

According to DiMaggio, psychology finds itself in a better position to develop more complex views of cognition that take account of cultural factors. One reason for this is psychology's successful rejection of behaviorism, which DiMaggio notes is largely irrelevant to culture. He also sees emerging signs that psychological research is more frequently considering cultural variables, and making reference to sociological topics such as crosscultural variations in cognition.

For DiMaggio, sociology and psychology are moving in a direction that can help to narrow the gap between external and subjective dimensions of culture. This is occurring despite the facts that the fit between the two disciplines is still poor, the bulk of psychological research is still irrelevant to sociology, and the orientation of most sociological study is still supra-individual in nature. Yet it is hoped that the future will see a growing amount of common ground that will permit an improved comprehension of culture's role in the cognition process.

ORGANIZATION AND CONTENT OF THIS VOLUME

This volume is divided into three parts. The first one, titled "Theoretical and Historical Perspectives," explores a number of general issues dealing with the concept of cultural cognition, including material explaining psychology's historical reluctance to appreciate the cultural origins of the cognitions that underlie psychopathology. Various theories of cultural cognition are discussed in a historical context, and there is also a detailed account of the specific cultural sources of cognition, which paves the way for an understanding of mental disturbance beyond the limited confines of the individual. Also in this section are anthropological perspectives on the relationship between cultural cognition and psychopathology.

Chapter 1, Tod Sloan's chapter, discusses the limitations of psychology's basic assumption of individualism in the wider context of new theoretical and philosophical perspectives that can shed new light on cultural aspects of cognition. While acknowledging that individualism is not entirely without redeeming features, he shows how it has caused cognitive psychologists to overlook key sociocultural realities that are involved in the mediation of consciousness, self, and personhood. More generally, Sloan explains that the assumption of individualism has prevented Western psychological theory from recognizing cultural processes at work in cognition, subjective experience, and psychopathology. After reviewing individualistic components of contemporary psychological thought and ideology, his chapter highlights the ways in which we need to reformulate the relationships between culture, cognition, and psychopathology. As part of this, Sloan argues that modern psychology must assign great significance to the issue of power as it plays a role in the manufacture of cultural cognition. He concludes by challenging the field of psychology to expand its theoretical and applied perspectives in order to contribute more toward social change and the serious global problems that face us today. This includes conceiving of many types of psychological disorders as manifestations of macroscopic sociocultural forces that impinge on community life and the lives of individual people.

In chapter 2, according to Harvey Whitehouse, both psychologists and anthropologists commonly distinguish two levels of explanation of human thought and behavior. One concerns causes internal to organisms (biological and psychological processes), and the other concerns causes external to organisms (sociocultural or, more generally, ecological processes). Theories of cultural cognition have tended to preserve rather than challenge this dichotomy, by focusing on how internal and external structures interact. Following a critical survey of anthropological perspectives on cultural cognition, Whitehouse argues that we need to go beyond interactionism, in the direction of a view of cognition as socioculturally constituted. He suggests that the activation and development of normal cognition and personality traits, as well as varieties of psychopathology, are most productively understood as outcomes of variable, socially regulated patterns of cultural transmission, encompassing processes that are located simultaneously within and among organisms.

Charles Nuckolls, in chapter 3, writes about the various interactions of cognition and culture, while providing an overview of experimental and observational evidence. The first interaction he considers is perception, and includes discussions of visual illusions and linguistic sound symbolism. Nuckolls also examines the cultural construction of reasoning and inference, with attention to moral thought and causal explanation. He next reviews the evidence for bodily based experiential schemas in language and reasoning. The rest of the chapter concerns the relationship between cognition and emotion. Nuckolls proposes a culturally informed theory that is then tested against ethnographic data, the first drawn from South India and the second from the diagnosis of personality disorders in American psychiatry.

Part II, "Cultural Cognition and Specific Disorders," contains chapters dealing with patterns of mental disturbance, including depression, anxiety, substance abuse, eating disorders, trauma, dissociative disorders, and schizophrenia. In each case, an attempt is made to expand existing etiological formulations by considering cultural components of underlying cognitive processes. In most cases, implications for treatment and future research are discussed. A number of the chapters incorporate material on crosscultural variations in the prevalence and manifestation of the disorder, which further enables a reformulation taking into account cultural inputs.

In chapter 4, John Schumaker develops a case for the etiology of clinical depression being closely related to predisposing patterns of cultural cognition that exist in contemporary Western culture. After summarizing research demonstrating that depression has increased dramatically over the past 50 years, he describes some non-Western cultures whose structures seem to immunize members from the experience of depression. Schumaker argues against the current diagnostic practice of cultural cleansing, which seeks to impose Western models of depression on non-Western expressions of psychopathology that should be understood in their own right. This chapter includes a section exploring the factors that increase cognitive vulnerability to depression among members of modern Western culture. Cognitive structuring of the so-called modern person is discussed in relation to the topics of constant change, infinite possibility, extremes of individualism, a dissolution of the commons, the commercialization of social relations, materialism, discontent related to artificial desire, and the increasing innerness of spirituality and transcendence. These and other cultural claims combine to create a situation of depression proneness in contemporary culture. However, the point is made that cognitive psychologists can improve their understanding of depression by recognizing pathological cognition that is socioculturally constituted. Schumaker outlines ways in which current psychotherapy approaches can be modified in order to incorporate cultural insights, and to intervene at the level of cultural cognition.

Joseph Westermeyer and Eric Dieperink begin chapter 5 by pointing out that, in and of itself, anxiety is not a symptom. Instead, it exists along a continuum from normal human experience at one end, to a terrifying state that results in maladaptation at the other. They go on to highlight the language differences that are involved in the expression of anxiety. A number of clinical presentations involving anxiety are culture related, or even culture bound, in nature, they claim. Westermeyer and Dieperink explore the relationships between alexithymia, anxiety, and culture, and in the process, a range of epidemiological, psychological, and clinical studies are reviewed. While considering the potential etiologies of cultural differences and similarities, the authors examine a variety of factors, including emotional responses to events, differences in levels of stress, culture as pathogen, culture as a preventive agent, and culturally sanctioned dissociation. Implications for psychotherapy are discussed, including those which are carried out in a cross-cultural context. Some case studies are presented to illustrate the ways in which an understanding of cultural influences can strengthen our current psychotherapeutic offerings.

Chapter 6 by M. Dawn Terrell explores the role of cultural cognitions in accounting for ethnocultural variations in patterns of substance use and abuse. An attempt is made to identify cognitions that may serve to protect some cultures from experiences of substance abuse or alcoholism, and to illuminate cognitions and circumstances that may predispose members of a culture to problematic substance use. She argues that culturally determined cognitions take the form of perceptions of mind-altering substances, norms concerning use of substances, and worldviews concerning appropriate solutions to substance abuse related problems. These comprise the cultural matrix for understanding an individual's experience of substance abuse and alcoholism. Such an understanding of the cultural matrix is critical for treating psychoactive substance abuse across cultures.

In chapter 7, Myra Cooper suggests a framework for linking eating disorders, culture, and cognition. Based on the available evidence, she suggests a preliminary synthesis between culture and cognition in eating disorders, which she argues may begin to help account for the differing incidence and prevalence of these disorders in different cultures. Cooper briefly summarizes the current evidence for cultural determinants of eating disorders, and then describes a basic "developmental" cognitive model of eating disorders, noting which aspects of cognition may be open to cultural influence. The author takes the main components of the model in turn and, by drawing on social cognition research, links their development in the individual to culturally determined beliefs. She also briefly examines cultural differences (current and historical) in the expression of eating disorders. Finally, in light of the synthesis suggested, Cooper discusses the usefulness of cognitive therapy in the treatment of eating disorders.

Chapter 8 by Gordon Hall and Amber Phung discusses the cultural influences that may affect one's cognitions about sexual abuse. The authors explain that sexual abuse in individualistic contexts is more likely to be determined by individual cognitions, whereas sexual abuse in collectivist contexts is likely to be determined by cognitions that are context-sensitive. While an individualist may make decisions about sexual abuse on an independent basis, a collectivist relies on authority figures and peers in such decisions. Both individual and contextual influences may determine the sexually aggressive behavior of persons who are exposed to individualist and collectivist cultures in a single context. Within a single cultural context, an individual's relative degree of individualism and collectivism, and his perceptions of the relative degree of individualism and collectivism of potential victims, may interact to create differing levels of risk for perpetration of sexual aggression.

Pittu Laungani begins chapter 9 with an overview of existing theory regarding susceptibility to trauma. A variety of personality, perceptual, affective, and cognitive factors are thought to influence trauma proneness. However, as Laungani observes, we often underestimate the role of culture in the trauma process. Culture shapes value systems, belief systems, attributional styles, and consciousness patterns, all of which can influence the likelihood that an event or experience will prove traumatic. Using examples from India for purposes of illustration, Laungani presents a conceptual model that can account for crosscultural variations in trauma proneness. Four interrelated factors are discussed in this regard. Existing along continua, these consist of (a) individualism and communalism, (b) cognitivism and emotionalism, (c) free will and determinism, and (d) materialism and spiritualism. According to Laungani, some events and experiences are universally recognized as traumatic, while others are specific to the cultures in which they are found. Cultural coping is also a factor that determines the ability of people to deal with potentially traumatic situations.

Joel Paris asserts in chapter 10 that personality disorders are shaped by a social and cultural context. This principle is supported by evidence that these diagnoses have a different prevalence in different societies, and that some disorders demonstrate cohort effects. Transitions from traditional to modern social structures, accompanied by social disintegration and rapid social change, could account for these phenomena. Paris writes that the main mechanisms of action would involve interference with family functioning, and with buffering from the social community.

In chapter 11, Martin Dorahy writes that through shared cognitions culture plays an important role in the development, phenomenology, and expression of psychopathology. He focuses specifically on the cultural factors that influence the manifestation of dissociative identity disorder (DID). The case is made that the development of DID is aided by cultural influences on dissociativity and by the nature of posttraumatic social support. In addition, Dorahy shows how culture impacts on the level of exposure to actual traumatic events, and shapes perceptions regarding the severity of emotive events. Through these and other characteristics, cultural elements combine with biological and psychological factors to influence the formation of DID.

Chapter 12 by Richard Siegert explains that schizophrenia is a major mental disorder that occurs globally and at fairly consistent rates. There are clear biological features of this disorder and also known neuropsychological deficits. The underlying cognitive mechanisms by which this disorder manifests itself in individuals from different cultures, however, seem much less clear. This chapter argues that in choosing which cognitive domains to focus on, schizophrenia researchers should use evolutionary psychology as a map. The central thesis is that to fully understand schizophrenia at a cognitive level we need to determine which cognitive modules that have evolved through natural selection are impaired in people with schizophrenia. Theory of mind is used to illustrate how this integration might provide promising new developments in understanding schizophrenia. At the same time, theory of mind is employed to demonstrate how careful attention to crosscultural differences is essential if this approach is to yield meaningful results.

Part III, "Applications and Implications," contains chapters highlighting ways in which the concept of cultural cognition can guide us toward more sophisticated theory, research, and treatment. It also includes a chapter that critically examines prevailing cultural assumptions in the context of social responsibility, social justice, and mental health problems related to oppressive conditions.

Junko Tanaka-Matsumi, Douglas Seiden, and Ka Nei Lam write in chapter 13 that psychotherapy is a social influence process by which a therapist performs a specific role to reduce a client's distress. The first stage in this process is typically an assessment interview, during which the therapist develops hypotheses regarding the client's presenting problems and their controlling variables. The authors present a conceptual framework for culturally informed assessment and therapy, and offer guidelines for conducting functional assessment in a crosscultural therapy situation. Their chapter expands on the Culturally Informed Functional Assessment (CIFA) interview and applies the CIFA's eight-step assessment to a more general practice of psychotherapy in multicultural contexts. The CIFA's eight steps include (1) assessment of cultural identity, (2) problem identification, (3) causal explanatory model elicitation, (4) functional assessment, (5) comparison and negotiation of the client's and therapist's explanatory models, (6) negotiation of treatment variables, (7) data collection procedures, and (8) discussion of treatment duration, course, and expected outcome.

Chapter 14 by Jo Thakker and Russil Durrant cites a growing body of research that elucidates the role of cultural factors in cognition. This, as well as available evidence for the crosscultural variability of psychopathology, provides rich lines of inquiry into the interrelationships between culture, cognition, and mental disorder. Thakker and Durrant provide a broad theoretical framework for understanding and exploring these relationships, which draws on some recent trends in the construction of cognitive theory. Specifically, the authors claim that an anti-individualist, domain-specific, and evolution-based approach to human cognition can provide an illuminating perspective on the relationships that occur between culture, cognition, and psychopathology. They illustrate the usefulness of this approach, drawing on the examples of phobia development and depression. A model of mental disorder is then presented that highlights the dynamic interrelationships between the multiple variables that need to be taken into account in the context of psychopathology. Thakker and Durrant argue for the need to emphasize the centrality of *context* as we strive toward a greater understanding of the nature of mental disorder.

In chapter 15, Tony Ward and Thomas Keenan argue that child molesters' cognitive distortions emerge from underlying culturally derived theories about the nature of their victims, the world, and themselves. These implicit theories function like scientific theories and are used to explain empirical regularities (e.g., other people's actions) and to make predictions about the world. The theories are relatively coherent and are constituted by a number of interlocking ideas and their component concepts and categories. Drawing on recent work in the cognitive distortions area, Ward and Keenan identify five core implicit theories. Each theory is described in detail and its relationship to cognitive distortions is discussed. Finally, the clinical and research implications of the implicit theory perspective are outlined.

In the final chapter, Isaac Prilleltensky writes about the cultural assumptions that exert an influence on social justice and mental health. He presents a model that views cultural assumptions as primary support mechanisms of the societal status quo, as well as the vehicles by which societal and psychological discourses are shaped. The actual content and design of cultural assumptions determine to a considerable degree the mental health status of members, as well as their chances of achieving social justice. For example, writes Prilleltensky, if our culturally constituted assumptions portray the good life as one of competition and personal achievement, we should not be surprised if the general social condition is marked by alienation, isolation, mindless consumption, and emotional detachment from others. He is especially concerned that existing cultural assumptions lead to distributive injustice as well as a variety of related psychological problems. The "spin doctors of globalization," as he terms them, have nearly erased the language of social justice from our contemporary vocabulary. The cultural themes of individualism, self-interest, and survival of the fittest have translated the problems of insufficient resources and poverty into a private matter. Prilleltensky observes that most Western nations are retreating from a model of social responsibility, which is having profoundly negative social and mental health effects on the poor. He writes that it is time for us to challenge current cultural assumptions, including the philosophy of individualism, in order to foster a process of conscientization. This entails a renewed awareness of the socioeconomic, cultural, political, and psychological circumstances that can generate oppressive conditions. As we seek new ways to promote social justice and wellness, we must extend our individual-based interventions to include strategies that are conducted at the level of community and society. By way of conclusion, Prilleltensky comments that psychology cannot afford to lose sight of predominant values and cultural assumptions since a number of these are destructive to mental health and the prospects of social justice.

NOTE

1. Some of the statements cited here by Marsella appeared in the first draft of his article and not in the final version.

REFERENCES

Al-Issa, I. (1995). The illusion of reality or the reality of illusion. *British Journal of Psychiatry, 166,* 368–373.

Bernal, M. E., & Castro, F. G. (1994). Are clinical psychologists prepared for service and research with ethnic minorities? *American Psychologist, 49,* 797–805.

D'Andrade, R. (1984). Cultural meaning systems. In R. A. Shweder & R. A. LeVine (Eds.), *Culture theory: Essays in mind, self, and emotion.* Cambridge, UK: Cambridge University Press.

D'Andrade, R. (1995). *The development of cognitive anthropology.* Cambridge, UK: Cambridge University Press.

DiMaggio, P. (1997). Culture and cognition. *Annual Review of Sociology, 23,* 263–287.

Hall, E. T. (1976). *Beyond culture.* Garden City, NY: Anchor/Doubleday.

Handwerker, W. P. (1991). Origins and evolution of culture. *American Anthropologist, 91,* 313–326.

Kazarian, S., & Evans, D. (1998). Introduction to cultural clinical psychology. In S. Kazarian & D. Evans (Eds.), *Cultural clinical psychology: Theory, research, and practice* (pp. 3–38). New York: Oxford University Press.

Levy, R. (1984). Emotion, knowing, and culture. In R. Shweder & R. A. LeVine (Eds.), *Cultural theory: Essays on mind, self, and emotion.* Cambridge, UK: Cambridge University Press.

Lumsden, C., & Wilson, E. O. (1981). Genes, mind, and behavior. Cambridge, MA: Harvard University Press.

Marsella, A. J. (1998). Toward a global community psychology. *American Psychologist, 53,* 1282–1291.

Sarason, S. B. (1981). An asocial psychology and a misdirected clinical psychology. *American Psychologist, 36,* 827–836.

Sayette, M. A., & Mayne, T. J. (1990). Survey of current clinical and research trends in clinical psychology. *American Psychologist, 45,* 1263–1266.

Serpell, R., & Boykin, A. W. (1994). Cultural dimensions of cognition: A multiplex dynamic system of constraints and possibilities. In R. J. Sternberg (Ed.), *Thinking and problem solving* (pp. 369–408). San Diego, CA: Academic Press.

Shore, B. (1991). Twice-born, once conceived: Meaning construction and cultural cognition. *American Psychologist, 93,* 9–27.

Sloan, T. (1996). Psychological research in developing countries. In S. Carr & J. Schumaker (Eds.), *Psychology and the developing world* (pp. 38–45). Westport, CT: Praeger.

Spiro, M. E. (1984). Reflections on cultural determinism and relativism. In R. A. Shweder & R. A. LeVine (Eds.), *Cultural theory: Essays on mind, self, and emotion.* Cambridge, UK: Cambridge University Press.

Spiro, M. E. (1987). Collective representation in religious symbol systems. In B. Kilborn & L. Langness (Eds.), *Culture and human nature.* Chicago: University of Chicago Press.

Spiro, M. E. (1994). *Culture and human nature.* Brunswick, NJ: Transaction Publishers.

Zerubavel, E. (1997). *Social mindscapes: An invitation to cognitive sociology.* Cambridge, MA: Harvard University Press.

PART I

Theoretical and Historical Perspectives

1

Culture, Cognition, and Psychological Individualism

Tod Sloan

Psychologists have struggled obsessively to present their discipline as a scientific, value-free enterprise unaffected by any biases stemming from its embeddedness in social and historical contexts. The public may have been fooled, but the field has in fact failed miserably in its attempt to transcend sociocultural conditioning. Perhaps the primary manifestation of this failure can be found in psychology's willingness to reproduce forms of individualism associated with industrial capitalism and liberal political philosophy. Another major example of failure that still merits attention, but that cannot be addressed here, is the field's adoption of research methods imported from the natural and physical sciences that are inherently inadequate to the understanding of subjective experience and that readily lend themselves to techniques for the exploitative control of populations.

Individualism is not inherently evil or perverse. Some aspects of individualism are not particularly problematic and actually represent cultural advances that have improved conditions for major sectors of society. For example, one certainly cannot complain about the contribution of liberal individualism to the growing global recognition of the rights and dignity of the individual. Modern scientific psychology, however, emerged in the late 1800s practicing a form of individualism that resulted from a patching together of contradictory elements of rationalism, empiricism, and materialism. This combination left the field with notions of mind and person as autonomous, self-contained, socially isolated, and disconnected from history.

Whether one considers the sort of individual consciousness described by Descartes or Locke, Hume or Kant, Helmholtz or Brentano, the focus is on an individual mind affected directly by its location in a body and only very indirectly, if at all, by its participation in society. Subsequent behaviorist emphases on the conditioning of the behavior of individual organisms by the immediate environment did little to undermine this basic focus on the individual as a separate object in the world. In general, behaviorist approaches effectively distracted psychological researchers from attending to the subjective experiences that would have evidenced the degree to which individual minds are understandable only in terms of sociocultural processes.

In the last few decades, researchers in cognitive psychology have begun to bump against the overlooked sociocultural realities that mediate self, consciousness, and personhood (which had never been forgotten in the sister disciplines of anthropology and sociology). They have been forced to ask, What in the world is culture anyway? and How are thought and culture connected (now that we have separated them so neatly)? Some interesting answers are emerging, but the field has a great deal of catching up to do just to get its concepts in order. Beyond that, much work is needed to assess the ramifications of these new perspectives for professional practice.

A curious contradiction thus drives a great deal of current work in cultural psychology. Unknowingly, psychology imported individualism into its theories and practices and thereby excluded culture as a constitutive element of the psyche. Now that it is obvious that culture must be taken into account, the field's individualistic theories and methods preclude a full appreciation of the culture/psyche complex. To complicate matters further, psychology itself has become a major player among the societal practices that shape modern individualities. As psychology's individualistic concepts of mind are translated into the institutional practices of schools, clinics, prisons, and factories, individual subjectivities increasingly mirror psychological theory and method. As Rose (1996, pp. 101–115) argues, psychological science functions as an "individualizing technology" by "disciplining difference," "inscribing identities," "materializing the mind," and "governing subjectivity." Thus as we confront our problems in living, including our psychological disorders, we cannot forget that psychological practices themselves shape the repertoires of modern persons.

In sum, individualism in Western psychological theory and practice prevents an adequate appreciation of the influences of sociocultural processes in cognition, subjective experience, and psychological disorders. In this chapter, I first review individualistic aspects of psychology and their ideological functions. I then demonstrate how the effects of such ideological occlusion of understanding can be overcome by rethinking the relations between culture, cognition, and psychopathology in terms of the interplay of culturally available discursive practices in everyday communication and action. In closing, I argue that to the extent that contemporary approaches in cultural psychology employ benign notions of culture that ignore ideological subjection and direct forms of exploitation and domination, they risk overlooking the forces that shape many manifestations of psychopathology. The consequences of this oversight are serious—not only for theory, but for practice; for the failure to take power relations into account can lead to practical responses (intervention, treatment, advocacy, etc.) that are considerably off track and therefore ultimately ineffective.

VARIETIES OF PSYCHOLOGICAL INDIVIDUALISM

How does Western individualism find expression in psychology? By artificially disentangling theory, method, and practice—for they are actually incredibly interwoven—it is possible to distinguish between different facets of psychological individualism.

Theoretical Individualism

Individualistic theories organize conceptual analyses around processes and structures within the individual or between a pregiven individual structure and the immediate social environment (e.g., family, peers). If culture, or society, is considered at all, it is taken into account only after the fact, added on as a categorical variable that mechanically interacts, or is regarded as a mediating influence, along with gender, age, and socioeconomic status. Most contemporary theoretical approaches (psychoanalysis, Piagetian theory, cognitive social psychology, existential-humanistic personality theory) by now have begun to build in a brief acknowledgement of the importance of considering sociocultural forces or factors beyond the individual level of analysis, although there are glaring exceptions (e.g., Power & Dalgleish, 1997). Similarly, sociological and behavioral perspectives that previously overlooked the role of individual agency and subjectivity in human action also have recently begun to correct for the opposite error by affirming a certain degree of agency and self-determination by individuals.

In numerous serious critiques, theoretical individualism has been linked fairly directly to social domination. For example, Sampson (1981) provides a powerful early critique of individualism in cognitive theory. He suggests that the conservative ideological functions of individualistic reductions give "primacy to the thinking and reasoning of the individual knower" (p. 730), and thereby excuse the social order for any systematic injustice and inequality that affect and heap blame on individuals for socially produced problems. From a Foucauldian angle, Henriques, Hollway, Urwin, Venn, and Walkerdine (1984) trace the detrimental impact of individualism in various applied subdisciplines of psychology. Prilleltensky (1994) also shows how pervasive individualism in contemporary psychological theory reproduces undesirable features of the societal status quo.

Methodological Individualism

Individualistic methods of investigation primarily assess relations between variables or characteristics at the level of the individual. They consider the individual's perceptions, judgments, attitudes, narratives, and patterns of action, and compare these to those of other individuals without regard for the life-historical, social, or cultural contexts from which all the foregoing derive their meanings. Individualistic methods reinforce theoretical individualism by documenting theorized relationships between aspects of individual personality and behavior (e.g., school performance and anxiety levels) without examining the construction of these individual-level aspects through sociohistorical processes (e.g., socioculturally determined forms of competition in the classroom and social-class affects on personal expectations).

Methodological individualism has been challenged by many alternative research methods that derive from feminist, social constructionist, poststructuralist, and critical theory perspectives. Many of these approaches may still appear to focus on the individual level of analysis in their case studies, but they often work explicitly against individualism by stressing the sociocultural mediation of discursive practices, narrative constructions, or subjectivity in general. The coming demise of acultural individualism in method may be further indicated by the fact that even mainstream social psychologists are hearing fervent calls from their peers to take culture deeply into account in their methods and theories (Fiske, Kitayama, Markus, & Nisbett, 1998).

Individualism in Practice

Most psychological practices focus on producing change at the level of the individual because the individual is defined, thanks to individualism, as the container of the problem. Individual counseling, psychotherapy, and psychopharmacological treatment are probably the most widespread examples of individualistic practice. Similarly, most psychological assessment techniques are inherently individualistic since they rely on input from individuals, even when the object of investigation is trans-individual, such as an organizational culture or climate. Group treatment modalities do not necessarily escape indictment as individualistic, for their usual aim is to bring about changes in individual behavior. In contrast, family systems interventions and some narrative therapy approaches explicitly aim to subvert individualism in treatment and often lead the charge to take sociocultural factors into account in psychological practice. The subdiscipline of community psychology also has been a major force in suggesting nonindividualistic forms of intervention (Marsella, 1998; Montero, 1994).

This triumvirate of individualism in psychological theory, method, and practice will be incredibly hard to overthrow both because the three modes (theory, method, and practice) reinforce each other, and because they in turn are still invigorated by Western individualism outside of psychology. Individualistic theory makes an individualistic research method look quite acceptable. Likewise, individualistic interventions seem appropriate in light of individualistic assessment techniques and the individualistic theories that inform them. Furthermore, the public demands such interventions because individuals have been taught to seek help individually. Since professional training puts its stamp of approval on individualistic theories, methods, and techniques, there is a tendency to look askance at proposals for nonindividualistic approaches. The latter simply do not sound or feel right because they do not fit with the dominant modes of conceiving human functioning.

It is in this context of hegemonic individualism in psychology that recent developments at the interface between cognitive psychology and cultural anthropology attain their importance. Put very simply, it has become glaringly obvious that we will understand neither culture nor cognition without a deep appreciation for the ways in which the two are inseparable from, but not reducible to, each other. As indicated by many of the citations above, the diagnosis of rampant individualism in psychology is already an old story. However, very few psychologists have demonstrated a full understanding of the problem by adjusting their theoretical perspectives and practical interventions accordingly. The remainder of this chapter offers a vision of how individualism can be overcome by putting together the pieces of the culture-cognition-psychopathology puzzle in a manner that transcends individualism and justifies a significantly different praxis in relation to psychopathology and to problems in living in general.

CULTURE AND COGNITION

Much of the work to be done requires a redefinition of basic terms in light of cultural psychological understandings (e.g., D'Andrade & Strauss, 1992). Recent developments in social and cultural theory are also relevant, in particular the emerging synthesis of critical-hermeneutic and poststructuralist perspectives (e.g., Kögler, 1996).

Since the 1960s, the relation between culture and thought or, more recently, cognition, has shifted from views of culture as external to, or interacting with, thought (e.g., Berry & Dasen, 1974) toward views that emphasize the radical inseparability of culture and cognition (e.g., Shore, 1996). This inseparability has been conceptualized in different ways: seeing culture as inherent in mind, culture as a set of practices emerging from the interaction of thought and action, or culture as the product of a person's efforts to interpret reality actively (Lemke, 1997; Lucariello, 1995). Concurrent with moves to break down the dichotomy between culture and cognition by demonstrating the role of culture in perception, memory, language, and reasoning (Altarriba, 1993) are efforts to bring psychological explanations into analyses of cultural meanings (Strauss & Quinn, 1997).

In general, these new views go far beyond the impoverished concepts of culture employed in most psychological literature, where *culture* means people living in a certain region of the world (e.g., Latin American culture), people whose ancestors came from a certain region of the world (e.g., Latino culture in the United States), people who speak the same language (Anglo-American culture), and so forth. It is not an overstatement to say that these examples are representative of what is meant when research reports assert that cultural variables were taken into account. Such thinking still plagues a great deal of mainstream social, clinical, and developmental psychology when culture or ethnicity is tacked on to research designs or theoretical models as a move dictated more by hopes of being politically correct than by an emerging understanding of cultural processes. Even the field of crosscultural psychology itself has long been hampered by misguided comparisons between the characteristics of members of one so-called cultural group with those of another. Contemporary views of culture very directly imply that to think of culture as a variable or a quantifiable dimension always has been a gross oversimplification, if not a horrendous misunderstanding, of culture.

A second area of consensus in the rethinking of culture and cognition, stemming in part from empirical work on cultural processes in narrative accounts and other forms of meaning making (e.g., Stromberg, 1986), is that it is far from useful to regard culture as a giant pulsing brain that tells every member of the culture to think, feel, and act in exactly the same way. Instead, cultural processes are part and parcel of the construction of individuality and agency, as individuals creatively work with combinations of the symbols or discourses that are readily available to them in everyday social interaction and communication (Cohen, 1994; Olson & Torrance, 1996). Culture and cognition are fused, not in a mechanistic one-way process, but in fragmented, experimental, and disparate schemas that guide action (DiMaggio, 1997).

As psychology's concept of culture has deepened, the concept of cognition has broadened considerably in the wake of cultural psychological contributions to cognitive psychology. Widespread notions such as scripts, narratives, discourses, subjectivities, and so forth are terms used to refer to processes previously understood as thought or cognition. The definitions of these terms all indicate that subjective experience is much more than thinking or information processing.

Thus for the purposes of this chapter, I will rely on a concept of cultural cognition to refer to shared modes of understanding (schema, interpretive frames) and related action possibilities (scripts, discursive practices) that emerge as people attempt to make sense of their experience and pursue their projects. Cultural cognitions are neither located in people's heads, nor in ethnographies. Instead, they are always already interactive and interpersonal in nature. For readers familiar with a critical phenomenological perspective, cultural cognition can be seen as a concept similar to communicative action in the lifeworld, the active and ongoing discursive practice in which possibilities for symbolic communication are refreshed through interpretation, negotiation, critique, and consensus formation in and against institutional forms and traditional practices. The concept of cultural cognition also overlaps considerably with poststructuralist concepts of subjectivity.

But why do we refer to cultural cognition as cultural? If cognition is always already cultural, why highlight its cultural aspect? This usage alludes to the fact that modes of cultural cognition are neither universal nor idiosyncratic, but shared within cultural groups of all sorts, for example, military families, Internet discussion groups, members of Alchoholics Anonymous, professors of engineering, or Greek Americans. To understand these shared modes of meaning-making, it is essential to recognize the ways in which they are *only* understandable in terms of meanings that are reproduced and reworked in and through the social relations that constitute a particular cultural group.

To illustrate the shift of perspective that occurs when one understands experience not individualistically in terms of cultureless thought, but rather in terms of cultural cognition, consider the difference between the following two ways of looking at a person's decision whether to marry. The first view might see the decision as a matter of considering the pros and cons of married life, the attractiveness of the potential spouse, the financial viability of the union, the opinions of relatives and friends, fantasies of what life would be like without the partner, and so on. All these ideas and associated feelings would somehow sort themselves out and lead to a conscious decision that would then be acted upon. This perspective may not seem strange to many Western readers because our subjective lives are generally constructed individualistically so we are prone to experience ourselves as relatively isolated thinking, deciding, and acting beings.

The process looks different, however, when the interpenetration of culture and cognition is highlighted. First of all, the cultural psychologist could point out that the very possibility of deliberating whether or not to be married is built into culturally available discourses regarding the course of romantic involvements. Depending on the historical juncture and the specific major and minor cultural groups in which the person's life projects are constructed, the meanings of getting married could range from the end of fun to the beginning of real life to what I must do to get out of my parent's house. The person might also understand that at a certain point one must make a decision about whether or not this love is for life.

Other culturally available discourses might also be tried to see if they fit more adequately with the complex of perceptions, sensations, feelings, values, and images that the person is aware of at disparate moments, and out of which the person strives to construct meaningful intention. For example, a person could experiment with the discourses of being just lovers or just friends by imaginatively or actually enacting them with a partner and learning from the partner's response. As the two dialogue further, they will find themselves drawing on and enacting other culturally available discourses, such as playing hard to get and desperately wanting to possess the loved person. To say that these discursive modes are culturally available does not imply that they are consciously thought, but they certainly could be at least partially articulated if the participants were asked to do so. The hard to get person might admit (to the cultural psychologist, at least) that he or she is really in love and expects to marry, but enjoys being pursued and does not want to be taken for granted. Furthermore, such discursive modes are recognizable by other people whose cultural worlds overlap sufficiently with theirs, even though they have never seen this exact form of the performance before.

This view may sound highly deterministic, but there is actually extensive room for variations upon the themes that culturally available discursive modes provide. This is not due to creativity but to the fact that each person automatically has an immensely different repertoire to draw on due to having been exposed to different novels, films, or television shows and having heard different family stories, played different roles in previous relationships, and developed different understandings of how a good person acts in such situations. Innovation is also engendered by the fact that each person plays out the scene in relation to the other's equally innovative performance and that discursive modes not previously combined in their experience might be joined, as would happen, for example, if the couple decided to get married but not live together.

Cultural Cognition and Psychopathology

The lack of attention to the nature of culture has also caught the attention of scholars focusing on crosscultural studies of psychopathology. For example, in a chapter entitled "Does Culture Make a Difference in Psychopathology?" Al-Issa (1982) concludes: "Although researchers have now accumulated substantial data that indicate[s] there is an association between cultural background and psychopathology, there is still very little known about the nature of the cultural processes underlying these associations. The nature of culture needs an extensive analysis before anyone can confidently describe how culture makes a difference in psychopathology" (p. 23).

Concepts of mental illness, psychological disorder, and psychopathology are also undergoing revision as the sociocultural contexts in which these concepts are employed are taken into account. As a result, assessments of what is normal and what is pathological are increasingly relativized. Wakefield (1992), for example, defines a psychological disorder as a harmful dysfunction, but readily acknowledges that cultural and historical contexts play an immense role in determining what is seen as harmful and what is seen as dysfunctional. In passing, it should be noted that while the cultural psychology has begun to address the interwoven nature of cognition and culture in psychopathology, there are similar, and equally important, efforts being made to understand cultural processes in normal and pathological emotion (e.g., Jenkins, 1996; Lutz & Abu-Lughod, 1990).

As cultural psychology and other interdisciplinary efforts chip away at individualistic and overly cognitive approaches to psychological disorders, room is being created for innovative accounts of psychopathology. In general, these approaches emphasize linguistic, symbolic, and performative aspects of communication action and the ways in which these degenerate in psychological disorders. These accounts have accorded new relevance to varieties of psychoanalytic thought that emphasize language, culture, narrative, and interpersonal processes rather than instinctual drives and intrapsychic structure. The cognitive therapies now in vogue look especially problematic from the perspective of the emerging cultural-linguistic-psychodynamic theories. They may work because they latch on to and rework cognitions, which are obviously an important part of emotional suffering, but in their search for practical effect, cognitive therapies bypass possibilities for developing deeper understandings of the psychocultural constitution of the client's problems.

One way of piecing together the emerging picture of psychopathology would be to understand psychological disorder as stemming from a systematic disruption of the congruence of feeling, thought, and action. This disruption is produced by the incapacity of the experiencing subject to grasp simultaneously the contradictory meanings associated with compelling but conflicting culturally available discursive practices. A desymbolization of experience occurs at the site of this contradiction, preventing certain intentions or desires from gaining expression while allowing others to shape action (Lorenzer, 1976; Sloan, 1996b). In object relations theory, the same process has been described at the intrapsychic level as a lack of differentiation of unconscious representations of self and other (e.g., Kernberg, 1977). However, such language tends to obscure the sociocultural and interpersonal origins of desymbolization, which occurs in the wake of unresolvable conflicts between compelling discursive possibilities. This general view is supported by Stromberg's (1993) work in psychological anthropology, which uses life-historical case studies to show that psychological processes related to identity confusion involve disruptions and reformulations of communication patterns.

To make all this more concrete, imagine that our person who is trying to decide whether to marry begins to have anxiety attacks, presenting symptoms such as not being able to cross the street, trembling when near members of the opposite sex, and having obsessive fears that the potential spouse will die in a horrible accident. The individualistic cognitive therapist treating these symptoms would search for the irrational cognitions that must underlie these symptoms. Perhaps the person is incorrectly linking marital commitment with the previous loss of a parent or thinking that being a good marital partner might limit opportunities for getting ahead in life or for enjoying friendship with the opposite sex. Whatever the assessment, the cognitive therapist would urge the client to rethink the situation realistically and not construct illogical connections between the current dilemma and past events.

From a cultural psychological perspective, the person's symptoms would not be automatically reduced to products of individual maladaptive thinking. The cultural psychologist might note that the person is not able to combine several culturally available discursive positions, each of which captures disparate and contradictory meanings related to action possibilities. For example, since the person has previously acted out the discourse of single, playing the field, and enjoyed it, he or she now must begin to practice the contradictory discourse of engaged, in love, and not available to others. A previous congruence of intention, feeling, and action is disrupted by the structural contradictions between these discourses. These provoke desymbolization and a reliance on another cultural script we might call being anxious about one's future, enacted with various idiosyncratic interpretations (miniscripts) such as expressing insecurity in the presence of the opposite sex, physical inability to cross the street, and catastrophic ideation symbolizing the seriousness of the matter as well as a way out of the dilemma. Note that although the focus of analysis in such cultural psychological interpretation is still on the individual, cultural process and discursive self-positioning are understood as one and the same. For other analytic purposes, the level of analysis could be shifted to understand, for example, why there is a demographic increase in unmarried cohabitation. In doing so, however, it would be important not to assume that all couples cohabit as an attempt to negotiate their way through exactly the same contradictory culturally available discourses related to living with an intimate partner. For instance, one can imagine that the same behavioral outcome would be arrived at through quite a different process by couples in a fundamentalist religious context as compared to couples in a bohemian arts community.

As mentioned above, this is just one way of piecing together the emerging perspective on cultural cognition and psychopathology. My way of putting things, which leans (probably more than others in this volume) on terminologies linked to post-structuralist psychoanalysis and critical hermeneutics, could probably easily be translated into a more familiar cognitive-cultural psychology vocabulary of goals, models, self-understandings, and schemas (D'Andrade & Strauss, 1992).

A Missing Piece of the Puzzle

An important piece of the culture-cognition-psychopathology puzzle is still missing in what I have presented above. To my mind, this missing piece is crucial. Approaches to psychopathology that do not take it into account risk missing the boat entirely, both in theory and practice. The missing piece is the play of power in intersubjective processes. Unless it is based on a biomedical disorder of some sort, psychopathology is always related to some form of disempowerment, subjection, oppression, or disenfranchisement and the attendant inability to articulate one's deepest needs and to pursue freely one's heartfelt projects. When the play of power is not at work, contradicting cultural cognitions simply contradict each other with no negative effect. The person can, for example, alternate his or her enactment according to the press of the situation. But if one fears loss of love, physical harm, or social rejection for enacting a particular cultural cognition, desymbolization kicks in as a way of managing fear and anxiety, thus breaking down the congruence of thought, feeling, and action. To continue with the example of the person facing the marriage dilemma, we might find that the stress of the decision is tolerable as long as everyone involved is understanding and conveys acceptance of whatever decision emerges, but frequently such decisions do not occur in benign circumstances. In my own research (Sloan, 1996b), a participant found herself caught between her emerging awareness that her husband-to-be was insanely jealous and prone to beat her when slightly provoked and, on the other hand, pressure from family and friends to go through with the elaborate wedding plans. A cognitive denial of the violence ensued, the wedding took place, and it was not until a few years later, when she was being beaten in front of her two small children, that she could acknowledge the nonviability of the relationship. Psychologists are just beginning to perceive the complete saturation of psychopathology by larger sociocultural processes, such as racism, sexism, and economic exploitation. This was demonstrated early on, however, when feminist researchers began to link high rates of depression in women to patriarchal societal relations underlying their suffering.

In my opinion, one of the most important and challenging tasks for cultural psychology is to demonstrate that progressive social change is necessary, not only because of the material suffering related to poverty, but also because the mental health consequences of social orders based on injustice and inequality are so extensive. In this regard, recent work demonstrates the negative mental health consequences of modernization (Sloan, 1996a; Sloan & Brownstein-Schroder, 1989), globalization (Sampson, 1989), immigration and refugee experiences (Marsella, 1998), and ethnic conflict (Comas-Diaz, Lykes, & Alarcon, 1998). Even where social change and social disruption do not occur at levels that are obviously traumatic, psychopathology is systematically produced by the rapidly shifting sociocultural sands, as we see in the fragmentation of postmodern selves (Sloan, 1996b; Strauss, 1997).

Our response to these global social processes must be more than academic or clinical. Those who benefit from cultural psychological insights, and seek to alleviate human emotional suffering, will need to develop new forms of nonindividualistic practice. We have seen many calls for this new psychology and consensus seems to be forming around the idea that it would operate at the level of communities rather than individuals. Nandy (1983) calls for a transcendence of Western ethnocentric and scientistic psychology toward a humane psychology that would refuse to medicalize individualistically the emotional consequences of social upheaval. More recently, Marsella (1998) urges the development of a global-community psychology. Montero (1994) argues for psychosocial community work to address the needs of marginalized communities. Prilleltensky (1994) lays out the principles that would guide a critical community psychology. There obviously will be as many forms of socially engaged psychology as there are psychologists, ranging from action research to overt political activism, but it is clear that the justifications for individualistic theories, methods, and practices are crumbling fast (Fox & Prilleltensky, 1996; Sloan, 2000). Those who care about finding solutions will need to comprehend psychological disorders as manifestations of global sociocultural processes that disrupt community life, and in turn work to respond energetically at the community and global levels as well as with compassion at the interpersonal level.

REFERENCES

Al-Issa, I. (Ed.). (1982). *Culture and psychopathology.* Baltimore: University Park Press.

Altarriba, J. (Ed.). (1993). *Cognition and culture: A cross-cultural approach to cognitive psychology.* Amsterdam: North-Holland/Elsevier.

Berry, J. W., & Dasen, P. R. (Eds.). (1974). *Culture and cognition: Readings in cross-cultural psychology.* London: Methuen.

Cohen, A. P. (1994). *Self consciousness: An alternative anthropology of identity.* London: Routledge.

Comas-Diaz, L., Lykes, M. B., & Alarcon, R. D. (1998). Ethnic conflict and the psychology of liberation in Guatemala, Peru, and Puerto Rico. *American Psychologist, 53*, 778–792.

D'Andrade, R. G., & Strauss, C. (Eds.). (1992). *Human motives and cultural models.* Cambridge: Cambridge University Press.

DiMaggio, P. (1997). Culture and cognition. *Annual Review of Sociology, 23*, 263–287.

Fiske, A. P., Kitayama, S., Markus, H. R., & Nisbett, R. E. (1998). The cultural matrix of social psychology. In D. T. Gilbert, S. T. Fiske, & G. Lindzey (Eds.), *The handbook of social psychology* (4th ed., Vol. 2, pp. 915–981). Boston: McGraw-Hill.

Fox, D., & Prilleltensky, I. (Eds.). (1996). *Critical psychology: An introduction.* London: Sage.

Henriques, J., Hollway, W., Urwin, C., Venn, C., & Walkerdine, V. (1984). *Changing the subject.* London: Methuen.

Jenkins, J. H. (1996). Culture, emotion, and psychiatric disorder. In T. R. Johnson (Ed.), *Medical anthropology: Contemporary theory and method* (Rev. ed., pp. 71–87). Westport, CT: Praeger.

Kernberg, O. (1977). *Object relations theory and clinical psychoanalysis.* New York: Aronson.

Kögler, H. H. (1996). *The power of dialogue: Critical hermeneutics after Gadamer and Foucault.* Cambridge, MA: MIT Press.

Lemke, J. L. (1997). Cognition, context, and learning: A social semiotic perspective. In D. Kirshner & J. A. Whitson (Eds.), *Situated cognition: Social, semiotic, and psychological perspectives* (pp. 37–55). Mahwah, NJ: Lawrence Erlbaum.

Lorenzer, A. (1976). Symbols and stereotypes. In P. Connerton (Ed.), *Critical sociology* (pp. 134–152). New York: Penguin.

Lucariello, J. (1995). Mind, culture, person: Elements in a cultural psychology. *Human Development, 38*, 2–18.

Lutz, C., & Abu-Lughod, L. (Eds.). (1990). *Language and the politics of emotion.* Cambridge, UK: Cambridge University Press.

Marsella, A. J. (1998). Toward a "global-community psychology": Meeting the needs of a changing world. *American Psychologist, 53*, 1282–1291.

Montero, M. (1994). Consciousness-raising, conversion and de-ideologization in community psychosocial work. *Journal of Community Psychology, 22*, 3–11.

Nandy, A. (1983). Towards an alternative politics of psychology. *International Social Science Journal, 35*, 323–338.

Olson, D., & Torrance, N. (1996). *Modes of thought: Explorations in culture and cognition.* New York: Cambridge University Press.

Power, M., & Dalgleish, T. (1997). *Cognition and emotion: From order to disorder.* East Sussex, UK: Psychology Press.

Prilleltensky, I. (1994). *The morals and politics of psychology: Psychological discourse and the status quo.* Albany, NY: SUNY Press.

Rose, N. (1996). *Inventing our selves: Psychology, power, and personhood.* Cambridge, UK: Cambridge University Press.

Sampson, E. E. (1981). Cognitive psychology as ideology. *American Psychologist, 36*, 730–743.

Sampson, E. E. (1989). The challenge of social change for psychology: Globalization and psychology's theory of the person. *American Psychologist, 44*, 914–921.

Shore, B. (1996). *Culture in mind: Cognition, culture, and the problem of meaning*. New York: Oxford University Press.

Sloan, T. S. (1996a). *Damaged life: The crisis of the modern psyche*. New York: Routledge.

Sloan, T. S. (1996b). *Life choices: Understanding dilemmas and decisions*. Boulder, CO: Westview.

Sloan, T. S. (Ed.). (2000). *Critical psychology: Voices for change*. London: Macmillan.

Sloan, T. S., & Brownstein-Schroder, S. (1989). Beyond cross-cultural psychology: The case of Third World factory women. *Psychology and Developing Societies, 1*, 137–151.

Strauss, C. (1997). Partly fragmented, partly integrated: An anthropological examination of "postmodern fragmented subjects." *Cultural Anthropology, 12*, 362–404.

Strauss, C., & Quinn, N. (1997). *A cognitive theory of cultural meaning*. Cambridge, UK: Cambridge University Press.

Stromberg, P. (1986). *Symbols of community: The cultural system of a Swedish church*. Tucson: University of Arizona Press.

Stromberg, P. (1993). *Language and self-transformation: A study of the Christian conversion narrative*. New York: Cambridge University Press.

Wakefield, J. C. (1992). The concept of mental disorder: On the boundary between biological facts and social values. *American Psychologist, 47*, 373–388.

2

Cultural Cognition and Psychopathology: Anthropological Perspectives

Harvey Whitehouse

Social and cultural theorists have, on the whole, been slow to take on board the increasingly persuasive models and findings of cognitive science. But, by the same token, many psychologists have failed to appreciate that cognition (both normal and abnormal) is socioculturally constituted. A relatively small number of cognitive anthropologists have, over several decades, struggled to reconcile theories that take the individual mind/brain as the primary unit of analysis with those that operate at the level of the society or culture.

Despite considerable progress in this area, a limitation of most theories of "cultural cognition" is that they tend to envisage all cultural knowledge as organized in semantic and procedural memory, resulting from incremental learning in response to recurrent experiences. Not all cultural transmission, however, is routinized. In this chapter, I argue for an alternative perspective on cultural cognition which, by focusing on the effects of variable transmissive frequency, reveals the need for a more thoroughgoing integration of social and cognitive theory.

SOCIAL THEORY AND COGNITION

Émile Durkheim, one of the founders of modern social theory, is often portrayed as having dismissed psychological explanations of social facts. But, notwithstanding some unfortunate rhetoric, Durkheim was really interested in the social origins of cognitive processes. His pioneering treatise on the elementary forms of religion (Durkheim, 1915) set out to demonstrate that concepts of time, space, class, and causality derive from social organization, rather than the other way around. An early member of the Durkheimian school, Maurice Halbwachs (1925, 1950), extended these arguments, proposing that memory is socially determined more generally. First, most of what people remember and recall is caused by social interaction in highly patterned ways. Second, the material environments in which humans live provide social groups, classes, etc., with distinctive mnemonic triggers. The memories elicited by material objects and their spatial organization are properties of society as much as of individuals. Thus Halbwachs rejected the idea that individual memory could be envisaged as distinct from what he called "la mémoire collective."

Anthropological theory has been substantially shaped by Durkheimian thinking. Bronislaw Malinowski (1944) happened to take up the functionalist strand of Durkheim's project, arguing, for instance, that the rationality of apparently absurd beliefs resided in their contribution to institutional stability. Later, such influential theorists as Claude Levi-Strauss (1963) and Mary Douglas (1966) developed Durkheim's ideas to unveil more substantially the isomorphy of social and cosmological systems of classification. In this post-structuralist era, the ideas of Halbwachs have enjoyed a sort of renaissance as a set of theories of social memory (for review, see Fentress & Wickham, 1992). The bulk of contemporary cultural theory, meanwhile, focuses on discourse analysis, and is concerned with historical contestations rather than functionally integrated systems. Within such approaches, however, mental processes are still commonly viewed in terms of fundamentally *social* properties and therefore are irreducible to the cognitive development of the individual mind/brain.

There remains a widespread skepticism among anthropologists and other social theorists toward individual psychology. It is true that psychologically oriented approaches have enjoyed a distinguished history in American cultural anthropology, exemplified by the culture and personality school (Benedict, 1935; Kardiner & Linton, 1949; Mead, 1950). Also, there has long been some general interest in cultural cognition, particularly in the study of complex taxonomic systems, such as ethnobotanical knowledge (Berlin, Breedlove, & Raven, 1974) and kinship terminology (Lounsbury, 1956). Nevertheless, cognitive anthropology has remained a somewhat marginal subfield, generating hypotheses and data that do not seem to bear substantially on the central concerns of social theory and, where they do, eliciting considerable suspicion.

Clifford Geertz's (1973) antipathy toward the notion of culture as something located in the mind reflects deeply rooted prejudices among social/cultural anthropologists, not only back in the 1960s and 1970s but continuing into the present. Some scholars recently have gone so far as to suggest that many central concepts of Western psychology are little more than folk categories cloaked in the language of natural science. Being unaware of the socially constructed character of psychological knowledge, cognitive scientists have been accused of producing visions of mental life that not only are ethnocentric but are unable to reflect on the conditions of their own genesis (Toren, 2000).

The general distrust of cognitive perspectives in social/cultural theory is closely connected to relativistic epistemology. For most anthropologists, culture provides the equipment by means of which reality is apprehended. There is no direct interaction between individuals and their environments because everything people do or experience is mediated by sociocultural forces, whether these are envisaged as structures and systems (in the early decades of anthropological theory) or as shifting power relations and contestations (in contemporary discourse analysis). According to this view, the determination of truth, meaning, and rationality are culturally relative, and can only be accessed through participation in the social praxis of the population in question. Although many anthropologists are prepared to countenance some limits to cognitive relativism, these limits typically are seen as more or less irrelevant to the task of ethnography.

To some extent, the tension between cognitive reductionism and cognitive relativism has tended to overlap with debates about the relative importance of genes and environment—or nature and nurture—in cognitive development. This is unnecessary, however, because the notion that cognition is culturally relative could very easily be hitched to strongly nativist assumptions (e.g., with regard to input systems, attention biases, conceptual domains, modular central processing, etc.). One could argue, in principle, that a great deal of cognitive architecture is genetically specified, but that culturally constituted processes of development lead to unlimited conceptual variability from one society to the next. The rejection of cognitive explanations of cultural phenomena would then follow on the grounds that one cannot explain variables in terms of constants. Conversely, approaches that focus on properties of the individual mind/brain might proceed from a tabula rasa starting point and account for the development of universal cognitive structures in terms of invariable features of the environment coupled with general-purpose learning equipment (e.g., standard Piagetian perspectives). Constructivist epistemology does not necessarily imply cognitive relativism.

What is obviously true is that the cognitive abilities of the individual develop through experience, regardless of how strongly that development is shaped by discrete, genetically specified mechanisms. The question addressed in this chapter is whether cognitive abilities, developing through experience, are most effectively analyzed at the level of social relations or at the level of the organism. In what follows I am going to suggest that many projects in social/cultural theory and cognitive science should aim to integrate both levels. The reason these two levels have tended to be studied separately has a great deal to do with the sociocultural conditions of academic research. After all, the development of academic discourse, just like any other body of cultural representations, is rooted simultaneously in processes within, but also quite extensively among, human minds.

THEORIES OF CULTURAL COGNITION

One way of attempting to overcome the limitations of cognitive approaches that treat the individual mind/brain as the unit of analysis is to envisage cognition as a process of interaction between mind and culture. This interactionist view is what is generally implied by the notion of cultural cognition. Research in this field has been concerned mostly with mapping the relations between cognitive entities known as schemas and a specified range of sociocultural arrangements, such as patterns of behavior between different categories of kin (D'Andrade, 1995).

George Mandler (1984) defines schemas as "abstract representations of environmental regularities" (pp. 55–56) but also as "processing mechanisms" enabling us to differentiate, interpret, and anticipate distinct patterns of experience. Insofar as schemas are widely shared (that is, enable a number of persons to form convergent inferences and expectations with regard to particular flows of events), they may be regarded as cultural. Cultural schemas are cognitive phenomena, internal to the individual mind/brain, but they are also outcomes of regularities in the experiences of entire populations. Schema theory has led to increasingly sophisticated models of memory and learning during the last couple decades, often in tandem with developments in neurology and artificial intelligence based on connectionist networks (Bechtel & Abrahamsen, 1991). The potential advantages of schema theory for the study of cultural cognition have recently been persuasively elucidated by Claudia Strauss and Naomi Quinn (1997), showing that such approaches not only parallel existing trends in social theory but, in certain respects, go beyond them in generating increasingly precise and empirically productive models.

Although it is generally assumed that schemas must be roughly shared in order to be classed as cultural, they do not have to be uniformly shared. Indeed, in any population there will be an uneven distribution of cultural schemas, acknowledged for instance as forms of specialist knowledge or expertise. This demonstrates once again the need to take the specified population, and not simply the individual mind/brain, as the unit of analysis in the study of cognition. Edwin Hutchins (1995) has recently argued that cognition should be regarded as distributed, further supporting the interactionist view outlined above.

If cognition is an outcome of interactions between processes at the level of the individual and the level of the population, it is clearly crucial to work out as precisely as possible the mechanisms by which such interactions occur. This is an underexamined area in the study of cultural cognition but some important suggestions have recently been formulated by Dan Sperber (no date). His starting point is the idea that all mental activity takes the form of cognitive causal chains (CCCs) in which processes such as remembering, perceiving, inferring information, and carrying out intentions are causally connected. Many CCCs (such as my having just taken a break from writing to make myself a cup of coffee, for example) do not engage the cooperation of others. But CCCs also can be social, involving, for instance, the satisfaction of one person's desire through compliance with a request on the part of another person. Social CCCs require the activation of similar or complementary CCCs on the part of more than one person.

Sperber argues that social CCCs link mental representations to what he calls public productions, that is, expressions of mental states that alter the environment. Some such productions or alterations to the environment are produced specifically for the purpose of causing others to perceive and form mental representations of them, and Sperber refers to such productions as public representations. For Sperber, the transmission of representations consists of the processes by which mental representations are converted into public representations and vice versa, and these processes occur through the activation of social CCCs.

Most social CCCs are simple and unique (e.g., my particular experiences of driving to work today) but they are organized according to reproducible CCCs (e.g., schemas for commuting by car, which include representations of how to respond to the signals of other motorists, how to plot a particular route from among a variety of alternatives, etc.). According to Sperber, comparatively stable and widespread representations constitute the phenomena that social scientists refer to as culture. Social CCCs that serve to reproduce cultural representations are described by Sperber as cultural cognitive causal chains (CCCCs).

As Sperber points out, many established approaches to the analysis of culture focus primarily on the semantic relations between representations. The analyst's models of how representations are linked through chains of logical implication, association, and so on, tend to overlook the actual social and psychological events in which the abstract system may be discerned. Sperber's concept of cognitive causal chains is intended to direct our attention to the way representations are linked, not just semantically, but also via countless oscillations between mental processes and public productions.

Sperber argues that, by focusing on the semantic relations between representations, cultural theorists sometimes raise to the level of analytic status a notion of representations as reified essences. He observes, for instance, that a particular narrative may seem to constitute a single design to which actual renderings are intended to conform. Thus the story of Goldilocks appears as a thing, capable of shaping each retelling of it. As Sperber puts it, however, "no teller of Goldilocks is guided in her telling by 'the tale of Goldilocks.' She is guided by her memory of previous tellings." By focusing on cognitive causal chains, the illusion of reified essences is avoided.

Thus it would seem that some recent developments in cognitive anthropology anticipate and overcome many of the objections of social/cultural theorists who are wary of the reductionist tendencies of individual psychology. At the same time, some of the limitations and fallacies of conventional anthropological theory have been identified and overcome. Nevertheless, theories of cultural cognition are currently incomplete. Research concerned, for instance, with cultural schemas, distributed cognition, and cultural cognitive causal chains is premised on the notion of an interaction between mechanisms engaged in incremental learning and highly repetitive forms of cultural transmission. Such approaches take little account of the fact that at least some aspects of cultural learning do not proceed incrementally and some forms of transmission are extremely infrequent.

Consider, for example, Sperber's argument that CCCs become cultural (CCCCs) only when they are stabilized through widespread and repetitive transmission in a similar form, or Mandler's notion of schemas as abstract representations of environmental regularities. Such perspectives are unable to envisage cultural representations that are neither abstract nor frequently transmitted. But a moment's reflection should convince us that such representations exist. The assassination of John F. Kennedy has been used frequently in the psychological literature on memory as an example of an event that is recalled as a distinctive, concrete, one-off episode in the life histories of those who remember it (Brown & Kulik, 1982; Conway, Rubin, Spinnler, & Wagenaar, 1992; Winograd & Killinger, 1983). The event itself, and people's recollections of it, are undoubtedly cultural. Indeed it has been observed that the possession of vivid memories of what one was doing when news of the assassination broke is a crucial element of American national identity. It may even be construed as un-American for people of an appropriate age not to be able to recall such details (Wright & Gaskell, 1992). What makes these patterns of recall cultural, at least in part, is precisely the fact that the episode contradicted people's normal expectations about presidential appearances in public, and about the security of the president personally. This was quite aside from the momentous implications for American society and government more generally. In arguing, like Sperber, that all social CCCs are molded in the direction of existing cultural CCCs, the fact is overlooked that representations can be contagious for exactly the opposite reason: because they depart radically from existing CCCCs.

TRANSMISSIVE FREQUENCY AND THE EPIDEMIOLOGY OF REPRESENTATIONS

One way of demonstrating the importance of transmissive frequency for a theory of cultural cognition is to consider what this might mean for epidemiological models of culture, as developed by Dan Sperber (1985, 1996) and Pascal Boyer (1993, 1994, 1996). Their starting point is the idea that representations are analogous to diseases insofar as the distribution of both can be partly explained in terms of organic susceptibilities. Given particular evolved cognitive architecture, humans are more likely to catch (i.e., encode, remember, and recall) certain representations than others. For instance, Sperber (1996) speculates that a set of perceptual mechanisms attuned to tonal variation and entailed in the evolution of language-processing equipment may help account for the fondness in humans for the production and appreciation of music. Since simple melodies are more contagious than, say, twenty-digit numbers, musical schemas are more likely to become widespread (i.e., shared and cultural) than are random numerical strings.

On the face of it, such an argument seems to demonstrate, after all, that properties of the *individual* mind/brain have direct causal implications for culture.

However, this impression is illusory. Sperber's argument overlooks the fact that the catchiness of a piece of music (e.g., the likelihood of a person humming or whistling a tune recently heard) is profoundly influenced by (among other things) the conditions of transmission and the listener's prior experience of the musical genre in question. This is so much the case that what some highly technical ethnomusicological accounts of Melanesian vocalizations regard as "singing" is described by indigenous performers as "weeping" (Feld, 1982). The untrained foreigner might not categorize it as music at all, and certainly would have difficulty reproducing it in a form that is recognizable to indigenes.

The issues here can be more precisely examined by considering Boyer's recent work, which greatly extends and enriches Sperber's original epidemiological approach. Boyer is concerned primarily with the distribution of religious concepts, especially concepts of extranatural agency. Such concepts systematically violate intuitive knowledge in highly patterned ways. Intuitive knowledge seems to be acquired according to a universal developmental schedule in human beings and is substantially compartmentalized. For example, from an early age children realize principles governing animate objects (e.g., that they are self-propelled by invisible intentions) do not apply to artifacts (e.g., that they have to be acted upon in order to be set in motion). Boyer points to evidence that children develop intuitive knowledge in a series of mental categories (e.g., person, animal, plant, artifact, etc.), which he describes as intuitive ontologies. This intuitive ontological knowledge appears to develop naturally in all humans, regardless of cultural differences.

Religious notions of extranatural agency seem to violate such universal intuitive knowledge by (a) canceling particular intuitive rules (e.g., canceling the physical principle of solidity, which normally applies to human bodies, producing a concept of spirit capable of passing through walls); and (b) transferring intuitive rules between ontological domains (e.g., transferring to an artifact the biological attributes of breathing, bleeding, or drinking, thereby producing sacred effigies that are regarded as alive). Boyer's argument is that the most widespread concepts of extranatural agency are ones that entail violations and transfers of particular sorts, while activating background intuitive knowledge by default. Whatever is strange about extranatural beings, as with nonstandard psychology, has to be explicitly transmitted; for example, spirits can read people's minds or see into the future, but many other things we know about such beings are no different from (and are extensions of) what we know about ordinary agents.

Thus on the basis of a combination of original and previously published experimental and ethnographic data, Boyer (2000) concludes:

The distribution of cultural representations seems to confirm the prediction that, all else being equal, representations that combine counter-intuitive principles and intuitive background in the way described here are more likely than others to be acquired, stored and transmitted, thereby giving rise to those roughly stable sets commonly described as cultural.

Boyer recognizes that the causes of those cultural distributions in which he is interested are numerous and complex. Therefore, of course, Boyer does not have to account for 100 percent of the variance among the phenomena he sets out to explain. Insofar as Boyer shows that certain religious representations are more likely than others to be globally recurrent, because the cognitive processes giving rise to these representations are globally recurrent, Boyer's theory shows that universal cognitive dispositions are among the causes of at least some cultural phenomena. This is an impressive achievement.

Nevertheless, if the sorts of representations that we are cognitively predisposed to remember are only memorable under most conditions, but not all, then the conditions of transmission must be a causal factor in the memorableness of *all* representations. In gathering experimental data in support of his argument, one might therefore have expected Boyer to attempt to reproduce a set of conditions that are typically present when concepts of extranatural agency are transmitted in human societies. On the contrary, however, Boyer explicitly designed his experimental procedures to neutralize rather than to reproduce the conditions of transmission in natural settings. Presumably, the strategy of neutralization works because certain social conditions of transmission, sufficiently similar to those created in Boyer's experiments, are recurrent in particular fields of human activity in the real world. It follows that, by specifying these particular conditions and seeking to reproduce them in experimental settings, the predictive power of Boyer's models would be increased. In the real world, as opposed to the psychologist's laboratory, religious representations are transmitted in social conditions that are systematically structured with regard to frequency, affectivity, and prior learning on the part of participants. We stand to gain from taking this into account.

In much of the tribal world, those religious occasions regarded as most sacred, revelatory, and costly (in terms of both material and social resources), also are often extremely infrequent. Fertility rites, installation ceremonies, initiations, and major sacrifices, for example, are commonly separated by periods of several years and, in some cases, are literally once-in-a-lifetime experiences. Not only is transmission rare or sporadic, but it often involves unusually intense affectivity, occasioned, for instance, by scarification, flagellation, mutilation, extreme exertion, fasting, sleep deprivation, and so on (Whitehouse, 1996). Very commonly, for example, tribal rituals violate established cultural schemas, like those concerning proper behavior between kinsmen, or procedural conventions (e.g., those relating to food preparation and consumption). Note that these violations do not necessarily exhibit counterintuitive properties, as defined by Boyer (although they might). In short, infrequent transmission, intense affectivity, and violation of cultural schemas are closely correlated variables in many tribal religions.

In two recent monographs (Whitehouse, 1995, 2000), I have argued that these forms of transmission constitute ideal conditions for the production of episodic memories for ritual performances and revelatory religious concepts. Such memories are often crucially important for patterns of group formation in such societies insofar as they specify coparticipants in rituals, and bind them together in enduring relations of social cohesion and solidarity.

All this, however, is a far cry from the highly routinized practices of most literate religions, in which doctrinal and ritual repetition may be as frequent as washing (and, in some cultures, provide the pretext for such mundane activities). Christian church services, like all repetitive rites, are remembered in much the same way as the story of Goldilocks or the meanings of road signs. Liturgical sequences are part of what psychologists call procedural and semantic memory. This is what the rest of us call habit and general knowledge. If you are a regular churchgoer, you will almost certainly not remember the specific details of a service in 1979 or even in 1998, but you will be able to provide a reasonably accurate description of what occurred on the basis of your knowledge of what a typical service is like.

Schema theory is well suited to the study of routinized religious ritual, and the other approaches to cultural cognition discussed above. Liturgical rituals tend to generate abstract conceptions of the religious community and the comparatively diffuse relations between anonymous members. This contrasts with the more concrete face-to-face cohesive relations among participants in tribal rites. Nevertheless, even in the most iconoclastic and puritanical religious traditions, outbursts of climactic, intense, revelatory ritual are often apparent, producing enduring episodic memories. These are moments of inspiration and high excitement that leave their mark on the religious imagination.

Thus the recurrence of any set of representations might be most effectively explained not in terms of properties of individual cognition, but in terms of cognitive adaptations to especially widespread social conditions of transmission. For example, although the concept of the Holy Trinity is counterintuitive in Boyer's terms, it condenses a body of complex cultural schemas that are peculiar to Christianity and require considerable effort to learn and transmit. Such concepts probably become stabilized only in conditions of theological specialization and routinized transmission. Boyer is not concerned with concepts of this sort. He focuses on simpler concepts such as ghost (e.g., normal psychology plus counterintuitive physics) or zombie (e.g., counterintuitive psychology plus normal physics).

These easy-to-construct concepts, although they may be found in complex doctrinal systems, are particularly widespread as relatively free-floating representations, poorly integrated into the wider corpus of cultural knowledge and invoked in an ad hoc way to explain anomalous events or misfortunes. Moreover, in many rarely performed ritual ordeals, what seems to matter is not that religious concepts are counterintuitive but that they systematically violate cultural schemas (e.g., normal expectations about behavior between categories of kin, the significance or uses of familiar objects/materials, etc.). The point, then, is that all representations come about through the adaptation of neural/mental activity to complex sociocultural conditions.

Boyer's work is pioneering, extremely ambitious, and on the whole persuasive. It would not take much to build his arguments into a theory of cognition as socially constituted, greatly increasing the precision and predictive power of epidemiological models. Once we recognize that cognition is not only cultural and distributed but also organized by a wider set of social conditions of transmission, and that cognition itself is a structured process of adaptation to these conditions, we find ourselves back in the theoretical milieu of Halbwachs and other Durkheimian scholars. The difference is that social theorists these days have access to vastly more sophisticated tools from the field of cognitive science and can no longer justify rhetorical opposition to psychological models.

CULTURAL COGNITION AND PSYCHOPATHOLOGY

The above arguments applied to normal cognition also apply to abnormal cognition, and to other varieties of psychopathology. It is true that some deviant forms of cognition and behavior may seem to be explainable in terms of properties of the individual mind/brain, such as personal developmental history, biochemical imbalances, genetic factors, neurological damage, or disease, etc. This sort of approach may be utilized even in studies where cultural factors shaping individual psychopathology are taken substantially into account. Theories of psychopathology, like most cognitive theories of culture, conventionally assume that there are some fixed properties or mechanisms within the individual mind/brain that account for certain recurrent features of clinical disorders, and cultural systems, respectively. But here too, it may be argued that those properties or mechanisms construed as operating at the level of the individual develop, and are activated through, systematically patterned regimes of social transmission.

This is not simply a matter of individual and cultural factors constraining psychological processes (whether normal or abnormal), as if both sets of factors could be studied from relatively independent but complementary viewpoints. It is rather that all forms of psychopathology, like all forms of normal cognition, are adaptations to social conditions of transmission. There are many possible ways of exploring the implications of this point for studies of psychopathology, but it is useful to focus briefly on the sorts of problems posed by crosscultural studies of so-called antisocial personality. This appears to be a globally recurrent disorder and therefore, one may be tempted to suppose, especially amenable to explanation in terms of dysfunctions at the individual level.

The label antisocial personality disorder (ASPD) refers to a pervasive tendency to disregard or violate others' rights. It is applied to subjects on the basis of behavioral criteria, including entrenched patterns of criminal, impulsive, and irresponsible behavior, and the absence of remorseful behavior. These criteria would need to be refined in order to allow universal application. For instance, the notion of criminality implies the presence of legal institutions that are lacking in some hunter-gatherer societies. Having an extremely limited material culture and highly fluid social groupings, individuals in such societies are able simply to walk away from conflicts and have no institutional mechanisms for sanctioning antisocial behavior. Even in the simplest hunter-gatherer bands, however, ASPD is probably not unknown (Lee, 1979).

Although ASPD, suitably defined, may be a universal form of psychopathology, its presence is highly variable crossculturally (Compton et al., 1991; Lee, Kovac, & Rhee, 1987) and rates may increase or decrease over time within a single society (Kessler et al., 1994). In accounting for the universality of ASPD, *and* the substantial variation in its prevalence crossculturally, it is tempting to speculate, as Paris does in this volume, that ASPD is an outcome of (a) individually variable temperamental dispositions toward antisocial behavior caused by genetically prespecified personality differences, and (b) culturally variable constraints on the expression of these dispositions caused by institutional differences. Such a strategy is similar to that adopted by Sperber and Boyer, in arguing that cognitive dispositions and susceptibilities account for the universality of certain cultural representations; it remains the task of social/cultural theory to account for specific local variation in the incidence of those representations. The problem for Paris, as for Sperber and Boyer, is that the dispositions/susceptibilities at issue are not (as Paris puts it, at least) present at birth, but are constructed through processes of social transmission. That is, cognitive and personality traits, in common with all phenotypic characteristics, are outcomes of highly structured developmental processes both within the organism *and* within its socially regulated environment.

A clue to why this is the case is provided by ethnopsychological evidence from Papua New Guinea concerning the causes of antisocial violent behavior among men. Prior to pacification by European governments over the last seventy years, many peoples living in the interior of Papua New Guinea were chronically at war with their neighbors. Mortality rates due to intergroup raiding were extremely high, and boys were raised in institutions (primarily systems of initiation) explicitly designed to foster aggressivity and homicidal behavior. In a recent monograph, Simon Harrison (1993) shows that the indigenous Melanesian theory of aggression is almost a precise inversion of Western folk and scientific theories. The latter tend to assume that a predisposition toward antisocial aggressive behavior is a panhuman characteristic, albeit stronger, perhaps, in some individuals than others. It is therefore the task of society to constrain and regulate this natural aggressivity. By contrast, the folk theory documented by Harrison in Papua New Guinea claims that the natural predisposition of humans is toward peaceful sociality and cooperation, and that this tendency has to be deliberately subverted by society in order to create warriors capable of maniacal, homicidal behavior. Such unnatural dispositions toward aggressivity then become problematic within the group. Great warriors are not only a source of protection against outsiders but also present a danger to those within the group. Their capacity for sudden, unprovoked violence means that they are feared as well as valued. Now, obviously, the Melanesian folk theory could be wrong from a psychological viewpoint. Nevertheless, there is good reason to suppose that the Melanesian theory is at least as plausible as the Western one.

Antisocial violent behavior in Papua New Guinea is especially prevalent among men who have undergone traumatic initiation rituals and have been forced, as Harrison puts it, to wear the mask of war. These rituals resemble extreme forms of child abuse, in that the boys (and, in some cases, girls) undergoing them are systematically tortured, both physically and psychologically. They are also unlike forms of child abuse in that everybody involved in these initiations, and society at large, considers these ordeals to be a necessary condition for physical and spiritual development. Among the psychological effects of initiation are enduring episodic memories of traumatic ritual experiences in which the members of one's own cohort are individually specified. Such memories provide a basis for enduring and intense cohesion within raiding parties, greatly reducing the risks of defection. At the same time, ritualized terrorism provides powerful motivations for subsequent violent behavior, which may be antisocial as well as being construed as serving the interests of a local group.

In many Melanesian systems of initiation, it is obvious to both participants and observers that antisocial aggressivity is being deliberately and systematically fostered by social institutions. Nevertheless, similar effects may be produced by social conditions of transmission that, although highly structured, operate on socially unrelated individuals rather than on cohorts of initiates. Examples of these might include patterns of child abuse intergenerationally transmitted within the family, or the recruitment of child soldiers in global theatres of chronic conflict. The point, however, is that all antisocial violent behavior develops through cognitive, affective, and behavioral patterns established within highly structured processes of social transmission. Arguably, both Melanesian and Western folk theories of these processes are misleading. Neither aggressivity nor peaceful sociality are naturally given, since both are constructed within socially regulated environments.

CONCLUSION

The conventional division of labor between cognitive and social/cultural explanations is premised upon an unnecessary fiction, namely, that at least some properties of the individual mind take the form of relatively fixed architecture, and that social and cultural factors merely serve to inhibit or foster the expression of these properties. The consequences of entertaining such a fiction are not necessarily disastrous. If they were, this fiction would not be so widespread among psychologists. But the consequences can reduce the explanatory potential of our models. In order for forms of psychopathology (such as ASPD) and certain aspects of normal cognition (such as the transmission of concepts of extranatural agency) to be universal, there must be some features of social transmission that are also universal. These features become theoretically relevant insofar as they have systematically observable effects on the development of both normal cognition and psychopathology in different populations across space and time.

REFERENCES

Bechtel, W., & Abrahamsen, A. (1991). *Connectionism and the mind: An introduction to parallel processing in networks.* Oxford: Blackwell.

Benedict, R. (1935). *Patterns of culture.* London: Routledge & Kegan Paul.

Berlin, B. O., Breedlove, D., & Raven, P. (1974). *Principles of Tzeltal plant classification.* New York: Academic Press.

Boyer, P. (Ed.). (1993). *Cognitive aspects of religious symbolism.* Cambridge, UK: Cambridge University Press.

Boyer, P. (1994). *The naturalness of religious ideas: A cognitive theory of religion.* Berkeley, CA: University of California Press.

Boyer, P. (1996). What makes anthropomorphism natural: Intuitive ontology and cultural representations. *The Journal of the Royal Anthropological Institute 2,* 1–15.

Boyer, P. (2000). Cultural inheritance tracks and cognitive predispositions: The example of religious concepts. In H. Whitehouse (Ed.), *Mind, evolution, and cultural transmission.* Cambridge, UK: Cambridge University Press.

Brown, R., & Kulik, J. (1982). Flashbulb memory. In U. Neisser (Ed.), *Memory observed: Remembering in natural contexts.* San Francisco: W. H. Freeman.

Compton, W. W., Helzer, J. E., Hwu, H.-G., Yeh, E.-K., McEvoy, L., Tipp, J. E., & Spitznagel, E. L. (1991). New methods in cross-cultural psychiatry: Psychiatric illness in Taiwan and the United States. *American Journal of Psychiatry, 148,* 1697–1704.

Conway, M. A., Rubin, D. C., Spinnler, H., & Wagenaar, W. A. (Eds.). (1992). *Theoretical perspectives on autobiographical memory.* Dordrecht, the Netherlands: Kluwer Academic Publishers.

D'Andrade, R. (1995). *The development of cognitive anthropology.* Cambridge, UK: Cambridge University Press.

Douglas, M. (1966). *Purity and danger.* London: Routledge & Kegan Paul.

Durkheim, E. (1915). *The elementary forms of the religious life.* London: Allen and Unwin.

Feld, S. (1982). *Sound and sentiment: Birds, weeping, poetics, and song in Kaluli expression.* Philadelphia: University of Pennsylvania Press.

Fentress, J., & Wickham, C. (1992). *Social memory.* Oxford, UK: Blackwell.

Geertz, C. (1973). *The interpretation of cultures.* New York: Basic Books.

Halbwachs, M. (1925). *Les cadres sociaux de la mémoire.* Paris: Presses Universitaires de France.

Halbwachs, M. (1950). *La mémoire collective.* Paris: Presses Universitaires de France.

Harrison, S. (1993). *The mask of war: Violence, ritual, and the self in Papua New Guinea.* Manchester, UK: University of Manchester Press.

Hutchins, E. (1995). *Cognition in the wild.* Cambridge, MA: MIT Press.

Kardiner, A., & Linton, R. (1949). *The individual and his society.* New York: Colombia University Press.

Kessler, R. C., McGonagle, K. A., Nelson, C. B., Hughes, M., Eshelman, S., Wittchen, H. U., & Kendler, K. S. (1994). Lifetime and 12-month prevalence of DSM-III-R psychiatric disorders in the United States. *Archives of General Psychiatry, 51,* 8–19.

Lee, K. C., Kovac, Y. S., & Rhee, H. (1987). The national epidemiological study of mental disorders in Korea. *Journal of Korean Medical Science, 2,* 19–34.

Lee, R. B. (1979). *The !Kung: Men, women and work in a foraging society.* Cambridge, UK: Cambridge University Press.

Levi-Strauss, C. (1963). *Totemism* (R. Needham, Trans.). Boston: Beacon Press.

Lounsbury, F. (1956). A semantic analysis of the Pawnee kinship usage. *Language, 32,* 158–194.

Malinowski, B. (1944). *A scientific theory of culture.* Chapel Hill: University of North Carolina Press.

Mandler, G. (1984). *Mind and body: The psychology of emotion and stress.* New York: Norton.

Mead, M. (1950). *Sex and temperament in three primitive societies.* New York: Mentor.

Sperber, D. (1985). Anthropology and psychology: Towards an epidemiology of representations. *Man, 20,* 73–89.

Sperber, D. (1996). *Explaining culture: A naturalistic approach.* Oxford: Blackwell.

Sperber, D. (no date). *Some conceptual tools for and epidemiology of representations.* Unpublished Manuscript.

Strauss, C., & Quinn N. (1997). *A cognitive theory of cultural meaning.* Cambridge, UK: Cambridge University Press.

Toren, C. (2000). The child in mind. In H. Whitehouse (Ed.), *Mind, evolution, and cultural transmission.* Cambridge, UK: Cambridge University Press.

Whitehouse, H. (1995). *Inside the cult: Religious innovation and transmission in Papua New Guinea.* Oxford, UK: Oxford University Press.

Whitehouse, H. (1996). Rites of terror: Emotion, metaphor, and memory in Melanesian initiation cults. *Journal of the Royal Anthropological Institute, 4,* 703–715.

Whitehouse, H. (2000). *Arguments and icons: The cognitive, social, and historical implications of divergent modes of religiosity.* Oxford, UK: Oxford University Press.

Winograd E., & Killinger, W. A. (1983). Relating age at encoding in early childhood to adult recall: Development of flashbulb memories. *Journal of Experimental Psychology: General, 112,* 413–422.

Wright, D., & Gaskell, G. D. (1992). The construction and function of vivid memories. In M. A. Conway, D. C. Rubin, H. Spinnler, & W. A. Wagenaar (Eds.), *Theoretical perspectives on autobiographical memory.* Dordrecht, the Netherlands: Kluwer Academic Publishers.

3

Cultural Sources of Cognition

Charles Nuckolls

The problem that confronts Theaetetus in the Platonic dialogue that bears his name is the same one that confronts psychologists and anthropologists when they consider cognition, and the extent to which the contents and processes of mind are shaped by culture. Socrates asks Theaetetus to tell him what knowledge is, and Theaetetus at first responds that it must be the same as sensory perception. Gradually, Socrates calls this judgment into question by showing that perception is constructed by experience and that experience necessarily varies. But that does not mean, says Socrates, that knowledge is infinitely variable, or that it cannot be described in generalizable terms. Socrates hedges, and in the end, the dialogue ends up not so much in solution as in a clear exposition of the problem—the problem that has not changed, except in the particulars, from Plato's time to the present (Burnyeat, 1990).

Is mind shaped by culture, and therefore relative to experience, or do its contents unfold in a manner governed more by the universalities of human information processing? Psychology and anthropology traditionally confront each other on this question. To simplify, answers have usually taken one of four forms, based on permutations of these two oppositions: internal versus external, and universal versus particular. These permutations can be represented schematically, generating as logical types the four positions that have dominated Western philosophies of mind:

Internal		Particular
	Knowledge	
External		Universal

Each combination is constitutive of a different domain of inquiry:

1. External/Particular: Knowledge is related to external reality, an indeterminate variable that is socially and historically constructed, and thus always particular. This proposition is inherent in most forms of cultural determinism and relativism (e.g., Geertz, 1973);

2. External/Universal: Knowledge is related to external reality, a set of nonarbitrary material circumstances that impose limiting conditions on knowledge. This proposition is inherent in most forms of cultural materialism and ecological determinism (e.g., Lutz, 1988);

3. Internal/Universal: Knowledge is a product of psychocultural evolution, a set of universal developmental stages that can be assessed crossculturally to generate comparative measures. This proposition is inherent in most forms of developmental evolutionism and genetic epistemology (e.g., Boyer, 1990); and

4. Internal/Particular: Knowledge is related to internal psychological processes, their realization is always specific to contextual problematics. This proposition is inherent in most forms of psychoanalytic interpretation (e.g., Spiro, 1984).

To maintain any of these positions exclusively, which is the unfortunate outcome of most discipline-based social science, leads to absurdities and conundrums: a psychological universalism so generalized that it completely bleaches out contextual variation, or a cultural relativism so particularistic that it never explains how crosscultural communication is possible. Integrative attempts are few and far between, but after reviewing some of the literature on culture and cognition, this essay will propose a step in that direction.

CULTURE AND COGNITION

The first empirically tractable scientific studies of cultural variation in mental processes were carried out at the turn of the century by A. C. Haddon and the members of the Cambridge University–sponsored Torres Straits Expedition. By training, Haddon was a marine zoologist, and he later became chair of the newly founded department of anthropology at Cambridge. While at Cambridge, Haddon appointed W. H. R. Rivers, a physician and psychiatrist, to conduct psychological experiments on sensory perception. The objective was to test the hypothesis that "savage and semi-civilized races [manifest] a higher degree of acuteness of sense than is found among Europeans" (Rivers, 1901, p. 12). Rivers and his colleagues (C. S. Myers and William McDougall) focused their experiments on visual acuity, color vision, visual spatial perception (including susceptibility to visual illusion), auditory acuity, smell, taste, tactile sensitivity, weight discrimination, and size-weight illusion.

For the most part, the experiments demonstrated that residents of the Torres Straits did not possess unusual powers of sensory acuity. Nevertheless, there were some important differences, evident when the natives employed their sensory skills in naturalistic settings. On one occasion, Rivers was sailing to one island from another when the three men in the boat (all island natives) remarked that there was already a boat in the harbor on the other side of the island to which they were bound. Rivers deduced that the men were able to see the tops of the ship's masts at this distance because they were accustomed to noticing such details. He concluded:

So far as our data go it seems that the savage starts with visual acuity which is but slightly superior to that of the average normal-sighted European. By long and continued practice, however, in attending to minute details in surrounding with which he becomes extremely familiar, the savage is able to see and recognize distant objects in a way that appears almost miraculous. (Rivers, 1901, p. 43)

Did the Torres Straits expedition demonstrate that human mental processes are the same, despite cultural differences, or that cultural differences are overwhelmingly important in all the contexts in which those processes are actually put to use?

Rivers' statement is important for two reasons. First, it suggests that controlled experimentation is insufficient when unaccompanied by naturalistic observation, and second, that sensory perception is highly context-specific. As a statement of scientific results, this is no less controversial now than it was at the turn of the century, because of widely, and nearly universally, shared assumption that the mind is a central processing unit. The contrary point of view, which is the context that not only directs but powerfully informs the processing of information, is seen as deeply problematic. This is because it puts at risk the experimental ideal of neutralizing context as an influencing variable. Theoretically and practically, this is the focus of the debate concerning the cultural sources of cognition, and provides much of the raison d'être of current research on both sides of the question. The point of this essay is not to decide the question one way or the other, or to make and support the claims of the various competing factions, but rather to examine the possibility that both are right in light of the best evidence available in the areas of perception, inference and memory, and the emotions.

PERCEPTION

To return to the Torres Straits, let us consider another of Rivers' experiments on native sensory perception, in this case perception of visual illusions. It was assumed at the time that "savages," given their greater attention to contextual details, would be more easily fooled than Westerners by illusions. This was because "savages'" cognitive processes were more bound up in the perception of immediate stimuli, and therefore less able to rise above it and reason in the abstract to a conclusion at variance with visual information. The Muller-Lyer illusion was the test Rivers used. It involves two horizontal lines that terminate either in convex or concave arrows, inducing the susceptible subject to conclude (falsely) that one line is longer than the other, when in fact the two lines are identical. Contrary to the hypothesis, Rivers found that the Torres Straits people were less susceptible to the Muller-Lyer illusion than European comparison groups. Even more surprising was the result that they were more susceptible to the horizontal-vertical illusion.

Many years later, Segall and his colleagues considered the results of the Rivers experiment and hypothesized that different susceptibilities to visual illusions were related to interactions with the environment. People living in highly "carpentered" environments would tend to interpret the drawings in terms of three dimensional objects: it therefore seemed likely they would be more susceptible to the Muller-Lyer illusion. On the other hand, people resident in rural areas and accustomed to scanning long-range distances would be more susceptible to the horizontal-vertical illusion. Unlike Rivers, Segall used a variety of measures and compared people from 14 non-European groups (13 African, 1 Filipino) and 3 groups of European origin (1 in South Africa, and 2 in the United States). The total number of subjects came to almost 1900, and the results confirmed Segall's hypothesis: Europeans were significantly more susceptible to the Muller-Lyer illusion while nonurban, non-European subjects were more susceptible to the horizontal-vertical illusion (Segall, Campbell, & Herskovitz, 1966). While questions still remain, the conclusion that perception is strongly influenced by cultural environment and attentional habits has held up (Segall, Dasen, Berry, & Poortinga, 1990).

Nevertheless, the phenomena are double-sided. The familiar idea is that culture influences perception and cognition of the environment, but recently the reverse hypothesis has attracted attention: that the environment influences perception and cognition. Consider the phenomenon of sound symbolism, when a sound unit of a language (a phoneme, syllable, feature, or tone) goes beyond its linguistic function to express directly some kind of meaning. Feld (1982) discovered that the Kaluli language of New Guinea features an abundant inventory of lexicalized sound imitative words. These words figure prominently in poetic evocations of bird cries, waterfall sounds and movements, and other environmental events. Bird sounds are especially significant, according to Feld, because they are more ecologically salient. In the jungle, one hears far better than one sees. Bird calls have an affective import that is evident in a Kaluli myth about a boy who asks his older sister for food but is ignored. The boy is then transformed into a muni bird, a kind of dove, whose cries represent sadness, and as such, provide a model for a mournful and melodic song pattern (Feld, 1982; Nuckolls, 1999).

Sound symbolism is important because it foregrounds an issue that arises in every aspect of the discussion of culture and cognition. It is necessary to ask how much of cognition should be attributed to variable cultural contexts and how much of it is influenced or determined by nonarbitrary features of the body in the environment. Years ago, Huttar (1968) pointed out that the pitch of a sound and its frequency are generally related, and that certain high frequency sounds are often associated with the idea of smallness (Ladefoged, 1975; Ultan, 1978). As Nuckolls (1999) points out, "the increasing tension used for higher pitch and the decrease in tension used for falling pitch have a universal tendency to be associated, metaphorically, with contrasting ideas of incompleteness (high pitch) and completeness (falling on low pitch)" (p. 5). Not coincidentally, as Bolinger (1978) says, breaks in utterances as well as asking questions are almost everywhere indicated with rising pitch, while terminal boundaries such as clauses or sentences are marked by falls in pitch.

Cultural anthropologists ever since Rivers' time have made it one of their goals to call into question and, if possible, confound the universalist claims of psychologists (as have economists, biologists, and theologians). It was de Saussure (1966) who insisted that arbitrariness always characterizes the relationship between signifier (sound image) and signified (concept). But if crosscultural communication is possible, as it surely must be in order for cultural anthropology to be possible, then some account must be given of the commonly shared mechanisms, whether cognitive or otherwise, that make this communication possible. Sound symbolism puts this issue directly before us, and it is odd that despite its ubiquity in so many of the world's spoken languages (including English), only a handful of scholars have developed explanations for it.

REASONING

Another Cambridge psychologist, Frederick Bartlett, began an important line of research into the effect of culture on memory. In the 1930s, Bartlett went to East Africa to study the extent to which the remembering of past events is filtered, or even distorted, by culturally shaped knowledge structures, which he called schemas. Sometimes the associated schema led to prodigious feats of recall. For example, Bartlett found Swazi herdsmen who could recall with astonishing accuracy the shape, color, and size of all the cattle bought and sold for the last ten years. Other kinds of schemas were found to be temporally organized, and to be associated with a style of reasoning that was very concrete and context-bound. In the following example (Bartlett, 1932, p. 265), taken from the transcripts of the colonial court, a woman is asked to explain the events that led up to an attack upon her by a man accused of attempted murder:

Magistrate: Now tell me how you got that knock on the head.

Woman: Well, I got up that morning at daybreak and I did (here followed a long list of things done, people met, things said). Then we went to so and so's kraal and we . . . (further lists here) and had some beer, and so and so said. . . .

Magistrate: Never mind about that. I don't want to know anything except how you got the knock on the head.

Woman: All right, all right. I am coming to that. I have not got there yet. And so I said to so and so . . . (there followed again a great deal of conversational and other detail). And then after that we went on to so and so's kraal.

Magistrate: You look here; if we go on like this we shall take all day. What about that knock on the head?

Woman: Yes; all right, all right. But I have not got there yet. So we . . . (on and on for a very long time relating all the initial details of the day). And then we went on to so and so's kraal . . . and there was a dispute . . . and he knocked me on the head, and I died, and that is all I know.

Bartlett was not an anthropologist, but recognized that there was more at work in this process than simply a failure to present a clear and concise account. He concluded that social context, including the value placed on a certain kind of memory, played a determining role.

The observation that people in traditional cultures show a preference for concrete and episodic models of remembering has been made repeatedly. As in Bartlett's day, the explanation given has often focused on the so-called intellectual predicament of primitive people. Their lack of education and exposure to abstract modes of thinking means they are limited to the particular, unable to reason outside or beyond the concrete pragmatics of the everyday (Horton, 1982). Bartlett (1932) himself attributed some aspects of native remembering to an unhurried way of life "where everything that happens is about as interesting as everything else" (pp. 265–266). Studies show that with exposure to Western education indigenous people from Asia and Africa do begin to reason abstractly and to remember events in more semantic terms, instead of episodically. But what, precisely, is being communicated in education?

In the 1980s, Shweder and his colleagues returned to the Bartlett hypothesis and tested its implications for moral thinking in India. Like the Swazi, Oriya-speaking residents of the temple town of Bhubaneshwar show a marked preference for concrete modes of thinking. Asked what someone is like, for example, they relate a series of cases and contexts. Shweder compared the Oriyas to a sample drawn from residents of Chicago, whom he found more prone to abstraction and generalization in personality assessment. The difference could be related to one or more of several factors. The Oriya language might lack terms of sufficient abstraction. The Oriyas themselves might be poorly educated, or unused to abstract reasoning in all contexts, even outside personality judgments. Or the Oriyas might live in a closed intellectual universe, so uniform and unchanging that reasoning across multiple contexts might be extremely difficult for them. As it happened, none of these factors proved valid, which left only one possibility, namely Oriya culture itself. Shweder & Bourne (1984) conclude that the Oriya worldview itself values context-dependent modes of thinking where reasoning about personality is concerned.

Another important test of the cultural construction of inference is in the use of syllogism, enshrined since Plato as one of the prime exemplars of correct thinking. In the 1920s, A. R. Luria submitted incomplete syllogisms to unschooled Central Asian peasants, with the following being a typical exchange between researcher and informant:

Ethnographer: In the far North, where there is snow, all bears are white. Novaya Zemlya is in the far North and there is always snow there. What color are the bears there?

Informant: We always speak only of what we see; we don't talk about what we haven't seen.

Ethnographer: But what do my words imply? (The syllogism is repeated.)

Informant: Well, it's like this: our tsar isn't like yours, and yours isn't like ours. Your words can be answered only by someone who was there, and if a person wasn't there he can't say anything on the basis of your words.

Ethnographer: But on the basis of my words, in the North, where there is always snow, the bears are white, can you gather what kind of bears there are in Novaya Zemyla?

Informant: If a man was sixty or eighty and had seen a white bear and had told about it, he could be believed, but I've never seen one and hence I can't say. That's my last word. Those who saw can tell, and those who didn't see can't say anything. (Luria, 1971, pp. 108–109)

Luria attributed the informant's reluctance to reason syllogistically to his lack of schooling, and to the absence of any need to think outside the narrow parameters of his immediate existence. Education, however, quickly changed informants' responses. But once again, the question was, Why?

In the 1970s, Cole and his colleagues conducted a similar project among the Kpelle. Cole found that, just as the Siberian peasants had done, the Kpelle preferred to restrict their thinking to the known. Cole categorized their responses as theoretical (responding on the basis of the information given in the problem) or empirical (responding on the basis of everyday information about the world). The tendency to theoretical reasoning, he found, increased exclusively as a function of years of education. This tallies with the results of other studies, which show that school attendance is correlated with a variety of cognitive abilities (Greenfield & Bruner, 1969; Stevenson, 1982). But as Cole points out, the development of these abilities is not necessarily generalizable. That is, they could be considered highly task or context specific: "Would the measurement of motor skills learned by the carpenter make him a skilled electrician or a ballet dancer, let alone a person with more highly developed sensorimotor and measurement skills?" (Sharp, Cole, & Lave, 1979, p. 81). The cognitive effects of schooling, in other words, simply could be a tautology: people do well on tests whose content they know and whose performance they have practiced.

Bartlett's line of inquiry has been extended further by Holland and Skinner (1987) in research on conceptual structures and simplified worldviews of college women in making decisions about romantic relationships. Like Bartlett, they hypothesized that people use a limited number of cognitive frameworks to make inferences, and that these frameworks, once activated, become a guide or map for action. For example, they found that college women maintain robust causal scenarios about the kinds of men there are, and that these scenarios are triggered by simple names and references. In the standard scenario, man and woman are equally attractive and equally attracted to each other. But as their attractiveness varies, the scenario allows for and even requires certain kinds of adjustments: "A relatively unattractive male can compensate for his lesser standing by making extraordinary efforts to treat her well and make her happy. A relatively unattractive female can compensate by scaling down her expectations of good treatment" (Holland & Skinner, 1987, p. 102). Other scenarios are organized around the categories of men whom women find unacceptable for special reasons: Don Juans, turkeys, gays, jocks, nerds, and chauvinists are among those who cause problems for women, and each category is associated with prototypical male/female relationships.

Even extremely mundane activities, such as adjusting the air conditioning or heating in the house, shows evidence of schematized information processing. For example, conventionalized and recurrent metaphors appear to guide inferential processes in matters so mundane that their operation goes completely undetected. Speakers of English are accustomed to talking about life as if it were a journey from one point to another, with direction, speed, and course. We speak of moving on with our lives or hitting a dead end, of setting a goal or hitting a fork in the road. While it is easy to dismiss metaphors like these as mere verbal artifice, psychological anthropologists have found that they enter deeply into the processes by which we make judgments and construct explanations. For example, Kempton (1987) found that typical Americans actually maintain radically different models of home heat control, based on different conceptual metaphors. According to some people, the thermostat is a like a person who senses when the house is cold and when the house is hot, and adjusts the temperature accordingly. Other people, in contrast, understand the thermostat as a kind of valve: turning it up releases more hot air, turning it down shuts the valve and cools the house. Kempton examined the thermostat control habits of a number of people, and found that the models he posited correctly predicted the adjustment patterns over a two-year period.

LINGUISTICS AND MENTAL PROCESSES

In the 1920s, Benjamin Whorf, in conjunction with his teacher Edward Sapir, developed several new and even radical hypotheses about the effects of language on the organization of thought. The first stated that the units of meaning of a language (the vocabulary or lexicon) strongly influence or even control perception, so that the availability of a certain term (e.g., *blue*) enables speakers of the associated language to see the color blue. The second hypothesis held that the structural components of a language (its grammar, or what Whorf called fashions of speaking) shaped and constrained thinking across a range of concepts, from time to personal identity. The difficulty with these hypotheses is that Whorf did not offer any independent measures for assessing the degree to which language actually shapes thinking. The only evidence offered was the language itself, or behavior related to the language. Other indicators were developed only later, and in general point to certain limitations on the original Whorf hypothesis, at least in terms of its more relativistic implications.

For example, Whorf asserted that natural language categories affect perception: if a language lacks color terms that differentiate green and blue, then native speakers of this language will not perceive the difference between green and blue objects. Probably no idea in the study of culture and mind has had more far-reaching impact than the idea that language directly affects perception. But it was not until many years later that it was actually put to the test, when Kay and Kempton (1984) used native speakers of English and Tarahumana, an Uto-Aztecan language of northern Mexico, which has only one term for both green and blue. Using color chips graded from pure green to pure blue, respondents in both languages were asked to decide which chip was the most different in color in selections of three chips. As the hypothesis predicts, English speakers were more inclined to discriminate between blue and green, whereas Tarahumara speakers were more inclined to see them as the same. How people label things, therefore, does affect their perception, and suggests that linguistic categories across a whole range of features could have demonstrable effects.

Whorf also found, or thought he found, that the temporal structures embedded in language, in the form of tense, for example, affect the speakers' perception of time. English makes fine distinctions between past, present, and future, and this helps to explain the peculiar fascination of English speakers with calculation and record keeping. The Hopi, on the other hand, speak a language that is more con-cerned with duration, and the relative absence of temporal punctiveness induces a sense of time that is much more fluid and organic. Things do not happen dis-cretely or all at once, but developmentally, in the manner of a plant growing from bud to blossom. Whorf speculated that people with a grammar that encodes a dis-crete view of time might tend to view each day as different, and therefore to expect change. People with a more organic view of time, however, might tend to view change as more continuous, or as less subject to intervention that would make change itself more radical.

In American culture, for example, it is conventional to speak of time as money: budget, spend, invest, profit, and loss are words equally applicable in both domains. We understand time as money, and vice versa, with the result that it is easy, even inevitable, that the two become synonymous with each other in prac-tical reasoning. Lakoff and Johnson (1999) provide an outline of the conceptual mapping of the two:

Money is mapped onto time

The user of money is mapped onto the user of time (agent)

The purpose that requires the money is mapped onto the purpose that requires time

The value of the money is mapped onto the value of time

The value of the purpose is mapped onto the value of time

Thus with the resources made available by the mapping of money onto time, we are able to comprehend utterances such as the following: I have to budget my time. I spent too much time on that. I've invested a lot of time on this project. You don't use your time profitably. That mistake resulted in considerable loss of time (Lakoff & Johnson, 1999, pp. 163–164). According to Lakoff and Johnson, the metaphorical structures of this kind are reified in institutions. One of them, of course, is the practice of paying people according to the time they work. Time clocks, business hours, deadlines, and appointment books, which are the practical mechanisms of life in a commercial and capitalist society, serve to reinforce and institutionalize the linguistic practices, and ultimately the beliefs that time is money and time is a resource.

From Whorf, and from those who followed him in this line of research, we know that in other cultures different concepts of time exist, with radically different implications for behavior. What would time be like, for example, for people who do not conceptualize time as extendible or expendable, that is, for people without the metaphors of direction and resource that we take for granted? Likewise, as Lakoff and Johnson point out, would time still be time for us if we could not waste it or budget it? There is a problem if the answer we give is too radically relativistic, since then the ontological question must arise, Is there such a thing as time at all independent of linguistic contrivance? This is where Lakoff and his colleagues go beyond Whorf, into a much more complex explanation of the relationship between the universals of human embodiment and the particularities of cultural experience, in a way that does not reduce one to the other.

The experience of time is structured by two processes, the first a correlation to the experience of the human body in space and the second an arbitrary mapping of experience onto cultural concepts whose variation is wide. The first is actually a process of metonymy, and is based on the experience of movement in space. Every day we participate in motion situations. That is, we move with reference to ourselves and the people around us, and we correlate that motion with those events that provide us with our sense of time. In these situations we are typically looking ahead in the direction of our motion and at those things moving toward us, and this provides us with the experiential resource whereby we imagine that future events are "ahead" of us. Metonymy thus refers to the co-occurrence of motion and time-defining events, such that the experience of one is mapped onto the experience of the other. For example, time duration can stand metonymically for distance, as in "Atlanta is two-and-a-half hours from Birmingham, Alabama." The metonymy is reversible, too. I can say, "Janis talked for a hundred miles while I drove," to signify that the distance corresponds to the amount of time talked (Lakoff & Johnson, 1999, pp. 151–152).

Lakoff and Johnson find that there are three great motion situations, which most (if not all) languages use to construct metonymies for time comprehension. As human beings, we are usually looking ahead, and thus we tend to conceptualize time as ahead of us, as moving toward us, or to conceptualize ourselves as moving toward time. Lakoff and Johnson offer the following positionality in relation to time:

Time Orientation: What we will encounter in the future is ahead of us. What we are encountering at present is where we are (present to us). What we encountered in the past is behind us.

Moving Time: What we will encounter in the future is moving toward us. What we are encountering now is moving by (passing) us. What we encountered in the past has moved past us.

Moving Observer: What we will encounter in the future is what we are moving toward. What we are encountering is now is what we are moving by. What we encountered in the past is what we moved past. (Lakoff & Johnson, 1999, p. 152)

What all human beings appear to share is a sense of their own bodies as fixed with respect to the passage of events, or as moving with respect to those events, and these experiences provide the fundamental groundwork for the conceptualization of time across languages. This is the universal. Variations occur with the cultural emphases given to the different metonymies, and to the metaphorical structures built with them. Thus there is no way to predict, based on the universals of human experience, that time will be conceptualized as money, or that time can be spent and saved, wasted or used wisely. Experiential gestalts derivative of basic bodily experience appear to undergird these, however, and provide the fundamental logic of temporal understanding. That time can be wasted, like money, is only comprehensible when one also has prior understanding of the fact that time is to be treated directionally, with objectives that can be met.

CULTURE AND MOTIVATED COGNITION

As we have seen, cognitive anthropology is influenced by recent work in cognitive science and linguistics. It is also beset with problems with a long philosophical pedigree. Chief among these problems is motivation. Given that people have the models cognitive anthropologists ascribe to them, what makes such models compelling? People do not merely have models and schemas, nor do they simply apply and reason about them. They also feel deeply about the knowledge they possess, and to a large extent, we cannot come up with a satisfying account of cultural cognition until we come to terms with this fact. Roy D'Andrade (1995) and Claudia Strauss (1992) have addressed this issue, redefining knowledge structures as goal-directed systems. The problem with this is that it tends to make us think in terms of discrete and isolable aims that are accessible to consciousness.

Edwin Hutchins (1987) and Drew Westen (1992) have attempted to incorporate Freudian psychoanalysis into their paradigm, in order to provide cognitive anthropology with a theory of deep motivation. Unfortunately, the ancient division of the field into the study of knowledge (cognition) and the study of motivation (psychoanalysis) makes a synthesis of the two difficult. For someone not familiar with the difference between cognitivists and psychoanalysts, or unaware of the mutual antipathy that divides them, the fact that the two have something to contribute to each other must seem obvious. It is not necessary to reduce one to the other in order to acknowledge that they might be related. What we need is a cultural theory of motivated knowledge that explains both how knowledge is organized and how it is motivated within different cultural domains. The whole concept of the schema needs to be rebuilt, to take into account dynamic processes.

The following proscription for refiguring schemas, I believe, is a step in the right direction: (1) Culturally constructed schemas summarize past experiences into holistic forms, allowing incoming information to be measured against the existing composite for goodness of fit. Incoming information may be distorted or partially deleted, in order to achieve this fit, thus explaining some of the errors or gaps in remembered accounts. Schemas enable rapid perception, as information is assimilated into the existing composite, but they also lead to patterned and recurrent distortions; (2) Multiple schemas may be applied simultaneously and unconsciously to the interpretation of information. Multiple channels operate in unconscious information processing, but conscious thought tends to proceed in one or only a few of these. As a result, there may be competition for priority among these multiple schemas; and (3) Conscious reflection on schemas may be possible, especially when schemas are given symbolic representation in words, signs, or gestures. This may facilitate changes in how the schemas are used in appraisals, decisions, and negotiations of meaning, leading to changes that can construct new schemata or that integrate old ones.

To create a dialogue between cultural cognition and psychoanalysis, let us posit the existence of a repertoire of schemas that contains archaic components, many formed in childhood, that can never be erased (Horowitz, 1988). Such early schemas of self and others are constrained by mature concepts of self that incorporate and integrate immature self schemas. Nevertheless, earlier forms continue an unconscious appraisal of current events. The link between the dynamic unconscious and cognitive schematic could then be stated as follows: Access to conscious symbol systems, including cultural images, words, and action scenarios, might occur only through the information organized by unconscious schemas, such that to instantiate one is to instantiate the other.

The Jalaris are a fishing caste people who live on the southeastern coast of India. They posit the existence of a variety of spirits, most of them female, known collectively as *ammavallu,* or mothers. The Jalaris associate terrible calamities, and dramatic events of all kinds (good and bad), with the *ammavalu.* Goddesses are binary agencies, made up of two aspects, one malign and the other benign, rather like split personalities. Sometimes goddesses do good things and sometimes they do bad things, but predicting their action is impossible: they are extremely fickle. Nevertheless, one must act toward them as if their behavior could be influenced, and that means giving them regular offerings of good things (meat, new clothes, and occasionally alcohol or even marijuana). People often forget to make offerings to the goddesses, and so when a goddess attacks and punishes them by inflicting disease or interrupting the fish catch, people say it is because she felt neglected. But would it have made any difference if they had made the offerings, in the correct amount and on time? The Jalaris doubt it.

If there seems to be a lot of ambivalence involved here, there is, and this is typical both of the goddesses themselves and the people who worship them. The goddesses are good and bad; people love them and hate them. No one is sure what to do, only that something must be done. When new calamities befall the

Jalaris, as during the occurrence of epidemic diseases, people interpret events according to the schema just described. It is full of conflicted images and emotions, and this is related both to the circumstances of Jalari childhood and to the structure of Jalari cosmology. A psychoanalytically informed model of development is needed here, because even though we can develop a satisfactory account of the cognitive schemas that inform Jalari goddess beliefs (Nuckolls, 1991), it is not adequate to explain them. We must take into account deep motivations in order to understand why people feel strongly about (and do not merely accept as true or false) propositions about supernatural agencies.

In Hindu South Asia ambivalence is central to the relationship between mother and child, and especially mother and son (Carstairs, 1958; Erikson, 1969; Kakar, 1981; Nuckolls, 1996; Obeyesekere, 1981; Roland, 1988; Trawick, 1990). On the one hand, a boy is drawn by memories of his mother's nurturing (far more long-lasting and intense in India than in the West) to idealize the feminine. On the other hand, fear that the mother may reject him, or worse, exploits him for the fulfillment of her own sexual needs, and compels him to constrain the feminine, to keep its power to envelop him under control. Children in Hindu South Asia, especially boys, appear to grow up with strikingly bifurcated images of their own mothers, and of women in general. It is therefore not surprising that images of the goddesses follow suit, with each goddess represented in both benign and malign aspects.

Cultural schemas relate the causes of misfortune (e.g., illness, death) to interventions by the goddesses. These episodically organized schemas can be described in great detail, in the manner that Holland and Skinner describe romantic knowledge structures among American college women, as follows: Social Dispute (leads to) Offertory Neglect (leads to) Goddess Attack (leads to) Misfortune. In other words, some kind of social dispute occurs, usually between close relatives, and this prevents family members from paying homage to their household goddesses. The goddesses attack and cause misfortune, and the only way to alleviate the misfortune is by identifying the source in divination and then promising the goddesses that the required offerings will take place in due course. The sequence is stereotypic and there are only minor variations from case to case. The cognitive account of this phenomenon describes the sequence and its contextual variations, as well as the inferential strategies used by the participants to argue toward a desired conclusion (Nuckolls, 1991). Where a combined cognitive and psychoanalytic account goes further, however, is in specifying the desires that inform and infiltrate schema use. If something bad happens, in other words, why is the Jalari individual predisposed to feel that it must be due to a supernatural agency he refers to as mother?

The cognitive account by itself cannot answer this question, nor is it meant to. That is because cognitivists almost always stop short of desire in motivation, and assume that instrumental consciousness is sufficient to account for goal-directed behavior involving schema use. This is hard to argue for except on narrow disciplinary grounds. A more fruitful approach would be to define cognitive schemas as knowledge structures that run simultaneously with elements in the dynamic unconscious. What sustains the causal schemas of the Jalaris is not simply habit, in other words, but the emotional homologies between mothers and goddesses. Caring and nurturing, cruel and punishing: mothers and goddesses are felt to be both, and this is why thinking about the causes of events in everyday life represents and partially resolves the deep-seated ambivalences that result.

THE CULTURAL PSYCHOLOGY OF MENTAL ILLNESS

Schematic representations sometimes conflict, not only in India but also in America, giving rise to the deep-seated and long-lasting ambivalences we identify with psychopathology. Dependency, for example, is probably a fact of human development, but so is the development of autonomy. Some cultures value autonomy over dependency, and encourage its development. For them, the desire for continued dependency is a sign of regression, and of the failure to grow up. Other cultures construe dependency as the supreme human good, and see proper human development as a return to a benign state of ego-less enmeshment. No matter what the goal or aim of life as constructed by different cultures, the tension between the desire for dependency and the desire for autonomy is common enough to be considered a human universal. The point is that only under particular circumstances does it lead to psychological distress or social dysfunction.

A case in point is the set of conditions termed in American psychiatry the personality disorders. These are chronic and long-lasting disorders, as opposed to the symptomatic psychiatric conditions, like mania or depression, that are considered more episodic in nature. The personality disorders are thought to reflect more basic emotional dysfunctions and to be less amenable to therapeutic change. What is most interesting, however, is the fact that they are all variations on a single theme: the opposition between the developmental ideals of dependency and autonomy. The disorders differ mainly in terms of the value represented (dependence or independence) and direction (active or passive), such that most of the ten currently recognized conditions can be understood as a combination of these two sets of terms, as follows:

Active-Independent	Active-Dependent
antisocial personality disorder	histrionic personality disorder
paranoid personality disorder	borderline personality disorder
Passive-Independent	Passive-Dependent
narcissistic personality disorder	dependent personality disorder
paranoid personality disorder	borderline personality disorder

What the chart reveals is that disorders of independence all represent a self-oriented approach to the world. The extent to which this approach is used is what distinguishes the least intense disorders of independence (antisocial and narcissistic), from the greatest (paranoid), as seen in the following clinical descriptions from the official diagnostic manual:

Antisocial: A pattern of disregard for, and violation of, the rights of others.

Narcissistic: A pattern of grandiosity, need for admiration, and lack of empathy.

Paranoid: A pattern of pervasive distrust and suspiciousness of others such that their motives are interpreted as malevolent.

These individuals do not understand, and cannot respond to, other peoples' needs and desires, and when not actually oblivious to others' feelings (as in narcissism), they seek to manipulate them (as in antisociality) in order to further their own ends. One may be actively independent, as in the case of the antisocial, or passively independent, as in the case of the narcissist, or somewhere in between. Paranoia, of course, is the structural obverse of antisociality. Instead of seeking control over others through guile and craftiness, paranoids fear that others are using these techniques against them.

The dependent personality disorders are all characterized by their need and other-directed approach to the world and vary (in terms of neediness and a disposition to psychotic features) from the least (histrionic and dependent) to the most (borderline). Actively dependent individuals are characterized by alertness, vigilance, persistence, and ambition, whereas passively dependent individuals display varying degrees of ineptness and tend to acquiesce to others' needs. The dependent personality disorders share a quality of neediness, which they express in different ways through submission and clinging in the case of the dependent personality, to outright demands and overt attention-seeking behavior in the case of the borderline personality:

Dependent: A pattern of submissive and clinging behavior related to an excessive need to be taken care of.

Histrionic: A pattern of excessive emotionality and attention seeking.

Borderline: A pattern of instability in interpersonal relationships and self-image, and a marked impulsivity.

The personality disorders are interesting because they represent, in extreme form, the values of independence and dependence that define American society. In American society, the disorders of dependence are diagnosed much more commonly among women than men. That is because the value of dependence has been allocated to women, and women are expected to manifest this value more. In the same way, men are diagnosed much more often than women with the disorders of independence. That is because men have been allocated the value of independence, and independent behavior is expected of them. Women and men who manifest the values that have been allocated to them in extreme form, or inappropriately, become diagnosed with the disorders of dependence and independence (Nuckolls, 1998).

The personality disorders of American psychiatry are culture-bound syndromes, the result of the long-standing historical tensions. It is important to understand that just because they are not simply or solely biological in origin does not make them any less real. On the contrary, they also reflect a particular cultural rendering of a universal human theme involving the difficulty of reconciling dependency needs with the development of autonomy. Their origin in the psyche make them even more fundamental to the human condition—not less so—than an explanation grounded in strict biological determinism. After all, one has to catch a disease, or be born with a peculiar predisposition to it, whereas the personality disorders reflect experiences all human beings share by virtue of their development. Of course the question must still be asked: Even with all that is shared, why do only some people manifest the psychological features we define as pathological? While there must be many answers, the one proposed by George Devereux (1980) in his articles on schizophrenia is still cogent. We need them. Personality disordered individuals help us to calibrate the scale according to which we measure our own normality (Nuckolls, 1998). In a sense, they set the scales at their upper limits, and while they point in the direction sanctified by cultural values, namely men toward independence and women toward dependence, they also say to us, "Do not go this far."

Ambivalence is a powerful motivator, both culturally and psychologically. Resolutions are sought, but the underlying conflicts always reassert themselves, and so the process continues. From the American cultural conflict between the values of independence and dependence, American psychiatry develops, in part, as a series of repeated attempts to resolve the ambivalence in favor of a purely reductive set of biogenetic constructs. If my account is correct, the effort is unlikely to succeed, because the underlying conflict is cultural, but founded ultimately on a deep-seated paradox in human development. This is the paradox of needing and wanting dependence even as we grow up (partially or wholly) rejecting it. The relationship between cultural schemas and psychological schemas is not a process of simple one-to-one matching. But the cultural process I just described cannot work without its counterpart in the human mind. The ambivalences we call social, in other words, must realize themselves partly in the psyche in order to become real. Obeyesekere (1981) calls this process objectification—the representation in the mind of the conflicts most members of a society share—and recommends a case-historical method to recover it.

CONCLUSION

Is knowledge best understood as the product of the world, a creation of external impingements, or as an outcome of internal processes inherent in the mind? This question was addressed in its classical form by Descartes. Unfortunately, the formulations in service today are little improved, since they continue to pit the external and internal against each other as if they are correctly interpreted as independent of each other. Modern disciplines are partly the result. Anthropologists have developed a cottage industry devoted to puncturing the universalistic assumptions of cognitive psychologists: culture in mind, they say, goes all the way down. Meanwhile, cognitivists have developed increasingly arcane models of storage and retrieval, with success measured in terms of how well a computer possessing artificial intelligence mimics the performance of real human beings on laboratory tasks. Integrative approaches are few and far between, but in this essay, I have tried to highlight the ones I consider most promising.

REFERENCES

Bartlett, F. (1932). *Remembering: An experiment in experimental and social psychology.* Cambridge, UK: Cambridge University Press.

Bolinger, D. (1978). Intonation across languages. In J. Greenberg, C. Ferguson, & E. Moravcshik (Eds.), *Universals of human language* (Vol. 2, pp. 471–524). Stanford, CA: Stanford University Press.

Boyer, P. (1990). *Tradition as truth and communication.* Cambridge, UK: Cambridge University Press.

Burnyeat, M. (1990). *The theaetetus of Plato* (M. Levett, Trans.). Indianapolis, IN: Hackett Publishing.

Carstairs, G. (1958). *The twice-born: A study of a community of high-caste Hindus.* Bloomington: Indiana University Press.

D'Andrade, R. (1995). *The development of cognitive anthropology.* Cambridge, UK: Cambridge University Press.

de Saussure, F. (1966). *Course in general lingusitics.* New York: McGraw-Hill.

Devereux, G. (1980). *Basic problems of ethnopsychiatry.* Chicago: University of Chicago Press.

Erikson, E. (1969). *Gandhi's truth.* New York: Norton.

Feld, S. (1982). *Sound and sentiment: Birds, weeping, poetics, and song in Kaluli expression.* Philadelphia: University of Pennsylvania Press.

Geertz, C. (1973). *Interpretations of culture.* New York: Basic Books.

Greenfield, P., & Bruner, J. (1969). Culture and cognitive growth. In D. Goslin (Ed.), *Handbook of socialization theory and research.* New York: Rand McNally.

Holland, D., & Skinner, D. (1987). Prestige and intimacy: The cultural models behind Americans' talk about gender types. In D. Holland & N. Quinn (Eds.), *Cultural models in language and thought.* Cambridge, UK: Cambridge University Press.

Horowitz, M. (Ed.). (1988). *Psychodynamics and cognition.* Chicago: University of Chicago Press.

Horton, R. (1982). Tradition and modernity revisited. In M. Hollis & S. Lukes (Eds.), *Rationality and relativism.* Cambridge: MIT Press.

Hutchins, E. (1987). Myth and experience in the Trobriand Islands. In D. Holland & N. Quinn (Eds.), *Cultural models in language and thought.* Cambridge, UK: Cambridge University Press.

Huttar, G. (1968). Relations between prosodic variables and emotions in normal American English utterances. *Journal of Speech and Hearing Research, 11,* 481–487.

Kakar, S. (1981). *The inner world: A psychoanalytic study of childhood and society in India.* New Delhi: Oxford University Press.

Kay, P., & Kempton, W. (1984). What is the Sapir-Whorf hypothesis. *American Anthropologist, 86,* 65–79.

Kempton, W. (1987). Two theories of home heat control. In D. Holland & N. Quinn (Eds.), *Cultural models in language and thought.* Cambridge, UK: Cambridge University Press.

Ladefoged, P. (1975). *A course in phonetics.* New York: Harcourt Brace Jovanovich.

Lakoff, G., & Johnson, M. (1999). *Philosophy in the flesh: The embodied mind and its challenge to Western thought.* New York: Basic Books.

Luria, A. (1971). Toward the problem of the historical nature of psychological processes. *International Journal of Psychology, 6,* 259–273.

Lutz, C. (1988). *Unnatural emotions.* Chicago: University of Chicago Press.

Nuckolls, C. (1991). Culture and causal thinking: Diagnosis and prediction in a South Indian fishing village. *Ethos, 19,* 3–51.

Nuckolls, C. (1996). *The cultural dialectics of knowledge and desire.* Madison: University of Wisconsin Press.

Nuckolls, C. (1998). *Culture: A problem that cannot be solved.* Madison: University of Wisconsin Press.

Nuckolls, J. (1999). The case for sound symbolism. *Annual Review of Anthropology. 28,* 225–252.

Obeyesekere, G. (1981). *Medusa's hair.* Chicago: University of Chicago Press.

Rivers, W. (1901). Vision. In A. C. Haddon (Ed.), *Report of the Cambridge anthropological expedition to the Torres Straits (Vol. 2).* Cambridge, UK: Cambridge University Press.

Roland, A. (1988). *In search of the self in India and Japan.* Princeton: Princeton University Press.

Segall, M., Campbell, D., & Herskovitz, M. (1966). *The influence of culture on visual perception.* Indianapolis, IN: Bobbs-Merrill.

Segall, M., Dasen, P., Berry, J., & Poortinga, Y. (1990). *Human behavior in global perspective: An introduction to cross-cultural psychology.* New York: Pergamon.

Sharp, D., Cole, M., & Lave, C. (1979). Education and cognitive development: The evidence from experimental research. *Monographs of the Society for Research in Child Development, 44,* nos. 1–2.

Shweder, R., & Bourne, E. (1984). Does the concept of the person vary cross-culturally? In R. Shweder & R. LeVine (Eds.), *Culture theory.* Cambridge, UK: Cambridge University Press.

Spiro, M. (1984). Some reflections on cultural determinism and relativism with special attention to reason and emotion. In R. Shweder & R. LeVine (Eds.), *Culture theory.* Cambridge, UK: Cambridge University Press.

Stevenson, H. (1982). Influences of schooling on cognitive development. In D. Wagner & H. Stevenson (Eds.), *Cultural perspectives on child development.* San Francisco: Freeman.

Strauss, C. (1992). Models as motives. In R. D'Andrade & C. Strauss (Eds.), *Human motives and cultural models.* Cambridge, UK: Cambridge University Press.

Trawick, M. (1990). *Notes on love in a Tamil family.* Berkeley, CA: University of California Press.

Ultan, R. (1978). Sound size symbolism. In J. Greenberg, C. Ferguson, & E. Moravcsik (Eds.), *Universals of human language (Vol. 2)*. Stanford, CA: Stanford University Press.

Westen, D. (1992). The cognitive self and the psychoanalytic self: Can we put ourselves together? *Psychological Inquiry, 3,* 1–13.

Whorf, B. (1956). *Language, thought, and reality.* Cambridge, MA: MIT Press.

PART II

Cultural Cognition and Specific Disorders

4

Cultural Cognition and Depression

John F. Schumaker

Over the years, a great many theories have emerged in order to understand the serious problem of depression. These have revolved around a wide range of biological, psychological, and environmental explanatory variables. A sense of urgency has crept into our search for an answer in light of research demonstrating that depression has reached epidemic proportions in Western cultural settings. A number of studies indicate that clinical depression is now approximately ten times more common than it was fifty years ago (Hagnell, Lanke, Rorsman, & Oejesjoe, 1982; Klerman, 1985; Sartorius, 1987; Schumaker, 1995; Seligman, 1990).

At the moment, biological and cognitive theories dominate our etiological formulations of depression. A number of physiological, neurochemical, and genetic factors are thought to underlie depression (e.g., Bertelsen, Harvald, & Hauge, 1977; Kendler, Heath, Martin, & Eaves, 1986). There is compelling evidence that some types of depression have a genetic component, and even that a depressive gene may cause some people to fall prey to depression. This general line of reasoning has been reinforced by the effectiveness of certain antidepressant medications.

One primary challenge to the biological models has to do with the large degree of crosscultural variation with regard to the occurrence of depression (Jenkins, Kleinman, & Good, 1991). If depression is, first and foremost, a biologically based disorder, one would expect to see fairly constant rates of depression across cultures. This is the case to a large extent with schizophrenia and other disorders that are predominantly organic in origin. In fact, evidence suggests that cultural shaping has considerably less to do with schizophrenia disorders than it does with depression (Draguns, 1995). Moreover, the variance with regard to cultural structures will also affect the likelihood that depression will emerge at all. As it turns out, clinical depression, with motivational, cognitive, emotional, and somatic symptoms, is far more prevalent in contemporary Western culture than in most non-Western ones. Some investigators have gone so far as to label clinical depression a Western culture-bound syndrome.

Those who insist that depression is a universal disorder frequently maintain that non-Western manifestations of depression are primarily somatic in nature. They generally concede that the familiar cognitive symptoms of depression (e.g., hopelessness, despair, sadness, guilt, feelings of inadequacy) are absent, with the same being true of motivational and emotional symptoms. But while noting that somatic symptoms still can be found in many non-Western cultures, they then argue that these somatic symptoms should be understood as depression even though three of the four symptom categories are often not represented.

This particular line of reasoning requires a leap in logic that cannot be justified by observable facts. It would require, for example, that we diagnose as depressed someone who reports gongs pounding in the head. In the absence of the other categories of symptoms that typically designate depression, one could just as easily diagnose this as an anxiety-related or stress-related disorder, or as any number of other disorders that have a somatic component. Jadhav (1995) is critical of the tendency of Western mental health practitioners to engage in what he refers to as cultural cleansing, as they persist in viewing depression as a constant feeling state that is universal, and that does nothing more than change its vocabulary over time and across cultures. They do not give sufficient attention to a variety of fundamental problems that shed doubt on depression as a universal entity. These include the high degree of crosscultural variation, radically different local categories of emotion, language variations across culture, difficulties in translating emotion-related vocabulary, and the lack of a universal biological indicator for depression.

To illustrate how cultural cleansing distorts an accurate picture of depression in India, Jadhav outlines some of the local idioms of distress that are currently classified as symptoms of depression. For example, in India a depressed person frequently presents the complaints *naara mein dard,* which means pain in the nerves, or *sar mein garmi,* which refers to heat in the head, or *badan mein Dard,* meaning pain in the body. According to Jadhav, mental health professionals, whose training typically revolves around the Western psychiatric diagnosis systems, tend to selectively prune or gloss over this information in order to fit the symptoms into conventional Western categories.

Once culture has been eliminated from the diagnostic equation, one loses the capacity to recognize important social and cultural variables that are involved in the etiology and manifestation of the disorder. Many of the unique symptom patterns are also sacrificed for cultural cleansing. With regard to the vast differences in the symptomatology of depression across cultures, Jadhav questions the practice of continuing to use the term depression for symptom patterns that bear little resemblance to Western depression. We do not have sufficient evidence to conclude that depression is an objective disease entity that can be transported, for purposes of convenience, from Western to non-Western settings. At the very least, we are forced to conclude that non-Western depression, if indeed it exists, represents an entity that deviates quite markedly from so-called clinical depression in Western cultural settings.

CULTURAL COGNITION AND DEPRESSION-RESISTANCE

The field of clinical psychology is dominated, and limited, by the deep-rooted assumption of individualism (Sloan, 1996). The prevailing cognitive models of depression tend to center on the core beliefs and automatic thoughts of isolated individuals (e.g., Beck, 1995), with little or no reference to the wider cultural context of those thoughts and beliefs. Apologists have responded to criticisms about excessive emphasis on individualism by arguing that cognitive theory and therapy have begun to take account of social influences. But this usually refers to factors operating in the family or local environment, rather than to the overarching cultural texts that underlie broad patterns of cognition. These latter elements are very important since they involve macroscopic structures of cultural cognition that precede, and are the building blocks of, individual cognition. It is essential that we gain a better understanding of the role of cultural cognition in depression, especially since it might help to explain why clinical depression seems to bind itself only to certain structures of cultural cognition.

While controversial, the argument that clinical depression is a Western culture-bound syndrome is supported by anthropological research demonstrating that entire cultures can be found that appear to be devoid of Western-style depression. For example, the Kaluli of New Guinea have been studied in relation to depression for over two decades, without discovery of a single case that resembled Western clinical depression. Schieffelin (1985) described the Kaluli as a people who benefit from "power cultural protection against depression as it is understood by many Western theories" (p. 115). The Kaluli are especially interesting in relation to the theories that regard depression as the result of the internalization, suppression, and/or repression of negative emotion. Members of that culture possess a remarkable "assertive energy" that manifests itself as "a tendency to get angry" (Schieffelin, 1985, p. 109). The emotional ethos in Kaluli culture encourages the externalization of toxic emotion, even defining male status partially in terms of the impressiveness of anger displays. One could argue that the apparent absence of depression among the Kaluli has to do with cultural messages and suggestions that, once absorbed, direct behavior in emotional expression patterns that are prophylactic in terms of depression. The logic of employing assertiveness to combat depression (as in some Western therapies) seems an in-built feature of Kaluli culture.

Of course, all this could be framed in terms of cultural cognition. For the most part, individual members of Kaluli culture are not employing private and personalized cognitions that lead them toward an assertive externalization of negative emotion. The cognitions involved are traceable to cultural constructions that predispose members toward certain beliefs, thoughts, and attitudes toward emotion. The same could be said about the Kaluli mindset that virtually eliminates the experience of loss. Referred to as social reciprocity, this cognitive construction informs members that all personal losses, injustices, and infractions will be reciprocated or rectified. Even loss of loved ones is reciprocated as members engage symbolically in practices that "get even" with the spiritual forces responsible for the loss.

It is misleading to depict Kaluli culture as one that has cognitive structures uniquely incompatible with the formation of depressive symptoms. This is because depression-resistant cultures can be found that have themes opposite to those of the Kaluli. For instance, the Toraja of Indonesia have a long tradition of discouraging expressions of negative emotion, in particular anger. It is a nonviolent society that attaches great meaning and significance to social harmony and group consensus. Outward expressions of hostility are so culturally unacceptable that they are deemed to be pathological, and even punishable by supernatural forces.

In light of the internalization models of depression, one might predict that the high levels of emotional containment in Toraja culture might result in high rates of clinical depression. The fact that this is not the case requires us to look more closely at what Hollan (1994) calls the cognitive work of culture (p. 74). In order to intercept the potential harmful consequences of extreme emotional control, Toraja culture evolved cognitive structures that keep issues related to anger at the forefront of people's consciousness, thereby preventing a true repression of these emotions. Thus we have another, although very different, example of cultural cognition that mediates emotional experience in order to minimize the risk of depression.

A sizable body of research also shows a large amount of crosscultural variation with postnatal depression, a disorder that frequently attracts biological explanations because of hormonal and various other physiological disruptions that accompany childbirth. But whereas 20 percent of Western women develop clinical depression after giving birth (Hopkins, Marcus, & Campbell, 1984), many non-Western cultures are completely free of this problem. In fact, after reviewing the crosscultural and anthropological literature, Stern and Kluckman (1983) were unable to find many indications of postnatal depression in the non-Western world, leading them to conclude that this may be another example of a Western culture-bound syndrome.

Harkness (1987), who also believes that postnatal depression is a Western culture-bound syndrome, gives a detailed account of the Kipsigis of Kenya, a cultural group who never suffer from postnatal depression. In her estimation, the "cultural structuring of childbirth" is such that Kipsigis women enjoy almost total immunity from this disorder. As part of this, the Kipsigis employ a range of customs and rituals, such as treating the new mother as a child and pampering her for an extended period of time. During this period, primary childcare responsibility is in the hands of the other women of the community.

Beyond thinking of these practices as cultural structuring, we can also understand them as mechanisms that result in collective modes of cognitive structuring, in this case ones that reduce vulnerability to depression. It still may be the case that the immunizing cognitions of new Kipsigis mothers are *self*-delivered, but they are actually interpretations of larger shared cognitions that are deeply embedded in wider Kipsigis culture. Western cognitive psychologists often pinpoint specific cognitions that may predispose a new mother to succumb to postnatal depression, for example, thinking "I must be constantly available for my baby" (Olioff, 1991). It may be that, in delivering this type of cognition to herself, the new mother invites feelings that she is sacrificing her freedom and running the risk of becoming personally overwhelmed by all the responsibility on her shoulders.

But rather than being an individual cognition, this particular one is a direct extension of the cognitive socialization, as well as the structural realities, that exist in contemporary Western culture. Likewise, a Kipsigis woman who thinks (or believes) "as a new mother, I am now important and deserve to be pampered," is also translating the cultural cognition available to her as part of her cognitive socialization in Kipsigis culture. She is employing what Jadhav (1995) describes as the cultural vocabulary that is an essential element in both normal and abnormal behavior. The historical vocabulary that predisposes many Westerners to depression revolves around such cultural themes as energy, fatigue, stress, and guilt. But Jadhav argues that the cultural vocabulary of many non-Western cultures is such that it does not lead to symptom formation patterns that are comparable to Western clinical depression. In this regard, Jadhav casts doubt on the crosscultural validity of depression, and dispels the notion of depression as a universal disorder.

Although it may be incorrect to conceptualize depression as a universal phenomenon, the crosscultural literature nonetheless contains reports of depression in the non-Western world. A wide amount of variation exists with regard to the mode of expression of these non-Western depressive disorders, but most tend to follow the previously mentioned somatic course of expression. This is well illustrated by so-called depression that is found in Chinese culture. There is no word in the Chinese language that conveys directly the notion of depression as we understand it in the West. The closest word to approximate it is *xin qing bu hao,* which refers to a state in which "the heart is not good," and one is in a bad mood (Kwong & Wong, 1981). Some research suggests that there is a very low rate of depression in China, but it is not without controversy. It has been claimed that these statistics are distorted due to diagnostic traditions that favor other categories of psychopathology (Kleinman, 1986).

Zhang (1995) summarized the history of depression in China, noting that it is most frequently given the diagnosis of neurasthenia, which entails such symptoms such as weakness, bitter taste in the mouth, dizziness, diarrhea, loss of appetite, insomnia, excessive dreaming, hypochondriacal pain, and chest discomfort. Zhang reasons that it is appropriate to conceptualize this constellation of symptoms as depression even though only the somatic category of symptoms is represented. He goes on to detail cultural and political arrangements in Chinese society that prevent depression from being expressed in ways other than somatic ones. The Chinese people, for example, are enculturated in order to express their emotions, and emotional disturbance, through physical and somatic symbolism. While bodily complaints are an accepted mode by which psychological distress is communicated in China, the opposite is true of direct expressions of psychological discomfort. In fact, as Zhang points out, there is even a strong political taboo against open expressions of distress. It reflects "incorrect" political thinking and a lack of allegiance to one's popular political ideology. Even though Chinese politics is undergoing considerable revision, it is still thought that former political conditioning continues to influence the choice of depressive symptoms.

From the above, it could be argued that existing patterns of cultural cognition in China limit the expression of depression solely to the somatic domain. This has been referred to as a somatic facade, wherein sadness and other types of dysphoria are coded through cognitive socialization in order to fall outside of conscious awareness (Cheung, Lau, & Waldmann, 1980). Zhang (1995) hypothesizes that, even when the Chinese become consciously aware of dysphoric states, they suppress and/or disguise them as they move along a culturally sanctioned avenue that translates depression into multiple somatic symptoms. Yet this type of speculation does not completely negate the argument that Chinese depression might be better understood in terms of a diagnostic category that is largely separate from Western clinical depression.

Especially interesting is the way in which historical developments and cultural evolution alter cognitive socialization patterns in such a way that the specific manifestations of the disorder are changed. For instance, Ullrich (1993) reports on depression among the Havik Brahmins, an orthodox caste in South India. Among these people, entry into marriage constitutes a socially defined pathway into a form of psychopathology that has been described as depression by some Western observers.

In a characteristic way, Havik depression is closely linked to the experience of women as they encounter the constraints of marriage, and simultaneously forfeit the support associated with close family ties. Historically, this marriage-linked female disorder took the form of possession, rather than one that carries the obvious hallmarks of Western clinical depression. Ullrich (1993) notes that the way in which Havik women became possessed was very similar from one case to another. Usually, upon entering her husband's house after visiting her parents, a spirit located in a treetop notices this "attractive" woman and descends in order to possess her. The possessing force identifies itself as the spirit of a dead person for whom the appropriate death ritual had not been performed. This aspect of the disorder reflects a symptom formation strategy that makes use of cultural cognitions that are embodied in Havik religious and spiritual beliefs.

Once the possession has taken place, the resultant symptoms generally involve sleep problems, loss of appetite, and an inability to work. Sometimes this is punctuated with energetic bursts of work, as well as a tendency to eat uncontrollably. According to Ullrich, the adaptive value of this disorder relates to the ability of the newly married woman to deflect onto a malevolent spirit the distress she is experiencing. Traditionally, family members would get involved in order to seek a cure. Often this would require exorcism by a religious healer, which proves effective in a high percentage of cases.

This traditional form of possession, with its largely somatic method of expression, has become less common in recent years. Ullrich observes that increasing levels of education have led to a decline in beliefs about spirits and their ability to possess people. In addition, spirit possession has been transformed by the rising status of the medical model into a pathological entity that no longer enjoys cultural endorsement and sanctioning. The end result is that straightforward possession disorders are becoming less common. In their place is a growing number of cases that, while still marriage based, resemble more closely the symptoms found in Western clinical depression.

One such case, as described by Ullrich, involves a 26-year-old Havik woman who got married to a young man she had met while at university. The woman experienced considerable difficulty in adjusting to the marriage. Reasons given for this adjustment problem included a lack of privacy, insufficient help with housework, and a husband who did not take her seriously. Consistent with the traditional mode of expression of this Havik marital depression, the woman developed sleeping problems, eating disruptions, and weight loss. In addition, however, she became tearful, lost interest in life, had decreased self-esteem, and reported depressed mood.

The social and religious changes that have taken place in Havik society have made it more difficult for young women to embark on the former somatic madness technique that resolved marital distress. The symptom pattern, as well as the outcome, have become much more diffuse as younger members of Havik society have come increasingly to view themselves as separate agents operating outside the realm of historical beliefs and reality constructions. Ullrich refers to the learned aspects of the traditional possession disorder, but these become less a part of the symptom constellation as the afflicted woman organizes her distress in an increasingly private and improvised fashion. In some respects, Western clinical depression may reflect a response to distress that cannot rely on preordained cultural constructions in structuring itself for coping purposes. As such, it often conveys the sense of individuals who have collapsed into themselves as they struggle alone to resolve their distress. This individualistic feature of Western depression may be an extension of the prevailing cultural theme of individualism, which is one of the sources of cultural cognition that predisposes so many Westerners to depression.

MODERN CULTURE AND COGNITIVE VULNERABILITY

Unlike Kaluli, Toraja, or Kipsigis culture, modern Western culture is highly complex, differentiated, fragmented, and hyperspecialized. This may be one reason that it cannot engage in a coordinated sort of cultural work that acts on behalf of the general psychological welfare of its members. In fact, when we speak of the age of depression, we are really talking about a recent development that has taken place in modern Western culture. It is essential that mental health professionals explore contemporary cultural structures in order to understand our current state of cognitive vulnerability toward depression. The rapidly growing problem of Western depression is part of a cultural crisis that has led some observers to speculate about a modern mental health crisis, as well as a modern person syndrome. This sometimes implies that the nature of modernity itself has the effect of increasing cognitive vulnerability toward a range of mental disorders, and in particular, depression. Because more than anything else, modernity is about constant change that imposes a temporality and impermanence on the beliefs, thoughts, and perceptions of cultural members. The cognitive world of modern Western people is dominated by the prospect that *infinite possibility* can generate negative emotion in those who perceive themselves as lacking the information necessary to experience a sense of certainty in decision-making, judgments, and appraisals. This diminished cognitive clarity entails an ambiguity that diminishes a person's sense of control and potency, thus rendering him or her more susceptible to the experience of depression. Some people thrive in a cultural condition in which change is constant, but a great many are demoralized by what Berman (1982) calls the endless flux of "incommensurable private languages" (p. 17) that preclude the reassurances that derive from consensus and predictability.

Seligman (1990) specifies a number of modern cultural themes that create fertile soil for the development of clinical depression. One of these is individualism, which is the tendency to assemble one's thoughts, beliefs, and perceptions in order to construct a self that is experienced as independent, distinct, and separate from the wider group. It ties in with other constructs such as self-reliance, competition, personal achievement, and self-centered hedonism (Schumaker, in press). As culture schemas promote an individualistic orientation, personal goals come to dominate the goals of the group, even when those goals can prove detrimental to the group. The independent self-construal strategies that accompany an individualistic orientation lead members to cope through personal control, direct action, and confrontation with other members. This differs dramatically from collectivist cultures, wherein cognitive socialization promotes interdependent self-construal techniques, and coping strategies that entail cooperative effort and group participation.

While individualistic structures carry certain advantages, they have been linked to a variety of social and psychological problems. Among these are depression and suicide, crime, violence, stress, and certain anxiety-related disorders (Schumaker, in press). Seligman (1990) maintains that modern Western culture has reached a degree of individualism that disconnects the individual from the commons. Social support and coping resources are lost as members become hedonistic self-serving islands.

Marsella (1985) also explains the problem of depression partially in terms of the individuated structure that is promoted in contemporary Western culture. The individuated self tends to personalize inner states of emotion, including distress resulting from adversity and painful life events. Depression and other emotional disorders become more likely as the individuated members bear the full emotional brunt of their problems. This contrasts, according to Marsella, to unindividuated cultures wherein the collective identity is able to absorb much of the individual's distress.

The psychological consequences of individualism are clearly related to perceived levels of social support. Research shows that high levels of social support reduce vulnerability to a wide range of mental disorders, including depression (Vaux, 1988). In cultural contexts that enfail a perceptible social network, cognition is patterned in order to comprehend the interconnectedness of social relations. This situation operates as a mental health prophylactic because the collective consensual element is experienced as a substantial coping resource (Oakley, 1992). On the other hand, members of cultures that have nonintegrated social ties develop cognitive schemas that incline them to experience their surrounding social world as a resource deficit.

Hirsch (1976) describes current patterns of cultural conditioning as "inherently antipathetic to sociality" (p. 88), which again diminishes social support and increases the risk of psychological disturbance. Schwartz (1994) takes this further in speaking of the depressing effects of "the commercialization of social relations" (p. 185) that has taken place in modern Western culture. Cognitive socialization in the Consumer Society implants a commercial interpretation of social dynamics that precludes the experience of others as a viable coping resource. As part of the commercialization of the Western self, members undergo a cognitive socialization that encourages a distinctly materialistic orientation. Of considerable interest is the body of research demonstrating that, without exception, materialism is detrimental to mental health. It has been associated with depression, low self-esteem, diminished life satisfaction, impaired social relations, and general unhappiness (Richins, 1996; Richins & Dawkins, 1992; Schumaker, in press).

Existing patterns of cognitive socialization also promote depression by reducing the quality and quantity of interpersonal relationships. Again this may be tied to some extent to the cultural theme of materialism. Baudrillard (1988) uses the label *Ego Consumens* to refer collectively to people in modern consumer culture.

They are conditioned to become preoccupied with personal needs, and to remain ever vigilant for opportunities to actualize their full potential, and to realize maximal consumption potential. According to Baudrillard, interpersonal relationships suffer as cultural conditioning creates individuals with a universal curiosity that revolves around a plethora of false needs.

In *Globalization: The Human Consequences,* Bauman (1997) singles out unsatisfied desire and discontent as major contributing factors in the genesis of depression, and in the modern mental health crisis generally. Bauman observes that consumer culture is linked to our contemporary economic strategies in such a way that unfulfilled desire is an ever-present feature of our cognitive worlds. Our socioeconomic system functions in relation to the motto Divided, We Move (Bauman, 1997). Relatedness needs are overwhelmed by a cognitive schema that renders members impervious to satisfaction, and incapable of stepping beyond repeated reminders of their discontent.

The poverty of interpersonal relationships is discussed by Ozanne and Murray (1996) in the context of conformist consumption. They cite evidence showing that the mentality and consequent lifestyle emerging from consumer culture causes a serious deterioration of interpersonal relationships. This reduces social support and forces less effective privatized coping strategies that, in turn, predispose members toward unhappiness and a range of adjustment problems. Ozanne and Murray assert that prevailing blueprints for cultural conditioning engage consumption as a social vision that destines members to a cultural code that interferes with the satisfaction of real needs. One could argue that this cultural code becomes the pool of cultural cognitions of which members avail themselves in directing their lives. Since this code appears to be toxic for mental health, Ozanne and Murray call for intervention strategies that promote a reflexive defiance in relation to certain key areas of cultural conditioning, in particular those that further a consumer consciousness at the price of human relationships. Goldhammer (1996) also sees considerable mental health benefits deriving from cultural deprograming techniques that can enable members to dissociate themselves from various collective currents, especially those that drive members toward a consumer orientation.

Seligman (1990) regards the waning of Western religion as another factor that predisposes members to depression. Similar to what was said above regarding the eclipse of social support, one could argue that cosmic and existential levels of support are being lost. Cultural cognitions are forged that do not permit the same degree of transcendental interpretation and attribution that was available in former ages when religion approximated a total way of life. A number of studies have shown that religious belief and practice can reduce the likelihood of depression (for review, see Schumaker, 1992). As religious cognitions become increasingly constrained by literal this-world frameworks, members are less able to draw on the coping strategies that immunize against depression. Neusch (1982) depicted the modern religious mentality as self-centered and lacking a "universally accepted organizing principle" (p. 215) that adds to the mental health crisis that features in the West. In a similar way, Turner (1985) writes about the increasing innerness of modern religious thinking, noting how it no longer contains the web of shared assumptions that offered followers a psychological "center." He argued further that his loss of a center helps to explain the modern predisposition toward depression, despair, and angst, as well as the chronic unrealized spiritual yearning that afflicts so many people today.

Several other elements of cognitive socialization have been implicated in the upsurge of depression in the West. These include status and self-esteem associated with competition, social alienation, overregulation of emotion (combined with low gratification yield) for purposes of image management, and personal identity tied to function and efficiency. It is beyond the scope of this chapter to deal separately with each of these. However, to understand why we have become a depression-prone culture, each of these must be examined more closely by psychologists in the future. After all, in many ways Western clinical depression can be understood as a crystallization of culture, a term that Bordo (1997) applied to anorexia nervosa but one that could just as easily be used to comprehend the current wave of depression.

IMPLICATIONS FOR TREATMENT

Whitehouse (this volume) points out how cognitive psychologists have been slow to realize that normal as well as pathological cognition is socioculturally constituted. If some types of psychopathology are a crystallization of certain predisposing features of cultural conditioning, it makes little sense to continue thinking exclusively in terms of treating isolated individuals. Typically, individual-based cognitive interventions do not even touch on the crucial cultural cognitions and associated behaviors that underlie the whole process of the depressive disorder. They also fail to take any account of possible pathogenic properties of culture that may infect the majority of members.

Kaiser, Katz, and Shaw (1998) comment specifically on cognitive-behavior therapy (CBT), which is one of the most popular psychological treatments of clinical depression. While many CBT therapists apply this technique within the narrow confines of self-delivered cognition at the level of the individual, Katz et al. state that CBT has the potential to be adapted to a variety of cultural contexts. They argue that key cognitive components of depression (e.g., helplessness, hopelessness, and worthlessness) manifest themselves differently in different cultures, and that CBT therapists must reshape their approach in order to account for these variations. As part of this, clinicians must familiarize themselves with normative cognitive processes and the attributions for illness of the different populations with whom they are working. Kaiser et al. comment that we must also modify the suitability criteria for CBT (Safran & Segal, 1990) in order to make room for cultural variations with regard to beliefs, attitudes, and perceptions. They give as an example the criterion that the person must be willing to take personal responsibility for emotional change. This is a popular Western theme that has found its way into current psychotherapeutic theory and practice. However, as Katz et al. observe, many non-Western cultures employ a wide range of external attributions that attach responsibility to spirit forces, or the controlling power of fate. Even so, there is plenty of scope for CBT to be tailored in order to accommodate cognitive patterns that do not necessarily fit the criteria that have been established for Western psychotherapy clients.

Mental health professionals need to think beyond individual dynamics, and to embrace the concept of cultural dynamics. Even when working with separate individuals, it would be possible to operate within a wider theoretical context that would invite an exploration of culturally-conditioned cognitions and ways to find healthier alternatives. The new culture-base cognitive therapies would not need to ignore factors and cognitions that are unique to the individual. Instead, they would increase the scope of psychotherapy in order that cultural insights could be a large part of the therapy process. It would require mental health professionals to move into new territories of knowledge that have not been traditional components of their training; they would have to begin thinking in terms of cultural health and, more specifically, how individual psychopathology is often a direct extension of cultural pathology. In general, the field of clinical psychology needs to progress further toward the goal of becoming, in Pedersen's (1995) words, "socially sensitive, culturally aware, and humanely oriented" (p. 47).

REFERENCES

Baudrillard, J. (1988). *Selected writings.* Stanford, CA: Stanford University Press.

Bauman, Z. (1997). *Globalization: The human consequences.* New York: Columbia University Press.

Beck, J. S. (1995). *Cognitive therapy: Basics and beyond.* New York: Guilford Press.

Berman, M. (1982). *All that is solid melts into air: The experience of modernity.* London: Verso.

Bertelsen, A., Harvald, B., & Hauge, M. (1977). A Danish twin study of manic-depressive disorder. *British Journal of Psychiatry, 130,* 330–351.

Bordo, S. (1997). Anorexia nervosa: Psychopathology as the crystallization of culture. In M. Gergen (Ed.), *Toward a new psychology of gender* (pp. 423–453). New York: Routledge.

Cheung, F., Lau, B., & Waldmann, E. (1980). Somatization among Chinese depressives in general practice. *International Journal of Psychiatry, 10,* 361–374.

Draguns, J. G. (1995). Cultural influences upon psychopathology: Clinical and practical implications. *Journal of Social Distress and the Homeless, 4,* 89–114.

Goldhammer, J. (1996). *Under the influence.* Amherst, NY: Prometheus.

Hagnell, O., Lanke, J., Rorsman, B., & Oejesjoe, L. (1982). Are we entering an age of melancholy?: Depressive illnesses in a prospective epidemiological study over 25 years. *Psychological Medicine, 2,* 279–289.

Harkness, S. (1987). The cultural mediation of postpartum depression. *Medical Anthropology Quarterly, 1,* 194–209, p. 207.

Hirsch, F. (1976). *Social limits of growth.* Cambridge, MA: Harvard University Press.

Hollan, D. (1994). Suffering and the work of culture: A case of magical poisoning in Toraja. *American Ethnologist, 21,* 74–87.

Hopkins, J., Marcus, M., & Campbell, S. B. (1984). Postpartum depression: A critical review. *Psychological Bulletin, 95,* 498–515.

Jadhav, S. (1995). The cultural origins of Western depression. *International Journal of Social Psychiatry, 42,* 269–286.

Jenkins, J. H., Kleinman, A., & Good, B. (1991). Cross-cultural studies of depression. In J. Becker & A. Kleinman (Eds.), *Psychosocial aspects of depression* (pp. 67–99). Hillsdale, NJ: Lawrence Erlbaum.

Kaiser, A. S., Katz, R., & Shaw, B. F. (1998). Cultural issues in the management of depression. In S. Kazarian & D. R. Evans (Eds.), *Cultural clinical psychology* (pp. 177–214). New York: Oxford University Press.

Kendler, K. S., Heath, A., Martin, N. C., & Eaves, L. J. (1986). Symptoms of anxiety and depression in a volunteer twin population: The antiologic role of genetic and environmental factors. *Archives of General Psychiatry, 43,* 213–221.

Kleinman, A. (1986). *Social origins of disease and distress: Depression, neurasthenia, and pain in modern China.* New Haven, CT: Yale University Press.

Klerman, G. L. (1985). Birth-cohort trends in rates of major depressive disorder among relatives of patients with affective disorder. *Archives of General Psychiatry, 42,* 689–695.

Kwong, B., & Wong, S. (1981). Physical presentations of psychological problems among Hong Kong Chinese: Cultural implications. *Journal of Hong Kong Psychiatric Association, 1,* 33–39.

Marsella, A. J. (1985). Culture, self, and mental disorder. In A. J. Marsella, G. De Vos, & F. L. K. Hsu (Eds.), *Culture and self.* London: Tavistock.

Neusch, M. (1982). *The sources of modern atheism.* New York: Paulist Press.

Oakley, A. (1992). *Social support and motherhood.* Oxford, UK: Blackwell.

Olioff, M. (1991). The application of cognitive therapy to postpartum depression. In M. Vallis, J. Howes, & P. Miller (Eds.), *The challenge of cognitive therapy* (pp. 111–133). New York: Plenum Press.

Ozanne, J. L., & Murray, J. B. (1996). Uniting critical theory and public policy to create the reflexively defiant consumer. In R. P. Hill (Ed.), *Marketing and consumer research in the public interest* (pp. 3–15). London: Sage.

Pedersen, P. (1995). Culture-centered ethical guidelines for counselors. In J. G. Ponterotto, J. Casas, L. Suzuki, & C. Alexander (Eds.), *Handbook of multicultural counseling* (pp. 33–49). Thousand Oaks, CA: Sage.

Richins, M. L. (1996). Materialism, desire, and discontent. In R. P. Hill (Ed.), *Marketing and consumer research in the public interest.* London: Sage.

Richins, M. L., & Dawkins, S. (1992). A consumer values orientation for materialism and its measurement. *Journal of Consumer Research, 19,* 303–316.

Safran, J. D., & Segal, Z. V. (1990). *Interpersonal process in cognitive therapy.* New York: Basic Books.

Sartorius, N. (1987). Cross-cultural research on depression. *Psicopatologia 7,* 115–120.

Schieffelin, E. L. (1985). The cultural analysis of depressive affect: An example from New Guinea. In A. Kleinman & B. Good (Eds.), *Culture and depression* (pp. 101–133). Berkeley, CA: University of California Press.

Schumaker, J. F. (1992). *Religion and mental health.* New York: Oxford University Press.

Schumaker, J. F. (1995). *The corruption of reality.* Amherst, NY: Prometheus.

Schumaker, J. F. (in press). *Modernity and mental health.* Westport, Conn: Praeger.

Schwartz, B. (1994). *The costs of living: How market freedom erodes the best things in life.* New York: W. W. Norton.

Seligman, M. E. P. (1990). Why is there so much depression today?: The waxing of the individual and the waning of the commons. In R. E. Ingram (Ed.), *Contemporary approaches to depression* (pp. 1–9). New York: Plenum Press.

Sloan, T. (1996). Psychological research methods in developing countries. In S. C. Carr & J. F. Schumaker (Eds.), *Psychology and the developing world* (pp. 38–45). Westport, CT: Praeger.

Stern, G., & Kluckman, L. (1983). Multi-disciplinary perspectives in post-partum depression: An anthropological critique. *Social Sciences and Medicine, 50,* 149–167.

Turner, J. (1985). *Without God, without creed.* Baltimore: The Johns Hopkins University Press.

Ullrich, H. E. (1993). Cultural shaping of illness: A longitudinal perspective on apparent depression. *The Journal of Nervous and Mental Disease, 181,* 647–649.

Vaux, A. (1988). *Social support.* New York: Praeger.

Zhang, D. (1995). Depression and culture: A Chinese perspective. *Canadian Journal of Counselling, 29,* 227–233.

5

The Cognitive Socialization of Stress and Anxiety

Joseph Westermeyer and Eric Dieperink

Anticipatory worry or concern are survival-oriented traits that may be thought of as adaptive anxiety. Should the concern become excessive and result in an anxiety attack, one then becomes less able to cope and more apt to view the experience in negative terms (e.g., being overwhelmed) rather than in positive terms (e.g., perceiving the experience as exciting). Thus, anxiety is not a symptom per se. Rather, it exists as a spectrum concept, from a normal, even necessary component of universal human experience to a dreaded state that can impede adaptation, and even produce severe maladaptation.

No one symptom is pathognomonic of anxiety disorder. However, there are prominent symptoms highly associated with anxiety disorders. These include symptoms across several physiological systems, including the autonomic nervous, cardiovascular, gastrointestinal, otolaryngology, neurological, pulmonary, urogenital symptoms system, and the central nervous systems. The DSM-IV classification of psychiatric disorders consists of five primary anxiety disorders, which differ considerably in their manifestations, course, epidemiological rates, and treatment (i.e., generalized anxiety disorder, obsessive-compulsive disorder, panic disorder, phobic disorder, and posttraumatic stress disorder). Several other disorders with prominent anxiety symptoms are described (i.e., adjustment disorder with anxiety, acute stress disorder, anxiety disorder due to a general medical condition, and substance-induced anxiety disorder). Anxiety disorders in children include overanxious disorder of childhood and separation anxiety disorder.

LANGUAGE DIFFERENCES IN EXPRESSING ANXIETY

Words structure our experience of and concepts regarding emotion. History, culture, literature, and the arts contribute to the construction of these words and concepts. For example, the English term *anxiety* derives from the Latin term *angere,* meaning to torment. In Webster's Dictionary II, the first definition for anxiety is "uneasiness or distress about future uncertainties." The second definition relates to the excessive or illness dimension of anxiety.

In English, the terms anxiety, fear (or phobia), and panic have technical meanings in our psychiatric jargon, and they are also known to the general population. This juxtaposition of technical and lay terms eases the ability of patients to communicate their distress to mental health clinicians. Indeed, English speakers have many folk or colloquial terms to describe various levels, or even contexts of anxiety (e.g., uptight, strung out, wired, tense). In many languages, however, a comparable term for anxiety does not exist. In Lao, a language with which the first author is familiar, there is a word for fear (*dyan*) but none for anxiety. People in that country do present with disorders that could be readily classified as anxiety disorders, but they might report only physical symptoms (e.g., headache, tachycardia, dyspnea without exertion, abdominal pain or cramping, diarrhea, urinary frequency, sweating), much as do some Anglophone patients. However, if they choose to focus on psychological distress, their language does not ease their communication task. They might say, "I feel afraid, but there is nothing to be afraid of," or "I feel afraid, but I don't know what I'm afraid of," or "I feel afraid, and I think a ghost is bothering me."

Anglophone patients may also mislead clinicians inadvertently as a result of their choice of words. For example, in the United States, young patients are apt to complain of feeling "paranoid." Further information seeking may reveal that they feel anxious in groups because they have a sense of people looking at them or judging them, but they do not believe that others have any malevolence toward themselves. Essentially, they are describing social phobia rather than paranoia.

In sum, the translation of terms involving anxiety symptoms can be problematic because of differences in connotation and denotation of terms specific to each language or dialect and its associated culture (Westermeyer, Janca, Sartorius, & Hughes, 1997). This can be true even in related languages. For example, the German word *angst* has the same Latin root as anxiety. However, as Wierzbicka has well described, the denotations and connotations of anxiety and angst overlap but also differ greatly (Wierzbicka, 1998).

PATHOPLASTICITY AND ANXIETY DISORDERS

Clinical presentations involving anxiety symptoms can differ greatly from one culture to the next. Such tremendous cultural variability is less evident with other disorders, such as dementia, delirium, schizophrenia, bipolar disorder, delusional disorder, substance abuse/dependence disorders, and even major depressive disorder (Beiser, 1985; Cox, 1988; Egeland, 1986; Westermeyer, 1986; Westermeyer,

1989; Zung, 1973). Indeed, even the folk criteria for major mental illnesses causing disability are surprisingly similar across cultures (Westermeyer, 1979). One might say that these disorders do not demonstrate as great pathoplasticity across cultures if compared to other disorders.

Some clinical presentations appear to be highly culture related (i.e., rates vary greatly from one culture to another), or even culture bound (the particular syndrome, or collection of signs and symptoms, occurs only in one or a few related cultures). Examples include cargo cult syndrome, brief or hysterical psychoses, neurasthenia, latah, amok, shinkeishitsu, and others (Friedman & Faguet, 1982; Lin, 1989; Simons, 1980; Simons & Hughes, 1985; Tseng et al., 1988). The term pathoplastic has been appended to these disorders, which tend to involve (1) brief symptoms, such as an acute self-limited hysterical outburst, or chronic but nondisabling signs and symptoms; (2) behavioral signs peculiar to the particular culture or syndrome; and (3) symptoms and signs often associated with anxiety (e.g., phobic behaviors, hyperventilation, and hyperarousal). However, psychiatric diagnoses do not typically have exact equivalents in these culture-related symptoms. Anxiety and/or nonpsychotic mood symptoms are often present in these conditions. For example, patients diagnosed in Japan as *shinkeishitsu* (a local diagnosis used in the professional literature in Japan) manifest social phobia, social withdrawal, and overconcern with one's social interactions (Westermeyer et al., 1997).

ALEXITHYMIA, ANXIETY, AND CULTURE

Alexithymia, literally the absence of words for feelings, involves the inability to discern one's own affect or emotion. This condition has been widely observed in combat veterans, rape victims, and other victims of violence. Although alexithymia has not been studied as a function of culture, there are reasons to believe that the ability to recognize and describe one's own affect might vary across cultures. Even within cultures, the ability to recognize one's own affect can differ with demographic characteristics. For example, some data indicate that alexithymia is more notable among men, those with less education, and those of lower socioeconomic status (Kirmayer & Robbins, 1993; Lane, Sechrest, & Riedel, 1998). These social influences could be related to child raising practices, ensocialization during childhood or adolescence, cultural roles, and other cultural influences.

Alexithymia may be more frequent in certain anxiety disorders, such as panic disorder (Zeitlin & McNally, 1993). Since panic disorder has been shown to vary as a function of culture, culturally prescribed alexithymia could conduce to higher rates of panic disorder. Alexithymia also has been more frequent among groups and subgroups who have experienced higher rates of life-threatening or horrific trauma (Hyer, Woods, Summers, Boudewyns, & Harrison, 1990). It is not clear at this point whether aspects of culture (such as child raising) or experiences of people in a particular culture can produce different rates of alexithymia.

EPIDEMIOLOGICAL STUDIES

The Epidemiological Catchment Area Study, a multisite study using DSM-III criteria, was undertaken around 1980 in five urban areas of the United States (Brown, Eaton, & Sussman, 1990). One of the more major interethnic differences concerned one month prevalence rates of phobic disorder. In both Baltimore and St. Louis, African Americans had significantly higher rates of current phobic disorder than Caucasian Americans in both places. However, the differences between Baltimore and St. Louis were also highly significant, with Baltimore having a rate about twice as high as that in St. Louis. The strongest predictor of social phobia was female gender. The next strongest predictor was location, with rates higher in Baltimore. The third predictor was ethnicity, with African Americans exceeding Caucasian Americans. More women had current phobia in both ethnic groups and in both sites.

Using the Epidemiological Catchment Area Study data, Karno and coworkers compared rates of psychiatric disorders between Mexican Americans and non-Hispanic White Americans in Los Angeles (Karno et al., 1987). In addition, Canino and coworkers used the same method to study psychiatric disorders in Puerto Rico (Canino et al., 1987). Rates of phobia, panic disorder, and obsessive-compulsive disorder, adjusted for sex and age, did not differ significantly among the three groups.

PSYCHOLOGICAL STUDIES OF
PATIENTS AND NORMALS

Leung and coworkers in Albany, New York, compared Chinese/Chinese Americans, Americans with social phobia (currently in outpatient treatment in a social phobia program), and American volunteers (Leung, Heimberg, Holt, & Bruch, 1994). The Chinese and American "normals" did not differ from one another on self-reported measures of anxiety, whereas both groups reported significantly less anxiety symptoms than those Americans with social phobia. With regard to their childhood experiences, the normal Chinese subjects and the American patients with social phobia were very similar (and quite unlike the normal Americans) in regard to the following parental child raising techniques: (1) parental emphasis on others' opinions (rather than the child's own opinion), (2) parental use of shaming techniques with their children, and (3) isolating children from nonfamily social activities.

As compared to both Chinese and American normal subjects, more American patients with social phobia reported that their families seldom interacted with other families during their childhood. These data suggest that the latter factor (i.e., familial isolation from other families) might be pathogenic in many cultures. On the other hand, the other factors (i.e., emphasizing others' opinions, shaming, restricting nonfamily interactions) might be pathogenic or be associated with pathogenicity in some cultures and not in other cultures. These data, while not the result of a definitive large-scale study, also indicate that anxiety levels are similar across normals using several self-rated scales (e.g., Social Interaction Anxiety Scale, Social Phobia Scale, and the Fear Questionnaire-Social Phobia Subscale), but are significantly greater in patients with social phobia. This study demonstrates the importance of not condemning child raising techniques of cultures simply based on studies comparing normals and psychiatric patients from one cultural group.

CLINICAL STUDIES

Friedman, Paradis, and Hatch (1994) studied African Americans and Caucasian Americans in a Brooklyn phobia-anxiety clinic. Both groups included more women than men (88% and 83% respectively) and had similar age and socioeconomic distribution. They also had similar durations of illness, numbers of panic attacks per week, types and distribution of anxiety symptoms reported, and score levels on several rating anxiety scales. Clinician ratings of improvement were comparable in both groups, however, African Americans were less apt to be currently married and were also more apt to have had emergency room treatment for panic symptoms. African American patients reported more mother loss, more father loss, more parental divorce, and more parental substance abuse. Conversely, Caucasian American patients reported more parental depression and childhood history of separation anxiety or school phobia. Comorbid sleep disorders were quite different in the two groups: African American patients reported significantly more isolated sleep paralysis. This study underscored remarkable syndromal similarities, but with many important differences perhaps related to socioeconomic and ethnic differences.

In our own study, we examined anxiety symptoms within a group of Hmong refugees one-and-a-half years after arriving in the United States (Westermeyer, Schaberg, & Nugent, 1995). This Asian group did not differ in their level of self-reported anxiety symptoms from a group of Mexican immigrants in the United States; in both studies, the anxiety scale on the 90-item symptom checklist was used to assess anxiety symptoms (Rodreguez & DeWolfe, 1990). In addition, neither the Hmong nor the Mexican group differed from the American norms on the anxiety scale (Derogatis, Lipman, & Covi, 1973). Within the Hmong group, those who lived closest to other Hmong or had more people in the household reported more anxiety symptoms, although we expected them to report fewer anxiety symptoms (Westermeyer et al., 1995). This finding suggests either that people with more anxiety tend to locate more closely to people of their own ethnic group, or that proximity to one's own ethnic group increases anxiety. We prefer the former explanation, but have no data to refute the latter interpretation. A multivariate analysis showed that those Hmong who reported more medical problems since arrival in the United States also reported more anxiety symptoms. Likewise, those who reported a poor future outlook also had more anxiety symptoms.

COMORBIDITY

Anxiety symptoms and disorders can differ across cultures in relation to the types of comorbidity found in various populations. In a pilot study, Neligh and coworkers studied a small group of Native American villagers. Although the sample was small, an unexpectedly high percentage of those studies met diagnostic criteria for panic disorder, and among those with panic disorder, alcohol abuse was frequent. In addition, panic disorder was also associated with depressive symptoms lasting two weeks or longer. Although the numbers were small, this study indicated that the high rate of panic disorder could be due to the high rate of comorbid alcoholism and depression, rather than simply to high rates of panic disorder by itself.

POTENTIAL ETIOLOGIES FOR OBSERVED
SIMILARITIES AND DIFFERENCES

Explanations for the Null Hypotheses.   One possible outcome of surveys might be that people selected to be homogeneous in other regards besides culture, would not show differences in anxiety symptoms or rates of anxiety disorder. Showing such similarity, however, does not prove the cause for the similarity. Alternative explanations for comparable anxiety symptom levels and/or rates of anxiety disorder are as follows:

Anxiety symptoms and disorders are hard wired into our genetic-constitutional systems, so that the entire species manifests similar distributions of symptoms and disorders.

Although there may be the potential for different expression of the anxiety disorder diathesis across groups, the commonality in group structure, process, and interaction results in rates that are highly similar.

Emotional Responses to Events.   Roseman and coworkers, in a comparison of college students from India and the United States, observed that students appraised their emotional responses to particular events in similar ways (Roseman, Dhawan, Rettek, Naidu, & Thapa, 1995). Both groups of students demonstrated a correlation between their cognitive judgments regarding the events and their emotional responses to the events, at least by retrospective self-report. However, the Indian students reported a higher threshold of distress than the American students. Stated differently, the Indian students reported less distress in relation to particular events than did the American students.

Differences in Levels of Stress.   Differences in levels and rates of trauma, stress, loss, and other pathogenic factors might account for observed differences in anxiety levels or rates of disorder. Posttraumatic stress disorder would comprise a model disorder, in which a high threshold of horrific experience or lethal threat appears necessary to activate the PTSD diathesis. Societies with high levels of violence or other victimization, or groups who have recently encountered war or refugee flight, could have higher levels of anxiety. Studies of special sub-groups, such as former prisoners of war, appear to bear this out, but larger-scale studies of victimized people would be necessary to demonstrate this more conclusively. (At the current time, we are undertaking such a study among East African refugees in the United States.)

Culture as Pathogen. As described above, shinkeishitsu is a relatively common syndrome in Japan, especially among young men. Japanese culture appears to foster this syndrome through its high valuation on concern about the feelings of others rather than one's own self, the importance of social image and "face," the exquisite protocol governing interpersonal interactions, and the ideal hierarchical nature of virtually all interpersonal relationships. In Taiwan, with Japanese influence but not Japanese culture, shinkeishitsu occurs infrequently (Lin, 1989).

Culture As Preventive Agent. Certain potential biological stressors in the life cycle can be ameliorated by culture. For example, menopause tends to be a benign psychosocial event in Japan, as compared to North America (Lock, 1993). Japanese women reported autonomic symptoms such as hot flashes and flushes at lower frequencies than the reported norms among American women. A specific lay term for menopause, as we have in English, does not exist in Japanese. Japanese women in mid-life tend to gain more independence, stature, and security than they have at earlier life stages. In this instance, Japanese culture may serve to insulate women from a life cycle stressor that often produces anxiety or loss in North America.

Culturally Sanctioned Dissociation. Religious groups and cultures can prescribe, or at least foster the use of dissociation to ameliorate, bind, or remove severe anxiety symptoms or disorders. Accomplishing willful dissociation involves alternative states of consciousness, usually described as trance or possession states (Cardeña, 1992). Trance typically requires that the individual undertakes certain physical and/or psychological exercises that conduce to this altered state. Possession implies that spirits, ghosts, or powers have taken over control of certain psychological or psychosensory capacities. The usual outcome from trance is an improvement, even if temporary, in the person's level of distress. However, occasional cases can be made worse by trance of possession states (Wintrob, 1966). Although these conditions are often associated with developing countries and tribal or peasant societies, they do occur in Anglophone countries as well (Pattison & Wintrob, 1981).

PSYCHOTHERAPY

Learning the patient's cognates in relation to his or her experiences and symptoms can present challenges across cultural and language barriers. However, with patience and curiosity, it can be accomplished. It helps to have some knowledge of differing worldviews and diverse cultures, but the patient must be the final arbiter of his or her own cognitions; books on anthropology cannot convey these to the clinician (although they can help). Of interest during the years that the first author worked in northern Laos, no one ever complained of fear of a heart attack in the midst of an anxiety attack, which people did indeed experience in that remote area. However, there was no folk concept of a heart attack in that region at that time. Thus, villagers would develop other culturally consistent explanations for their symptoms (e.g., being smothered by a ghost, for example). Both these examples suggest that healers themselves may contribute to the cultural construction of attributions made in the midst of an anxiety attack. That is, Americans have learned from their physicians to be wary of heart attacks when suffering shortness of breath and chest pain. Laotian villagers, on the other hand, have been influenced by their spirit healers to consider ghost-induced illness in association with the same symptoms.

Cognitive Therapies: Cognitive Behavioral Therapy, Cognitive Restructuring. These psychotherapeutic approaches can be readily applied in a variety of settings. For example, a therapist conducting crosscultural psychotherapy can apply such methods without necessarily knowing a great amount about the patient's culture. In addition, cognitive therapies can work equally well with illiterate as well as highly literate patients. Moreover, the benefits of this approach usually are soon apparent to both patient and clinician. If the patient fails to benefit in a timely manner, the clinician can reassess the diagnosis and/or treatment. Treatment in the following cases was conducted by the first author.

Case Example

A 34-year-old refugee woman from Southeast Asia presented with a fear of imminent death. An illiterate widow and mother of four children, she had developed symptoms of anxiety and depression following a mugging in a grocery store parking lot (she was pushed to the ground, her money and some of her groceries taken). The woman had begun having a dream in which her deceased grandmother would approach her from a distance, looking at her but saying nothing. As the grandmother drew closer, the woman would awake frightened and fearing death.

Additional information from the patient and ethnic peers revealed that dreams in which deceased people appeared could be seen as a harbingers of death. From her cultural viewpoint, the deceased person had left the land of the dead to make a visit to the living person for a specific reason. One of these reasons could have been to foretell the person's death, so that the individual would prepare to die. However, other reasons could also account for such visitation.

At our second meeting I suggested to the patient that her grandmother could be visiting her for another reason. For example, her grandmother may want to support her during this critical time. I added that her grandmother surely must know that there was no one else to care for her granddaughter's four children, and that the grandmother would be concerned about the future of these great-grandchildren.

At the next visit, the patient reported that she no longer dreaded the appearance of her grandmother in her dream. And indeed, "Grandmother's visit" provided her with a sense of support and relief rather than dread. Moreover, the cognitive restructuring of the dream's meaning let us put that major complaint aside while we addressed other, more fundamental issues. At the same time, through paradoxical intention, we were able to turn a symptom into a support.

In order to undertake cognitive work of this kind, one must first become familiar with the patient's cognitions. Such work may not fit neatly into any one therapeutic modality.

Psychodynamic Thinking and Cognitive Therapies.   In undertaking such work, it can be useful to think psychodynamically as well as cognitively and behaviorally. Psychodynamic formulations often can guide cognitive interventions.

Case Example

A 38-year-old married man with three children, also a refugee from Southeast Asia, developed comorbid anxiety mood disorders within several weeks after having been laid off from his factory during an economic slump. During this period, he began to have a recurrent nightmare in which his former army squad members were chasing him. In the dream, fearing they would kill him, he would flee. As they caught up with him, he would awake in a sweat. Like the woman described above, he took the dream to be an omen of his own inevitable and imminent death.

All of the men in the dream were deceased members of an army squad that he had led during the war in Southeast Asia. In a particular battle, the patient was wounded early on in the battle and removed to a place of safety. Subsequently, his squad members were all killed in the attack. The patient experienced survival guilt as a result, but did not develop full-blown PTSD until he was laid off from work. In his thinking, his being laid off from work comprised a failure similar to that of his squad being overrun and killed. He felt that he was letting down his wife and children, who depended on him for a living.

The patient had never grieved for these dead comrades, in part because no ceremony was ever held. Thus I chanced suggesting to him that in the next dream, he should not run from the ghosts of his dead squad members, but rather, he should let them catch up to him. Then he should ask them what they wanted. At our next visit, smiling broadly, he reported that the dream went exactly as I suggested. Upon my asking what the men had to tell him, he responded, "They said, don't forget us." We spent the remainder of the session discussing how he might meet this request. He decided to build them a small altar of honor in his home, to have an annual dinner to honor their memory, and to tell his own children and other children related to the young dead soldiers about their brave relatives.

As with the previous case, therapy involved taking the beliefs and concerns as expressed by the patient and working with them. It made no sense to try and dissuade these patients from their cultural belief in dreams as occurring in an alternate world that existed between the living and the dead, a place where the living and the dead could communicate and interact. In addition, it made no sense to try and convince them that their interactions in the dream grew out of their own minds; they clearly perceived these dream events as real interactions with actual people, albeit deceased people. Rather, the task was to refocus them away from their fears and toward redefining their relationship with the deceased person(s), who had highly important meaning to the two patients. In addition, settling the dream issue allowed us to move on to other relevant material (e.g., the woman's sense of vulnerability and inability to care for herself and her children in a new and sometimes dangerous society, the man's sense of being an incompetent or star-crossed leader).

Behavioral Modification. Behavioral techniques also work nicely regardless of the patient's literacy, education, and cultural beliefs. Although we as clinicians may not think of them as having a cognitive component, this may not be true from the patient's perspective. In the following case, the patient associated the dark with the ghost of her deceased daughter.

Case Example

A 46-year-old illiterate widow, a refugee from Southeast Asia, presented with opium addiction. Following detoxification in a hospital setting, it became apparent in the subsequent weeks that she had the following psychiatric disorders: major depressive disorder (MDD), phobia (to being in the dark) with panic (precipitated by exposure to the dark). Her MDD and phobia with panic had begun the previous year, following the death of her husband. She had started smoking opium as a means of getting to sleep and allaying her fears of the dark. Initially, opium did relieve her insomnia and fear of the dark; but eventually her insomnia and fears returned.

Darkness was associated with the fear that her deceased daughter's ghost would harm her in the darkness. This daughter, her firstborn child, was mortally wounded during a mortar attack on her village in Laos. Although the women tried to carry the 8-year-old child, she could not hurry her three younger children out of harm's way and carry her injured daughter. Certain that her daughter was mortally wounded (her heart and one lung were visible in the wound, and the child was unconscious and breathing in gasps), she decided to leave her daughter. Before doing so, however, she scooped out some earth and laid her child in the shallow hole, covering it with sticks and stones to keep animals away (a traditional burial practice in that culture). Then, as mortar rounds continued to fall, she shepherded her other children to safety. In the subsequent weeks and months, during which survival was difficult, she did not grieve for this child.

Initial treatment consisted of grief therapy and antidepressant medication, both for her MDD and to block her panic attacks. Since these therapies did not alleviate her darkness phobia, she was exposed to gradually increasing lengths of time alone in a dark room. During initial exposures, her pulse regularly rose to 160 per minute and she left the room with considerable apparent anxiety. However, with repeated exposures, anxiety decreased and she was able to tolerate darkness well.

In this case, we did not change the patient's cognates regarding her daughter's ghost and the presence of her ghost in darkened places. Moreover, neither grief therapy nor alleviation of her MDD ameliorated her phobia to darkness. However, desensitization therapy did produce virtually complete alleviation of her darkness phobia. As she became unafraid in the dark, she perceived that her daughter's ghost was leaving this world and going on to the place of the dead. She interpreted this as meaning that her daughter knew now that her mother loved her, and that her hasty burial and lack of mourning were not a sign that she did not.

CONCLUSIONS

Language used to describe anxiety is developed through a cultural context, including personal experience, religion, art, literature, and history. Anxiety may be manifest in culture-related syndromes, so that culture may play a larger role in structuring the clinical presentation and clinical phenomenology in anxiety disorders than in comparison to other psychiatric disorders. Despite potential differences among cultures, several studies using the same instrument revealed comparable rates of anxiety symptoms, even among migrants and refugees. Moreover, women tended to report more anxiety symptoms and have higher rates of anxiety disorder than men in all cultures studied.

Although rates of anxiety symptoms appear highly similar across cultures, rates of specific anxiety disorders may differ. For example, epidemiological studies of social phobia in the United States showed a difference between African Americans and Caucasian Americans in prevalence rates of phobic disorder. However, Hispanic Americans and Caucasian Americans did not differ greatly in regard to rates of anxiety disorder, including phobic disorder.

It is not clear how culture might influence the rates of psychiatric disorder. However, this chapter has suggested a few means by which culture could affect prevalence rates. One of these could be the training of children in the use of dissociation, or alexithymia, as a means of coping with stress. Culture may serve as a pathogenic agent, or as a preventive agent, or perhaps both vis-à-vis anxiety disorder. More investigation will be needed before we can begin to see discernible patterns in the relationship between culture, anxiety symptoms, and anxiety disorders.

78   *Cultural Cognition and Psychopathology*

REFERENCES

Beiser, M. (1985). A study of depression among traditional Africans, urban North Americans and Southeast Asian refugees. In A. Kleinman & B. J. Good (Eds.), *Culture and depression* (pp. 272–298). Berkeley, CA: University of California Press.

Brown, D. R., Eaton, W. W., & Sussman, L. (1990). Racial differences in prevalence of phobic disorders. *Journal of Nervous Mental Disease, 178,* 434–440.

Canino, G. J., Bird, H. R., Shrout, P. E., Rubio-Stipec, M., Bravo, M., Martinez, R., Sesman, M., & Guevara, L. M. (1987). The prevalence of specific psychiatric disorders in Puerto Rico. *Archives of General Psychiatry, 44,* 727–735.

Cardeña, E. (1992). Trance and possession as dissociative disorders. *Transcultural Psychiatric Research Review, 29,* 287–300.

Cox, J. L. (1988). Postnatal depression: A comparison of Scottish and African women. *Social Psychiatry, 18,* 25–28.

Derogatis, L. R., Lipman, R. S., & Covi, L. (1973). The SCL-90: An outpatient psychiatric rating scale. *Psychopharmacology Bulletin, 9,* 13–28.

Egeland, J. (1986). Cultural factors and stigma for manic-depression: The Amish study. *American Journal of Social Psychiatry, 14,* 279–286.

Friedman, C. T. H., & Faguet, R. A. (1982). *Extraordinary disorders of human behavior.* New York: Plenum Press.

Friedman, S., Paradis, C.M., & Hatch, M. (1994). Characteristics of African-American and White patients with panic disorder and agoraphobia. *Hospital Community Psychiatry, 45,* 798–803.

Hyer, L., Woods, M. G., Summers, M. N., Boudewyns, P., & Harrison, W. R. (1990). Alexithymia among Vietnam veterans with posttraumatic stress disorder. *Journal of Clinical Psychiatry, 51,* 243–247.

Karno, M., Hough, R. L., Burnam, A., Escobar, J. I., Timbers, D. M., Santana, F., & Boyd, J. H. (1987). Lifetime prevalence of specific psychiatric disorders among Mexican Americans and non-Hispanic Whites in Los Angeles. *Archives of General Psychiatry, 44,* 695–701.

Kirmayer, L. J., & Robbins, J. M. (1993). Cognitive and social correlates of the Toronto Alexithymia Scale. *Psychosomatics, 34,* 41–52.

Lane, R. D., Sechrest, L., & Riedel, R. (1998). Sociodemographic correlates of alexithymia. *Comprehensive Psychiatry, 39,* 377–385.

Leung, A. W., Heimberg, R. G., Holt, C. S., & Bruch, M. A. (1994). Social anxiety and perception of early parenting among American, Chinese American, and social phobic samples. *Anxiety, 1,* 80–89.

Lin, T. Y. E. (1989). Neurasthenia in Asian cultures. *Culture Medicine Psychiatry, 13,* 105–241.

Lock, M. (1993). *Encounters with aging: Mythologies of menopause in Japan and North America.* Berkeley, CA: University of California Press.

Pattison, E. M., & Wintrob, R. M. (1981). Possession and exorcism in contemporary America. *Journal of Operational Psychiatry, 12,* 13–20.

Rodreguez, R., & DeWolfe, A. (1990). Psychological distress among Mexican American and Mexican women as related to status on the new immigration law. *Journal of Consulting Clinical Psychology, 58,* 548–553.

Roseman, I. J., Dhawan, V., Rettek, S. I., Naidu, R. K., & Thapa, S. (1995). Cultural differences and cross-cultural similarity in appraisal and emotional responses. *Journal of Cross-Cultural Psychology, 26,* 23–48.

Simons, R. C. (1980). The resolution of the latah paradox. *Journal of Nervous and Mental Disorders, 168,* 195–206.

Simons, R. C., & Hughes, C. C. (Eds.). (1985). *The culture-bound syndromes.* Dordrecht: Reidel Publishing Company.

Tseng, W.-S., Kan-Ming, M., Hsu, J., Li-Shuen, L., Li-Wah, O., Guo-Qian, C., & Da-Wei, J. (1988). A sociocultural study of Koro epidemics in Guangdong, China. *American Journal of Psychiatry, 145,* 1538–1543.

Westermeyer, J. (1979). Folk concepts of mental disorder among the Lao: Continuities with similar concepts in other cultures and in psychiatry. *Cultural and Medical Psychiatry, 3,* 301–17.

Westermeyer, J. (1986). Two self-rating scales for depression among Hmong refugees: Assessment in clinical and nonclinical samples. *Journal of Psychiatric Research, 20,* 103–113.

Westermeyer, J. (1989). Paranoid symptoms and disorders among 100 Hmong refugees: A longitudinal study. *Acta Psychiatrica Scandinavia, 80,* 47–59.

Westermeyer, J., Janca, A., Sartorius, N., & Hughes, C. C. (1997). *Lexicon of cross-cultural terms in mental health.* Geneva: World Health Organization.

Westermeyer, J., Schaberg, L., & Nugent, S. (1995). Anxiety symptoms in Hmong refugees. *Journal of Nervous Mental Disease,* in press.

Wierzbicka, A. (1998). Angst. *Culture and Psychology, 4,* 161–188.

Wintrob, R. M. (1966). Psychosis in association with possession by Genii in Liberia. *Psychopathologie Africaine, 2,* 249–258.

Zeitlin, S. B., & McNally, R. J. (1993). Alexithymia and anxiety sensitivity in panic disorder and obsessive-compulsive disorder. *American Journal of Psychiatry, 150,* 658–660.

Zung, W. W. K. (1973). A cross-cultural survey of symptoms in depression. *American Journal of Psychiatry, 126,* 116–121.

6

The Role of Cultural Cognition in Substance Abuse and Alcoholism

M. Dawn Terrell

There is widespread concern about the abuse of psychoactive substances, particularly in areas of the world where use of drugs or alcohol is a relatively new phenomenon or where traditional and culturally sanctioned patterns of use are giving way to misuse and addiction. The World Health Organization (WHO), for example, has noted concerns about increasing rates of alcohol consumption and drug related problems in all WHO regions, including countries with long traditions of abstinence (Grant & Weir, 1991). Both the World Health Organization and the United Nations have called for the development of coordinated efforts to stem the rising tide of substance abuse and alcoholism around the world (U.N. International Drug Control Programme, 1997). These initiatives are sparked in part by recognition of the enormous toll exacted by alcoholism and drug addiction in health costs, social disruptions, and lost productivity.

The move to bring a global perspective to problems of substance abuse and alcoholism has increased attention to the role of ethnocultural factors in patterns of use and misuse. A host of monographs (e.g., Rebach, Bolek, Williams, & Russell, 1992; Trimble, Padilla, & Bell, 1987) have documented different patterns of drug and alcohol abuse among ethnic groups in the United States, while a growing body of literature examining rates of use and abuse around the world also points to significant cultural variations in patterns of psychoactive substance use (e.g., Adrian, 1996; Heath, 1995; U.N. International Drug Control Program, 1997).

Despite the oft reported findings of ethnocultural differences in psychoactive substance abuse, there have been relatively few attempts to fully articulate the possible pathways of cultural influence on substance abuse and alcoholism. Much of the limited work that has been done in this area points to the importance of cultural cognition in shaping patterns of substance use and abuse (e.g., Heath, 1995; Westermeyer, 1984, 1995, 1996). More specifically, it appears that culturally determined norms, attitudes, and beliefs concerning substances may help to explain patterns of use within and across cultures (Heath, 1999).

The central thesis of this chapter is that culturally informed cognition (here taken to include perceptions, worldviews, beliefs, attitudes, norms, and values) is critically important in understanding and treating substance abuse related phenomena. A basic assumption underlying the work is that an individual's psychological, social, and biological experiences—in this case, experiences associated with the use and misuse of psychoactive substances—are mediated by the cognition provided by cultural models (D'Andrade & Strauss, 1992). Cultural cognition is the filter through which individuals understand their experiences (Strauss & Quinn, 1997), and thus this cognition provides the interpretive framework, or cultural meanings attached to experiences with drugs and alcohol.

The goal of the chapter is not to pose a cultural model of substance abuse in opposition to biopsychosocial models, but rather to delineate some of the ways in which cultural cognition may account for differential patterns of use and abuse of psychoactive substances across cultures. After briefly reviewing some of the theory and research pointing to the importance of cultural cognition for understanding substance abuse and alcoholism, an attempt will be made to identify culturally informed cognition that may predispose a culture to higher rates of substance use and abuse, as well as those that may serve to protect members of a culture from problems of abuse or alcoholism. As part of this discussion, examination will be made of cultural variations in cognition concerning mind-altering substances—both in norms dictating appropriate and inappropriate use, and in views about how to address problems of excessive use and abuse. Finally, the implications of cultural cognition for understanding and treating substance abuse are examined.

CULTURAL COGNITION AND MODELS OF ALCOHOLISM AND DRUG ABUSE

In an early examination of patterns of alcohol use across cultures, Bales (1946) proposed that cultural differences in rates of alcoholism could be explained by norms and attitudes that either fostered a climate for excessive alcohol consumption or supported alternative methods of tension reduction. Bales argued that cultures with norms that increase the experience of tension (e.g., that restrict expression of sexual or aggressive feelings), and that condone the use of alcohol as a means of tension reduction, are likely to have comparatively high rates of alcoholism. In contrast, cultures with attitudes and norms favoring abstinence or that call for use of alcohol only as part of ritualized practices, and that provide alternative means of tension reduction, will have lower rates of alcohol use.

Bales also proposed that cultures in which success strivings were emphasized but unlikely to be fulfilled might have high rates of alcohol consumption because of the inherent frustration for individuals unable to achieve the upward mobility expected in the culture (Valentine, 1998). This theme of thwarted social mobility fostering a climate for substance abuse is also a key feature of more recent discussions of the possible linkages between cultural factors and psychoactive substance use.

Oetting and his colleagues (Oetting, Donnermeyer, Trimble, & Beauvais, 1998) have offered the primary socialization theory of adolescent drug use in which they argue that the experience of cultural failure leads to low identification with cultural values. This is true whether the cultural failure is caused by structural factors such as blocked access to the means to achieve cultural success, or whether it occurs as a consequence of the failure of the primary socialization sources to provide an adequate foundation for meeting cultural demands. They suggest that it is this low level of cultural identification, as well as the experience of failure itself, that leads to an increased likelihood of drug use. Individuals with low levels of cultural identification are less likely to be protected from drug use by cultural norms proscribing drug use. They are also more likely to turn to associations with deviant peers, and thus be exposed to subcultural norms tolerant of drug and alcohol use.

Oetting et al. have accorded cultural norms and cultural identification a critical role in accounting for differential rates of drug and alcohol use. Cultural norms are transmitted via the primary socialization sources, which for the adolescent will include the family, school, and peer clusters. It is assumed that in most instances the norms transmitted through the family and school will be prosocial norms that protect the adolescent from drug or alcohol abuse. Peer clusters, however, may hold conflicting subcultural norms that foster deviant behavior, including drug or alcohol use. According to this model, higher rates of drug and alcohol abuse are likely to occur in cultures that have more tolerant norms concerning drug use, or that allow peer clusters to have the central socializing role (rather than family or school).

Culturally determined cognition such as norms and attitudes toward use may not only influence rates of alcohol and drug use, but also influence the experience and expression of intoxication. In the classic work, *Drunken Comportment*, MacAndrew and Edgerton (1969) review extensive crosscultural data on alcohol intoxication to bolster their argument that the behavior and demeanor displayed by intoxicated individuals will depend on culturally determined beliefs and attitudes about intoxication. They contend that "the way people comport themselves when they are drunk is determined not by alcohol's toxic assault upon the seat of moral judgement, conscience or the like, but by what their society makes of and imparts to them concerning the state of drunkenness" (p. 165).

Goode (1984) takes a similar stance with regard to drug intoxication. He suggests that the cultural meanings associated with a particular drug, as well as the sociocultural context of drug use, will not only determine the way the drug's effects are experienced but also whether the use is considered appropriate or inappropriate. He cites as an example the very different effects of morphine on the street addict who is seeking euphoria and pleasure compared to the hospitalized patient who experiences neither when administered an equal dose of morphine as part of a medical regime. The addict's use is considered illicit, and is condemned, while morphine used medicinally is deemed entirely appropriate.

While the foregoing discussion points to the significance of culturally determined cognition for understanding variations in the use and experience of psychoactive substances, cultural cognition has been given relatively short shrift in many contemporary models of addiction. Acknowledged as contributing factors, culturally determined beliefs, attitudes, and norms concerning substance use are nevertheless typically relegated to the sidelines when compared to the emphasis on the explanatory potential of biological or psychological factors. Even cognitive models of addiction (e.g., Beck, Wright, Newman, & Liese, 1993; Marlatt & Gordon, 1985), which give primacy to the role of beliefs and expectancies in producing addictive behavior, focus more on the conditions under which beliefs lead to decisions to use and abuse drugs or alcohol than on the cultural underpinnings for those beliefs.

The irony, of course, is that *all* models of addiction are themselves cultural constructions, reflecting the beliefs, norms, and conventions of the sociocultural context in which they are developed (Shaffer & Robbins, 1995). Thus we had the moral model of alcoholism prominent in the eighteenth and early nineteenth centuries in Europe and America, which held that abusive drinking is primarily an individual choice and a sign of moral weakness. Public policies such as prohibition in the United States were designed to remove temptation from morally weak individuals. In turn, the *medical model* gained ascendancy during the middle decades of this century. In this model, alcoholism was seen as a disease in which the addictive properties of alcohol itself, along with biologically determined predispositions toward alcoholism, account for an individual's dependence on and cravings for the substance (Valentine, 1998). Rather than condemning the alcoholic as weak, treatment was seen as necessary to help an individual cope with cravings and remain abstinent.

The shift to the medical model coincided with both an increasing understanding of the biological contributions to alcoholism and cultural shifts away from ascribing moral meaning to the act of imbibing (with concomitant increases in per capita alcohol consumption). Many cultures worldwide continue to hold worldviews concerning substance use that fit either a moral or a medical model of addiction, although both models have been largely supplanted in the professional literature on psychoactive substance abuse by biopsychosocial theories that focus on the complex interaction of multiple factors in producing addiction. Culturally determined cognition, in this case worldviews (i.e., characteristic ways of understanding the world), thus can be seen to profoundly shape not only patterns of use and the experience and expression of substance use, but also the way in which cultures understand and seek to address problems associated with use.

VARIATIONS IN COGNITION CONCERNING SUBSTANCE USE AND ABUSE

There are enormous variations both within and across cultures in cognition concerning psychoactive substance use and abuse. Cultures vary in how they perceive psychoactive substances, in their norms dictating what is appropriate or inappropriate use, and in the way they approach instances of inappropriate use or abuse. An examination of some of these variations may help to determine whether there is cognition that makes a culture more vulnerable to high rates of use and abuse of psychoactive substances or that, conversely, provides some inoculation against substance abuse and alcoholism.

Perceptions of Psychoactive Substances

Several authors (e.g., Bales, 1946; Heath, 1995; MacAndrew & Edgerton, 1969) have noted that cultures that perceive psychoactive substances in terms of their tension reducing or intoxicating properties often have more tolerant views concerning use of psychoactive substances, and hence higher rates of use and abuse. Heath (1995) has also noted that cultures in which alcohol consumption is viewed as indicative of valor or "manliness" may be more tolerant of alcohol use (at least by men), and hence may have higher rates of alcohol consumption and abuse. Conversely, cultural perceptions of psychoactive substances that emphasize nutritive, medicinal, and spiritual uses may serve to immunize members of the culture from excessive use, especially when these perceptions are coupled with norms proscribing use of substances beyond their valued function. For example, alcohol is widely viewed as a food substance in cultures around the world, and cultures that restrict use to meals tend to have lower rates of alcoholism (Bales, 1946). In contrast, cultures like France, which not only emphasize drinking as part of a meal, but also tolerate imbibing alcohol apart from meals, will typically have higher rates of alcoholism (Heath, 1995).

In addition to being valued for its nutritive properties, alcohol historically has been revered for its medicinal properties in many cultures (Adrian, 1996; Westermeyer, 1995). Heath (1995) notes that cultural perceptions concerning alcohol's healing properties continue in many contemporary societies, including among indigenous populations in China, India, and Nigeria, which "specifically use alcohol as medicine and as an integral part of curing rites" (p. 344). Ironically, this view of alcohol as medicinal often persists in spite of public policies that seek to restrict access to alcohol because of its potential deleterious impact on public health. It should be noted, however, that even in cultures that view alcohol primarily as medicinal, there may also be a perception that excessive use of alcohol is unhealthy (Heath, 1995).

As mentioned earlier, Goode (1984) has noted that where drugs are seen as medicinal rather than as intoxicants—as in the case of morphine—use is typically condoned when restricted to medicinal purposes. It is interesting to note historical shifts in a culture's views of a particular psychoactive substance with regard to its medicinal or healing value. While cocaine is now considered one of the most addictive—and therefore most dangerous—narcotics, as recently as the late 1800s and early 1900s it was widely hailed as a virtual panacea by prominent citizens in Europe (Heath, 1996), and was widely prescribed for a variety of ills, including alcoholism. Similar shifts have occurred in attitudes toward heroin and opium, and marijuana (Adrian, 1996; McNeece & DiNitto, 1998).

Drugs and alcohol have traditionally held religious as well as medicinal significance for many cultures (Heath, 1995; Westermeyer, 1995). Some cultures, for example, include alcohol in religious rites through offerings or as part of the sacraments, while other cultures may view intoxication as a spiritual experience (Heath, 1995; MacAndrew & Edgerton, 1969). Other psychoactive substances have been similarly perceived as having important religious significance. Examples include the hallucinogen peyote in the Native American Church, tobacco in other Native American tribes, and the mild stimulant khat among some East African groups (Adrian, 1996; Westermeyer, 1995).

Westermeyer (1995) notes that for many cultures use of drugs or alcohol as part of religious rites is not only acceptable, but required. He suggests that members of a cultural group rarely develop patterns of abuse of psychoactive substances whose use is culturally prescribed, though he notes exceptions. The exceptions typically occur in cultures where use of a substance is not restricted to religious rites, as, for example, the many cultures in which alcohol use is prescribed as part of religious rites but is also tolerated for nonreligious purposes.

Many cultures hold negative views of alcohol and other psychoactive substances on religious grounds (Heath, 1995). Such cultures are usually entirely abstinent, or at least espouse abstinence as a cultural ideal (Heath, 1995; Westermeyer, 1996). Thus use of all potential intoxicants is prohibited by the Mormon religion, and Muslims are expected to be abstinent, as are some Protestant sects, even though alcohol may be used as part of particular religious rites (Heath, 1995). In the latter instance, it is presumed that there will be low levels of alcohol abuse because of the cultural proscriptions against use outside of the narrow confines of a religious rite—as long as members of the culture remain strongly identified with the culture and adhere to the cultural norms and beliefs concerning alcohol (Westermeyer, 1995).

The problem, of course, is that cultural perceptions and norms concerning psychoactive substances may not be shared equally by all members of a culture, reducing the potential protective value of the perceptions linking psychoactive substance use to religious, medicinal, or nutritive uses. There may be a failure in the enculturation process, so that individuals have not adequately absorbed the protective perceptions and norms (Westermeyer, 1995). It is also possible, as mentioned earlier, that individuals will not identify with the cultural perceptions and norms because of structural barriers to their full participation in the culture and/or because of participation in a deviant subculture (Oetting et al., 1998; Westermeyer, 1996). The inoculation provided by protective cultural perceptions and norms concerning drug and alcohol use is also likely to be disrupted in instances of rapid social change or cultural disintegration, placing individuals within the culture at risk for substance abuse (U.N. International Drug Control Programme, 1997).

Oetting and Beauvais (1991) have noted that it is possible for individuals to maintain multiple cultural identifications, perhaps with conflicting perceptions and norms concerning drugs and alcohol. This is often the case with immigrants who come into contact with differing cultural models of substance use in their host society (Adrian, 1996; Terrell, 1993). Individuals who are minimally identified with protective cultural perceptions and associated norms concerning substances, or who have competing identifications, may be at higher risk for substance use and abuse, particularly if they are exposed to more tolerant perceptions and norms concerning alcohol and drug use through deviant subcultural associations (Oetting et al., 1998) or acculturation experiences (Anderson, 1998; Terrell, 1993).

Norms Concerning Appropriate and Inappropriate Use of Substances

Heath (1995) notes that attitudes concerning alcohol use in a given culture, particularly norms about what is considered appropriate or inappropriate use (and by whom), often reflect the social organization of the culture. Indeed, prescriptions and proscriptions concerning alcohol and drug use have traditionally been one way in which cultures sought to reinforce social organization. Many cultures around the world, for example, have sought to restrict access to alcohol or other psychoactive substances to the more powerful members of the culture as a means of enforcing power differentials. Thus there were laws prohibiting sale of alcoholic beverages to indigenous populations in Australia, the United States, and Canada (Adrian, 1996). Conversely, in some societies those with higher status may be less likely to use alcohol, as is the case in Sri Lanka and India (Heath, 1995). Sometimes the status differential is marked not by whether one uses alcohol, but rather by the type of beverage imbibed, as in cases where higher status individuals drink spirits while drinking beer or wine is associated with lower status individuals.

One important consequence of the relationship between social organization and cultural prescriptions and proscriptions concerning substance use is that in instances of upward mobility, individuals may begin using substances new to them, without being fully enculturated into patterns of appropriate use (Westermeyer, 1995). New users may apply rules appropriate for other substances, but not psychoactive substances, as has been the case with some indigenous peoples who upon gaining access to alcohol consume it in much the same way they would consume food substances: all at one sitting (Adrian, 1996).

Another way in which cultural attitudes concerning appropriate and inappropriate use of psychoactive substances reflect the social organization of a society is the widely observed gender difference in prescriptions and proscriptions concerning use (Coupe, 1991; Heath, 1995). Where alcohol use by males, and even public intoxication, is condoned in many cultures as an appropriate male bonding ritual, most cultures have expectations that women will imbibe less than their male counterparts, if at all, and will certainly not drink to excess (Heath, 1995) or use illicit drugs (U.N. International Drug Control Programme, 1997). Conversely, women's use of psychotropic medications is socially acceptable in many cultures. Studies have shown that women are far more likely to be prescribed psychotropic medications than are men in the United States, Guatemala, Brazil, and Jamaica (U.N. International Drug Control Programme, 1997). Strong cultural proscriptions against illicit drug and alcohol use may place women at a disadvantage in seeking treatment for substance abuse or alcoholism (Coupe, 1991), while the acceptability of using prescribed psychotropics may place them at higher risk for addiction to licit drugs.

As in instances of upward mobility, women who move from cultural settings with strong proscriptions against substance use to settings with more tolerant views may be at risk for substance abuse because they lack a fully ingrained cultural model for appropriate use. There is some indication that women's substance use increases as part of the process of becoming acculturated to a new culture with more tolerant attitudes concerning women's substance use (e.g., Balcazar, Peterson, & Cobas, 1996; Gilbert, Mora, & Ferguson, 1994), or where social change within a culture has meant a shift in norms (U.N. International Drug Control Programme, 1997).

As noted earlier, rapid social change within a culture may be a general risk factor for increased rates of substance abuse. This is particularly the case where new substances, or more potent forms of already used substances, are being introduced into the culture (Adrian, 1996; Westermeyer, 1995). As an example, Adrian (1996) describes how the use of kava (a mild hypnotic) in Polynesia has moved from nonproblematic, quasiceremonial use by individuals who produced their own supplies to problematic use and potential abuse as a consequence of new modes of administration. Rather than chewing the kava root, individuals may now consume commercially produced kava for sale in the form of beverages at local bars. It is thus possible to consume a much greater quantity of kava in a single sitting. As the use of kava, which has been viewed as culturally appropriate, has shifted from chewing the root to imbibing kava based drinks, the use of alcoholic beverages has also gone up, perhaps because the cultural acceptance of kava use is being shifted to alcohol.

It is typically only after a culture has noted significant harmful effects from use of a psychoactive substance that cultural norms concerning use are developed to limit or contain use, often accompanied by legal sanctions against use (Westermeyer, 1995). This process is sometimes complicated by economic and political factors, as in the case where there are economic benefits to some members of the culture for continuing to produce or distribute a substance (Westermeyer, 1996). Despite draconian policies against the use of crack cocaine, for example, its use reached epidemic proportions in some parts of the world in the 1980s in part because the sale and distribution of crack provided substantial economic opportunities in otherwise severely depressed communities (Terrell, 1993; U.N. International Drug Control Programme, 1997).

The relationship between cultural attitudes toward use and economic factors also can be seen in countries where production and distribution of psychoactive substances is a significant contributor to the nation's economy. So, for example, the wine producing regions of southern Europe typically have cultural norms that are tolerant of consumption of alcohol (Heath, 1995), while many of the opium producing countries of Asia likewise have long histories of tolerating opiate use, which may account for continued high rates of consumption in some countries (e.g., Vietnam, Laos, Cambodia, Burma) despite severe legal penalties against use (Westermeyer, 1996).

Cultural Approaches to Substance Abuse Related Problems

Economic factors also may play a part in the way a society responds to problems of substance abuse and alcoholism. Thus societies that rely on income from production of alcoholic beverages often turn a blind eye toward problematic drinking (Moser, 1991). This is particularly the case when, as noted above, the production of alcohol is related to a cultural tradition of tolerance toward alcohol consumption, as in Ireland (McNeece & DiNitto, 1998). If the negative consequences of excessive consumption become abundantly apparent, such cultures may move toward promoting "responsible" or moderate use of alcoholic substances through educational campaigns and the like, eschewing strategies for addressing alcoholism that call for abstinence.

With regard to strategies for addressing problems of excessive alcohol consumption, Room (1992) notes that cultures have been classified as either temperance cultures such as the United States or Canada in which the traditional approach has been to seek to restrict drinking by reducing the physical and cultural availability of alcohol, or wet cultures such as Australia or Finland, in which the aim is to reduce problematic drinking by better integrating drinking into the culture. Temperance cultures tend to be more concerned with the potential negative health consequences of excessive consumption, while cultures seeking wet solutions tend to be more concerned about the impact of intoxication on the social fabric. Societies may move between stances, prompted by social change or the perceived failure of a prior stance. In fact, neither strategy has demonstrated unequivocal success, although temperance solutions that effectively cut consumption are more successful in reducing rates of alcohol related problems than are wet solutions.

Several authors (e.g., McNeece & DiNitto, 1998; Westermeyer, 1996) have noted that the most successful models for changing patterns of alcohol consumption or drug use are those in which there is significant cultural impetus for change rather than merely for a change in public policy. In fact, Westermeyer (1996) argues that imposition of culturally based sanctions on those who use drugs or alcohol excessively is a very powerful mode of addressing problematic use in monocultural societies where cultural integration is highly valued. These sanctions may take the form of shaming or extrusion, and they may be more powerful even than formal, legal sanctions (U.N. International Drug Control Programme, 1997).

Cultural sanctions against excessive use can be a double-edged sword, however. The risk for increased substance abuse for those who experience marginalization or low cultural identification, which are the potential consequences of extrusion, has already been noted. It is also the case that cultural taboos against excessive use may make it less likely that chemically dependent members seek treatment for substance abuse related problems. For example, it has been noted that the taboo against acknowledging excessive use of drugs or alcohol in Asian cultures means that individuals from these cultures are less likely to seek treatment for chemical dependency (e.g., Cheung, 1991; Ja & Aoki, 1993).

The way a culture approaches instances of substance abuse or alcoholism will reflect its more general worldview concerning the causes and meaning of illness or deviance, and cultural beliefs about how change in behavior is best induced (or even whether behavior can be changed). In cultures with supernatural worldviews, for example, use of spiritual healing practices or exhortations about the supernatural consequences for transgressing cultural norms may be called on to address problems of excessive use (Westermeyer, 1996). Watts and Gutierres (1997) suggest the cultural significance of such practices in facilitating recovery among Native Americans who are chemically dependent. Cultures that emphasize the impact of an individual's behavior on the family and collective, including many Asian cultures, may try to handle the behavior within the context of the family, using shaming and the threat of extrusion to try to shape behavior (Ja & Aoki, 1993).

IMPLICATIONS FOR UNDERSTANDING AND TREATING SUBSTANCE ABUSE

Worldviews concerning the causes of substance abuse and cultural beliefs about the process of change comprise an individual's explanatory model of substance abuse (Tang & Bigby, 1996). This explanatory model, along with culturally determined perceptions of substances and norms concerning appropriate and inappropriate use, provide the cultural matrix out of which an individual's experiences with use and abuse of psychoactive substances will be formed. As has been shown, some of the cultural cognition embedded in this matrix may provide protective functions, making it less likely that an individual will experience substance abuse or alcoholism. Other cognition may foster use and thus, potentially, abuse of psychoactive substances. What should be clear from the foregoing discussion is that any effective model for understanding and treating substance abuse and alcoholism must take into account the cultural matrix out of which the disorder arises.

Lack of understanding of the role of cultural cognition in an individual's experience of substance abuse may be one reason that treatment models designed in one cultural context have often been found to have limited utility when applied across cultures (e.g., Perez-Arce, Carr, & Sorensen, 1993; Smith, Buxton, Bilal, & Seymour, 1993; Watts & Gutierres, 1997). Smith et al. (1993) outline cultural points of resistance to the oft used 12-step model of recovery, for example, to the concept of powerlessness. Perez-Arce et al. (1993) note that the confrontational methods often employed in substance abuse treatment are less effective with some cultural groups and with women. Rather than simply pointing out the limitations of traditional treatment approaches, some authors have discussed the utility of designing treatment programs that specifically incorporate the cultural cognition and themes of the individuals for whom the treatment is intended (e.g., Smith et al., 1993; Watts & Gutierres, 1997). Such programs may have the added benefit of reducing low cultural identification or marginalization (Terrell, 1993; Watts & Gutierres, 1997). More generally, effective treatment approaches will need to match the cultural matrix of the clients. As Smith et al. (1993) note:

Internationally, one cannot simply take a treatment program that is successful in New York or Seattle, replicate it in Florence or Addis Ababba, and expect it to be entirely successful. While the technical aspects of drug dependence may be similar, addiction takes place in and must be treated within a culturally specific milieu. (p. 101)

Another implication of our discussion of cultural cognition and use of psychoactive substances is that individuals may be most at risk for substance abuse when there is a disruption in their cultural matrix, whether the disruption is caused by acculturation experiences, cultural disintegration, or marginalization experiences. There is an ample body of literature (e.g., Anderson, 1998; Oetting et al., 1998; Tang & Bigby, 1996; Terrell, 1993; U.N. International Drug Control Programme, 1997) that attests to the heightened risk for substance abuse associated with these experiences, though the risk has not necessarily been linked to disruptions in an individual's cognitive set. What has been noted, however, are the distinctive changes in an individual's cognition that accompany the process of becoming chemically dependent.

Westermeyer (1984, 1996) notes that once an individual begins to use alcohol or drugs, the power of culturally informed perceptions and norms is vastly reduced as the user "gradually places a higher and higher value on the chemical experience" (1984, p. 13). Beck et al. (1993) concur with this observation, and argue it is in fact a distinguishing characteristic of the individual who becomes chemically dependent on psychoactive substances that the substance "seems to take control. . . . [G]oals, values, and attachments become subordinate to the drug using" (p. 23). In effect, the user moves from identification with the culture of origin and its potentially protective cognition to identifying with the substance abuse subculture, with its own set of shared cognition (Westermeyer, 1984).

The process through which protective cultural perceptions and norms are shed for beliefs that foster use of psychoactive substances is not clearly understood, although the Oetting et al. primary socialization model offers possible pathways. There is a large body of research literature documenting that alcohol and drug use typically follow a progression from mild to moderate to heavy (McNeece & DiNitto, 1998), which suggests that there also may be a progressive shift in cognition. There is some empirical data to suggest that as individuals gain experience with psychoactive substances, their perceptions of those substances become more differentiated and complex, and they may be less likely to consider psychoactive substances as potentially harmful and also to see more positive outcomes from use (e.g., Fabricius, Nagoshi, & MacKinnon, 1993).

Clearly, much more research is necessary to better understand the role that shifts in culturally determined cognitions concerning substances may play in the process of addiction. Further research is also necessary to better understand both the potential protective and the risk inducing functions of cultural cognitions in accounting for crosscultural differences in rates and experiences of substance abuse and alcoholism. In particular, it will be important to understand the role of cultural cognitions in an increasingly complex world, where cultural hybridization and interconnectedness have led to the transformation of cultural practices and identities throughout the world (Herman & Kempen, 1998).

REFERENCES

Adrian, M. (1996). Substance use and multiculturalism. *Substance Use and Misuse, 31,* 1459–1501.

Anderson, T. L. (1998). Drug identity change processes, race, and gender: Explanations of drug misuse and a new identity-based model. *Substance Use and Misuse, 33,* 2263–2279.

Balcazar, H., Peterson, G., & Cobas, J. A. (1996). Acculturation and health-related risk behaviors among Mexican-American pregnant youth. *American Journal of Health Behavior, 20,* 425–433.

Bales, R. F. (1946). Cultural differences in rates of alcoholism. *Quarterly Journal of Studies on Alcohol, 6,* 480–499.

Beck, A. T., Wright, F. D., Newman, C. F., & Liese, B. S. (1993). *Cognitive therapy of substance abuse.* New York: Guilford.

Cheung, Y. (1991). Ethnicity and alcohol/drug use revisited: A framework for future research. *The International Journal of the Addictions, 25,* 581–605.

Coupe, J. (1991). Why women need their own services. In I. B. Glass (Ed.), *The international handbook of addiction behavior* (pp. 168–178). London: Tavistock.

D'Andrade, R. G., & Strauss, C. (Eds.). (1992). *Human motives and cultural models.* Cambridge, UK: Cambridge University Press.

Fabricius, W. V., Nagoshi, C. T., & MacKinnon, D. P. (1993). Beliefs about the harmfulness of drug use in adults who use different drugs. *Psychology of Addictive Behaviors, 7,* 52–65.

Gilbert, M., Mora, J., & Ferguson, L. (1994). Alcohol-related expectancies among Mexican-American women. *International Journal of the Addictions, 29,* 1127–1147.

Goode, E. (1984). *Drugs in American society.* New York: Alfred Knopf.

Grant, M., & Weir, M. (1991). The World Health Organization. In I. B. Glass (Ed.), *The international handbook of addiction behavior* (pp. 326–330). London: Tavistock.

Heath, D. B. (Ed.). (1995). *International handbook on alcohol and culture.* Westport, CT: Greenwood.

Heath, D. B. (1996). The War on Drugs as a metaphor in American Culture. In W. K. Bickel & R. J. DeGrandpre (Eds.), *Drug policy and human nature: Psychological perspectives on the prevention, management, and treatment of illicit drug abuse* (pp. 279–299). New York: Plenum.

Heath, D. B. (1999). Culture. In P. J. Ott & R. E. Tarter (Eds.), *Sourcebook on substance abuse: Etiology, epidemiology, assessment, and treatment* (pp. 175–183). Boston: Allyn & Bacon.

Herman, H. J. M., & Kempen, H. J. G. (1998). Moving cultures: The perilous problems of cultural dichotomies in a globalizing society. *American Psychologist, 53,* 1111–1120.

Ja, D. Y., & Aoki, B. (1993). Substance abuse treatment: Cultural barriers in the Asian-American community. *Journal of Psychoactive Drugs, 25,* 61–71.

MacAndrew, C., & Edgerton, R. B. (1969). *Drunken comportment: A social explanation.* New York: Aldine.

Marlatt, G. A., & Gordon, J. R. (1985). *Relapse prevention: Maintenance strategies in the treatment of addictive behaviors.* New York: Guilford.

McNeece, C. A., & DiNitto, D. M. (1998). *Chemical dependency: A systems approach.* Boston: Allyn & Bacon.

Moser, J. (1991). What does a national alcohol policy look like? In I. B. Glass (Ed.), *The international handbook of addiction behavior* (pp. 313–319). London: Tavistock.

Oetting, E., & Beauvais, F. (1991). Orthogonal cultural identification theory: The cultural identification of minority adolescents. *The International Journal of the Addictions, 25,* 655–685.

Oetting, E. R., Donnermeyer, J. F., Trimble, J. E., & Beauvais, F. (1998). Primary socialization theory: Culture, ethnicity, and cultural identification. The links between culture and substance use. *Substance Use and Misuse, 33,* 2075–2107.

Perez-Arce, P., Carr, K. D., & Sorensen, J. L. (1993). Cultural issues in an outpatient program for stimulant abusers. *Journal of Psychoactive Drugs, 25,* 35–44.

Rebach, H. M., Bolek, C. S., Williams, K. L., & Russell, R. (1992). *Substance abuse among ethnic minorities in America: A critical annotated bibliography.* New York: Garland.

Room, R. (1992). The impossible dream?: Routes to reducing alcohol problems in a temperance culture. *Journal of Substance Abuse, 4,* 91–106.

Shaffer, H. J., & Robbins, M. (1995). Psychotherapy for addictive behavior: A stage-change approach to meaning making. In A. M. Washton (Ed.), *Psychotherapy and substance abuse: A practitioner's handbook* (pp. 103–12). New York: Guilford.

Smith, D. E., Buxton, M. E., Bilal, R., & Seymour, R. B. (1993). Cultural points of resistance to the 12-step recovery process. *Journal of Psychoactive Drugs, 25,* 97–108.

Strauss, C., & Quinn, N. (1997). *A cognitive theory of cultural meaning.* Cambridge, UK: Cambridge University.

Tang, W. W. H., & Bigby, J. (1996). Cultural perspectives on substance abuse. In L. Freidman, N. F. Fleming, D. H. Roberts, & S. E. Hyman (Eds.), *Source book on substance abuse and addiction* (pp. 41–56). Baltimore, MD: Williams & Wilkins.

Terrell, M. D. (1993). Ethnocultural factors and substance abuse: Toward culturally sensitive treatment models. *Psychology of Addictive Behaviors, 7,* 162–167.

Trimble, J. E., Padilla, A. M., & Bell, C. S. (1987). *Drug abuse among ethnic minorities* (office of science monograph series). Rockville, MD: National Institute on Drug Abuse.

United Nations International Drug Control Programme. (1997). *World drug report.* Oxford, UK: Oxford University Press.

Valentine, P. V. (1998). The etiology of addiction. In C. A. McNeece & D. M. DiNitto, *Chemical dependency: A systems approach* (pp. 23–37). Boston: Allyn & Bacon.

Watts, L. K., & Gutierres, S. E. (1997). A Native American-based cultural model of substance dependency and recovery. *Human Organization, 56,* 9–18.

Westermeyer, J. (1984). The role of ethnicity in substance abuse. In B. Stimmel (Ed.), *Cultural and sociological aspects of alcoholism and substance abuse* (pp. 9–18). New York: Haworth.

Westermeyer, J. (1995). Cultural aspects of substance abuse and alcoholism. Assessment and management. *The Psychiatric Clinics of North America, 18,* 589–605.

Westermeyer, J. (1996). Cultural factors in the control, prevention, and treatment of illicit drug use. The earthlings' psychoactive task. In W. K. Bickel & R. J. DeGrandpre (Eds.), *Drug policy and human nature: Psychological perspectives on the prevention, management, and treatment of illicit drug abuse* (pp. 99–124). New York: Plenum.

7

Eating Disorders, Culture, and Cognition

Myra Cooper

There is growing evidence, both crossculturally and historically, for the importance of culture in the development and expression of eating disorders. There is also increasing interest in cognitive factors in anorexia nervosa and bulimia nervosa. This chapter will suggest a framework for linking eating disorders, culture, and cognition. Based on the available evidence, it will suggest a preliminary synthesis between culture and cognition that may begin to help account for the differing incidence and prevalence of eating disorders in different cultures.

After a brief note on the relationship between culture and cognition, the chapter will summarize the current evidence for cultural determinants of eating disorders. It will then describe a basic "developmental" cognitive model of eating disorders (Cooper, Todd, & Wells, 1998), noting which aspects of cognition may be open to cultural influence. It takes the main components of the model in turn and, by drawing on social cognition research, links their development in the individual to culturally determined beliefs. It then briefly examines historical and cultural differences in the expression of eating disorders. Finally, it discusses briefly the usefulness of cognitive therapy in the treatment of eating disorders.

Shared cognitions and shared cognitive processes are an integral part of culture. Haviland (1997), for example, has recently defined culture as "the abstract values, beliefs, and perceptions of the world that lie behind people's behavior and which are reflected in their behavior" (p. 345). Traditionally, cognitive psychology has not focused on culture or cultural aspects of the mind. However, there have been some recent moves to include and draw attention to cultural factors. In this regard, Bruner (1990) notes that the fundamental question in cognitive psychology is not only how people create meaning but the importance of culture in this act.

An increasing number of empirical studies support the suggestion that culture plays an important role in the development of eating disorders (for a review, see Fedoroff & McFarlane, 1998), including both anorexia nervosa and bulimia nervosa. The accumulating evidence suggests that eating disorders are most common in those from Western economically developed countries, and much less common in those from developing countries. However, ethnic groups from developing countries now living in Western cultures are more at risk than those who remain in their culture of origin. Moreover, the more acculturated individuals are, the greater is the risk.

It also seems that, as Western cultural values spread, cases in developing countries, while still infrequent, are becoming slightly more common. In most cases sufferers primarily are young and female, which means that any cultural factors implicated in eating disorders must act selectively on young women. Studies also show that many of the risk factors identified by cognitive models vary crossculturally, and show the same cultural distribution as diagnosed eating disorders (see Fedoroff & McFarlane, 1998). This includes the presence of dieting, the desire to be thin, and the presence of concerns about weight and shape. Eating disorders, and risk factors, thus seem to be most common in cultures where it is fashionable and acceptable to diet.

COGNITIVE THEORY IN EATING DISORDERS

Clinicians have long noted the existence and importance of a cognitive disturbance in anorexia nervosa (Bruch, 1973). A similar disturbance has also been noted in bulimia nervosa (Russell, 1979). At present, two cognitive models are commonly used as a basis for cognitive therapy in eating disorders, one designed for anorexia nervosa (Garner & Bemis, 1982) and one designed for bulimia nervosa (Fairburn, Cooper, & Cooper, 1986). Both assign unusual beliefs and attitudes, often referred to as underlying assumptions, a causal role in the maintenance of the two disorders. Both are primarily models of maintenance and do not describe how eating disorders might develop.

Although developmental elements are not included in either of the models, other researchers have begun to address this issue by highlighting the importance of self-schemata (Vitousek & Hollon, 1990) or personal identity structures (Guidano & Liotti, 1983), the content of which appears to refer to what Young (1990) has called core beliefs. Processes driven by core beliefs (e.g., selective attention and selective memory, to use cognitive psychology terminology; or schema compensation, avoidance, and maintenance, to use clinical cognitive psychology terminology) have also been highlighted (Vitousek & Hollon, 1990).

More recently, a detailed developmental cognitive model of eating disorders (including both anorexia nervosa and bulimia nervosa) has been proposed (Cooper, Todd, & Wells, 1998). This model draws on existing theory, on the developmental issues mentioned above, and on recent empirical work (Cooper, Todd, & Wells, 1998). In this model it is suggested that eating disorders are characterized by negative self-beliefs (e.g., I'm a failure, I'm worthless) that arise from early traumatic or negative experiences. Underlying assumptions then develop, often encouraged by family, social, or cultural pressures related to weight and shape, as a way to overcome these negative self-beliefs.

Three types of underlying assumptions have been identified as having a central role: weight and shape as a means to self-acceptance (e.g., If I lose weight, I'll be a better person), weight and shape as a means to acceptance by others (e.g., If I diet, others will like me more), and assumptions reflecting control over eating (e.g., If I eat less, it means I'm more in control). These assumptions are examples of schema compensation strategies (Young, 1990). They provide a way, through controlling weight and shape, for the person to overcome or make up for negative views about themselves. This model is primarily a model of the development of eating disorders. It emphasizes the conjunction of negative self-beliefs and underlying assumptions. Both are needed for an eating disorder to develop.

In this model, cultural influences may be evident in the content of cognition (e.g., underlying assumptions that reflect schema-driven processes) and negative self-beliefs. They can also reveal themselves in the structure and actual existence of both these constructs. This includes the structure and existence of schema-driven processes that seek to compensate for perceived negative attributes or qualities.

Little research has been conducted on the link between the individual factors identified in cognitive theories of eating disorders and cultural beliefs. However, the developmental theory of eating disorders outlined above (Cooper, Todd, & Wells, 1998) links to cognitive theories, especially social cognition theories (and concepts) in nonclinical psychology, in which some work linking cognition to cultural factors has been conducted. Examination of this link in these theories may be relevant to the relationship between individual cognition and culture in eating disorders. Indeed, social cognition theories, unlike cognitive theories of eating disorders, often have several facets or strands that may help to provide a more detailed and complex analysis of the relationship between eating disorders, culture, and cognition. Possible links between culture, cognitive psychology, and the individual factors identified as important in the developmental model of eating disorders will be outlined below.

CULTURE AND COGNITION IN EATING DISORDERS

Social inference theory, "the core of social cognition" (Hogg & Vaughan, 1998, p. 71), which investigates the way in which we form impressions and make judgments, may be particularly relevant to understanding underlying assumptions in eating disorders. Specifically, it may be relevant to the way in which we make judgments about the meaning of weight and shape, and eating or not eating. Both the content of judgments as well as the inferential processes and the heuristics used are open to cultural influence. In Western cultures, and with respect to content, culturally held beliefs state that fat is bad, and thin is good.

For instance, Kurman (1978) found that thinness was associated with positive personality traits. This included traits of self-discipline and self-control (Garner & Garfinkel, 1982), which are positively valued in Western cultures. At the same time, fat is stigmatized and evaluated negatively (Brownell & O'Neil, 1993).

Evidence suggests that even young children in Western cultures attribute negative qualities to larger body shapes (Staffieri, 1967). Little empirical research has been conducted on what it means to be fat and thin in non-Western cultures. Nevertheless, anecdotal psychological and anthropological reports suggest that the content of inferences differs from that identified in Western cultures. In particular, most non-Western cultures associate plumpness with desirable social status. For example, plumpness is an overt sign of wealth when food is not abundant (Rudofsky, 1972), and is associated with fertility (in women), strength, and prosperity (Buhrich, 1981). Such cultural differences could affect vulnerability to eating disorders. Though little crosscultural work relevant to eating disorders has been conducted on the different types of inferential processes themselves or on the heuristics associated with them, it is possible that these also could differ crossculturally, and affect vulnerability to eating disorders.

Underlying assumptions contain implicit causal attributions. Therefore, attributional theory (Weiner, 1995), which attempts to explain how people construct explanations, may also be relevant to understanding underlying assumptions in eating disorders. It may be particularly relevant to how people construct explanations for individual characteristics. Both the inferential processes and the heuristics used to construct explanations in attributional theories, especially the tendency to make dispositional attributions, are open to cultural influence. In Western cultures, and in relation to eating disorders, causal attributions are reflected in the culturally held belief that everyone could and should achieve a healthy weight, and that if they do not or cannot they have only themselves to blame.

This reflects a tendency in the West to make internal causal attributions. However, with respect to inferential processes and heuristics, crosscultural research has been conducted on the bias to make dispositional attributions for others' behavior, known as the fundamental attribution error (Ross, 1977). It found that this heuristic occurs much less often in those from non-Western cultures (Miller, 1984). Thus, in non-Western cultures, being fat or thin is less likely to be interpreted as saying something about the individual and more likely to be viewed as related to the individual's context. Such cultural differences could affect vulnerability to eating disorders.

As with social inference theory, there might also be crosscultural differences in the inferential processes, as well as in other heuristics besides the fundamental attribution error. These may also affect vulnerability to eating disorders.

Women and Eating Disorders

It is generally accepted that Western cultural beliefs about what it means to be fat or thin have a greater impact on women than men in the West (Wooley &

Wooley, 1980). This suggests that increased vulnerability to eating disorders in women may, at least in part, be linked to recent cultural forces acting selectively on women. Relevant forces include female sexual liberation (Bennett & Gurin, 1982), changes in the role of women, and changes in cultural demands and expectations. These pressures can be linked to specific beliefs, at the cultural or subcultural level, about what it means to be fat or thin. Among other things, it has been suggested that thinness represents a rejection of the feminine stereotype (Szyrynski, 1973), and/or an expression of female sexual liberation (Bennett & Gurin, 1982), with the attributes or meanings associated with thinness (e.g., athleticism, nonreproductive sexuality) representing a kind of androgynous independence. Others, such as Bruch (1978), have emphasized the process rather than the meaning and have suggested that, faced with too many conflicting demands and choices, some women choose weight and shape as means to control their lives or as realms to be "successful" in. This is described by Vitousek and Hollon (1990) as a New Years' resolution style of cognitive process. As well as affecting vulnerability, it also is possible that cultural pressure acting on women and not men may affect the expression of eating disorders. Western women are, traditionally and unlike men, rewarded for affiliation and dependence. Thus self-esteem, as well as being tied to internal or dispositional factors, also tends to be more strongly tied to interpersonal approval (Bardwick, 1971). These two processes may be reflected in women's vulnerability to develop weight and shape assumptions tied to both self-acceptance and to acceptance by others.

Eating disorders are more likely to develop in adolescent girls and young women. It has been suggested that adolescence is more difficult for girls than for boys in Western culture (Hsu, 1990). In particular, it has been suggested that the onset of puberty may make denial or avoidance of the expectations associated with adolescence more difficult for girls and that, in the West, recent cultural changes may magnify the stress.

Negative Self-Beliefs

The concept of schemas (Neisser, 1967) may be relevant to understanding negative self-beliefs, particularly the concept of self-schemas. A schema may be defined as "a cognitive structure that represents knowledge about a concept or type of stimulus, including its attributes and the relations among those attributes" (Fiske & Taylor, 1991). A self-schema is a schema about oneself; that is, ones' self-concept. Negative self-beliefs represent the content of schema. Such structures possess schematic properties that influence the way we perceive, understand, make sense of, and recall the information presented to us (Eysenck, 1993). Cultural forces might influence the existence of negatively toned schemas, their structure, and the processes associated with them.

Typically, a self-schema includes objective information or descriptions of physical characteristics (e.g., I'm female, I'm tall, I'm fat) as well as personality descriptors (e.g., I'm honest, I'm successful, I'm caring). To date, it is usually the more objective or physical descriptors that have been studied (Markus, Hamill, & Sentis, 1987). While social cognition theory tends to treat these two types of schema as equivalent, this tendency is not apparent in cognitive theories of eating disorders. In particular, personality descriptors appear to exist at a deeper level of meaning than physical descriptors, particularly the belief that one is fat or thin. They can be derived from physical/objective descriptors by asking, What does being (believing that you are) fat mean or say about you? This level of meaning lies at the core of the self-concept in cognitive theory and therapy for eating disorders. Despite this difference in view of the self, the concept of self-schema remains useful as a framework for furthering our understanding of cultural influences on eating disorders.

With respect to the existence of negatively toned schemas, preliminary evidence suggests that the self-concept or self-schema may be similar in women with eating disorders and women with depression, at least in Western cultures (Cooper & Hunt, 1998); that is, in the presence of negative self-beliefs. With respect to cultural differences, Koenig (1997) notes that depression may manifest itself in different ways in West and non-Western cultures. In particular, cognitive/motivational symptoms (e.g., guilt, self-deprecation, despair, suicidal ideation) seem to be more common in Western cultures. Koenig links this difference in symptoms to differences in the cultural selfway (Markus, Mullally, & Kitamaya, 1997).

Selfways are characteristic ways of engaging in the social world. Defined as "a pattern that establishes or strengthens certain kinds of self-concepts" (Neisser, 1997, p. 5), selfways, like the individual self-concept, have schematic properties. They guide "what people notice and think about, what they feel moved to do, what they feel, how they feel, and how they organize, understand and give meaning to their experiences" (Markus, Mullally, & Kitamaya, 1997, p. 15).

In Western cultures, the cultural selfway is reflected in the drive to be distinct and unique, as compared to many non-Western cultures where the drive is to fit in and be a useful member of the group. This difference means that, in the West, negative affect is linked to low self-esteem, which is then reflected in negative self-beliefs. In non-Western cultures, however, negative affect is linked to not fitting in, and does not have the effect of encouraging the development of negative self-beliefs. This may, at a broad level, increase vulnerability to the development of an eating disorder.

Within a specific cultural selfway, and consistent with the suggestion made earlier, Markus et al. (1997) also note that females' experience may be rather different from that of men, particularly in the West where cultures are more likely to emphasize dependent selves to women; that is, maintaining relationships and connection to others. However, in the West, connecting to others is a distinguishing attribute of the self, not fitting in or being part of a relationship. This means that women in the West appear to have both positive, strong, articulated selves and an emphasis on connectivity and relatedness to others. These two themes in the self-concept may help to explain, more clearly and in more detail than previous researchers have done, why women with eating disorders are concerned not only about weight and shape as a means to enhance their own self-esteem, but also about weight and shape as a means to be accepted by others.

Differences in the type of selfway developed and the emphasis on a dependent self for women in Western cultures may affect vulnerability to eating disorders. Different cultures may also stress different kinds of self-concept. The type found in Western cultures may not be universal and may also relate, at a general level, to vulnerability to eating disorders. For example, the Penobscot Indians have a concept of the self in which each individual is made up of two parts, the body and a vital self dependent on the body but able to have out of body experiences (Speck, 1920). This structure differs from the coherent, whole, and integrated structure characteristic of the Western self-concept.

Attributional theory may also be extended to negative self-beliefs, specifically to the attribution of responsibility for the belief that one is, for example, a failure or worthless. As with underlying assumptions, responsibility for being worthless or a failure can be located in the self or in external factors. As with its application to underlying assumptions, both the inferential processes and the heuristics used to construct explanations may be open to cultural influence. Again, differences between cultures in these may affect the likelihood of developing eating disorders.

Schema-Driven Processing

Attributional theory is also applicable to schema-driven processing. In relation to eating disorders, the self-serving bias (i.e., the tendency to enhance or protect self-esteem) is relevant to schema compensation in which dieting is seen as a way to overcome or make up for perceived negative qualities. The existence of this bias is open to cultural influence. In the developmental cognitive theory outlined above, schema compensation processes reflect dieting as a means to overcome negative self-beliefs. This process, self-esteem enhancement, seems analogous to the concept of self-serving biases that, within the context of attributional theory, serve to protect or enhance self-esteem or self-image.

While research in Western cultures finds self-serving and self-protective biases in which individuals take credit for their success and attribute it to their own abilities, the opposite pattern is found in other cultures. In Japan, for example, individuals explain success in terms of situational factors (Kitayama, Takagi, & Matsumoto, 1995). Cultural differences in the existence of the self-serving bias may contribute to individual vulnerability to developing eating disorders.

Culture and the Expression of Eating Disorders

It seems clear that there are cultural differences in the expression of eating disorders, both currently across cultures and historically within cultures. Cases of eating disorders in some less developed countries do not always appear to have all the typical features of those in Western cultures. For instance, fear of fatness may not be common in non-Western anorexia nervosa (Khandelwal, Sharan, & Saxena, 1995). Instead, decrease in food intake may be related to fasting for religious purposes or to eccentric nutritional ideas. It has been suggested that degree of Westernization may affect findings such as this (Fedoroff & McFarlane, 1998), with atypical presentations being more common in less Westernized cultures. Historically, symptoms are not always related to a sense of fatness or to pressure against fatness (Littlewood, 1995).

Cultural differences can, within a cognitive framework focused on the cultural meaning system (D'Andrade, 1984), explain these differing manifestations. In Western cultures, DSM-IV (American Psychiatric Association, 1994) provides a set of rules that create eating disorders. These include a focus on dieting or not eating to avoid becoming fat. An examination of subjective experience can highlight many different culturally determined meanings for refusal to eat. In the Middle Ages one got closer to God through fasting. It was this that made fasting/dieting good and acceptable. Exploring differences in cultural meaning also may help to explain the rather different meanings attached to weight loss and dieting. For example, the emphasis on control (Fairburn, Shafran, & Cooper, 1999), as opposed to other outcomes (e.g., self-acceptance), may simply be another instance of a culturally determined meaning attached to dieting and/or fasting.

COGNITIVE THERAPY FOR EATING DISORDERS

Cognitive therapy is widely regarded as the treatment of choice for bulimia nervosa, particularly for more severe bulimia nervosa. Although not extensively evaluated, it is also considered to be useful in the treatment of anorexia nervosa. Traditionally, it focuses on cognitions at the level of automatic thoughts and underlying assumptions, and not on negative self-beliefs and schema-driven processes. Traditional cognitive therapy does not help everyone. Many do not recover completely, and some who have recovered relapse (Cooper, 1997). This suggests that it may be useful and important to broaden cognitive therapy to include an emphasis on negative self-beliefs and schema-driven processes.

The evidence discussed here suggests that some of the cognitive content, structures, and processes that characterize eating disorders may simply be absent in cultures where eating disorders are rare. However, in some cultures eating disorders take on different forms, especially with regard to the meaning of symptoms; for example, what it means to be fat or thin. This reflects differences in underlying assumptions, and in the location of the core psychopathology of eating disorders (Vitousek & Hollon, 1990). Cognitive therapy, with its explicit focus on the meaning of symptoms, is ideally suited to explore culturally determined meanings of dieting and fasting. It can deal usefully with both crosscultural and within-cultural manifestations of eating disorders. A range of focuses could be employed, including weight and shape, asceticism and spirituality, or control. As such, cognitive therapy may be applicable across all cultures in which eating disorders are found, regardless of how they are manifested.

CONCLUSIONS

This chapter has suggested a framework for linking eating disorders, culture, and cognition. Based on the available evidence it has suggested a synthesis between culture and cognition, particularly social cognition, that may begin to account for the differing incidence and prevalence of eating disorders in different cultures. It also begins to explain cultural differences in the expression of eating disorders. It is suggested that cognitive therapy, with its emphasis on meaning, may be a particularly useful treatment for eating disorders, in which the meaning of symptoms is, at least in part, often culturally determined.

REFERENCES

American Psychiatric Association. (1994). *Diagnostic and statistical manual of mental disorders* (4th ed.). Washington, DC: Author.

Bardwick, J. (1971). *Psychology of women: A study of bio-cultural conflicts.* New York: Harper & Row.

Bennett, W. B., & Gurin, J. (1982). *The dieter's dilemma: Eating less and weighing more.* New York: Basic Books.

Brownell, K. D., & O'Neil, P. M. (1993). Obesity. In D. H. Barlow (Ed.), *Clinical handbook of psychological disorders: A step-by-step treatment manual.* New York: Guilford.

Bruch, H. (1973). *Eating disorders: Obesity, anorexia nervosa and the person within.* New York: Basic Books.

Bruch, H. (1978). *The golden cage.* Cambridge, MA: Harvard University Press.

Bruner, J. S. (1990). *Acts of meaning.* Cambridge, MA: Harvard University Press.

Buhrich, N. (1981). Frequency of presentation of anorexia nervosa in Malaysia. *Australian and New Zealand Journal of Psychiatry, 15,* 153–155.

Cooper, M. J. (1997). Cognitive theory in anorexia nervosa and bulimia nervosa: A review. *Behavioural and Cognitive Psychotherapy, 25,* 113–145.

Cooper, M. J., & Hunt, J. (1998). Core beliefs and underlying assumptions in bulimia nervosa and depression. *Behaviour Research and Therapy, 36,* 895–898.

Cooper, M. J., Todd, G., & Wells, A. (1998). Content, origins and consequences of dysfunctional beliefs in anorexia nervosa and bulimia nervosa. *Journal of Cognitive Psychotherapy, 12,* 213–230.

D'Andrade, R. G. (1984). Cultural meaning systems. In R. A. Shweder & R. A. LeVine (Eds.), *Culture theory: Essays on mind, self, and emotion.* Cambridge, UK: Cambridge University Press.

Eysenck, M. W. (1993). *Principles of cognitive psychology.* Hove, UK: Erlbaum.

Fairburn, C. G., Cooper, Z., & Cooper, P. (1986). The clinical features and maintenance of bulimia nervosa. In K. D. Brownell & J. P. Foreyt (Eds.), *Physiology, psychology and treatment of the eating disorders.* New York: Basic Books.

Fairburn, C. G., Shafran, R., & Cooper, Z. (1999). A cognitive behavioural theory of anorexia nervosa. *Behaviour Research and Therapy, 37,* 1–13.

Fedoroff, I. C., & McFarlane, T. (1998). Cultural aspects of eating disorders. In S. S. Kazarian & D. R. Evans (Eds.), *Cultural clinical psychology*. New York: Oxford University Press.

Fiske, S. T., & Taylor, S. E. (1991). *Social cognition*. New York: McGraw-Hill.

Garner, D. M., & Bemis, K. M. (1982). A cognitive-behavioural approach to anorexia nervosa. *Cognitive Therapy and Research, 6,* 123–150.

Garner, D. M., & Garfinkel, P. E. (1982). Anorexia nervosa: A multidimensional perspective. New York: Brunner/Mazel.

Guidano, V. F., & Liotti, G. (1983). *Cognitive processes and emotional disorders: A structural approach to psychotherapy.* New York: Guilford Press.

Haviland, W. A. (1997). *Anthropology.* Fort Worth, TX: Harcourt Brace College Publishers.

Hogg, M. A., & Vaughan, G. M. (1998). *Social psychology.* Hertfordshire, UK: Prentice Hall.

Hsu, L. K. G. (1990). *Eating disorders.* New York: Guilford Press.

Khandelwal, S. K., Sharan, P., & Saxena, S. (1995). Eating disorders: An Indian perspective. *International Journal of Social Psychiatry, 41,* 132–146.

Kitayama, S., Takagi, H., & Matsumoto, H. (1995). Causal attributions of success and failure: Cultural psychology of the Japanese self. *Japanese Psychological Review, 38,* 247–280.

Koenig, L. J. (1997). How is the self conceptualised? Variations among cultures. In U. Neisser & D. A. Jopling (Eds.), *The conceptual self in context.* Cambridge, UK: Cambridge University Press.

Kurman, L. (1978). An analysis of messages concerning food, eating behaviours, and ideal body image on prime-time American network television. *Dissertation Abstracts International, 39,* 1907.

Littlewood, R. (1995). Psychopathology and personal agency: Modernity, culture change and eating disorders in South Asian societies. *British Journal of Medical Psychology, 68,* 45–63.

Markus, H. R., Hamill, R., & Sentis, K. P. (1987). Thinking fat: Self-schemata for body weight and the processing of weight relevant information. *Journal of Applied Social Psychology, 17,* 50–72.

Markus, H. R., Mullally, P. R., & Kitayama, S. (1997). Selfways: Diversity in modes of cultural participation. In U. Neisser & D. A. Jopling (Eds.), *The conceptual self in context.* Cambridge, UK: Cambridge University Press.

Miller, J. G. (1984). Culture and the development of everyday social explanation. *Journal of Personality and Social Psychology, 46,* 961–978.

Neisser, U. (1967). *Cognitive psychology.* Englewood Cliffs, NJ: Prentice Hall.

Neisser, U. (1997). Concepts and self-concepts. In U. Neisser & D. A. Jopling (Eds.). *The conceptual self in context.* Cambridge, UK: Cambridge University Press.

Ross, L. (1977). The intuitive psychologist and his shortcomings. In L. Berkowitz (Ed.), *Advances in experimental social psychology* (Vol. 10). New York: Academic Press.

Rudofsky, B. (1972). *The unfashionable human body.* New York: Doubleday.

Russell, G. F. M. (1979). Bulimia nervosa: an ominous variant of anorexia nervosa. *Psychological Medicine, 9,* 429–448.

Speck, F. G. (1920). Penobscot shamanism. *Memoirs of the American Anthropological Association, 6,* 239–288.

Staffieri, J. R. (1967). A study of social stereotype of body image in children. *Journal of Personality and Social Psychology, 7,* 101–104.

Szyrynski, V. (1973). Anorexia nervosa and psychotherapy. *American Journal of Psychotherapy, 27,* 492–505.

Vitousek, K. B., & Hollon, S. D. (1990). The investigation of schematic content and processing in the eating disorders. *Cognitive Therapy and Research, 14,* 191–214.

Weiner, B. (1995). *Judgements of responsibility.* New York: Guilford Press.

Wooley, O. W., & Wooley, S. (1980). The Beverly Hills eating disorder: The mass marketing of anorexia nervosa. *International Journal of Eating Disorders, 1,* 57–69.

Young, J. E. (1990). *Cognitive therapy for personality disorders: A schema focused approach.* Sarasota, FL: Professional Resource Exchange.

8

Cognitive Enculturation and Sexual Abuse

Gordon C. Nagayama Hall and Amber H. Phung

Sexual abuse is a widespread societal problem. As many as one in four adults have been involved with sexual abuse as a perpetrator or as a victim (Koss, Gidycz, & Wisniewski, 1987; Mills & Granoff, 1992; Urquiza & Goodlin-Jones, 1994). Most sexual aggression is perpetrated by males, which will be the focus of this chapter. The role of cognitive processes in the perpetration of sexually aggressive behavior will be examined. It is contended that such cognitive processes differ across cultural groups and that there are culturally specific determinants of sexually aggressive behavior.

Cognitive schemata have been conceptualized as implicit theories that are used to explain, predict, and interpret interpersonal phenomena (Ward, in press). Schemata function as scripts based on social experiences that provide the context for what is perceived to be socially appropriate or deviant, and schemata regulate behavior. Schemata can affect the manner in which information is perceived and interpreted, can guide behavior, and can organize the memory of events (Yee, Santoro, Paul, & Rosenbaum, 1996). Once such schemata are established, they may resist inconsistent evidence (Fiske & Taylor, 1991). Moreover, cognitive schemata do not necessarily reflect the actual world, but represent an individual's unique conception of a situation or themselves (Ward, Keenan, & Hudson, in press).

Cognitive schemata are influenced by one's cultural context and cognitions that support or discourage sexual abuse may differ across cultural groups. There is some consensus among researchers that culture involves shared cognitions, standard operating procedures, and unexamined assumptions (Triandis, 1996). Cognition itself has been defined as inherently cultural (Rogoff & Chavajay,

1995) and cultural behavior patterns may be acquired and transmitted via beliefs and implicit theories (Butcher, Nezami, & Exner, 1998). The content of individuals' cognitions are strongly influenced by their participation in cultural practices and contexts (Fiske, Kitayama, Markus, & Nisbett, 1998). Thus it is possible that perceptions of what qualifies as sexual abuse and cognitive distortions may differ according to cultural context.

Given that broad categorizations of cultural groups involve the combination of heterogeneous subgroups of individuals, major ethnic differences in rates of sexually aggressive behavior would appear unlikely. Ethnicity has been recently defined as referring to cultural norms and values, ethnic identity, and minority status (Phinney, 1996). Ethnicity subsumes race, a term for which there is much disagreement on its meanings and use (Yee, Fairchild, Weizmann, & Wyatt, 1993; Zuckerman, 1990). Rates of rape victimization are generally similar among American women in different ethnic groups, ranging from 7 to 40 percent (Koss, Gidycz, & Wisniewski, 1987; Mills & Granoff, 1992; Urquiza & Goodlin-Jones, 1994). Relatedly, perpetration of rape is admitted to by 0 to 10 percent of American men across ethnic groups (Koss et al., 1987; Mills & Granoff, 1992). Koss et al. (1987) have contended that ethnic differences in sexual aggression, some of which may be statistically significant, are not substantive and that variables other than ethnicity, such as attitudes, may be more relevant predictors of sexual aggression. Therefore, the evidence suggests that sexually aggressive behavior is not endemic to any particular ethnic group. The issue, then, is to identify particular risk and protective factors that may be more or less prominent in particular cultural groups.

The strength of one's identification with their ethnic group, or ethnic identity, might be more directly associated with behavior than broad ethnic categorizations. Ethnic identity involves the attitudes and feelings associated with a sense of membership in an ethnic group (Phinney, 1996). Ethnic identity is not as salient for European Americans as it is for ethnic minority Americans because the particular ethnicity of most European Americans is not obvious (Phinney, 1996). Ethnic group membership is much more evident, and therefore more salient, for persons of color in the United States.

Strength of ethnic identity may be reflected in one's relative degree of individualism or collectivism. In individualistic cultures, the self is defined as independent and autonomous (Triandis, 1996) and therefore motivation for behavior tends to be internally and individually based (Markus & Kitayama, 1991). From this cultural perspective, being unique and the assertive expression of personal desires are central; personal goals take priority over the goals of groups. Social behavior tends to be shaped by individual attitudes and the anticipated consequences for the person in question (Triandis, 1996). There are often multiple, sometimes conflicting, cultural norms for which violation is often not punished (Triandis, 1995). Individualists emphasize equality and there tends to be a lack of hierarchical structure with respect to authority figures (vertical individualism) and to peers (horizontal individualism) (Triandis, 1995).

In collectivist cultures, the self is defined as an aspect of a group (Triandis, 1996) and individual goals are subordinated to those of the group. Accordingly, motivation for behavior tends to depend on the relevant social context rather than individual desires and beliefs. The powerful influence of the social context on cognitions has been discussed in connectionist theories of cultural meaning (Strauss & Quinn, 1997). Collectivist cultures emphasize attending to others, fitting in, and interpersonal harmony (Markus & Kitayama, 1991). Social behavior is regulated by norms, duties, and obligations, and there are clear sanctions for violations (Triandis, 1995, 1996). Collectivism may be reflected in deference to authority figures (vertical collectivism) or to peers in one's group (horizontal collectivism). Unlike the emphasis on individualism in mainstream American culture, American ethnic minority cultures often emphasize collectivist values (Greenfield, 1994; Hill et al., 1994). Although it may be more likely that ethnic minority Americans would have a collectivist orientation than would European Americans, it would be inappropriate to assume that all ethnic minority Americans are collectivists.

SEXUAL AGGRESSION IN INDIVIDUALIST CULTURES

Individualism or collectivism does not place a person at risk for engaging in sexually aggressive behavior per se. However, the determinants of sexually aggressive behavior may differ in individualist versus collectivist settings. Cultural contexts may create conditions under which sexually aggressive behavior may become acceptable (Baumeister & Heatherton, 1996). When individual desires take precedence over the rights of others, personal fulfilment might include the violation of others' rights. In fact, satisfying one's own needs at the expense of others may be viewed as a moral right or a definition of freedom in individualist cultures (Schmidt, 1995). Fulfilment of desires for individual enhancement at the expense of others could be associated with many forms of violent behavior, including sexual aggression (Baumeister, Smart, & Boden, 1996; Hall & Barongan, 1997). In individualist cultures, ego-focused emotions, including anger, frustration, and pride, that are self-serving are common (Markus & Kitayama, 1991). The expression of such ego-focused emotions may occasionally lead to overt aggression. One's personal welfare in individualist cultures depends primarily on personal resources and is not necessarily dependent on the welfare of others. If one is not personally fulfilled, but feels entitled to fulfilment, then others may simply be regarded as vehicles to be used to become fulfilled. The suffering and harm that victims of aggression experience may not be a deterrent to an aggressive individual whose primary goal is self-fulfilment. In fact, reducing another person's sense of superiority may be the motivation for some who are aggressive (Baumeister et al., 1996). Prevention of victimization and recovery from it may even be regarded as the victim's responsibility. Thus, in individualist cultures, *intra*personal constructs may be more important than *inter*personal ones.

Individual cognitive distortions have been proposed as the basis of the perpetration of sexual abuse (Hall, 1996; Hall & Barongan, 1997; Murphy, 1990; Ward, Hudson, Johnston, & Marshall, 1997; Ward, Hudson, & Marshall, 1995). Two major functions of cognitive distortions involve (a) the misperception of sexually aggressive behaviors as nonaggressive or normal, and (b) the minimization of the impact of sexual aggression. Many men are socialized to be aggressive and to have multiple sexual partners. Thus for some men, being sexually coercive is part of the male role, and may be perceived as perfectly acceptable or even normal (Mosher, 1991; Mosher & Tomkins, 1988; Zaitchik & Mosher, 1993). Forcing a person who does not want to be sexual to engage in sexual activity may be part of a conquest script for some men and could be viewed as more of a challenge and perhaps even more sexually arousing than consensual sexual behavior. Even sexual contact with children may be viewed as normal by some men who regard children as part of their property. Although most men, including nonoffenders, exhibit sexual arousal to sexually aggressive stimuli, a minority of men are more aroused by sexually aggressive stimuli than by consenting sexual stimuli (Hall, Shondrick, & Hirschman, 1993). Nevertheless, the relatively large minority of men who engage in sexually aggressive acts may cause some men to believe that this type of behavior is prevalent. In ambiguous sexual situations, a perpetrator may selectively attend to cues that apparently indicate consent (e.g., she agreed to go on a date with me) and selectively ignore cues that indicate nonconsent (e.g., she is disinterested in sex; Craig, 1990; Ward, Fon, Hudson, & McCormack, 1998).

The popular media is also replete with support for sexual aggression. *Gone With the Wind* is a classic example of a woman's token resistance to a man's sexual advances. Currently popular movies often combine sexually arousing and violent images (Hall, 1996). Pornographic material and discussion groups available over the Internet may be perceived by some men as support for the normalcy of sexual aggression, including child molestation. Repeated personal or vicarious exposure to sexual aggression may desensitize men to its harm to victims. Such desensitization might result in cognitive distortions that allow men to believe that sexual abuse is enjoyable, beneficial, or at least not harmful to victims (Lonsway & Fitzgerald, 1994). As with other stereotypes, an individual may recall such examples of support for a cognitive distortion and ignore examples that are inconsistent (Lonsway & Fitzgerald, 1994).

Some men may recognize that sexually aggressive behavior is inappropriate, but view it as permissible when there are mitigating circumstances. For these men, cognitive distortions serve to minimize the impact of sexual aggression. Victims are often perceived by perpetrators (and, unfortunately, often by the legal system) as provoking sexual aggression by their appearance or behavior. For example, a woman who wears revealing clothing, or who invites a man into her apartment for a drink, may be perceived as inviting sexual activity. A child's apparent friendliness or physical contact, such as hugging or wrestling, may be interpreted as a desire for sexual contact. What is missing from the analysis, of course, is the man's responsibility to determine whether such cues are invitations for sexual activity or not. Justifications of child sexual abuse involve greater levels of distortion than sexual abuse involving adult victims (Hall, 1996). Some common minimizations of child sexual abuse are that it is part of a child's sexual education or that the child was perceived as somehow seductive.

SEXUAL AGGRESSION IN COLLECTIVIST CULTURES

Interpersonal conflict and violence tend to be minimal in collectivist cultures because individual goals are subordinated to those of the group, social support is high, and competitiveness is low (Markus & Kitayama, 1991; Triandis, 1995). Indeed, satisfying one's personal goals may require meeting others' goals (Markus & Kitayama, 1991). Persons having interdependent self construals tend to be more concerned about negative evaluations by others than do those having independent self construals (Okazaki, 1997). Being unique and asserting one's personal desires are de-emphasized insofar as they may interfere with group harmony. An aggressive act may be regarded as a crime against a whole community or society rather than as an isolated act involving two individuals (Hall & Barongan, 1997).

The importance of fitting in with the group may cause group norms to be more influential in collectivist than in individualist cultures. Deviant behavior may result in loss of face, or the threat of loss of one's social integrity (Sue & Morishima, 1982). In collectivist settings, the important consequences of loss of face are not their impact on an individual, but on the group. Personal consequences of deviant behavior are secondary. Thus an individual who engages in deviant behavior is shamed more because the deviant behavior results in loss of face for the whole group than because of any negative individual consequences. Loss of face may be a more important mediator of behavior among collectivist than among individualist Americans (Zane, 1991).

Loss of face might serve as a protective or risk factor associated with sexual aggression, depending on one's reference group. In collectivist cultures, vertical (superiors) and horizontal (peer) relationships serve as reference groups. A general respect for authority is an example of the value placed on vertical relationships. Authority figures typically disapprove of sexually aggressive behavior. Fear of disapproval or punishment by authority figures (e.g., parents, employer, police, legal/judicial system) may be more of a deterrent against acting out in collectivist cultures than in individualist cultures (Hill et al., 1994). Peer disapproval may also serve as a deterrent against sexual aggression in collectivist cultures. In collectivist cultures in which the self is not separate from others, any behavior that serves to upset group interdependence is not approved of (Markus & Kitayama, 1991, 1994). Both aggressive behavior and unrestricted sexual behavior may interfere with group harmony (Bond, 1991). To be sexually aggressive could be a violation of group norms in a collectivist culture. Loss of face could also serve as a risk factor for sexual aggression. If one's reference group is other aggressive and sexually aggressive men, it may appear manly to engage in sexually aggressive behavior (Malamuth et al., 1991; Malamuth et al., 1995). Thus loss of face could occur if a man does not engage in aggressive and sexually aggressive behavior against women to fulfill the perceived masculine role.

A collectivist orientation may particularly increase the risk of aggression against those in outgroups. Outgroup aggression typically has no direct bearing on ingroup harmony, and thus is not necessarily disapproved of. If women are perceived by men as part of the outgroup (e.g., nonmale), then a collectivist orientation may not deter aggression against women, including sexual aggression (Hall, Windover, & Maramba, 1998). Men who are strongly allied with other men may consider relationships with women as interfering with these alliances (Smuts, 1992). Such alliances with other men may be particularly likely when men's dominance is threatened, such as by a women's movement within a culture (Staub, 1996). Women may be devalued and aggressive acts, including sexual aggression, may be more likely for men who have strong alliances with other men as an effort to reestablish their superiority. Although women may be viewed as an outgroup by men of any culture, such an ingroup/outgroup distinction might be more salient and have a greater effect on the behavior of men from group-oriented, collectivist cultures (Rhee, Uleman, & Lee, 1996; Triandis, 1995).

Moreover, the patriarchal structure of collectivist cultures may also create risk factors for sexual aggression (Hall & Barongan, 1997; Hall et al., 1998). Women and children often have a subordinate status and may be oppressed in collectivist cultures (Ho, 1990; Okazaki, 1998). Suffering and persevering without complaining, and acceptance of fate are Asian values that may encourage abuse (Chen & True, 1994; Ho, 1990; Yoshihama & Sorenson, 1994). However, patriarchy in non-European cultures may operate somewhat differently than in cultures of European origin. For example, although machismo in Latino cultures usually is associated with sexist behaviors, a positive aspect involves a man's responsibility for the welfare of his family (Sorenson & Siegel, 1992). Moreover, roles in collectivist cultures tend to be complementary and power tends to be shared, and there may be less of a power imbalance between men and women than there is in individualist cultures (Malik & Lindahl, 1998). Thus, it may be the abuse of the power of the patriarchal role rather than the role itself that is associated with sexual abuse in collectivist cultures.

WITHIN-CULTURE VARIABILITY AND
RISK FOR SEXUAL AGGRESSION

Although cultural groups may be broadly categorized as relatively individualist or collectivist, there exists heterogeneity within cultural groups. There are relatively collectivistic persons in individualist cultures as there are relatively individualistic persons in collectivist cultures. Perpetrators' perceptions of the cultural characteristics of potential victims may be associated with relative levels of risk for sexually aggressive behavior.

A model of relative risk for sexual aggression based on perpetrator and victim cultural characteristics is presented in Table 8.1. This model is based on perpetrators' perceptions of victims and does not necessarily mean that actual victim characteristics somehow precipitate sexual abuse. In fact, perpetrators' perceptions of the cultural characteristics of potential victims may be based on stereotypes. Nevertheless, it is possible that such perceptions may influence the likelihood of perpetrators engaging in sexually aggressive behavior.

Table 8.1
Relative Risk for Sexual Abuse Among
Individualists and Collectivists Within a Single Context

Perpetrator	Victim			
	Ingroup		Outgroup	
	Individualist	Collectivist	Individualist	Collectivist
Individualist	Medium risk	High risk	Medium risk	High risk
Collectivist	Low risk	Low risk	Medium risk	Medium risk

The risk for developing cognitions supportive of sexual aggression and subsequent sexually aggressive behavior would appear to be highest in individualist cultures. Tolerance of divergent ideas, including deviant thinking, may be greater in individualist cultures. Cultural norms may be less specific, and defiance of cultural norms may be supported to some degree as part of the individuation process. Conversely, cognitions supportive of sexual aggression would have to be normative to be accepted in collectivist cultures. Thus, an individual may be relatively unlikely to develop such cognitions in the absence of social support for sexual aggression. Nevertheless, such social support could be identified relatively easily, insofar as a significant minority of men are sexually aggressive (Hall et al., 1998; Koss et al., 1987). The risk for sexually aggressive cognitions and behavior in a collectivist culture would be a function of perceived societal acceptance of sexual aggression.

Risk for engaging in sexually aggressive behavior may involve an interaction between a potential perpetrator's cognitions about the acceptability of sexual aggression and his perceptions of the vulnerability of potential victims. The highest risk situation would involve an individualist perpetrator and potential victims who are collectivists. The individualist may perceive the collectivist as vulnerable and unlikely to resist sexual aggression or to retaliate because such actions would disrupt interpersonal harmony. A collectivist victim might also not want to bring attention to themselves by reporting that they had been sexually victimized. Thus, an individualist perpetrator might perceive a relatively low likelihood of any form of negative sanctions for victimizing someone having a collectivist cultural orientation.

Whether the potential victim is an outgroup or ingroup member would be less critical for individualist than for collectivist perpetrators. Nevertheless, individualist perpetrators may believe that there will be less retribution for victimizing outgroup than ingroup individuals. For example, an ethnic minority person may be perceived as an outgroup member who may have difficulty achieving recourse against an ingroup perpetrator insofar as the ingroup controls the means of recourse (e.g., legal punishment). Similarly, children may be perceived as an outgroup by some child molesters. Individuals more vulnerable to acts of sexual aggression and violence tend to be those with less power or status in society (Sorenson & Siegel, 1992). In collectivist cultures where preservation of the community and upholding the good name of the family may be stressed, a woman or child may be encouraged to keep their victimization experiences a secret for the greater good of the family and her community. It may well be the case that they feel compelled to behave within the norms and roles that have been established for women or children within that cultural context and community in order to preserve harmony.

A medium risk situation would involve an individualist perpetrator and an individualist victim. Although individualist cultures may have an inherent risk for deviant cognitions and behavior, there is also more of an acceptance of one individual challenging and criticizing the actions of another individual. The perceived likelihood that an individualist victim would resist, retaliate, or report the offense might be a deterrent for many potential perpetrators.

A second cultural combination in the medium risk category would involve a collectivist perpetrator and a collectivist or individualist victim from an outgroup. This combination is considered a medium risk because sexually aggressive norms would be a prerequisite for sexually aggressive cognitions and behavior in a collectivist context, whereas such norms would not be required in individualist sexual aggression. Sexual aggression against an outgroup member for a collectivist perpetrator may be viewed as having no bearing on the ingroup. An outgroup person is likely to have less power and less recourse in society than ingroup members. Presumably an outgroup individualist would be more likely to seek recourse for being sexually abused than would an outgroup collectivist. In the United States, most individualists are part of the ingroup. Thus a situation involving an outgroup individualist victim would be rare. Perhaps this might involve an individualist from another culture (e.g., an immigrant) who is not considered part of the ingroup in the United States. The risk of sexual aggression by a collectivist perpetrator against an outgroup individualist victim might be higher in a collectivist culture in which it might be difficult for an individual to challenge or influence the status quo.

Lower risk situations would involve collectivist perpetrators and ingroup victims. Sexual aggression against an ingroup member would be undesirable because it would upset ingroup harmony. Nevertheless, if sexual aggression were considered acceptable in a collectivist cultural group, perceptions of potential victims as compliant or vulnerable (e.g., compliant with men as authority figures) would create a risk for sexual aggression. The lowest risk for sexual aggression might involve a collectivist perpetrator and an ingroup individualist victim. For example, an individualist could be viewed as part of a collectivist ingroup if the individualist was from the same ethnic background as the collectivist.

CONCLUSIONS

Cognitive enculturation may influence the determinants of sexually aggressive behavior. Sexual aggression in individualist contexts is more likely to be determined by individual cognitions, whereas sexual aggression in collectivist contexts is likely to be determined by cognitions that are context sensitive. Both individual and contextual influences may determine the sexually aggressive behavior of persons who are exposed to individualist and collectivist cultures in a single context. Within a single cultural context, an individual's relative degree of individualism and collectivism, and his perceptions of the relative degree of individualism and collectivism of potential victims, may interact to create differing levels of risk for perpetration of sexual aggression.

Cultural models of sexual aggression have implications for clinical treatment and prevention with potential perpetrators. Individual cognitions, such as rape myths and hostility toward women, would appear to be the most relevant focus of interventions in individualist contexts. Interventions at a group level, such as the family or community, would appear relevant in collectivist contexts. Both approaches present unique challenges. Although changing individual cognitions may appear easier than changing whole groups, the idiosyncratic nature of individual cognitions that justify sexually aggressive behavior requires treatment approaches that may differ for each individual. Moreover, it is possible that deviant individual cognitions may be resistant to group-based preventive interventions (e.g., sexual abuse education in school settings) unless these interventions happen to address the particular cognitions that are relevant to the individual. The challenge in collectivist contexts is to gain access to the power structure of the group and to convince those within the power structure that sexually aggressive behavior is maladaptive. Such interventions at the group level may be particularly difficult in groups where sexual aggression is normative. Although it may be less difficult to change individual norms than group norms, successful interventions at the group level may have a broader impact than those at the individual level.

REFERENCES

Baumeister, R. F., & Heatherton, T. F. (1996). Self-regulation failure: An overview. *Psychological Inquiry, 7,* 1–15.

Baumeister, R. F., Smart, L., & Boden, J. M. (1996). Relation of threatened egotism to violence and aggression: The dark side of high self-esteem. *Psychological Review, 103,* 5–33.

116   *Cultural Cognition and Psychopathology*

Bond, M. H. (1991). *Beyond the Chinese face: Insights from psychology.* New York: Oxford University Press.

Butcher, J. N., Nezami, E., & Exner, J. (1998). Psychological assessment of people in diverse cultures. In S. S. Kazarian & D. R. Evans (Eds.), *Cultural clinical psychology: Theory, research, and practice* (pp. 61–105). New York: Oxford University Press.

Chen, S. A., & True, R. H. (1994). Asian/Pacific Island Americans. In L. D. Eron, J. H. Gentry, & P. Schlegel (Eds.), *Reason to hope: A psychosocial perspective on violence and youth* (pp. 145–162). Washington, DC: American Psychological Association.

Craig, M. E. (1990). Coercive sexuality in dating relationships: A situational model. *Clinical Psychology Review, 10,* 395–423.

Fiske, A. P., Kitayama, S., Markus, H. R., & Nisbett, R. E. (1998). The cultural matrix of social psychology. In D. T. Gilbert, S. T. Fiske, & G. Lindzey (Eds.), *The handbook of social psychology,* 4th ed. (pp. 915–981). New York: Oxford University Press.

Fiske, S. R., & Taylor, S. E. (1991). *Social cognition* (2nd ed.). New York: Random House.

Gaines, S., & Reed, E. (1995). Prejudice from Allport to DuBois. *American Psychologist, 50,* 96–103.

Greenfield, P. M. (1994). Independence and interdependence as developmental scripts: Implications for theory, research, and practice. In P. M. Greenfield & R. R. Cocking (Eds.), *Cross-cultural roots of minority child development* (pp. 1–37). Hillsdale, NJ: Erlbaum.

Hall, G. C. N. (1996). *Theory-based assessment, treatment, and prevention of sexual aggression.* New York: Oxford University Press.

Hall, G. C. N., & Barongan, C. (1997). Prevention of sexual aggression: Sociocultural risk and protective factors. *American Psychologist, 52,* 5–14.

Hall, G. C. N., & Hirschman, R. (1991). Toward a theory of sexual aggression: A quadripartite model. *Journal of Consulting and Clinical Psychology, 59,* 662–669.

Hall, G. C. N., Shondrick, D. D., & Hirschman, R. (1993). The role of sexual arousal in sexually aggressive behavior: A meta-analysis. *Journal of Consulting and Clinical Psychology, 61,* 1091–1095.

Hall, G. C. N., Sue, S., Narang, D. S., & Lilly, R. S. (1999). *Culture-specific models of men's sexual aggression: Intra- and interpersonal determinants.* Manuscript submitted for publication.

Hall, G. C. N., Windover, A. K., & Maramba, G. G. (1998). Sexual aggression among Asian Americans: Risk and protective factors. *Cultural Diversity and Mental Health, 4,* 305–318.

Hill, H. M., Soriano, F. I., Chen, S. A., & LaFromboise, T. D. (1994). Sociocultural factors in the etiology and prevention of violence among ethnic minority youth. In L. D. Eron, J. H. Gentry, & P. Schegel (Eds.), *Reason to hope: A psychosocial perspective on violence and youth* (pp. 59–97). Washington, DC: American Psychological Association.

Ho, C. K. (1990). An analysis of domestic violence in Asian American communities: A multicultural approach to counseling. *Women and Therapy, 9,* 129–150.

Koss, M. P., Gidycz, C., & Wisniewski, N. (1987). The scope of rape: Incidence and prevalence of sexual aggression and victimization in a national sample of higher education students. *Journal of Consulting and Clinical Psychology, 55,* 162–170.

Lonsway, K. A., & Fitzgerald, L. F. (1994). Rape myths: In review. *Psychology of Women Quarterly, 18,* 133–164.

Malamuth, N. M., Linz, D., Heavey, C. L., Barnes, G., & Acker, M. (1995). Using the confluence model of sexual aggression to predict men's conflict with women: A 10-year follow-up study. *Journal of Personality and Social Psychology, 69,* 353–369.

Malamuth, N. M., Sockloskie, R. J., Koss, M. P., & Tanaka, J. S. (1991). Characteristics of aggressors against women: Testing a model using a national sample of college students. Special Section: Theories of sexual aggression. *Journal of Consulting and Clinical Psychology, 59,* 670–681.

Malik, N. M., & Lindahl, K. M. (1998). Aggression and dominance: The roles of power and culture in domestic violence. *Clinical Psychology: Science and Practice, 5,* 409–423.

Markus, H. R., & Kitayama, S. (1991). Culture and the self: Implications for cognition, emotion, and motivation. *Psychological Review, 98,* 224–253.

Markus, H. R., & Kitayama, S. (1994). The cultural construction of self and emotion: Implications for social behavior. In S. Kitayama & H. R. Markus (Eds.), *Emotion and culture: Empirical studies of mutual influence* (pp. 89–130). Washington, DC: American Psychological Association.

Mills, C. S., & Granoff, B. J. (1992). Date and acquaintance rape among a sample of college students. *Social Work, 37,* 504–509.

Mosher, D. L. (1991). Macho men, machismo, and sexuality. *Annual Review of Sex Research, 2,* 199–247.

Mosher, D. L., & Tomkins, S. S. (1988). Scripting the macho man: Hypermasculine socialization and enculturation. *Journal of Sex Research, 25,* 60–84.

Murphy, W. D. (1990). Assessment and treatment of cognitive distortions in sex offenders. In W. Marshall, D. Laws, & H. Barbaree (Eds.), *Handbook of sexual assault* (pp. 331–342). New York: Plenum Press.

Okazaki, S. (1997). Sources of ethnic differences between Asian American and White American college students on measures of depression and social anxiety. *Journal of Abnormal Psychology, 106,* 52–60.

Okazaki, S. (1998). Teaching gender issues in Asian American Psychology: A pedagogical framework. *Psychology of Women Quarterly, 22,* 33–52.

Phinney, J. S. (1996). When we talk about American ethnic groups, what do we mean? *American Psychologist, 51,* 918–927.

Rhee, E., Uleman, J. S., & Lee, H. K. (1996). Variations in collectivism and individualism by ingroup and culture: Confirmatory factor analyses. *Journal of Personality and Social Psychology, 71,* 1037–1054.

Rogoff, B., & Chavajay, P. (1995). What's become of research on the cultural basis of cognitive development? *American Psychologist, 50,* 859–877.

Schmidt, M. (1995). Anglo Americans and sexual child abuse. In L. A. Fontes (Ed.), *Sexual abuse in nine North American cultures* (pp. 156–175). Thousand Oaks, CA: Sage.

Smuts, B. (1992). Male aggression against women: An evolutionary perspective. *Human Nature, 3,* 1–44.

Sorenson, S. B., & Siegel, J. M. (1992). Gender, ethnicity, and sexual assault: Findings from a Los Angeles study. *Journal of Social Issues, 48,* 93–104.

Staub, E. (1996). Cultural-societal roots of violence: The examples of genocidal violence and of contemporary youth violence in the United States. *American Psychologist, 51,* 117–132.

Strauss, C., & Quinn, N. (1997). *A cognitive theory of cultural meaning.* Cambridge: Cambridge University Press.

Sue, S., & Morishima, J. (1982). *The mental health of Asian Americans.* San Francisco: Jossey-Bass Publishers.

Triandis, H. C. (1995). *Individualism and collectivism.* Boulder, CO: Westview Press.

Triandis, H. C. (1996). The psychological measurement of cultural syndromes. *American Psychologist, 51,* 407–415.

Uba, L. (1994). *Asian Americans: Personality patterns, identity, and mental health.* New York: Guilford Press.

Urquiza, A. J., & Goodlin-Jones, B. L. (1994). Child sexual abuse and adult revictimization with women of color. *Violence and Victims, 9,* 223–232.

Ward, T. (in press). Sexual offenders' cognitive distortions as implicit theories. *Aggression and Violent Behavior.*

Ward, T., Fon, C., Hudson, S. M., & McCormack, J. (1998). A descriptive model of dysfunctional cognitions in child molesters. *Journal of Interpersonal Violence, 13,* 129–155.

Ward, T., Hudson, S. M., Johnston, L., & Marshall, W. L. (1997). Cognitive distortions and sexual offending: An integrative review. *Clinical Psychology Review, 17,* 479–507.

Ward, T., Hudson, S. M., & Marshall, W. L. (1995). Cognitive distortions and affective deficits in sex offenders: A cognitive deconstructionist interpretation. *Sexual Abuse: A Journal of Research and Treatment, 7,* 67–83.

Ward, T., Keenan, T., & Hudson, S. M. (in press). Understanding cognitive, affective, and intimacy deficits in sex offenders: A developmental perspective. *Aggression and Violent Behavior.*

Yee, A., Fairchild, H., Weizmann, F., & Wyatt, G. (1993). Addressing psychology's problems with race. *American Psychologist, 48,* 1132–1140.

Yee, P. L., Santoro, K. E., Paul, J. S., & Rosenbaum, L. B. (1996). Information processing approaches to the study of relationship and social support schema. In G. R. Pierce, B. R. Sarason, & I. G. Sarason (Eds.), *Handbook of social support and the family* (pp. 25–42). New York: Plenum.

Yoshihama, M., & Sorenson, S. B. (1994). Physical, sexual, and emotional abuse by male intimates: Experiences of women in Japan. *Violence and Victims, 9,* 125–138.

Zaitchik, M. C., & Mosher, D. L. (1993). Criminal justice implications of the macho personality constellation. *Criminal Justice and Behavior, 20,* 227–239.

Zane, N. (1991, August). *An empirical examination of loss of face among Asian Americans.* Paper presented at the American Psychological Association Convention, San Francisco.

Zuckerman, M. (1990). Some dubious premises in research and theory on racial differences. *American Psychologist, 45,* 1297–1303.

9

Culture, Cognition, and Trauma: Crosscultural Evaluations

Pittu Laungani

The term trauma has been investigated from several different theoretical and applied perspectives: medical, organic, genetic, biological, psychological, social anthropological, sociological, and crosscultural, to name but a few. Each theoretical perspective offers its own concepts, terminologies, meanings, nuances and configurations, and diagnostic nomenclature. In addition, each one has its own research methodologies, therapeutic strategies, and outcome measures. Such a state of affairs tends to make commensurability a serious problem.

But as Lakatos (1971) points out in his brilliant analysis of the methodology of scientific research programs, dissent and diversity are often seen as healthy signs. This is because they indicate that the discipline is active, vibrant, and the subject of competing research programs, some of which will lead eventually to degeneration and decay and some to progress and growth.

In medical terms, the word trauma refers to a morbid condition of body produced by a serious physical wound or external injury, or by an act of violence. However, in recent years the term trauma has exceeded its medical usage and is used extensively by psychiatrists, psychotherapists, psychologists, and a variety of other health professionals.

In its simplest form, trauma refers to a state of physical and/or emotional shock, which may be a result of real, anticipated, imagined, or forgotten (repressed) experiences or encounters. Trauma may occur at an individual level, a group level, or a cultural level. The traumatic experiences may occur instantly, or in certain instances, may remain repressed in one's psychic system for several months or even years, before emerging to the surface of one's consciousness, as posttraumatic stress disorders.

The experience leading to trauma may be sudden and unexpected, such as when an individual may be a victim of an accident or physical attack. On the other hand, the experience may be anticipated and predictable, as when passengers in an aircraft may become aware of its impending crash. Trauma may occur from imagined catastrophes, such as those highlighted by Festinger in his famous book *When Prophecy Fails* (1964), in which he examined the anxieties and traumas experienced by a group of believers whose leader (unsuccessfully) predicted the end of the world. One might also recall Freud's famous study of the Rat Man, who was totally traumatized by his own dreams. He called this a form of psychical trauma. To Freud (1955/1974), "any experience which calls up distressing affects—such as those of fright, anxiety, shame or physical pain—may operate as trauma of this kind; and whether it in fact does so depends naturally enough on the susceptibility of the person affected" (p. 56).

Freud explained an individual's affective response to a stimuli in terms of the person's susceptibility, a term that is difficult to explain in any precise terms. In general terms, however, the term susceptibility suggests a form of a personality proneness that predisposes some individuals to experiencing events in terms of trauma. Freud's explanation would suggest that certain types of personality characteristics predispose an individual to labeling certain perceptual experiences as being traumatic. In labelling a perceptual experience, Freud implied that some form of cognitive appraisal, whether conscious or unconscious, is involved.

Yet this observation is not as straightforward as it seems. As Eysenck and Keane (1998) observe, there are disputes within cognitive psychology whether the perception of an affective stimulus involves some form of cognitive appraisal, is independent of cognitive appraisal, precedes cognitive appraisal, or whether affect and appraisal are two independent systems. These intriguing theoretical questions have been argued by Zajonc (1980, 1981, 1984), who supports the notion of independent systems, and by Lazarus (1982, 1984), who disagrees with Zajonc and contends that cognitive appraisal plays a crucial role in emotional experience, and generally precedes any affective reaction.

Fifty years of sustained research in the field of perception has established quite clearly that perception is not as straightforward a phenomenon as one might wish to believe. Perception is influenced by a variety of psychological factors, which may include internal mental states, levels of motivation, mental set, past experience and learning, anticipated reinforcement contingencies, personality factors, one's predilections and expectations, and one's beliefs, attitudes, and values. Culture, too, exercises a powerful influence on one's perception of phenomena, as has been demonstrated by a variety of crosscultural studies on perception that have been undertaken in recent years (Ekman, 1972, 1973, 1985, 1994; Ekman & Friesen, 1975; Ekman & Heider, 1988; Matsumoto, 1989, 1992, 1996). Although, at first sight, the range of the studies appears to be comprehensive, most of them have concentrated on cultural variations in social cognitive processes, emotionality, morality, and the process of attribution (Markus & Kitayama, 1991; Matsumoto, 1996; Mishra, 1997; Shweder & Sullivan, 1993).

CULTURAL VARIATIONS IN THE COGNITIONS OF TRAUMA

It now seems reasonable to posit the idea that certain kinds of experiences, such as natural disasters, earthquakes, tornados, volcanic eruptions, or flooding would be universally perceived as being traumatic. On the other hand, certain events that occur at a specific cultural level may be collectively perceived by members of that culture as being extremely traumatic, whereas persons from another culture, unfamiliar with the norms, values, and mores of the people of the first culture, may fail to perceive the same events in a like manner.

Common sense, too, confirms the observation that cognition of an event varies from one individual to another, from one group to another, from one time to another, and from one culture to another. An event, or a set of stimuli, perceived as being stressful or traumatic on one occasion might be seen as being exciting on another occasion. A person unused to public speaking may find the experience extremely traumatic, but with practice and encouragement the same experience on another occasion might seem quite exhilarating. Moreover, one individual's trauma might be another individual's thrill. For those living in the Sahara desert, the perception of stressors is likely to be significantly different from those living in the rain forests of the Amazon. However, cultures vary not merely in climatic conditions but also in terms of their political, social, economic, and environmental conditions, each exerting their own sets of influences.

Cultures also vary in terms of their value systems. Values may be defined as the currently held normative expectations underlying individual and social conduct (Laungani, 1995). Values form the bases of social, political, and religious order. They may be the result of past religious and philosophical legacies, and although we may not be consciously aware of their precise origins, we nonetheless take them in. Since they are passed on over centuries, their roots get deeper and deeper and are not easily severed. Over time, values become an integral part of our unique cultural psyche; we carry them around us as securely as a tortoise carries its shell. To a large extent, values remain stable, but gradually over years, they may change. Several factors such as migration, and political, religious, scientific, and technological upheavals, may result in rapid changes in an individual's personal behavior and value-system.

CULTURE-SPECIFIC TRAUMA

Let us take an example to illustrate the cultural specificity of an experience that may be construed as being traumatic. Anantha Murthy in his book *Samskara* (1978) discusses in detail the events that follow the death of a high-caste Hindu Brahmin in a small village in South India. The Brahmin dies in the home of a prostitute with whom he had formed a sexual relationship. The prostitute, it turns out, comes from the Sudra caste, the lowest caste of untouchables. In accordance with Hindu religious texts, a Brahmin under no circumstances is allowed to have any sexual relationships with an untouchable. Nor is he allowed to eat animal flesh, drink alcohol, or befriend people of the lower castes. To enter the home of an untouchable is to become spiritually contaminated. In forming a sexual relationship with a person from the Sudra caste, he is likely to lose his own high-caste status, and may himself be identified as being an untouchable.

In *Samskara,* the main question that arises for the deceased's family members, for his entire village, and in particular for the high priest in the village, is how they shall perform the funeral rites. In keeping with Hindu tradition, *all* the funeral rites are performed by the deceased's family members, with the entire ceremony guided and overseen by the Brahmin priest. The high priest in the village, who is the most revered and respected member of the community, is totally traumatized by this event and does not know what he should do. Given the dramatic changes in the deceased's circumstances, he does not know how the funeral rites should be performed.

Under no circumstances can the priest or the family members of the deceased enter the house of the prostitute: to do so would result in further spiritual pollution. The priest cannot perform the funeral rites that normally would be accorded to a Brahmin, because in forming a sexual liaison with a prostitute and dying in her home the Brahmin has forfeited all his rights to a proper Brahmin funeral. And since the funeral rites have to be performed by the family members, the priest cannot request another person to perform the funeral rites. Neither can the corpse be left unattended in the house of the prostitute. On the other hand, not to accord the deceased the full Brahmin funeral rites would be to undermine his own high status within his community. The high priest consults all the religious texts, talks to other priests from neighboring villages, and is unable to find a satisfactory solution. The moral and caste-related transgressions of the deceased bring untold misery and sorrow upon all the family members. They also lead to devastating consequences for the entire village and for the high priest who ultimately is destroyed by this event.

This event, despite its rarity, is of immense magnitude when seen within the context of orthodox Hindu society. The tragedy that befalls the family members of the deceased and the high priest of the village (who was unable to perform the funeral rites), fits into a neat cultural pattern that can be understood by most members of that culture. To an outsider, however, who does not share the norms and mores of that culture and has little or no awareness of the religious rites and rituals that govern social practices, the same event would appear totally bewildering, and he or she would be able to make no sense of it whatever.

Because I myself am Hindu and can readily understand the feelings of the family members and high priest, I chose to discuss this particular episode with some of my European and American friends and colleagues and several of my graduate students, whose initial responses were of incredulity. They claimed that there was nothing extraordinary about the event for it to be labelled as a traumatic event. If anything, the event was seen as an over reaction. To them, the deceased's sexual relationship with the prostitute was a private affair, of no concern to others. To perceive it in such terms was in keeping with the Western notion of individualism. Consequently, they were unable to appreciate that a sexual liaison with the prostitute was construed as a serious moral and sexual transgression by the people in the village, a transgression that led to untold harm for the deceased's family and for the high priest. When they had had time to reflect, they wondered why the funeral arrangements could not have been passed on to undertakers. Such an arrangement seemed feasible to them, and offered a neat solution to an otherwise insolvable problem. Once again, a Western solution was being offered to a culturally unique Indian problem. Sadly, there was no understanding on their part that Hindus, for a variety of religious, philosophical, and cultural reasons, do not have undertakers. A variety of other plausible explanations and seemingly "rational" solutions were also proposed, but none of them seemed conceivable, let alone acceptable, within the context of Hindu culture. As shown by this story, the notion of rationality needs to be seen as a cultural construct, and not as something superordinate to all cultures.

The point that is being made is this. It is difficult, if not impossible, for outsiders observing a series of events, such as the ones described above, to construe accurately the meaning and significance assigned to those events. To assign an accurate meaning to an event one needs to be either an integral part of that cultural group, or to have acquired a close and intimate knowledge of the culture in question. Otherwise, one is likely to fall into the trap of offering etic explanations of an event which is uniquely emic in its construction.

It is not my intention to get embroiled in the emic–etic debate about which so much has already been written (Berry, 1969; Berry & Sam, 1997; Jahoda & Krewer, 1997; Kagitcibasi, 1997; Lonner, 1980; Miller, 1997; Segall, Dasen, Berry, & Poortinga, 1999; Segall, Lonner, & Berry, 1998; Triandis, 1995), and for which valuable suggestions and recommendations have been offered to deal with this vital methodological issue. Although the emic–etic debate is an important methodological problem, in the final analysis methodology needs to serve the interests of theory, not the other way around. Therefore, what is far more important is to formulate a comprehensive theoretical system that allows us to understand the nature of trauma across cultures as well as the manner in which it is conceptualized, appraised, and dealt with.

A catalogue of descriptive accounts of trauma across cultures would be an excellent starting point. Descriptive accounts, however, have one fatal flaw. While they may enable us to formulate meaningful categories and even taxonomies, they do not allow us to offer valid explanations of the observed phenomena. A descriptive model is often based on a form of inductive reasoning, and as a result, it falls into the inductive fallacy trap, first highlighted by David Hume in the eighteenth century (e.g., Chalmers, 1978; Cottingham, 1984; Popper, 1963, 1972). Referring to the example quoted earlier, we know how strongly

Hindus, particularly the high-caste Brahmins, feel about preserving their caste purity. We also know what they feel about caste-contamination in the face of death. We know too that certain behaviors that deviate from established norms are perceived as being extremely traumatic. With respect to rites and rituals related to dying, cremation, and grieving, we know what Hindus did in the past, and continue to do at present. But what we do not know and have no way of knowing is what Hindus will do or will continue to do in future because our descriptive account does not allow us to make those predictions.

While knowledge of the past may throw some light on the present, the present offers us no guide whatever into the future because of our inability to predict the future. It is necessary therefore to go beyond a head count, so to speak, and offer meaningful explanations that would enhance our understanding of the problem. The questions that are of importance therefore are, How do people from different cultures cognitively construe an event as being traumatic? How do they arrive at such constructions? What are the variables within a given culture that influence such attributions? What makes a particular event traumatic in one culture and not in another? A comprehensive theory should also explain satisfactorily both between-group and within-group differences.

CONCEPTUAL MODEL OF CULTURAL DIFFERENCES

Over the years, my associates and I have proposed a theoretical model that argues that there are four interrelated core values, or factors, that distinguish Western cultures from Eastern cultures and, more specifically, English culture from Indian culture, in terms of their salient value systems (Laungani, 1991, 1992, 1993, 1994, 1995, 1996, 1997, 1998, 1999; Laungani & Sookhoo, 1995; Sachdev 1992; Sookhoo, 1995).

The four values or factors are:

Individualism ....Communalism (collectivism)
Cognitivism......................Emotionalism
Free will..........................Determinism
Materialism ....Spiritualism

It should be noted that the two concepts underlying each factor are not dichotomous. They need to be understood as extending along a continuum starting at, say, Individualism, at one end, and extending into Communalism or Collectivism at the other. A dichotomous approach tends to classify people in either-or terms. As Schwartz (1990) points out, such an approach is limited in its usefulness. People seldom fit into neat theoretically formulated and/or empirically derived categories. The sheer complexity and variability of human behaviors precludes serious attempts at dichotomous or categorical classifications. Categorical approaches were popular four or five decades ago, but were abandoned and replaced by more complex, multifactorial models.

A dimensional approach, on the other hand, takes account of human variability. It has the advantage of allowing us to measure salient attitudes and behaviors at any given point in time, as well as over time. It also enables us to hypothesize expected theoretical and empirical shifts in positions along the continuum both within and between cultural groups. Each of the hypothesized dimensions subsumes within it a variety of attitudes and behaviors which, to a large extent, are influenced by the norms and values operative within that culture. Robust empirical validation of the four factors has been provided by Laungani & Sookhoo (1995), Sachdev (1992), Sookhoo (1995), and Laungani & Williams (1997).

The concepts on the left side of each factor are applicable more to the British and to Western societies in general, and those on the right side are applicable more to the Indians and to Eastern cultures in general. Let us now examine each concept briefly, and trace its relationship to trauma.

INDIVIDUALISM-COMMUNALISM (COLLECTIVISM)

Several thinkers, particularly in America, have written on the concepts of Individualism and Collectivism (Bellah, 1985; Hofstede, 1980, 1991; Hui & Triandis, 1986; Kagitcibasi, 1997; Kim, 1997; Kim, Triandis, & Yoon, 1992; Lukes, 1973; Matsumoto, 1996; Spence, 1985; Triandis, 1995; Waterman, 1981). Many of them have come to see Individualism and Collectivism as two sides of the same coin.

Insofar as the concept Collectivism is concerned, I prefer the word Communalism instead. A culture is not just a motley crowd or collection of people; it is much more. In selecting a word that is seemingly neutral in its social and political connotations, there is the implicit danger of reintroducing the old notion of group mind, which was abandoned several decades ago.

Individualism has come to acquire several different meanings: an ability to exercise a degree of control over one's life, the ability to cope with one's problems, an ability to change for the better, reliance on oneself, being responsible for one's actions, self-fulfilment and self-realization of one's internal resources, and the pursuit of one's own chosen goals in a culture that respects and cherishes pluralistic (and even conflicting) values. Triandis (1994) points out that individualism, in essence, is concerned with giving priority to one's personal goals over the goals of one's ingroup. While Triandis (1995) distinguishes between vertical and horizontal individualism, Kim (1997) characterizes individualism in terms of three features, which he refers to as: (1) emphasis on distinct and autonomous individuals; (2) separation from ascribed relationships such as family, community, and religion; and (3) emphasis on abstract principles, rules, and norms that guide the individual's thoughts, feelings, and actions. According to Kim (1997), individualism asserts the positions of rationalism, universalism, detachability, and freedom of choice, and rejects a traditional, ascribed, communal, and medieval social order.

How does the notion of individualism enable us to understand trauma? What are the factors within the philosophy of individualism that are likely to lead to stress and trauma?

Individualism tends to create conditions that do not permit an easy sharing of one's personal problems and concerns with others. It does not offer the social and familial support systems that are so easily available in non-Western cultures. The emphasis on self-reliance, the expectation of being responsible for one's own success or failure, which is integral to the notion of individualism, imposes severe stress on the individual. Additionally, individualistic societies, in their espousal of pluralistic values, do not offer clear and culturally defined indicators or markers as to how a variety of negative emotional events ought to be construed. Thus the same event may be perceived in a variety of different ways by people in individualistic cultures. A brief example may be given to illustrate the last point.

A person is picked up by the police and taken into custody for questioning in relation to a particular crime that has been committed. After a few hours of questioning, the person concerned is released without charge.

Can this be labelled a traumatic event, whose consequences can be devastating for the individual concerned? Would it be perceived as a traumatic event by everybody? In the absence of any specific guidelines or cultural norms, the same event is likely to be perceived in different ways. To some, it might seem an extremely traumatic event; a few might construe it as a nuisance; others might find it distressing and frightening; and a few might even regard it a challenge in which they can test their wits against the police. However, it is unlikely that the same event will be perceived the same by all in terms of trauma. In an individualistic culture, an individual, to a large measure, is free to act in accordance with his or her own inclinations. There are no clearly defined guidelines, norms, or rules concerning appropriate or inappropriate behaviors, other than those that may involve legal infringements. Thus the onus of defining an affective event as being traumatic comes to rest on the individual.

Traumas in Western individualistic cultures are not related to religious or theological teachings. In the past, religious transgressions might have been considered traumatic, as they are in non-Western cultures, but given the decline in religious beliefs in Western societies in general (Parkes, Laungani, & Young, 1997), religion and theology play but minimal roles in accounting for what might constitute traumatic experiences. Traumas have become secularized in the West.

Another important distinction of individualistic as opposed to collectivist culture, is that within an individualistic culture there is also the expectation that the individual concerned will attempt to find a satisfactory solution to the type of event described above. Failure on the part of the individual to cope with the problem may result in the individual's seeking professional help from those specially qualified to deal with traumatic or posttraumatic stress disorders.

Communalism (Collectivism)

Indian society, not unlike other Eastern societies, is a family based and community oriented society (Kakar, 1981; Koller, 1982; Lannoy, 1976; Laungani, 1997, 1998; Mandelbaum, 1972; Saraswathi & Pai, 1997; Sinari, 1984; Sinha & Kao, 1997). A community, in the sense in which it is understood in India, has several common features. People within a group are united by a common caste, religious grouping, and linguistic and geographical boundaries. There are similarities in dietary customs, religious beliefs and practices, and leisure pursuits. All the members within a community generally operate on a ranking or a hierarchical system. Elders are accorded special status within the community and are generally deferred to. In Indian family life, one's individuality is subordinated to collective solidarity, and one's ego is absorbed into the collective ego of the family and one's community. The prescriptive norms of the community serve as markers that help to define behaviors, including those considered traumatic. Consequently, when an emotional problem affects a given individual in a family, it tends to get perceived as a communal event, affecting the entire family and, in certain instances, the subcommunity. The family concerned makes a concerted attempt to find a satisfactory solution to the problem.

Other collectivist cultures, including China, Taiwan, Korea, Hong Kong, the Philippines, Thailand, Nepal, Pakistan, Iran, Turkey, Portugal, Mexico, Peru, Venezuela, and Colombia, also share most of the features described above (Cheng, 1996; Gulerce, 1996; Hofstede, 1980; Jing & Wan, 1997; Kim, 1997; Matsumoto, 1996; Sinha, Mishra, & Berry, 1996; Ward & Kennedy, 1996; Yang, 1997). For instance, Kuo-Shu Yang (1997), in his excellent analysis of the traditional Chinese personality, refers to the tight, close-knit bond between the individual and his or her family. He points out that

Chinese familism disposes the Chinese to subordinate their personal interests, goals, glory, and welfare to their family's interests, goals, glory, and welfare to the extent that the family is primary and its members secondary. (p. 245)

Again, Kuo-Shu Yang (1997) points out that in order to attain harmony within the family it is essential for the individual to "surrender or merge into his or her family, and as a result, lose his or her individuality and idiosyncrasies as an independent actor" (p. 245).

To remain part of the family, the individual is expected to submit to familial and communal norms, and is expected not to deviate to an extent where it becomes necessary for the deviant to be dealt with severely. The pressure to conform to family norms and expectations necessarily entails an inability or unwillingness to assert one's independence with regard to the choice of one's occupation, one's friends, even one's marriage partner. This can be an extremely traumatic experience for the individual concerned and can, in some instances, lead to psychotic disorders and hysteria (Channabasavanna & Bhatti, 1982; Sethi & Manchanda, 1978). The very act of living together in a crowded physical environment, with little room for physical privacy, creates its own sets of stressors. On the whole, however, it would appear that extended family networks provide built-in safety measures against stress and mental disturbances. The emotional and physical intimacy shared by all members within a family group acts as a buffer against stressors, stressors from which the Indian's European counterpart is not protected.

A Case of Cultural Misperceptions

In India it is a fairly common practice for parents to perform what is referred to as the *mundan* ceremony of their male child. Between the ages of three and five, the child is taken to a temple of a mother goddess. In some regions of North India the child may be taken to the banks of the river Ganges. There the baby hair of the child is shaved and is offered to the goddess. Amid this joyous ceremony to which relatives and friends are invited, the child is then dressed up in a new outfit that is a miniature replica of the clothes worn by adult members of his community. The ceremony has the important symbolic function of representing the child's individuation and separation from its mother. The offering of the fetal hair, as Kakar (1981) points out, marks "the death of the mother-infant symbiosis and the psychological birth of the child as a separate individual" (p. 206). Kakar points out that the symbolism of death and rebirth lies at the heart of many rituals connected with *chudakarana,* or the rituals associated with tonsure. There are regional variations in this practice in terms of the age at which, and the manner in which, this ceremony is performed. But the importance of the ceremony cannot be overstated. It is only after the child's tonsure that he is considered ready for the process of discipline and the family's attempts at socialization. It might be of interest to note that among certain Hindus, and the Sindhi Hindus in particular, the ritual is not confined to boys alone. Girls are also included in these symbolic representations of individuation. This practice, over the years, has also spread to the Muslims in India and elsewhere.

The mundan ceremony is practiced freely by Asians in Britain. A serious problem arose within the social services department in one of the larger cities in England in relation to this ceremony. A health professional, unacquainted with the above cultural practices, and ignorant of the underlying importance of such a practice, accused the parents of traumatizing the child. Seeing the child with its tonsured head, the health professional concerned perceived such a ceremony as a ritualized form of child abuse.

From an Indian cultural perspective, it needs to be pointed out that in shaving off the child's hair, there is no intended harm. The intentions, if anything, are honorable, for the ceremony signifies what is a positive good in the community: the child's severance of its symbiotic relationship with its mother and the assertion of its individuality. There is no evidence to support the argument that as a result of the tonsure the child will experience serious trauma that will have a long-lasting deleterious effect on the child's development or personality. Such arguments are misguided at best, and irresponsible at worst. At a deeper level, they suggest an unconscious intolerance of cultural variations, where intolerance masquerades as paternalistic concern for the welfare of children.

COGNITIVISM — EMOTIONALISM

This factor is concerned with the way in which the British, and in particular the English, construe their private and social worlds and the ways in which they form and sustain social relationships.

Cognitivism

It has been suggested by Pande (1968) that Western society in general is a work-and-activity-centered society, and Indian society, in contradistinction, is a relationship-centered society. These different constructions of two different social worlds are not accidental cultural developments. They stem from the inheritance of two different philosophical legacies. In a work-and-activity-centered society, people are more likely to operate on a cognitive mode, where the emphasis is on rationality, logic, and control. Public expression of feelings and emotions, especially among the middle classes in England, is often frowned upon. The expression of negative feelings causes mutual embarrassment and is often construed as being vulgar.

Within a cognitivist framework, there is a cultural expectation that persons in most social situations will exercise a high degree of self-control. Stress and trauma in such a framework arises from the cultural expectation of reliance on self-control, and the cultural embargo on the expression of feelings and emotions in public. Even in situations where it would seem legitimate to express feelings openly and without inhibition, at funerals for instance, the English are guided by self-control, which requires that one must not cry in public, one must at all times put on a "brave" face, and one must, above all, never lose one's dignity. Dignity is preserved, or even perpetuated, through restraint. The unwillingness or inability to express emotions openly is a theme that has caused some worry to other writers in the field (Gorer, 1965; Hockey, 1993; Sarbin, 1986).

Given the paucity of social support systems, it is inevitable that in a work-and-activity-centered society a need arises for the creation of professional and semi-professional settings that permit the legitimate expression of specific feelings and emotions and their handling by experts trained in specific areas, including cognitive behavior therapy, rational-emotive therapy, and others. Thus one sees in Western society the growth of specialist counselors and psychotherapists of a variety of theoretical and clinical persuasions.

Another major feature of the work-and-activity-centered society is its emphasis on time. Work and its relation to self-esteem acquire meaning only when seen against the background of time. In a work-and-activity centered society, one's working life, including one's private life, to a large measure, is organized around time. To ensure the judicious use of time, one resorts to keeping appointment books, calendars, and computer-assisted diaries. One fixes time schedules, sets deadlines, and tries to keep within one's time limits. One is constantly aware of the swift passage of time, and to "fritter it away" is often construed as an act of criminality. McClelland (1961) has shown that people in general, and high achievers in particular, use metaphors such as "a dashing waterfall" or "a speeding train to describe time." In high-achieving Western environments even casual encounters between friends or colleagues at work are time related and operate on covert agendas. One seldom gets together with coworkers as an end in itself. Instead, meeting people at work is construed as a means to an end, with time playing a significant role. Running out of time, and therefore not being able to meet one's deadlines, is one of the greatest stressors in Western society.

Emotionalism

Non-Western societies tend to be relationship centered and to operate in an emotional mode. The fact that people live in close physical proximity and share their lives with one another forces them into this emotional mode. In such a society, feelings and emotions are not easily repressed, and their expression in general is not frowned upon. Crying, mutual interdependence, and excessive emotionality are not in any way considered signs of weakness. Emotional outbursts are generally accepted by family members, and quite often help the individual to cope with a trauma.

The factor of time, so important in Western societies, does not have the same meaning in a relationship-centered society. Time, in Indian metaphysics, is not conceptualized in linear terms, in which there is a beginning, a middle, and an end, or in other words, a past, a present, and a future. Time, in Indian philosophy, is conceptualized in circular terms, which means that it has no beginning, no middle, and no end, or if there is a beginning, it remains unknown. These different conceptualizations have serious implications for our understanding of stress and trauma in the two different cultures.

For instance, at a day-to-day observational level, one does not notice among Indians the same sense of urgency that appears to have become the hallmark of Western society. Time, in India, is often viewed as a quiet, motionless ocean, or a vast expanse of sky. It is interesting to note that in Hindi there is only one word, *kal,* which stands for both yesterday and tomorrow. The word kal also symbolizes death. The flexible Indian attitude to time is often reflected in social engagements as well. Indians tend to be quite casual about keeping appointments. Being late for an appointment, or keeping another person waiting, does not appear to cause undue stress.

There are, however, exceptions to this flexible construction of time. They occur in socially significant situations such as undertaking an important journey, or fixing the times of christenings, betrothals, weddings, and funerals. In such important situations one is expected to consult the family Brahmin priest, who then consults an almanac from which he (most Brahmin priests are male) calculates the best time for the commencement of that particular activity. Because of their religious significance, such events are seldom left to chance; one seeks divine guidance in their planning and execution. Unprecedented delays in the performance of religious ceremonies tend to cause acute anxiety. Should a chance adverse event cause a delay or the inappropriate performance of a ceremony, it may be attributed to divine retribution, and the family concerned may feel traumatized.

FREE WILL—DETERMINISM

The issues related to the nature of free will, predestination, determinism, and indeterminism are still hotly debated in philosophical and scientific journals. No satisfactory solutions have been found to these age-old issues. Although the Aristotelian legacy has undergone several transformations, it has remained with us for over two thousand years (Flew, 1989). In the past, prior to Newton's spectacular achievements, determinism was entangled in its theistic and metaphysical connotations. But after the publication of Newton's *Principia* in 1687, the concept of determinism was partially freed from its theistic connotations, and a nontheistic and mechanistic view of determinism in science, and indeed in the universe, gained prominence. A scientific notion of determinism, with its emphasis on causality, or conversely, its denial of noncausal events, found favor among the rationalist philosophers who embraced it with great fervor (Popper, 1972). However, it was not until the emergence of quantum mechanics in the early twentieth century that determinism in science, if not in human affairs, once again came to be seriously questioned.

Free Will

There is a peculiar dualism in Western thinking concerning free will and determinism. Scientific research in medicine, psychiatry, psychology, biology, and other related disciplines is based on the acceptance of a deterministic framework, hence the concern with seeking causal explanations and with predictability in accordance with rational scientific procedures. Yet at social, psychological, and common sense levels there is a strong belief in the notion of free will.

Free will might be defined as a non-causal, voluntary action. However, at a commonsense level, it is defined as exercising voluntary control over one's actions. Thus free will allows an individual to do what he or she wills and, in so doing, take credit for his or her successes and accept blame for his or her failures and mishaps. Therefore a person is forever locked into the consequences of his or her own actions. This feature of Western society entraps people in their own existential predicaments, from which there does not appear to be an easy way out. If, however, the label trauma is changed into posttraumatic stress disorder (PTSD), then PTSD becomes "an attractive explanatory model for many people because it places responsibility for their suffering on factors outside themselves, factors over which they often had neither responsibility nor control" (Friedman, 1999, p. 1).

Determinism

Indians, by virtue of subscribing to a deterministic view of life, in a teleological sense, at least, are prevented from taking final responsibility for their own actions. The notion of determinism plays a crucial role in Indian thinking. The law of karma, which involves determinism and fatalism, has shaped the Indian view of life over centuries (Herman, 1976; O'Flaherty, 1976, 1980; Reichenbach, 1990; Sinari, 1984; Weber, 1963).

In its simplest form, the law of karma states that happiness and sorrow are the predetermined effects of actions committed by people either in their present lives or in one of their numerous past lives. Things do not happen because *we* make them happen. Things happen because they were *destined* to happen. If people's present lives are determined by their actions in their previous lives, it follows that any problem that affects an individual was destined to happen because of past actions.

A belief in the law of karma does not necessarily negate the notion of free will. As von Furer-Haimendorf (1974) has pointed out, in an important sense karma is based on the assumption of free will. The theory of karma rests on the idea that individuals have the final moral responsibility for each of their actions and therefore the freedom of moral choice.

Pandey, Srinivas, and Muralidhar (1980) in a study of informants of psychiatric patients in India found that the most commonly stated causes of psychotic disorders and other traumatic experiences were attributed to sins and wrong deeds in previous and present lives. These findings have been corroborated by Srinivasa and Trivedi (1982) who, in their study of 266 respondents selected from three villages in South India, attributed, among other factors, "God's curse" as one of the most common causes of stress leading to mental disorders. Such a belief has a positive effect in Indian cultural terms: It takes away the blame that might otherwise be apportioned to the individual concerned.

A belief in determinism is likely to engender in the Indian psyche a spirit of passive, if not resigned, acceptance of the vicissitudes of life. This prevents a person from experiencing feelings of guilt, a state from which Westerners, because of their fundamental belief in the doctrine of free will, cannot be protected. One of the many disadvantages of determinism lies in the fact that it often leads to a state of existential, and in certain instances moral resignation, compounded by a profound sense of inertia. Indians do not take immediate proactive measures; they merely accept the vicissitudes of life without qualm. While this may prevent a person from experiencing stress, it does not allow the same person to make individual attempts to alleviate his or her unbearable condition.

MATERIALISM—SPIRITUALISM

Materialism

Materialism refers to a belief in the existence of a material world, or a world composed of matter. What constitutes matter is itself debatable, and the question has never been satisfactorily answered (Trefil, 1980). Matter may consist of atoms, but it appears atoms are made of nuclei and electrons. Nuceli in turn are made up of protons and neutrons. What are protons and neutrons made of? Gell-Mann (see Davies, 1990) suggests quarks. But are quarks really the final answer? The assumed solidity of matter may turn out to be a myth (Davies, 1990).

The notion of the solidity of matter was robustly debated by Heisenberg in his now famous research paper on indeterminacy in quantum theory in 1927 (Heisenberg, 1930). However, such debates are confined to journals of philosophy and science. At a practical level, one accepts the assumed solidity of the world that one inhabits, but not without paying a heavy price. Such an acceptance gives rise to the popular myth that all explanations of phenomena, ranging from lunar cycles to lunacy, from stress to trauma, need to be sought within the (assumed) materialist framework. This is evidenced by the profound reluctance among psychiatrists, medical practitioners, and psychologists, particularly in the West, to entertain any explanations that are of a nonmaterial or supernatural nature.

A materialist philosophy also tends to engender in its subscribers the belief that our knowledge of the world is external to ourselves; reality is, as it were, "out there," and it is only through objective scientific enterprise that one will acquire an understanding of the external world and, with it, an understanding of "reality." Nonmaterial explanations are seen to fall within the purview of *prescientific* communities, or in other words, superstitious and backward societies, to be found mainly in underdeveloped countries.

Spiritualism

In Indian thinking, the notion of materialism is a relatively unimportant concept. The external world to Indians is not composed of matter. It is seen as being illusory. It is *maya*. The concept of maya, as Zimmer (1951/1989) points out, "holds a key position in Vedantic thought and teaching" (p. 19). Since the external world is illusory, reality, or its perception, lies within the individual, and not, as Westerners believe, outside the individual. This, according to Zimmer (1951/1989) tends to make Indians more inward looking and Westerners more outward looking. Also, given the illusory nature of the external world, the Indian mind remains unfettered by materialistic boundaries. It resorts to explanations where material and spiritual, physical and metaphysical, and natural and supernatural explanations of phenomena coexist with one another. What to a Western mind, weaned on Aristotelian logic, nourished on a scientific diet, socialized on materialism, empiricism, and positivism might seem an irreconcilable contradiction, leaves an Indian mind relatively unperturbed. To a Westerner if A is A, A cannot then be not-A. If dysentery is caused by certain forms of bacteria, it cannot then be due to the influence of the evil eye; the two are logically and empirically incompatible. But contradictions to Indians are a way of life. A is not only A, but under certain conditions, A may be not-A.

One of the most interesting differences between Indian thinking and Western thinking is this: Indians believe intuitively and spiritually the external world to be illusory without actually "knowing" it, while Westerners "know" it to be illusory, without actually believing it. This differential construction of one's physical world has an important bearing on the perception of stress and the methods employed for coping with it. In Indian thinking, a traumatic event can be unleashed by an army of unseen, unknown, evil, and malevolent spirits, ghosts, devils, and demons, whose devastating powers would need to be quashed in order for the person concerned to survive the trauma.

COPING WITH TRAUMA:
CROSSCULTURAL VARIATIONS

We have seen that trauma is a common human experience. Some events and experiences, such as natural disasters, accidents, floods, fires, and violence, are universally recognized as being traumatic, and others tend to be specific to the culture in which they occur. There are personality differences in people that affect their appraisal of, and reaction to, trauma.

Coping strategies tend to be indigenous to the culture. The methods of coping with trauma in Western societies are too well known to merit a detailed discussion here. They range from a variety of conventional individual and group psychotherapies, which include cognitive centered approaches and cognitive restructuring (Hoyt, 1999), brief group counseling (Zaidi, 1994), rational-emotive therapy, confrontational techniques, nondirective client-centered therapies, and psychoanalytic therapies. There are also the less conventional techniques such as expressive art therapy, letter writing, audiotaping, videotaping exercises (Meichenbaum, 1999), aerobics, and sextherapy. The efficacy of many of these therapeutic processes remains a debatable question.

In Eastern cultures, particularly in India, traumas related to natural disasters, acute poverty and starvation, overcrowding, shortage of safe drinking water, caste-related violence, communal riots, political exploitation, endemic corruption, chronic illnesses, disease, child prostitution, child labor, and high levels of infant mortality, are everyday events. Although the effects of these traumas are devastating, they seldom come within the care and attention of trained experts. India does not have the trained psychiatric and psychological personnel to offer Western-type therapies to its people, an estimated population of 943 million. What then, are the therapeutic alternatives available in India?

Psychiatric Treatment

Wig and Saxena (1982) point out that psychiatrists in India continue to use the classificatory systems of ICD-9 and the DSM-III (and more recently, the DSM-IV) in their clinical work. Psychiatric treatments include confinement in a psychiatric institution, use of drugs, electroconvulsive therapy (ECT), custodial care, and so forth. Several psychiatrists, however, have expressed dissatisfaction with the classificatory systems highlighted in the DSM-IV and have suggested changes and revisions that would take into account important social and cultural factors in classification. In any event, the uses of the above classificatory systems are limited for at least two reasons.

First, the ratio of psychiatrists to the general population in India is a little over one psychiatrist to every million people (Rao, 1986). There are only about 50 mental hospitals in the entire country. There is hardly any undergraduate training in psychiatry in the medical schools. It is estimated that mental illness and other stress related disorders affect some two to seven persons per 1000 population in India (Rao, 1986). In India, between two and four million are affected by stress related disorders of one form or other. Given the size of the population, the regional and linguistic variations, and the great rural-urban divide in terms of social, educational, and economic differentials, it is impossible for the present psychiatric services to meet the needs of the afflicted persons in India. It is evident therefore that the various forms of psychiatric treatment, including the use of psychotropic drugs, ECT, and other forms of therapies, are limited in their uses. They are confined to psychiatric institutions, which are located mainly in the urban areas of the country. Moreover, psychiatric institutions in India tend to be overcrowded and understaffed. In addition to the above problems, there are limited economic resources, lack of trained personnel, limited availability of drugs, high drop-out rates from treatment, lack of awareness among general medical practitioners, and lack of integration of indigenous and modern systems of medicine.

Second, psychiatric institutions arouse pejorative, stigmatizing, and even hostile images in the minds of people. A person's being admitted to a psychiatric institution is the ultimate admission of a family member's insanity. It is a label that families, for social reasons, are anxious to avoid. The label often transfers to the entire family, making it difficult in many cases for parents to find suitable spouses for their children, particularly for their daughters. Parents of eligible daughters are loathe to consider forming marital liaisons with families where there is known psychiatric or stress related traumatic disorder. Thus people in general are profoundly reluctant to have their loved ones admitted to psychiatric institutions, unless of course they feel they have no choice. Admission to a psychiatric institution may often be seen as the last resort after all other alternatives have been tried and exhausted.

Yoga Therapy

In India there is greater reliance on indigenous therapeutic treatments than on Western therapeutic models. The World Health Organization (WHO) report (1978) points out that there are over 108 colleges of indigenous medicine in India, with over 500,000 practitioners of one of the following indigenous forms of healing: Ayurveda, Unani, and Yoga. Yoga appears to be the most popular form of treatment used in psychological disorders all over the country. Evidence of the efficacy of yoga therapy is quite convincing (Satyavathi, 1988). Encouraged by the results of yoga therapy, Vahia (1982) even suggested that yoga represents a new conceptual model of health and disease. Although several studies have pointed to the effectiveness of yoga therapy (Bhole, 1981; Dharmakeerti, 1982; Neki, 1979; Nespor, 1982), it is not seen as a panacea for all types of disorders.

Religious Counseling

Since trauma is often perceived as a visitation from malevolent gods, it is an accepted practice to take the afflicted person to a well-known shrine, a temple, or to a Muslim *darga*. It might be of interest to note that in this instance there is a powerful pragmatic mixture of religious beliefs. Hindus frequently visit Muslim dargas, and Muslim families undertake to visit a temple or a well-known Guru attributed with divine healing powers. Sudhir Kakar (1982), in his excellent book *Shamans, Mystics and Doctors* cites remarkable case studies describing this. The visitations to shrines, temples, and mosques may take several forms. The afflicted person surrenders his or her will to the guru by sitting near and "feasting" his or her eyes on the guru. The *darshan* (blessed vision) of the guru is attributed with immense spiritual and healing powers. In other instances, the guru may encourage the person to recite prayers, meditate, read from the scriptures, or perform religious rites, all of which are attributed with healing properties. Special emphasis is paid to the intense and symbiotic relationship between the guru and the follower. The guru-follower therapeutic procedure tends to adopt a directive approach, rather than a nondirective one. The guru attempts to guide the afflicted person through all his or her afflictions, and offers hope and prayer. In return, it is beholden upon the follower to abide by all the teachings and prescriptions of the guru. For the therapeutic enterprise to progress smoothly, it is essential that the guru be perceived as a person of immense sagacity and wisdom. The guru must have no obvious pecuniary interests in the outcome of the treatment. The guru must also be seen to be living on the margins of society. In other words, the guru, in keeping with Indian cultural traditions, must be seen as being truly and totally detached from material comforts and aspirations.

The well-to-do often undertake long, arduous, and expensive pilgrimages to the holy cities, such as Benaras, Hardwar, Vrindavan, and Rishikesh. There they perform elaborate religious ceremonies, feed hundreds of mendicants, or bathe the victim and themselves in the river Ganges, which is attributed to have divine cleansing powers. At home, the women pray, undertake regular fasts, refrain from eating meat, and practice extremely severe austerities to ensure the restoration of the victim's mental and physical health.

Demonological Therapies

Trauma, as was stated earlier, is also explained in terms of sorcery, bewitchment, and evil spirits (Kakar, 1982). The patient afflicted by these disorders is considered blameless because the illness is seen as the work of demons and other malevolent spirits, or *shaitans,* who take possession of the patient. Why a demonic spirit should take possession of one individual and not another is attributed to the belief that spirit possession is due to the envy of neighbors at the visible affluence and success and good health of the afflicted person. Belief in the evil eye, commonly referred to as *najar* or *dishti,* is quite strong and widespread among Indians. A child who meets with an accident or falls seriously ill and contracts an infectious disease might be the victim of an evil eye (Fuller, 1992; Laungani, 1988). Social acceptance of such attributions has served to legitimize belief in the evil eye and its malevolent variants. In addition to wearing charms, amulets, and sacred threads (the symbol of the twice-born high-caste Hindu), parents might symbolically blacken the child's face with ash or coal dust or even kohl to ward off the dangers of the evil eye. A plain or "ugly" child is less likely to become a victim of the evil eye than is a pretty child.

But when such prophylactic measures fail, persons specially qualified to remove spells and counterspells, and exorcise demons and other spirits such as *bhoots, balas,* and shaitans, are summoned by the family members of the afflicted persons. All over India one finds an army of faith healers, mystics, shamans, *pirs* (holy men), *bhagats* (religious persons), and gurus. They are accorded the same respect and veneration as medically trained psychiatrists in Western countries. It is not uncommon to find the concerned relatives of a distressed person consulting some, if not all, of these specialists for effective treatment.

Astrological Therapies

Belief in astrology and the malevolent influences of planets on one's life is strongly ingrained in the Indian psyche. It is quite customary to have a child's horoscope read upon its birth. The heavenly configuration of planets at the moment of birth is seen as a determinant of life chances. A carefully cast horoscope reveals the person's fate, which is written on his or her forehead (Fuller, 1992). Astrologers are also consulted prior to finalizing betrothals. In the event of a serious planetary mismatch in the horoscopes of the couple, the parents may decide not to proceed with the engagement of their children, or may decide to undertake arduous religious ceremonies that would propitiate the evil influences of the planets on the future of the couple. Traumas may occur as a result of the malevolent influence of the planets, particularly *shani* or Saturn. Shrines containing images of Saturn and other planets are found in all parts of India. On the day when Saturn moves from one house to another, people all over India offer prayers. Some express relief at having survived the last thirty months, and others are fearful and anxious at having to get through the next thirty months without calamitous misfortunes (Fuller, 1992).

Indigenous Ayurvedic Therapies

Ayurveda is a traditional Indian system of medicine. Its fundamental goal is to bring about and maintain a harmonious balance between the person, the person's body, and the person's psyche. In modern Western terminology it might be construed as a form of holistic medicine. Its roots, however, run deeper. There is a shared belief among Indians and people from South Asia that Ayurvedic medicine has no beginning since it reflects "the laws of nature inherent in life and living beings and thus mirrors their unchanging essence" (Kakar, 1982, p. 221). Ayurvedic medicine is focused more on treating the person rather than the disease. Illness occurs when there is an humoral imbalance between the psyche-soma identity, leading to different types of insanities due to specific imbalances.

For effective treatment it is as important to understand the person as it is the disease to be treated. The emphasis of treatment is on purification, which may often consist of purges, emetics, enemas, and bleeding. However, these practices appear to have fallen into disuse in many areas, even though they are still practiced in certain parts of South India. They have been replaced by other traditional herbal remedies. Since the Ayurvedic goal is to restore a harmonious balance, the treatment procedures tend to be diverse. There is a strong emphasis on rigid dietary practices, which is in keeping with the belief that certain types of foods produce certain mental states (both desirable and undesirable) and therefore can be eaten only at certain times of the day. The patient is also encouraged to undertake regular physical exercises, including breathing exercises, or *pranayanas*. The final emphasis is on the acquisition of desirable personal and social habits, which include ways of relating to oneself and to others, and the attaining of those thoughts, attitudes, beliefs, and values that promote a harmonious balance between the person, the soma, and the psyche.

CONCLUDING COMMENT

No culture or society appears to have all the answers concerning the problems related to trauma and stress related disorders. It is important therefore that cultures meet on equal terms, as equal partners, and express genuine willingness to learn from each other, so that answers might be found to questions that concern us all.

REFERENCES

Anantha Murthy, U. R. (1978). *Samskara.* New York: Oxford University Press.
Bellah, R. N. (1985). *Habits of the heart: Individuation and commitment in American life.* Berkeley, CA: University of California Press.

Berry, J. W. (1969). On cross-cultural comparability. *International Journal of Psychology, 4,* 119–128.

Berry, J. W., & Sam, D. (1997). Acculturation and adaptation. In J. W. Berry, M. H. Segall, & C. Kagitcibasi (Eds.), *Handbook of cross-cultural psychology: Social behavior and applications.* Boston: Allyn & Bacon.

Bhole, M. V. (1981). Concept of relaxation in shavasana. *Yoga Mimamsa, 20,* 50–56.

Chalmers, A. F. (1978). *What is this thing called science?* Milton Keynes, UK: The Open University Press.

Channabasavanna, S. M., & Bhatti, R. S. (1982). A Study on interactional patterns and family typologies in families of mental patients. In A. Kiev & A. V. Rao (Eds.), *Readings in transcultural psychiatry* (pp. 149–161). Madras, India: Higginbothams.

Cheng, C. H. K. (1996). Towards a culturally relevant model of self-concept for the Hong Kong Chinese. In J. Pandey, D. Sinha, & D. P. S. Bhawuk (Eds.), *Asian Contributions to Cross-Cultural Psychology* (pp. 235–254). New Delhi, India: Sage Publications.

Cottingham, J. (1984). *Rationalism.* London: Paladin.

Davies, P. (1990). *God and the new physics.* London: Penguin.

Dharmakeerti, U. S. (1982). Review of "yoga and cardiovascular management." *Yoga, 20,* 15–16.

Ekman, P. (1972) Universals and cultural differences in facial expressions of emotion. In J. Cole (Ed.), *Nebraska symposium of motivation* (Vol. 19). Lincoln: University of Nebraska Press.

Ekman, P. (1973). *Darwin and facial expression.* New York: Academic Press.

Ekman, P. (1985). *Telling lies.* New York: Norton.

Ekman, P. (1994). Strong evidence for universals in facial expressions: A reply to Russell's mistaken critique. *Psychological Bulletin, 115,* 268–287.

Ekman, P., & Freisen, W. V. (1975). *Unmasking the face.* Englewood Cliffs, NJ: Prentice-Hall.

Ekman, P., & Heider, K. (1988). The universality of a contempt expression: A replication. *Motivation and Emotion, 12,* 303–308.

Eysenck, M., & Keane, M. T. (1998). *Cognitive psychology: A student's handbook.* London: Taylor & Francis.

Festinger, L. (1964). *When prophecy fails.* New York: Harper & Row.

Flew, A. (1989). *An introduction to western philosophy (Rev. ed.).* New York: Thames and Hudson.

Freud, S. (1955/1974). *Studies on hysteria.* The Pelican Freud Library (Vol. 3). London: Penguin.

Friedman, M. J. (1999). PTSD diagnosis and treatment for mental health clinicians. In M. J. Scott & S. Palmer (Eds.), *Trauma and post-traumatic stress disorder.* London: Cassess.

Fuller, C. J. (1992). *The camphor flame: Popular Hinduism and society in India.* Princeton, NJ: Princeton University Press.

Gorer, G. (1965). *Death, grief, and mourning in contemporary Britain.* London: Cresset Press.

Gulerce, A. (1996). A family structure assessment device for Turkey. In J. Pandey, D. Sinha, & D. P. S. Bhawuk (Eds.), *Asian contributions to cross-cultural psychology* (pp. 108–118). New Delhi, India: Sage.

Heisenberg, W. (1930). *The physical principles of the quantum theory.* Berkeley, CA: University of California Press.

Herman, A. L. (1976). *The problem of evil and Indian thought.* New Delhi, India: Motilal Banarasidass Publishers.

Hockey, J. (1993). The acceptable face of human grieving? The clergy's role in managing emotional expression during funerals. In D. Clark (Ed.), *The sociology of death* (pp. 129–148). Oxford, UK: Blackwell.

Hofstede, G. (1980). *Culture's consequences: International differences in work-related values.* Beverly Hills, CA: Sage.

Hofstede, G. (1991). *Cultures and organizations: Software of the mind.* London: McGraw-Hill.

Hoyt, M. F. (1999) Cognitive-behavioural treatment of PTSD from a narrative, constructivist perspective: A conversation with Donald Meichenbaum. In M. J. Scott & S. Palmer (Eds.), *Trauma and post-traumatic stress disorder: A reader.* London: Cassell.

Hui, C. H., & Triandis, H. C. (1986). Individualism-collectivism: A study of cross-cultural researchers. *Journal of Cross-Cultural Psychology, 17,* 222–248.

Jahoda, G., & Krewer, B. (1997). History of cross-cultural and cultural psychology. In J. W. Berry, Y. H. Poortinga, & J. Pandet (Eds.), *Handbook of cross-cultural psychology: Theory and method* (pp. 1–42). Boston: Allyn & Bacon.

Jing, Q., & Wan, C. (1997). Socialization of Chinese children. In H. S. R. Kao & D. Sinha (Eds.), *Asian perspectives on psychology* (pp. 25–39). New Delhi, India: Sage.

Kagitcibasi, C. (1997). Individualism and collectivism. In J. W. Berry, M. H. Segall, & C. Kagitcibasi (Eds.), *Handbook of cross-cultural psychology: Social behavior and applications* (pp. 1–49). Boston: Allyn & Bacon.

Kakar, S. (1981). *The inner world: A psychoanalytic study of children and society in India.* Delhi, India: Oxford University Press.

Kakar, S. (1982). *Shamans, mystics and doctors.* London: Mandala Books.

Kim, U. (1997). Asian collectivism: An indigenous perspective. In H. S. R. Kao & D. Sinha (Eds.), *Asian perspectives on psychology* (pp. 147–163). New Delhi, India: Sage.

Kim, U., Triandis, H. C., & Yoon, G. (1992). (Eds.). *Individualism and collectivism: Theoretical and methodological issues.* Newbury Park, CA: Sage.

Koller, J. M. (1982). *The Indian way: Asian perspectives.* London: Collier Macmillan.

Lakatos, I. (1971). Falsification and the methodology of scientific research programmes. In I. Lakatos & A. Musgrave (Eds.), *Criticism and the growth of knowledge.* London: Cambridge University Press.

Lannoy, R. (1976). *The speaking tree.* Oxford, UK: Oxford University Press.

Laungani, P. (1988). Accidents in children: An Asian perspective. *Public Health, 103,* 171–176.

Laungani, P. (1991, June). *Preventing child abuse and promoting child health across cultures.* Paper presented at the United Nations Conference on Action for Public Health, Sundsvall, Sweden.

Laungani, P. (1992). Assessing child abuse through interviews of children and parents of children at risk, *Children and Society, 6,* 3–11.

Laungani, P. (1993). Cultural differences in stress and its management. *Stress Medicine, 9,* 37–43.

Laungani, P. (1994). Cultural differences in stress: India and England. *Counselling Psychology Review, 9,* 25–37.

Laungani, P. (1995). Stress in Eastern and Western cultures. In J. Brebner, E. Greenglass, P. Laungani, & A. O'Roark (Eds.), *Stress and emotion* (pp. 265–280). Washington, DC: Taylor & Francis.

Laungani, P. (1996). Research in cross-cultural settings: Ethical considerations. In E. Miao (Ed.), *Cross-cultural encounters: Proceedings of the 53rd annual convention of international council of psychologists* (pp. 107–136). Taipei, Taiwan: General Innovation Service.

Laungani, P. (1997). Patterns of bereavement in Indian and English Society. In J. D. Morgan (Ed.), *Readings in thanatology* (pp. 67–76). Amityville, NY: Baywood Publishing.

Laungani, P. (1998). Client-centred or culture-centred counselling? In S. Palmer & P. Laungani (Eds.), *Counselling across cultures*. London: Sage.

Laungani, P. (1999). Cultural influences on identity and behaviour: India and Britain. In Y.-T. Lee, C. R. McCauley, & J. Draguns (Eds.), *Through the looking glass: Personality in culture* (pp. 191–212). Boston: Lawrence Erlbaum.

Laungani, P., & Sookhoo, D. (1995, July). *Myocardial infarction in British white and Asian adults: Their health beliefs and health practices.* Paper read at the 4th European Congress of Psychology, Athens, Greece.

Laungani, P., & Williams, G. (1997). Patient focused care: Effects of organizational change on the stress of community health professionals. *International Journal of Health Education, 35,* 109–114.

Lazarus, R. S. (1982). Thoughts on the relations between emotion and cognition. *American Psychologist, 37,* 1019–1024.

Lazarus, R. S. (1984). On the primacy of cognition. *American Psychologist, 39,* 124–129.

Lonner, W. J. (1980). The search for psychological universals. In H. C. Triandis & W. W. Lambert (Eds.), *Handbook of cross-cultural psychology: Perspectives* (pp. 143–204). Boston: Allyn & Bacon.

Lukes, S. (1973). *Individualism.* Oxford, UK: Basil Blackwell.

Mandelbaum, D. G. (1972). *Society in India.* Berkeley, CA: University of California Press.

Markus, H. R., & Kitayama, S. (1991). Culture and the self: Implications for cognition, motivation, and emotion. *Psychological Review, 98,* 224–253.

Matsumoto, D. (1989). Cultural influences on the perception of emotion. *Journal of Cross-Cultural Psychology, 20,* 92–105.

Matsumoto, D. (1992). American-Japanese cultural differences in the recognition of universal facial expresssions. *Journal of Cross-Cultural Psychology, 23,* 72–84.

Matsumoto, D. (1996). *Culture and psychology.* San Diego, CA: Brooks/Cole Publishing.

McClelland, D.C. (1961). *The achieving society.* Princeton, NJ: Van Nostrand.

Meichenbaum, D. (1999). Letter writing, audiotaping and videotaping as therapeutic tools: Use of "healing" metaphors. In M. J. Scott & S. Palmer (Eds.), *Trauma and post-traumatic stress disorder: A reader* (pp. 96–101). London: Cassell.

Miller, J. (1997). Theoretical issues in cultural psychology. In J. W. Berry, Y. H. Poortinga, & J. Pandey (Eds.), *Handbook of cross-cultural psychology: Theory and method* (pp. 85–128). Boston: Allyn & Bacon.

Mishra, R. (1997). Cognition and cognitive development. In J. W. Berry, P. R. Dasen, & T. S. Saraswathi (Eds.), *Handbook of cross-cultural psychology: Basic processes and human development* (pp. 143–175). Boston: Allyn & Bacon.

Neki, J. S. (1979). Psychotherapy in India: Traditions and trends. In M. Kapur, V. N. Murthy, K. Satyavathi, & R. L. Kapur (Eds.), *Psychotherapeutic processes* (pp. 113–134). Bangalore, India: National Institute of Mental Health and Neurosciences.

Nespor, K. (1982). Yogic practices in world medical literature. *Yoga, 20,* 29–35.

O'Flaherty, W. D. (1976). *The origins of evil in Hindu mythology.* Berkeley, CA: University of California Press.

O'Flaherty, W. D. (1980). *Karma and rebirth in classical Indian traditions.* Berkeley, CA: University of California Press.

Pande, S. (1968). The mystique of "Western" psychotherapy: An Eastern interpretation. *The Journal of Nervous and Mental Disease, 146,* 425–432.

Pandey, R. S., Srinivas, K. N., & Muralidhar, D. (1980). Socio-cultural beliefs and treatment acceptance. *Indian Journal of Psychiatry, 22,* 161–166.

Parkes, C. M., Laungani, P., & Young, W. (Eds.). (1997). *Death and bereavement across cultures.* London: Routledge.

Popper, K. (1963). *Conjectures and refutations.* London: Routledge.

Popper, K. (1972). *Objective knowledge: An evolutionary approach.* Oxford, UK: The Clarendon Press.

Rao, V. (1986). Indian and Western psychiatry: A comparison. In J. L. Cox (Ed.), *Transcultural Psychiatry* (pp. 291–305). London: Croom Helm.

Reichenbach, B. R. (1990). *The law of karma: A philosophical study.* Honolulu: University of Hawaii Press.

Sachdev, D. (1992). *Effects of psychocultural factors on the socialisation of British born Indian children and indigenous British children living in England.* Unpublished doctoral dissertation, South Bank University, London.

Saraswathi, T. S., & Pai, S. (1997). Socialization in the Indian context. In H. S. R. Kao & D. Sinha (Eds.), *Asian perspectives on psychology: Cross-cultural research and methodology series* (pp. 74–92). New Delhi, India: Sage.

Sarbin, T. R. (1986). Emotion and act: Roles and rhetoric. In R. Harre (Ed.), *The social construction of emotions.* Oxford, UK: Blackwell.

Satyavathi, K. (1988). Mental health. In J. Pandey (Ed.), *Psychology in India: Organizational behaviour and mental health* (pp. 217–288), New Delhi, India: Sage.

Schwartz, S. H. (1990). Individualism-collectivism: Critique and proposed refinements. *Journal of Cross-Cultural Psychology, 21,* 139–157.

Segall, M. H., Dasen, P, R., Berry, J. W., & Poortinga, Y. H. (1999). *Human behaviour in global perspective: An introduction to cross-cultural psychology.* Boston: Allyn & Bacon.

Segall, M. H., Lonner, W. J., & Berry, J. W. (1998). Cross-cultural psychology as a scholarly discipline: On the flowering of culture in behavioural research. *American Psychologist, 53,* 1101–1110.

Sethi, B. B., & Manchanda, R. (1978). Family structure and psychiatric disorders. *Indian Journal of Psychiatry, 20,* 283–288.

Shweder, R. A., & Sullivan, M. A. (1993). Cultural psychology: Who needs it? *Annual Review of Psychology, 44,* 497–527.

Sinari, R. A. (1984). *The structure of Indian thought.* Delhi, India: Oxford University Press.

Sinha, D., & Kao, H. S. R. (1997). The journey to the East: An introduction. In H. S. R. Kao & D. Sinha (Eds.), *Asian perspectives on psychology: Cross-cultural research and methodology series* (pp. 9–22). New Delhi, India: Sage.

Sinha, D., Mishra, R. C., & Berry, J. W. (1996). Some eco-cultural and acculturational factors in intermodal perception. In J. Pandey, D. Sinha, & D. P. S. Bhawuk (Eds.), *Asian contributions to cross-cultural psychology* (pp. 151–164). New Delhi, India: Sage.

Sookhoo, D. (1995). *A comparative study of the health beliefs and health practices of British whites and Asian adults with and without myocardial infarction.* Paper read at the 53rd Annual Convention of the International Council of Psychologists, Taipei, Taiwan.

Spence, J. T. (1985). Achievement American style: The rewards and costs of individualism. *American Psychologist, 40,* 1285–1295.

Srinivasa, D. K., & Trivedi, S. (1982). Knowledge and attitude of mental diseases in a rural community of South India. *Social Science Medicine, 16,* 1635–1639.

Trefil, J. (1980). *From atoms to quarks: An introduction to the strange world of particle physics.* New York: Charles Scribner.

Triandis, H. C. (1994). *Culture and social behaviour.* New York: McGraw-Hill.

Triandis, H. C. (1995). *Individualism and collectivism.* Boulder, CO: Westview.

Vahia, N. S. (1982). Yoga in psychiatry. In A. Kiev & A. V. Rao (Eds.), *Readings in transcultural psychiatry* (pp. 11–19). Madras, India: Higginbothams.

von-Furer-Haimendorf, C. (1974). The sense of sin in cross-cultural perspective. *Man, 9,* 539–556.

Ward, C. A., & Kennedy, A. (1996). Crossing cultures: The relationship between psychological and socio-cultural dimensions of cross-cultural adjustment. In J. Pandey, D. Sinha & D. P. S. Bhawuk (Eds.), *Asian contributions to cross-cultural psychology* (pp. 289–306). New Delhi, India: Sage.

Waterman, A. A. (1981). Individualism and interdependence. *American Psychologist, 36,* 762–773.

Weber, M. (1963). *The sociology of religion.* London: Allen & Unwin.

WHO Report. (1978). *The promotion and development of traditional medicine.* WHO Technical Report Series No. 622. Geneva, Switzerland: WHO.

Wig, N. N. & Saxena, S. (1982). Recent developments in psychiatric diagnosis and classification. *Continuing Medical Educational Programme, 1,* 53–62.

Yang, K. S. (1997). Theories and research in Chinese personality: An indigenous approach. In H. S. R. Kao, & D. Sinha (Eds.), *Asian perspectives on psychology* (pp. 236–264). New Delhi, India: Sage.

Zaidi, L. Y. (1994). Group treatment of adult male inpatients abused as children. *Journal of Traumatic Stress, 7,* 719–728.

Zajonc, R. B. (1980). Feeling and thinking: Preferences need no inferences. *American Psychologist, 35,* 151–175.

Zajonc, R. B. (1981). A one-factor mind about mind and emotion. *American Psychologist, 36,* 102–103.

Zajonc, R. B. (1984). On the primacy of affect. *American Psychologist, 39,* 117–123.

Zimmer, H. (1951/1989). *Philosophies of India.* Princeton, NJ: Princeton University Press.

10

Cultural Risk Factors in Personality Disorders

Joel Paris

Personality is a construct describing those behaviors, cognitions, and affects that are unique to individuals. These characteristics have multiple sources, being shaped by temperament, by social learning, and by culture (Rutter, 1987). Personality traits vary continuously within populations, and therefore can be considered dimensions that can be assessed by self-report instruments. These methods provide reasonably valid measures of traits, and researchers have used them to conduct crosscultural studies of personality (McCrae & Costa, 1997).

Personality disorders are pathological amplifications of these normal traits. DSM-IV (American Psychiatric Association, 1994) describes a personality disorder as "an enduring pattern of inner experience and behavior that deviates markedly from the expectations of the individual's culture," and goes on to stipulate that the pattern be inflexible, pervasive, stable over time, and lead to clinically significant distress and impairment. Three clusters of disorders are described, one involving unusual cognitions (schizoid, schizotypal, and paranoid disorders), one involving impulsive behavior (antisocial, borderline, narcissistic, and histrionic disorders), and one involving social anxiety (avoidant, dependent, and compulsive disorders.)

In community studies, personality disorders are found to lie on a spectrum with normal trait dimensions (Livesley, 1998). This supports the interpretation that disorders are amplified traits that have become exaggerated to a point where they seriously interfere with functioning (Paris, 1996). The underlying mechanisms determining the process of amplification are biopsychosocial (i.e., a combination of abnormal temperament, psychological adversities, and cultural influence).

PERSONALITY AND CULTURE

Paradoxically, the fact that culture plays a crucial role in personality has been most clearly demonstrated by behavioral genetic studies (Reiss, Plomin, & Hetherington, 1992; Plomin, Defries, & McClearn, 1997). This research shows that about half the variance on any trait dimension is heritable. The genetic component corresponds to the construct of temperament, individual differences in behavior, cognition, and affect that are present at birth. Temperament, personality traits, and personality disorders have a hierarchical relationship.

Of particular relevance to cultural studies is the other half of the variance in personality: the environmental component. The effects of environment are divided by behavioral genetic methods into shared and unshared components, depending on whether or not they are related to growing up in a particular family. The environmental contribution to personality traits is almost entirely unshared. This finding suggests that the most important influences on personality may not be related to parental rearing style, as has been previously believed. Instead, traits may be shaped to a large extent by the larger social environment and culture (Paris, 1996).

Bronfenbrenner (1979) was among the first to note this relationship, describing how community values create an ecological system that has a profound influence on personality structure. Behaviors and cognitions in children are influenced by the culture through several mechanisms: by peer groups (Harris, 1995, 1998), by community leaders in schools, churches, and ethnic groups (Rutter & Rutter, 1993), and by the media (Millon, 1993).

Given the strength of these social factors, one would expect personality profiles to demonstrate crosscultural differences. Research has generally supported this hypothesis (Eysenck, 1982; McCrae & Costa, 1997), although variations between individuals in any society are much larger than variations between one society and another.

Crosscultural differences in personality could also reflect biological variations at the population level (Eysenck, 1982; Kagan, 1994). Nonetheless, a vast literature supports the hypothesis that personality is shaped, at least in part, by differential social learning patterns that influence cognition (Durham, 1992). Cultures reinforce and model different patterns, reducing the frequency of some traits, and increasing the frequency of others.

Individual variations in traits ultimately represent alternative strategies for adaptation (Beck & Freeman, 1990). There are both advantages and disadvantages to temperamental characteristics that make one odd, impulsive, or anxious. The crucial issue is whether the culture is flexible enough to allow everyone to find a social niche.

For example, societies differ as to how much they tolerate impulsivity. This is reflected in consistent crosscultural differences between the behavioral problems seen in children, which are probably indicators of differential socialization processes. Those brought up in traditional structures tend to have more symptoms associated with overcontrol, while those raised in modern structures tend to have more symptoms associated with undercontrol (Weisz, Sigman, Weiss, & Mosk, 1993).

Emotional expressiveness demonstrates a similar cultural variability (Leff, 1981). Families in traditional societies tend to encourage the repression of emotion more than those in modern societies (Murphy, 1982). These differences also reflect variations in how much societies value conformity to the group, as opposed to encouraging autonomy (Berry, Poortinga, Segall, & Dasen, 1992; Lewis-Fernandez & Kleinman, 1994).

Thus traditional societies are more likely to encourage overcontrol and repression, while modern societies are relatively more tolerant of impulsivity and expressiveness. The increasing prevalence of impulsive disorders in Western countries supports this principle (Paris, 1996). These differences could exist without any major crosscultural variations in temperament and personality, since whether or not traits become dysfunctional usually depends on the social context.

The more trait profiles correspond to social expectations, the less likely they will be considered pathological. For example, odd cognitions might be less of a problem in agricultural societies. Similarly, the rapid responses to environmental challenges associated with impulsivity might be of advantage in warriors (Beck & Freeman, 1990). Kagan (1989) has suggested that anxious traits are associated with good functioning in cultures that value emotional control, and in societies that promote high levels of family and community cohesion.

CROSSCULTURAL STUDIES
OF PERSONALITY DISORDERS

To determine whether personality disorders demonstrate crosscultural variability in prevalence requires the solution of thorny methodological problems. A crossculturally valid classification system is a necessary prerequisite to study the relationship between culture and mental disorders (Fabrega, 1994). Even within Western societies, problems with the validity of personality diagnoses have impeded research. The only category to merit serious epidemiological study has been antisocial personality, with its relatively clearcut behavioral criteria (Robins & Regier, 1991).

The World Health Organization (WHO) took a first step to addressing this problem through an international study in clinical settings at sites on several continents (Loranger et al., 1994). The project developed an interview measure for diagnosis, the International Personality Disorders Examination (IPPE). All the disorders listed in the WHO system (International Classification of Diseases, World Health Organization, 1992) as well as in the American system (DSM-IV, American Psychiatric Association, 1994) could be identified at all the sites in the study (Bangalore, Geneva, Leiden, London, Luxembourg, Munich, Nairobi, New York, Nottingham, Oslo, Tokyo, Vienna).

But the WHO study only examined patients in tertiary care centers, and these individuals are not representative of community populations. We would need epidemiological studies to determine whether personality disorders can be found outside of these cosmopolitan enclaves. Given the potential expense, we may have to wait many years before this kind of research is conducted.

Yet there are several reasons to expect that the prevalence of personality disorders should show prominent crosscultural differences. First, if trait profiles are known to show significant differences between cultures, then the disorders that are amplifications of these dimensions should vary accordingly. Second, disorders that reflect discrepancies between cultural expectations and individual characteristics should be exquisitely sensitive to culture.

The best evidence for this hypothesis derives from research on antisocial personality disorder (ASPD). This condition, most frequently found in men, is defined by DSM-IV as " a pervasive pattern of disregard for and violation of the rights of others," with specific criteria describing a long-term pattern of impulsivity, criminality, irresponsibility, and lack of remorse.

Epidemiological studies have shown that ASPD is remarkably rare in some cultures. In particular, samples from urban and rural areas of Taiwan (Hwu, Yeh, & Change, 1989; Compton et al., 1991) show a very low prevalence of ASPD, ranging from 0.03 to 0.14 percent. Although no systematic studies have been carried out in mainland China, low rates may apply there (Cheung, 1991). ASPD has also been found to be rare in primary care settings in Japan (Sato & Takeichi, 1993). A low prevalence of ASPD is not, however, universal in East Asia: South Korea, where alcoholism is also frequent, has a much higher prevalence of ASPD (Lee, Kovac, & Ree, 1987). Finally, ASPD has doubled in prevalence since the Second World War in most Western countries (Robins & Regier, 1991; Kessler et al., 1994), suggesting that social change influences the development of the disorder.

Borderline personality disorder (BPD) resembles ASPD in many ways, but is much more common in women. BPD is described by DSM-IV as "a pervasive pattern of instability of interpersonal relationships, self-image, and affects" that is accompanied by marked impulsivity. Although borderline patients are more likely to hurt themselves (usually through suicide attempts) than to hurt others, this disorder might still reflect the same trait matrix as ASPD, with its overt symptoms being shaped by female gender (Paris, 1997). Indirect evidence, deriving from crosscultural differences in the prevalence of symptoms such as parasuicide, suicide, antisocial behavior, and substance abuse (Millon, 1987, 1993; Paris, 1992, 1994), suggests that BPD is more frequent in modern than in traditional societies.

There is also suggestive evidence pointing to a recent increase in the prevalence of BPD in Western cultures (Millon, 1987, 1993; Millon & Davis, 1995; Paris, 1992). This conclusion is based on increases in its characteristic symptoms, most particularly parasuicide in young women (Bland, Dyck, Newman, & Orn, 1998), a characteristic symptom of borderline personality. Moreover, BPD can be diagnosed in about a third of cases of completed suicide among young people (Lesage, Boyer, Grunberg, Morisette, & Vanier, 1994).

As cultures change, the range of trait variation can become skewed, with more individuals shifted to an extreme on a distribution. Crosscultural and cohort differences probably reflect underlying trends affecting the prevalence of impulsive personality traits. Social stressors in modern societies may have greater effects on these individuals, whose temperament would have been contained in another cultural setting. When these trait profiles become more prevalent, we can expect to see parallel increases in the prevalence of specific impulsive disorders.

SOCIAL STRUCTURES: TRADITIONAL AND MODERN

To understand the role of sociocultural factors in the personality disorders, we need a general model describing how cultures differ from each other, as well as how cultures change over time. For this purpose, social structures can be broadly dichotomized as traditional or modern (Inkeles & Smith, 1974; Lerner, 1958). Although this dichotomy describes ideal types never seen in pure form, the distinction is useful for understanding social factors in personality development.

Throughout human history, most cultures have been traditional (i.e., characterized by slow rates of social change, intergenerational continuity, family and community cohesion, and clear social roles). Modern societies, in contrast, are characterized by rapid social change, intergenerational discontinuity, decreased family and community cohesion, and unclear social roles.

Although there are important differences between societies that can be classified as traditional, they share a crucial structural factor, namely the provision of predictable expectations. Traditional societies provide a buffer against many forms of psychopathology, most specifically those associated with impulsivity. In contrast, modern societies are marked by the breakdown of stable structures, and their replacement by less stable ones. These conditions of rapid social change lead to an instability in the social fabric, increasing the risk for some forms of psychopathology, most particularly impulsive personality disorders.

One of the primary mechanisms of cultural influence on personality disorders involves the availability of social roles. Traditional societies, which provide relatively secure and predictable occupational and family roles for every individual, protect their most vulnerable members from feeling useless or socially isolated. Since traditional societies tend to encourage conformity with the expectations of family and community, their structures will promote behavioral patterns characterized by inhibition and constriction of emotion. Essentially, the structures of these societies have less tolerance for deviance, and tend to outgroup individuals whose behaviors fail to meet expectations.

By contrast, modern societies do not provide most people with readily available social roles, but expect them to find or create them on their own. Modernity therefore demands a high level of autonomy, rewarding behaviors associated with a more active and expressive personality style, while remaining relatively more tolerant of deviance.

SOCIOCULTURAL MECHANISMS ASSOCIATED WITH INCREASED RISK FOR PERSONALITY DISORDERS

Sociocultural factors can be hypothesized to influence the risk for personality disorders through two mechanisms: (1) interference with the social buffering of psychological risks, and (2) increases in social stressors as well as rapid social change.

Society and the Family

Applying a biopsychosocial model (Engel, 1980), personality disorders arise out of complex interactions between biological predispositions, psychological adversities, and social influences (Paris, 1993, 1996). The impact of social and cultural factors on personality depends in part on temperament (Paris, 1996) since, for the most part, stressors have greater effects on individuals with trait vulnerabilities that make them sensitive to their environment (Kendler & Eaves, 1986). In addition, sociocultural factors may be particularly important in individuals who have suffered psychological adversities. Disorders are particularly likely to develop when breakdown in the functioning of the community interferes with the social buffering of biological and psychological risks. Amato and Booth (1997) have described this mechanism linking psychological and social factors as mediation (i.e., the influence of social structures on family stability, and the ability of social structures to buffer family dysfunction).

The overall risk for mental disorders is elevated when family dysfunction is associated with community dysfunction (Leighton, Harding, & Macklin, 1963). Breakdown of extended family ties, absence of a sense of community, normlessness related to the loss of consensual values, difficulty in developing social roles, problems in choosing an occupation and a partner, and the fragility of social networks all constitute additional stressors for children raised in dysfunctional families. These effects will be even more potent in individuals who are temperamentally vulnerable.

At the same time, social change is making the family less of a haven. Modern families, as compared to those in traditional societies, are smaller and less stable. Nuclear families easily become overburdened because geographical and social mobility uproots them from their networks in extended family and community. Yet given the lack of alternatives, individual needs for nurturance in the family may be higher than they have ever been. The quality of marital satisfaction has gone down, largely as a result of unrealistic expectations that contribute to marital instability (Amato & Booth, 1997). When families do break down, there are fewer outside supports to buffer effects on children.

Research on resilient children (Werner & Smith, 1992) provides evidence for these mechanisms. Networks and social supports are crucial protective factors against many forms of adversity. Most of the psychological risk factors for personality disorders are associated with family dysfunction, but children exposed to defective parenting need not develop psychopathology if they can find alternative attachments, either through extended family or community (Garmezy & Masten, 1994).

Crosscultural research on antisocial personality sheds light on the interface between social and family structures. As noted above, ASPD is unusually rare in Taiwan, a society noted for high levels of family and social cohesion. In fact, the Confucian family, with its emphasis on rules and structures, is a virtual mirror image of the risk factors for ASPD.

A parallel model can be applied to BPD. Linehan (1993) hypothesizes that this disorder involves an interface between a constitutionally determined emotional instability and an invalidating environment. Essentially, patients who develop borderline personality require higher levels of emotional buffering and support. The modern world, which demands greater individual autonomy, and which allows less dependence on or attachment to others, interferes with the ability of children with these needs to obtain the level of care they require.

We might apply a similar model to anxious cluster personality disorders (Paris, 1998). Anxious temperament is more common in Asian populations (Kagan, 1994). In Japanese society (Iwawaki, Eysenck, & Eysenck, 1977), these variations are associated with a higher prevalence for social phobia (Kirmayer, 1991), a condition that greatly resembles avoidant personality disorder. Overprotective parenting is an additional risk factor, since it interferes with the deconditioning of anxious temperament (Kagan, 1994). We do not know whether anxious cluster personality disorders are more common in Japan or the West. However, the effects of overprotection should be greater in societies where children are raised in nuclear rather than extended families, and where they can spend longer periods at home with their families, with proportionally less time involved in peer groups and community activities.

Social Disintegration and Social Change

Social stressors have a direct effect on the risk for mental disorders. The mechanisms need not necessarily involve effects on family functioning, but could be mediated through breakdown in the social fabric. This can be demonstrated by changes in the form taken by psychological distress over time. Social forces can have remarkable effects on symptomatology (Al-Issa, 1982). For example, clinicians in the West in recent decades (e.g., Kohut, 1970) have reported seeing fewer neurotic symptoms, and more personality pathology. We can observe parallel changes as traditional societies become modernized. In a follow-up study of a village clinic in India in the 1960s and 1980s, Nandi et al. (1992) found that whereas conversion symptoms among female patients had previously been very common, these phenomena became much less frequent, replaced by a higher prevalence of suicide attempts.

Leighton et al. (1963) introduced the construct of social disintegration to describe the cumulative impact of stressors on the social fabric. Levels of social integration help explain differences in the prevalence of psychopathology in different communities. Its opposite, social disintegration, is similar to the classical construct of anomie (Durkheim, 1951) associated with suicide rates.

The association between social disintegration and psychopathology is particularly striking in societies that have undergone rapid social change. Cohort effects in the frequency of impulsive personality disorders may be one example, and youth suicide is another. Suicide occurs in all cultures, but is less common in traditional societies, particularly among the young (Murphy, 1982). A study of the high suicide rates found in Canadian Inuit populations, and concentrated in young males, concluded that the causes lay with the breakdown of a traditional way of life (Kirmayer, 1994). Similar findings have been reported all over the world (Jilek-Aall, 1988), suggesting that as traditional societies break down, they undergo an epidemic of pathology associated with impulsivity and affective instability.

The fact that both suicide and crime among young people has increased during the period of unprecedented prosperity since the Second World War also reflects a breakdown in the social fabric (Rutter & Rutter, 1993). In the last hundred years, Western societies have experienced accelerating rates of social change, resulting in the breakdown of many norms. The most unique aspect of modernity is the continuous acceleration of these changes. In recent decades, these effects have irreversibly changed traditional societies all over the globe.

All societies have had their own share of social and family pathology (DeMause, 1974). There are many social tensions in traditional cultures (Freeman, 1983; Edgerton, 1992), as well as within traditional subcultures in developed societies (Srole & Fischer, 1980). We should not, therefore, idealize tradition. However, the problem with rapid social change is that it replaces predictable expectations with choices. When the norms for role performance that were valid for an older generation are no longer useful, young people face the stressful task of forging a personal identity without useful models. Contemporary social demands therefore act as a selection pressure. Modernity benefits those who can achieve autonomy, and hurts those with stronger needs for affiliation.

In traditional societies, the family and the community, not the individual, would have been responsible for choices of work, partners, and community affiliations, leading to greater intergenerational continuity. In modern societies, identity formation demands a high level of individuation and autonomy. Young adults must adapt to a number of new challenges, including an increased life span, a decrease in family size, changes in family structure, new conditions of work, and ideological confusion (Westen, 1985). Young people need more, not less, social support to achieve these difficult tasks.

RESEARCH IMPLICATIONS

The hypotheses developed in this paper can be tested. They would lead to the following predictions:

1. To the extent that sociocultural factors are important in shaping personality disorders, they should be reflected in major differences in crosscultural prevalence.
2. To the extent that modern societies increase the risk for personality disorders, most particularly those in the impulsive group, we should observe cohort increases in prevalence in many societies undergoing rapid change.
3. There should be large differential prevalences for personality disorders between cultural subpopulations within the same society.
4. Personality disorders are not purely a cultural phenomenon, but should be most frequent among those exposed to multiple and interacting risk factors, including temperamental vulnerabilities and psychological adversities.

REFERENCES

Al-Issa, I. (1982). Sex differences in psychopathology. In I. Al-Issa (Ed.), *Culture and psychopathology* (pp. 3–32). Baltimore: University Park Press.

Amato, P., & Booth, A. (1997). *A generation at risk.* Cambridge, MA: Harvard University Press.

American Psychiatric Association (1994). *Diagnostic and statistical manual of mental disorders* (4th ed.). Washington, DC: American Psychiatric Association.

Beck, A. T., & Freeman, A. (1990). Cognitive therapy of personality disorders. New York, Guilford Press.

Berry, J. W., Poortinga, Y. H., Segall, M. H., Dasen, P. R. (1992). Cross-cultural psychology: Research and applications. Cambridge, MA: Cambridge University Press.

Bland, R. C., Dyck, R. J., Newman, S. C., & Orn, H. (1998). Attempted suicide in Edmonton. In A. A. Leenaars, S. Wenckstern, I. Sakinofsky, R. Dyck, M. J. Kral, & R. C. Bland (Eds.), *Suicide in Canada* (pp. 136–150). Toronto, Canada: University of Toronto Press.

Bronfenbrenner, U. (1979). *The ecology of human development.* Cambridge, MA: Harvard University Press.

Cheung, P. (1991). Adult psychiatric epidemiology in China in the 1980s. *Culture, Medicine, Psychiatry, 15,* 479–496.

Compton, W. W., Helzer, J. E., Hwu, H.-G., Yeh, E.-K., McEvoy, L., Tipp, J. E., & Spitznagel, E. L. (1991). New methods in cross-cultural psychiatry: Psychiatric illness in Taiwan and the United States. *American Journal of Psychiatry, 148,* 1697–1704.

DeMause, L. (Ed.). (1974). *The history of childhood.* New York: Psychohistory Press.

Durham, W. H. (1992). *Co-evolution: Genes, culture, and human diversity.* Stanford, CA: Stanford University Press.

Durkheim, E. (1951). *On suicide.* New York: Free Press.

Edgerton, R. B. (1992). *Sick societies: Challenging the myth of primitive harmony.* New York: Free Press.

Engel, G. L. (1980). The clinical application of the biopsychosocial model. *American Journal of Psychiatry, 137,* 535–544.

Eysenck, H. J. (1982). Culture and personality abnormalities. In I. Al-Issa (Ed.), *Culture and psychopathology* (pp. 277–308). Baltimore: University Park Press.

Fabrega, H. (1994). Personality disorders as medical entities: A cultural interpretation. *Journal of Personality Disorders, 8,* 149–165.

Freeman, D. (1983). *Margaret Mead and Samoa.* Cambridge, MA: Harvard University Press.

Garmezy, N., & Masten, A. S. (1994). Chronic adversities. In M. Rutter & L. Hersov (Eds.), *Child and adolescent psychiatry: Modern approaches* (3rd ed.) (pp. 191–208). London: Blackwell.

Harris, J. R. (1995). Where is the child's environment? A group socialization theory of development. *Psychological Review, 102,* 458–489.

Harris, J. R. (1998). *The nurture assumption.* New York: Free Press.

Hwu H. G., Yeh, E. K., & Change, L. Y. (1989). Prevalence of psychiatric disorders in Taiwan defined by the Chinese diagnostic interview schedule. *Acta Psychiatria Scandinavia, 79,* 136–147.

Inkeles, A., & Smith, D. H. (1974). *Becoming modern: Individual change in six developing countries.* Cambridge, MA: Harvard University Press.

Iwawaki, S., Eysenck, S. B. G., & Eysenck, H. J. (1977). Differences in personality between Japanese and English. *Journal of Social Psychology, 102,* 27–33.

Jilek-Aall, L. (1988). Suicidal behavior among youth: A cross-cultural comparison. *Transcultural Psychiatric Research Review, 25,* 87–105.

Kagan, J. (1989). *Unstable ideas: Temperament, cognition and self.* Cambridge, MA: Harvard University Press.

Kagan, J. (1994). *Galen's prophecy.* New York, Basic Books.

Kendler, K. S., & Eaves, L. J. (1986). Models for the joint effect of genotype and environment on liability to psychiatric illness. *American Journal of Psychiatry, 143,* 279–289.

Kessler, R. C., McGonagle, K. A., Nelson, C. B., Hughes, M., Eshelman, S., Wittchen, H. U., & Kendler, K. S. (1994). Lifetime and 12-month prevalence of DSM-III-R psychiatric disorders in the United States. *Archives of General Psychiatry, 51,* 8–19.

Kirmayer, L. (1991). The place of culture in psychiatric nosology: Taijin kyofusho and DSM-III-R. *Journal of Nervous and Mental Disorders, 179,* 19–28.

Kirmayer, L. (1994). Suicide among Canadian aboriginal peoples. *Transcultural Psychiatric Research Review, 31,* 3–58.

Kohut, H. (1970). *The analysis of the self.* New York: International Universities Press.

Lee, K. C., Kovac, Y. S., & Rhee, H. (1987). The national epidemiological study of mental disorders in Korea. *Journal of Korean Medical Science, 2,* 19–34.

Leff, J. P. (1981). *Psychiatry around the globe.* New York: Dekker.

Leighton D. C., Harding J. S., & Macklin D. B. (1963). *The character of danger: Psychiatric symptoms in selected communities.* New York: Basic Books.

Lerner, D. (1958). *The passing of traditional society.* New York: Free Press.

Lesage A. D., Boyer, R., Grunberg, F., Morisette, R., & Vanier, C. (1994). Suicide and mental disorders: A case control study of young males. *American Journal of Psychiatry, 151,* 1063–1068.

Lewis-Fernandez, R., & Kleinman, A. (1994). Culture, personality, and psychopathology. *Journal of Abnormal Psychology, 103,* 67–71.

Linehan, M. M. (1993). *Cognitive behavioral treatment of borderline personality disorder.* New York: Guilford.

Livesley, J. (1998). Suggestions for a framework for an empirically based classification of personality disorder. *Canadian Journal of Psychiatry, 43,* 137–147.

Loranger, A. W., Sartori, N., Andreoli, A., Berger, P., Bucheim, P., Channabasavanna, S. M., Coid, B., Dahl, A., Diekstra, R. F. W., Ferguson, B., Jacobsberg, L. B., Mombour, W., Pull, C., Ono, Y., & Regier, D. A. (1994). The international personality disorder examination. *Archives of General Psychiatry, 51,* 215–224.

McCrae, R. R., & Costa, P. T. (1997). Personality trait structure as a human universal. *American Psychologist, 52,* 509–516.

Millon, T. (1987). On the genesis and prevalence of borderline personality disorder: A social learning thesis. *Journal of Personality Disorders, 1,* 354–372.

Millon, T. (1993). Borderline personality disorder: A psychosocial epidemic. In J. Paris (Ed.), *Borderline personality disorder: Etiology and treatment* (pp. 197–210). Washington, DC: American Psychiatric Press.

Millon, T., & Davis, R. (1995). *Personality disorders: DSM-IV and beyond.* New York: Wiley.

Murphy, H. B. M. (1982). *Comparative psychiatry.* New York: Springer.

Nandi, D. N., Bznerjee, G., Nandi, S., & Nandi, P. (1992). Is hysteria on the wane? *British Journal of Psychiatry, 160,* 87–91.

Paris, J. (1992). Social factors in borderline personality disorder: A review and a hypothesis. *Canadian Journal of Psychiatry, 37,* 480–486.

Paris, J. (1993). Personality disorders: a biopsychosocial model. *Journal of Personality Disorders, 7,* 255–264.

Paris, J. (1994). *Borderline personality disorder: A multidimensional approach.* Washington, DC: American Psychiatric Press.

Paris, J. (1996). *Social factors in the personality disorders.* New York: Cambridge University Press.

Paris, J. (1997). Antisocial and borderline personality disorders: Two separate diagnoses or two aspects of the same psychopathology? *Comprehensive Psychiatry, 38,* 237–242.

Paris, J. (1998). Anxious traits, anxiety disorders, and anxious cluster personality disorders. *Harvard Review of Psychiatry, 6,* 142–148.

Plomin R., DeFries J. C., & McClearn G. E. (1997). *Behavioral genetics: A primer* (3rd ed.). New York: W. H. Freeman.

Reiss, D., Plomin, R., & Hetherington, E. M. (1992). Genetics and psychiatry: An unheralded window on the environment. *American Journal of Psychiatry, 149,* 147–155.

Robins, L. N., & Regier, D. A. (Eds.). (1991). *Psychiatric disorders in America.* New York: Free Press.

Rutter, M. (1987) Temperament, personality, and personality development. *British Journal of Psychiatry, 150,* 443–448.

Rutter, M., & Rutter, M. (1993). *Developing minds: Challenge and continuity across the life span.* New York: Basic Books.

Sato, T., & Takeichi, M. (1993). Lifetime prevalence of specific psychiatric disorders in a general medicine clinic. *General Hospital Psychiatry, 15,* 224–233.

Srole, L., & Fischer, A. K. (1980). The midtown Manhattan longitudinal study vs. "the mental paradise lost doctrine." *Archives of General Psychiatry, 37,* 209–218.

Weisz, J. R., Sigman, M., Weiss, B., & Mosk, J. (1993). Parent reports of behavioral and emotional problems among children in Kenya, Thailand, and the United States. *Child Development, 64,* 98–109.

Werner, E., E., & Smith, R. S. (1992). *Overcoming the odds: High risk children from birth to adulthood.* New York: Cornell University Press.

Westen, D. (1985). *Self and society: Narcissism, collectivism and the development of morals.* New York: Cambridge University Press.

11

Culture, Cognition, and Dissociative Identity Disorder

Martin J. Dorahy

Schumaker (1995) has suggested that one of the cognitive byproducts of being human is our spontaneous, involuntary ability to regulate sensory information. This cognitive ability allows the manipulation of psychosensory stimuli so as to fit personal and cultural schemas. Schumaker argues that our view or perception of the world, or what he terms personal reality, is not an exact representation of the empirical world we live in. Rather, we add representations, interpretations, clarifications, and explanations to the sensory stimuli we obtain. A primary influence on shaping our mental view of the world is culture.

Marsella and Kameoka (1989) suggest that culture is psychologically represented as collective beliefs, values, attitudes, and thinking styles. These culturally derived and fostered schemas may be understood as cultural cognitions. From birth, culture is a continual provider of messages and suggestions that shape our view of the world. Through shared cognitive schemas, culture also provides a template for emotional expression and behavior, both at individual and group levels. The critical role of culture in constructing and influencing cognitions and behaviors does not stop at healthy, adaptive functioning but also is evident in psychopathology.

The influence of culture on dissociative disorders is exposed most fully in crosscultural differences in the shape, form, and distinctiveness of dissociative identity disorder (DID) alters. For example, Castillo (1997) notes that, in line with their cultural beliefs, people in traditional cultures usually manifest nonhuman, supernatural alters, such as gods and ghosts. Alexander (1956) presents an Indian case study where the alter personalities were believed by the patient and her family to be incarnations of a deceased aunt and neighbor. He notes that similar cases will exist in any culture that propagates beliefs of spirit possession. In contrast, DID alters in secular-oriented Western cultures typically take the form of human entities (Castillo, 1997). However, Putnam (1989) has suggested that religious alters, such as angels or demons, are particularly common in people raised in strict religious settings. These examples highlight the impact of culture on the perceived nature and identity of alters in DID.

Given the relationship between culture and DID, this chapter has two distinct goals. First, it explores the connection between DID and culture, arguing that their relationship is intrinsic, not tenuous. The focus is directed away from an exclusive analysis of the current controversy surrounding the existence of DID. However, by the very nature of the debate it is unavoidable in a chapter on culture, cognition, and DID to ignore completely these issues. The second goal is to highlight and briefly explore some of the cultural factors that may impact on the development of DID. Ross (1995) has suggested that the human mind is ripe for dissociative experiences but that cultural mores largely shape their nature and expression. While others have remarked on this issue (e.g., Castillo, 1997; Golub, 1995), the focus here is on cultural factors in the formation, rather than expression, of DID.

CULTURE, COGNITION, AND DID

DID is a disorder of fragmented information processing and maladaptive psychological coping. It falls under the dissociative disorders category of DSM-IV and the neurotic, stress-related, and somatoform disorders category of ICD-10. DID is characterized by the existence of two or more subjectively experienced ego states that take recurrent control of the individual's behavior (Kluft, 1993). Also evident are marked anomalies of memory that manifest as amnesia for significant autobiographical events (American Psychiatric Association, 1994; World Health Organization, 1994).

Like all other mental pathologies, DID is formed through, and characterized by, a complex mix of cultural, psychological, and biological factors (Kirmayer, 1994). Increasing numbers of scholars are highlighting cultural influences in the understanding of psychopathology. They are noting that psychiatric categories are not inherent, universal human expressions. Rather, they are a complicated mixture of individual and cultural determinants (e.g., Brody, 1994). Kleinman (1988) has been instrumental in reminding us that psychopathology is not a *thing* but a *process*. The categories we give to these individual processes (e.g., Schizophrenia, PTSD, DID) are not intrinsic givens and are always influenced by culture (Martinéz-Taboas, 1995). Moreover, they are usually pathological expressions of underlying human mental mechanisms or capacities. Just as delusions are pathological extensions of the innate human ability to manipulate or distort reality,

DID is a pathological expression of the innate human ability to dissociate. Even though the nature and influence of this innate ability in the development of DID is still under scrutiny (Jang, Paris, Zweig-Frank, & Livesley, 1998; Waller & Ross, 1997), psychiatric categories are culturally derived labels that attempt to define and explain maladaptive expressions of underlying human mental processes.

DeVries (1996) suggests that Western psychiatry has mistakenly focused on decontextualizing mental illness. He argues instead that our attention should be drawn away from "overly concrete definitions of psychological illness as a thing in itself, bringing us back to the person's experience and the meaning which he or she assigns to it" (DeVries, 1996, p. 399). Like other psychiatric conditions, DID requires us to acknowledge biological and psychological factors enmeshed within the context and confines of the overarching framework of culture. Consequently, pathological expressions of dissociation will not always manifest as the same set of symptoms across cultures, even if their underlying mental structure is similar. Additionally, when the experiences (e.g., symptoms) are similar they will be interpreted in ways consistent with cultural beliefs, values, and norms (Golub, 1995). Marsella, Friedman, and Spain (1994) suggest that there is most likely a universal neurobiological response to trauma, but cultural differences exist in the manifestation (and explanation) of this response.

Due to the influence of culture, the expression of underlying dissociative pathology will never display a discrete set of universal signs and symptoms directly comparable across all cultures. Yet across many cultures, DID has proved a relatively stable psychiatric condition. Cases have been widespread and include reports from Australia, India, New Zealand, North and South America, Turkey, Israel, Switzerland, Japan, the Netherlands, France, Belgium, Germany, Scandinavia, Scotland, and England. Moreover, the symptom profile across these cultures is remarkably similar (Coons, Bowman, Kluft, & Milstein, 1991). This suggests that the biological, psychological, interpersonal, and cultural conditions favor this pathological manifestation of dissociation in many countries and cultures.

Differing cultural cognitions and mores ensure that cultures have different views of self, which influence phenomenological experience as well as symptom expression (Marsella et al., 1994). As Golub (1995), among others, has suggested, DID development is reliant on specific cultural cognitions and conditions. For example, she argues that DID is likely to be evident in cultures that tolerate the maltreatment of children and devalue interdependency by propagating the group cognition of individualism. Cultures not characterized by these features are less likely to report cases of DID, even though other forms of pathological dissociation may be apparent. In discussing the relationship between culture and DID in the West, Martinez-Taboas (1995) states:

It is possible that our own idiosyncracies, our construction of self, cultural stressors, and the prevailing set of cultural experience and expectations favor the use of this type of dissociative mechanism [DID] in some individuals. Similarly, in other places with cultural and religious idiosyncracies different from ours, the dissociative mechanisms may express themselves in ways that seem to conflict with our prevailing world-view, as trance and possession states rather than as multiple personality (p. 176).

Indeed, many traditional cultures interpret as spirit possession signs and symptoms consistent with dissociative pathology and DID. It is unlikely that every case of spirit possession is directly analogous to DID (see Cardeña, 1992; Varma, Bouri, & Wig, 1981). Yet the expression of spirit possession is consonant with cultural schemas and preestablished indigenous modes of behavior. The so-called alter personality, or new identity, typically present as a ghost, god, or other supernatural entity is enmeshed within cultural cognitions (Castillo, 1997; Suryani & Jensen, 1993). Moreover, Castillo (1997) suggests that if the imposing entity is perceived as a benevolent force, such as a cherished god or goddess, it will be interpreted in a positive light and treatment will not be sought. However, if a malevolent force is believed to be the source of possession, vigorous treatment will ensue. Not surprisingly, treatment methods will also follow cultural norms and explanatory idioms. Dissociative pathology is treated in the West via psychotherapy, whereas spirit possession is treated in traditional cultures via exorcism or other purging rituals.

In previous centuries the use of exorcism in Western culture to cure individuals of their alterations in identity reflected cultural cognitions at the time (Wright, 1997). The cultural dominance of religious explanations and healing methods has since been superseded by secular perspectives more aligned with the positivist views currently favored in Western culture (Ellenberger, 1970). As the religious framework brought with it explanation and treatment strategies, so modern psychiatry has its own explanations and interventions.

DeVries (1996) states that healers in traditional societies never detach the body from the mind and the mind from the cultural context. Much is to be learned from this simple axiom. For example, arguments against the existence of DID are in danger of detaching culture from the analysis. By stating that DID cannot exist in Western culture, adherents of this view appear to detach the core symptom profile, and the diagnostic category it is given in Western psychiatry (i.e., DID), from cultural influences and the impact these have on individual and social affect, cognition, and behavior. Suggesting that DID *cannot* exist immediately implies that this psychopathology is perceived as an intrinsic category or "thing" rather than as a "process" or psychiatric categorization enmeshed and influenced by cultural and individual factors (see Kleinman, 1988). The ultimate existence of this diagnosis, or any other psychiatric diagnosis, is not analogous to that of a physical injury, such as a broken arm. No matter how universally experienced and accepted a mental illness may be, psychiatric categories exist within the larger framework of cultural values, idioms, and beliefs. To suggest that DID cannot exist is to detach the mental phenomenology from the cultural context, thus subjecting the potential existence of this form of pathological dissociation to a culturally insensitive analysis of psychopathology.

CULTURAL DETERMINANTS OF DID DEVELOPMENT

As outlined above, culture is inherently connected to all psychopathology, including DID. Marsella et al. (1994) suggest that cultural factors are intertwined with all aspects of mental illness, from etiology through to treatment. In the case of DID, etiological factors have typically had an intrapersonal, psychological focus. Kluft (1993) offers a four-factor model for the development of DID. He suggests that a child must have the innate psychological capacity to dissociate (factor 1) and must experience sufficiently traumatic stimuli to evoke dissociative defenses (factor 2). Moreover, the individual's psychological architecture, as well as the cultural mores within which he or she lives, must favor DID development. These factors will also shape the expression of DID (factor 3). Finally, social support and other inlets for soothing and psychological rejuvenation must be absent (factor 4).

This section will use factors 1, 2, and 4 of Kluft's (1993) model to briefly identify and outline some of the cultural and cognitive factors that may also contribute to DID development. In doing so, this analysis will highlight much of Kluft's (1993) third factor by identifying some of the cultural aspects that may favor DID development. However, it should be remembered that cultural determinants in no way solely account for the development of dissociative disorders. Rather, an intricate interaction of individual and cultural factors are at work. As Kleinman (1988) eloquently warns, mental illness is a complex interplay of biological, psychological, and cultural sources of vulnerability.

Capacity to Dissociate

Kluft's (1993) first factor in DID etiology is the mental capacity to dissociate. Individuals who are psychologically accustomed to using dissociation as a dominant coping strategy for everyday stress are believed to be susceptible to dissociative disorders if exposed to other necessary conditions (Irwin, 1998; Spiegel, 1986). Culture may have a role in fashioning an individual's proneness to dissociate. Martinéz-Taboas (1995) has suggested that the "dissociative potential of some people is mediated by expectations and cultural beliefs" (p. 175). He goes on to say that culturally derived cognitions lead to greater levels of stress, particularly in Western culture, and that these stressors initiate dissociative process. In outlining these culturo-cognitive stressors, Martinéz-Taboas states:

It is possible that our culture—with its strong taboos against incest and sex at an early age, with the alarming increase in physical and sexual abuse, and with our ideological acceptance of the existence of an unconscious life and the notion that the "self" must be unique, autonomous and individual—tacitly exposes the person to a series of stressors and beliefs that do not occur, or occur less often in other cultural environments (p.175).

Okano (1997) makes a similar point when suggesting that sociocultural cognitions, in the form of beliefs, values, and norms, impact on an individual's level of dissociation. He notes that traumatic stress created by cultural mores underlies much of the dissociative pathology in Japan. For example, in Japanese culture individual emotional expression is often suppressed in favor of group harmony. According to Okano this characteristic often leads to what he calls "relationship stress," or a welling of inexpressible affects in day-to-day relationships (e.g., employer-employee, husband-wife). Pathological dissociative conditions, such as fugue and amnesia, appear to be a common means of dealing with this culturally induced stressor (Okano, 1997). Hence cultural dynamics may inadvertently influence an individual's ability to dissociate.

Trauma: Actual and Perceived

In support of Kluft's (1993) second factor, there is now a burgeoning empirical literature that documents the precipitating effect of childhood overwhelming experience in the development of DID (e.g., Coons, 1994; Lewis, Yeagar, Swica, Pincus, & Lewis, 1997; Swica, Lewis, & Lewis, 1996). While some have focused primarily on child abuse and neglect (e.g., Wilbur, 1984), which may differ across cultures (Coons et al., 1991), traumatic antecedents of DID development are in no way limited to intrafamilial and extrafamilial child maltreatment. Other childhood events reported by DID patients are prolonged periods of isolation, confinement, witnessing a violent death, especially of a family member, accidents, prolonged physical pain through illness or injury, and exposure to war (Kluft, 1984; Putnam, Guroff, Silberman, Barban, & Post, 1986; Wilbur, 1985). Childhood exposure to traumatic events is not culture bound, nor is the relationship between childhood trauma and DID. Research from Australia (e.g., Middleton & Butler, 1998), Turkey (e.g., Sar, Yargic, & Tutkan, 1996), the Netherlands (e.g., Boon & Draijer, 1993), and Puerto Rico (e.g., Martinéz-Taboas, 1995), among many other countries, has underscored the existence of severe aversive childhood experience in DID patients.

However, little work on the genesis of DID has gone beyond interpersonal stressors. The role of traumatic experience emanating from cultural, ethnocultural, and social conditions on DID development is still to be explored. These may include the impact of growing up in a society or culture punctuated by incessant gang-warfare, terrorism, political violence, famine, natural disasters, and war. Marsella et al. (1994) have recently alluded to the notion of trauma cultures, or cultures that expose members to high levels of socially sanctioned trauma. While these cultures may have historic ties to continued conflict, the spread of intracultural and intercultural conflict can quickly transform a passive cultural fabric into one of violence and aggression. This severs the once serene environment of previous generations and brings children face-to-face with otherwise unknown traumas.

Another variable that at a cultural level may impact on the development of DID is the perception of specific events as traumatic. Perception plays a primary part in determining the traumatic nature of an event (Dorahy, Lewis, Millar, &

Gee, 1999; Laungani, chapter 9, this volume; van der Kolk, van der Hart, & Marmar, 1996) and cultural cognitions influence perceptions. Carlson (1997) suggests that an event is traumatic when it is perceived as sudden, severely aversive, and beyond control. Culturally derived cognitions impact on all three perceptions to the point that ethnocultural differences are evident in perceived traumatic events (Laungani, chapter 9, this volume; Okano, 1997). An anecdotal source may be most useful in illustrating cultural difference in perceiving emotive events as traumatic. Until recently, street rioting had become a common ethnocultural expression of social and political dissatisfaction in some parts of Northern Ireland. It was not unusual to see young children actively involved in this violence. The children's perception of this event, while no doubt emotionally arousing, was nevertheless strikingly different to that of a child tourist mistakenly caught up in one of these skirmishes. The local child was not overcome with the terror that characterized the tourist's experience. Thus while the event remains constant, each child's perception determines the emotional valance of the experience and, as the example suggests, cultural and ethnocultural influences may impact on this perception.

Social Support and Cultural Attachment

Ethnocultural and cultural perceptions of traumatic events can inoculate children against the development of trauma-induced psychiatric conditions like DID. Yet these perceptions may also make children vulnerable to the development of DID. In discussing the ethnocultural aspects of PTSD, Marsella et al. (1994) suggest that an individual's vulnerability to PTSD is largely determined by ethnocultural factors. The same argument could be made for DID. Culturally derived cognitions provide a platform for reinterpreting ongoing ethnoculturally sanctioned hostilities, so the trauma-ladenedness of these aversive events is reduced. Cultural cognitions therefore offer a culturally prescribed inoculation against exposure to these sanctioned events. For example, in Northern Ireland Wilson and Cairns (1996) suggest that a number of socially mediated cognitive strategies operate to reduce the overwhelming psychological effects of political violence. These include making light of violence, distorting the reality of violence, and ignoring its existence.

However, in terms of the possibility of dissociative disorder development, culturally derived perceptions of trauma also have the potential to downplay or minimize individual support following events that a child perceives as traumatic. This characteristic provides the cultural context for Kluft's (1993) fourth factor in the etiology of DID. DeVries (1996) states that "culture plays a key role in how individuals cope with potentially traumatizing experiences by providing the context in which social support and other positive and uplifting events can be experienced" (p. 400). Yet in cultures where highly emotive events are normalized, children often may be inadvertently overlooked by the cultures' "inoculating fabric." Social support is a well-known means of stemming the development of long-term effects in the aftermath of trauma (Carlson, 1997; Irwin, 1996; McFarlane & Van der Kolk, 1996). Yet if ethnocultural mores play down the reality or effects of a child's perceived experience, support may not be forthcoming. In this case the child's cognitions are at odds with cultural cognitions and the latent effect can be damaging for both the individual and the culture.

Consequential to the issue of emotional support, cultural attachment is a further cultural determinant of dissociative disorders that relates to Kluft's (1993) fourth factor. Cultural attachment can be thought of as the extent to which an individual bonds to, relies on, and identifies with social and cultural supports, knowledge, values, and norms (deVries, 1996). Thus cultural attachment is partly reliant on the extent to which an individual is socialized. In recent years increased attention has been given to the nature of child-caregiver attachment in people with dissociative disorders (e.g., Barach, 1991; Liotti, 1992). Similar principles may also be evident at a cultural level. The quality of, and reliance on, cultural attachment is likely to be one mediating factor between childhood trauma and the development of dissociative psychopathology. While the complexities and nomenclature are undeveloped and not comparable with our understanding of infant-caregiver attachment, attachment to culture warrants attention due to the impact of culture on psychopathology.

The aspects of cultural attachment that may provide inoculating influences will not have the same opportunity to supply their nullifying effects if the traumatic experience remains an intrapersonal experience hidden from the cultural psyche. This is often the case in instances of child abuse. Moreover, childhood traumatic experiences, such as betrayal trauma (Freyd, 1996), which remain hidden from social and cultural life, are likely to have adverse effects on the child's attachment to their culture. Fear, mistrust, and anger are likely to impede the growth of cultural attachment, inhibiting valuable communal support and nurturance that buffer against the effects of trauma. In this situation the traumatized individuals are isolated and must fall back on their own cognizing to attribute meaning and understanding. Not surprisingly, the opposite tends to occur when society is under threat or the traumatized are known. Here attachment relations typically increase and individuals are privy to the resultant inoculating effects (McFarlane & Van der Kolk, 1996).

Detachment from culture and its emotional consequences are magnified when the traumatized are displaced from their ethnocultural setting (Marsella et al., 1994). Refugee children, child immigrants, and young displaced victims of war and other atrocities not only have to deal cognitively with their own interpersonal traumas, but they lack the emotional support that comes with acculturation and cultural attachment. It is at this point that the inoculating effects of culture are most conspicuous by their absence. Kluft (1993) has noted that cultural dislocation may precipitate dissociative defenses which, in the presence of other conditions, could ultimately lead to DID formation.

The importance of social support and cultural attachment in buffering against DID development is compounded in Western culture by the erosion of family stability. Paris (chapter 10, this volume) has noted that modern families are smaller and less stable units than those in traditional cultural settings. In this context the opportunities for support and nurturence are greatly reduced in comparison to families from traditional societies. Additionally, extended family ties are less evident. These characteristics of the modern family are likely to affect the genesis of DID, as they do other disorders (see Paris, chapter 10, this volume). Tillman, Nash, and Lerner (1994) point out that family dynamics are an often ignored, but highly important, component in the development of pathological dissociation. Abusive families may already lack the characteristics needed to protect against dissociative disorder development. Yet children exposed to nonabusive trauma may also have less access to exogenous buffers due to the nature of modern family dynamics. Thus in Western culture changes in the family dynamic heighten the importance of social support and cultural attachment. These mechanisms cushion the effects of traumatic experience and reduce pathological dissociative coping and DID development.

In sum, the cultural fabric may be a determinant of the degree of perceived or actual trauma to which an individual is exposed. Through shared cognitions culture may influence an individual's proneness to dissociativity. Cultural cognitions also play a part in what events are interpreted as traumatic and what are not. Individuals exposed to culturally identified trauma will benefit from the protection and support that characterize the cultural fabric. Thus if cultural mores decree an event to be traumatic, social support will be forthcoming. This inlet for posttraumatic emotional sustenance may be even more important in light of changes in family dynamics in Western cultures. Yet if a childhood experience is not decreed traumatic, culture will not bear witness to the emotional pain of the child and its inoculating effects will be greatly reduced. The same outcome is evident if the trauma remains hidden from culture, as in many cases of child abuse. The degree of cultural inoculation is partly dependent on the quality of attachment that individuals have to the cultural beliefs and norms around them. People such as refugees, living in cultures that do not share their ethnocultural cognitions and who fail to adopt their new cultures' cognitions, risk abandonment. In this case, the posttraumatic soothing functions of culture will not be evident.

CULTURE, DID, AND THE SOCIOCOGNITIVE MODEL

As culture is inherently related to DID, a final consideration must be given to the sociocognitive perspective that suggests that dissociative behavior is wholly culturally constructed. Due to cultural influence and the role of cultural cognitions and suggestions on behavior, the sociocognitive theory has something to offer a complete understanding of DID. The sociocognitive view of DID states that the disorder is a socially fashioned and validated role-play (Spanos, 1996). The condition rarely exists in and of itself, being primarily a complex artifact of social learning and shaping (Lilienfeld et al., 1999). While it is unlikely that the sociocognitive model can offer a universal account of DID, there seems little doubt that cultural and social factors can influence behavior, including those manifest as psychopathology. The behavior of DID patients may be influenced in part by media fascination with the condition, academic and clinical publications, and phenomenological accounts from those diagnosed with this disorder.

In providing a descriptive model to account for the diversity of dissociative experience, Krippner (1997) cautions against a purely sociocognitive explanation for dissociative behaviors, including DID. However, he concedes that "most complex social activity is role-driven to some extent" (Krippner, 1997, p. 16), and psychopathology is no exception. Similarly, Ross (1997) has suggested that all psychopathology is influenced to some degree by sociocognitive forces. Yet while the sociocognitive model adds to the understanding of cultural influence on DID, it operates most effectively when incorporated with traumagenic accounts (e.g., Kluft, 1993). This is because the role-play or sociocognitive model struggles to account for objective evidence supporting the disorder's existence, such as physiological and neurological variations across alter states (e.g., Miller, 1989, Putnam, Zahn, & Post, 1990; Tsai, Condie, Wu, & Chang, 1999). In addition, the model does not provide a telling explanation for nonvolitional human responses to prolonged childhood traumatic stress and posttraumatic coping. But it does purport to account for the behavioral expressions manifest by DID patients (e.g., Spanos & Burgess, 1994). Thus the sociocognitive account overestimates cultural influence, especially on the development of DID. Moreover, the sociocognitive view gives little credit to pathological manifestations of the innate human ability to dissociate. Therefore it is argued that the sociocognitive and traumagenic accounts are not mutually exclusive models of DID. Rather, a complete understanding of DID may be best served by a combination of both frameworks.

CONCLUSION

Given that psychopathology cannot be understood outside culture, culture is a necessary condition for understanding DID. Moreover, cultural influences, through such things as shared cognitions, influence the development and expression of DID. In lieu of adequate intrapersonal resources and interpersonal support, culture interplays with psychological and biological processes in DID nosology. Yet cultural, psychological, and biological factors also play their part in predisposing a child to DID development. Marsella et al. (1994) suggest that at least three dimensions of human functioning need to be examined when studying psychopathology: the universal, the cultural, and the individual. The importance of all three factors should not be downplayed by the cultural focus offered here.

Acknowledgment

I would like to thank Harvey Irwin for his valuable comments on an earlier draft of this paper.

REFERENCES

American Psychiatric Association. (1994). *Diagnostic and statistical manual of mental disorders* (4th ed.). Washington, DC: Author.

Alexander, V. K. (1956). A case study of a multiple personality. *Journal of Abnormal and Social Psychology, 52,* 272–276.

Barach, P. M. (1991). Multiple personality disorder as an attachment disorder. *Dissociation, 4,* 117–123.

Boon, S., & Draijer, N. (1993). *Multiple personality disorder in the Netherlands: A study on reliability and validity of the diagnosis.* Amsterdam: Swets & Zeitlinger.

Brody, E. B. (1994). Psychiatric diagnosis in sociocultural context. *Journal of Nervous and Mental Disease, 182,* 253–254.

Cardeña, E. (1992). Trance and possession as dissociative disorders. *Transcultural Psychiatric Research Review, 29,* 287–300.

Carlson, E. B. (1997). *Trauma assessment: A clinician's guide.* New York: Guilford Press.

Castillo, R. J. (1997). *Culture and mental illness: A client-centered approach.* Pacific Grove, CA: Brooks/Cole.

Coons, P. M. (1994). Confirmation of childhood abuse in child and adolescent cases of multiple personality disorder and dissociative disorder not otherwise specified. *Journal of Nervous and Mental Disease, 182,* 461–464.

Coons, P. M., Bowman, E. S., Kluft, R. P., & Milstein, V. (1991). The cross-cultural occurrence of MPD: Additional cases from a recent survey. *Dissociation, 4,* 124–128.

DeVries, M. W. (1996). Trauma in cultural perspective. In B. A. Van der Kolk, A. C. McFarlane, & L. Weisaeth (Eds.), *Traumatic stress: The effects of overwhelming experience on mind, body and society* (pp. 398–413). New York: Guilford Press.

Dorahy, M. J., Lewis, C. A., Millar, R. G., & Gee, T. (1999). *Correlates of non-pathological dissociation in Northern Ireland: The affects of trauma and exposure to political violence.* Unpublished manuscript.

Ellenberger, H. F. (1970). *The discovery of the unconscious: The history and evolution of dynamic psychiatry.* New York: Basic Books.

Freyd, J. J. (1996). *Betrayal trauma: The logic of forgetting childhood abuse.* Cambridge, MA: Harvard University Press.

Golub, D. (1995). Cultural variations in multiple personality disorder. In L. Cohen, J. Berzoff, & M. Elin (Eds.), *Dissociative identity disorder: Theoretical and treatment controversies* (pp. 285–326). Northvale, NJ: Aronson.

Irwin, H. J. (1996). Traumatic childhood events, perceived availability of emotional support, and the development of dissociative tendencies. *Child Abuse and Neglect, 20,* 701–707.

Irwin, H. J. (1998). Affective predictors of dissociation-II: Shame and guilt. *Journal of Clinical Psychology, 54,* 237–245.

Jang, K. L., Paris, J., Zweig-Frank, H., & Livesley, W. J. (1998). Twin study of dissociative experience. *Journal of Nervous and Mental Disease, 186,* 345–351.

Kirmayer, L. J. (1994). Pacing the void: Social and cultural dimensions of dissociation. In D. Spiegel (Ed.), *Dissociation: Culture, mind, and body* (pp. 91–122). Washington, DC: American Psychiatric Press.

Kleinman, A. (1988). *Rethinking psychiatry: From cultural categories to personal experience.* New York: Free Press.

Kluft, R. P. (1984). Treatment of multiple personality disorder: A study of 33 cases. *Psychiatric Clinics of North America, 7,* 9–29.

Kluft, R. P. (1993). Multiple personality disorder. In D. Spiegel (Ed.), *Dissociative disorders: A clinical review* (pp. 17–44). Lutherville, MD. Sidran Press.

Krippner, S. (1997). Dissociation in many times and places. In S. Krippner & S. M. Powers (Eds.), *Broken images, broken selves: Dissociative narratives in clinical practice* (pp. 3–40). Washington, DC: Brunner/Mazel.

Lewis, D. O., Yeagar, C. A., Swica, Y., Pincus, J. H., & Lewis, M. (1997). Objective documentation of child abuse and dissociation in 12 murderers with dissociative identity disorder. *American Journal of Psychiatry, 154,* 1703–1710.

Lilienfeld, S. O., Lynn, S. J., Kirsch, I., Chaves, J. F., Sarbin, T. R., Ganaway, G. K., & Powell, R. A. (1999). Dissociative identity disorder and the sociocognitive model: Recalling the lessons of the past. *Psychological Bulletin, 125,* 507–523.

Liotti, G. (1992). Disorganized/disoriented attachment in the etiology of the dissociative disorders. *Dissociation, 5,* 196–204.

Marsella, A. J., Friedman, M. J., & Spain, E. H. (1994). Ethnocultural aspects of posttraumatic stress disorder. In J. M. Oldham, M. B. Riba, & A. Tasman (Eds.), *Review of Psychiatry* (Vol. 12, pp. 17–41). Washington, DC: American Psychiatric Press.

Marsella, A. J., & Kameoka, V. A. (1989). Ethnocultural issues in the assessment of psychopathology. In S. Wetzler (Ed.), *Measuring mental illness: Psychometric assessment for clinicians* (pp. 229–256). Washington, DC: American Psychiatric Press.

Martinéz-Taboas, A. (1995). *Multiple personality: An Hispanic perspective.* San Juan, PR: Puente Publishing.

McFarlane, A. C., & Van der Kolk, B. A. (1996). Trauma and its challenge to society. In B. A. van der Kolk, A. C. McFarlane, & L. Weisaeth (Eds.), *Traumatic stress: The effects of overwhelming experience on mind, body, and society* (pp. 24–46). New York: Guilford Press.

Middleton, W., & Butler, J. (1998). Dissociative identity disorder: An Australian series. *Australian and New Zealand Journal of Psychiatry, 32,* 794–804.

Miller, S. D. (1989). Optical differences in cases of multiple personality disorder. *Journal of Nervous and Mental Disease, 177,* 480–486.

Okano, K. (1997). The notion of "dissociogenic stress." *Dissociation, 10,* 130–134.

Putnam, F. W. (1989). *The diagnosis and treatment of multiple personality disorder.* New York: Guilford Press.

Putnam, F. W., Guroff, J. J., Silberman, E. K., Barban, L., & Post, R. M. (1986). The clinical phenomenology of multiple personality disorder: Review of 100 recent cases. *Journal of Clinical Psychiatry, 47,* 285–293.

Putnam, F. W., Zahn, T. P., & Post, R. M. (1990). Differential autonomic nervous system activity in multiple personality disorder. *Psychiatric Research, 31,* 251–260.

Ross, C. A. (1995). The validity and reliability of dissociative identity disorder. In L. Cohen, J. Berzoff., & M. Elin. (Eds.), *Dissociative identity disorder: Theoretical and treatment controversies* (pp. 65–84). Northvale, NJ: Aronson.

Ross, C. A. (1997). *Dissociative identity disorder: Diagnosis, clinical features, and treatment of multiple personality.* New York: Wiley.

Sar, V., Yargic, L. I., & Tutkan, H. (1996). Structured interview data on 35 cases of dissociative identity disorder in Turkey. *American Journal of Psychiatry, 153,* 1329–1333.

Schumaker, J. F. (1995). *The corruption of reality: A unified theory of religion, hypnosis and psychopathology.* New York: Prometheus Books.

Spanos, N. P. (1996). *Multiple identity and false memories: A sociocognitive perspective.* Washington, DC: American Psychological Association.

Spanos, N. P., & Burgess, C. (1994). Hypnosis and multiple personality disorder: A sociocognitive perspective. In S. J. Lynn & J. W. Rhue (Eds.), *Dissociation: Clinical and theoretical perspectives* (pp. 135–155). New York: Guilford Press.

Spiegel, D. (1986). Dissociating damage. *American Journal of Clinical Hypnosis, 29,* 123–131.

Suryani, L. K., & Jensen, D. J. (1993). *Trance and possession in Bali: A window on Western multiple personality disorder and suicide.* Kuala Lumpur, Malaysia: Oxford University Press.

Swica, Y., Lewis, D. O., & Lewis, M. (1996). Child abuse and dissociative identity disorder/multiple personality disorder: The documentation of childhood maltreatment and the corroboration of symptoms. *Child and Adolescent Psychiatric Clinics of North America, 5,* 431–447.

Tillman, J. G., Nash, M. R., & Lerner, P. M. (1994). Does trauma cause dissociative pathology? In S. J. Lynn & J. W. Rhue (Eds.), *Dissociation: Clinical and theoretical perspectives* (pp. 395–414). New York: Guilford Press.

Tsai, G. E., Condie, D., Wu, M. T., & Chang, I. W. (1999). Functional magnetic resonance imaging of personality switches in a woman with dissociative identity disorder. *Harvard Review of Psychiatry, 7,* 119–122.

Van der Kolk, B. A., Van der Hart, O., & Marmar, C. R. (1996). Dissociation and information processing in posttraumatic stress disorder. In B. A. Van der Kolk, A. C. McFarlane, & L. Weisaeth (Eds.), *Traumatic stress: The effects of overwhelming experience on mind, body, and society* (pp. 303–327). New York: Guilford Press.

Varma, V. K., Bouri, M., & Wig, N. N. (1981). Multiple personality in India: Comparisons with hysterical possessions states. *American Journal of Psychotherapy, 35,* 113–120.

Waller, N. G., & Ross, C. A. (1997). The prevalence of pathological dissociation in the general population. *Journal of Abnormal Psychology, 106,* 499–510.

Wilbur, C. B. (1984). Multiple personality and child abuse: An overview. *Psychiatric Clinics of North America, 7,* 3–7.

Wilbur, C. B. (1985). The effects of childhood abuse on the psyche. In R. P. Kluft (Ed.), *Childhood antecedents of multiple personality disorder* (pp. 21–35). Washington, DC: American Psychiatric Press.

Wilson, R., & Cairns, E. (1996). Coping processes and emotions in relation to political violence in Northern Ireland. In S. Joseph & G. Mulhern (Eds.), *Psychosocial perspectives on stress and trauma: From disaster to political violence* (pp. 19–28). Leicester: British Psychological Society.

World Health Organization (1994). *ICD-10: Classification of mental and behavioral disorders.* Geneva, Switzerland: Author.

Wright, P. A. (1997). History of dissociation in Western Psychology. In S. Krippner & S. M. Powers (Eds.), *Broken images, broken selves: Dissociative narratives in clinical practice* (pp. 41–60). Washington, DC: Brunner/Mazel.

12

Culture, Cognition, and Schizophrenia

Richard J. Siegert

Schizophrenia is a major mental disorder that is characterized by a range of symptoms that may include auditory hallucinations, paranoid delusions, flattened affect, catatonia, thought disorder, apathy, and social withdrawal. It is typically a severe disorder that, unless carefully managed, can cause major impairment in most aspects of daily living, and considerable emotional distress to the person with schizophrenia and their family.

A substantial body of evidence now exists for a biological basis for this disorder. This evidence for a biological etiology includes studies supporting a genetic predisposition (e.g., Gottesman & Shields, 1972), studies implicating the role of the neurotransmitter Dopamine (e.g., Davis, Kahn, Ko, & Davidson, 1991), and studies demonstrating the presence of structural brain abnormalities in persons with schizophrenia (e.g., Chua & McKenna, 1995). A further line of support for a biological basis is the finding that schizophrenia occurs around the world (wherever epidemiological studies are conducted), and the prevalence rates are generally quite consistent (typically between 0.5%–1%). While cultural factors are important to consider in the presentation of the disorder, and even more so in the treatment and management of schizophrenia, only the most extreme relativist would argue that it is primarily a cultural, rather than a biological, phenomenon.

Curiously, in the crosscultural literature on schizophrenia, the focus remains on either greater precision in specifying local prevalence rates and prognosis, or on identifying unique variations in symptom presentation. These are important and useful endeavors to be sure. However, this focus on local variations in the presentation of the disorder obscures some more fundamental and scientifically important issues. Specifically, which domains of cognition that can be observed across different cultures are impaired in schizophrenia? It is a curious anomaly that while the universality of schizophrenia is generally accepted, and this is typically seen to reflect its biological underpinnings, there has to date been almost no attempt to specify how this might be reflected at a cognitive level. Certainly, there is a substantial body of data on the neuropsychology of schizophrenia. However, this literature seems to have little connection theoretically or empirically with the crosscultural research, probably because one emphasizes a relativist, and the other a nativist, position. However, if we are ever to truly make sense of schizophrenia, it behooves us to attempt an integration of data from biological, cognitive, and cultural domains.

The present paper will first review some important historical issues concerning the diagnosis and classification of schizophrenia and then consider its prevalence across cultures. A brief summary of some of the major findings regarding the neuropsychology of the disorder will then be made. The question as to what extent specific "domains of mind" can be demonstrated across diverse cultures will then be considered. Next, it will be argued that to understand schizophrenia at a cognitive level, we must determine which mental modules that are believed to occur in all human beings regardless of culture, might best account for schizophrenic symptomatology. Lastly, some speculative answers based on cognitive anthropology and evolutionary psychology will be advanced.

THE CLASSIFICATION OF
SCHIZOPHRENIA: THE HISTORICAL BACKGROUND

The identification of schizophrenia as a disease entity in its own right began with the German psychiatrist Emil Kraepelin who first used the term *dementia praecox* late in the nineteenth century (Bentall, 1992; Davison & Neale, 1996). This term reflected Kraepelin's opinion that schizophrenia involved the early onset of a progressive intellectual deterioration. Kraepelin observed three major subtypes of schizophrenia, which were the catatonic, the hebephrenic, and the paranoid. The next major advance in the classification of this disorder came through the work of Bleuler (1930) who introduced the name schizophrenia, meaning a split between thought and feeling, and separated the concepts of schizophrenia and dementia. Bleuler placed greater diagnostic importance on the symptoms, rather than the course of the disorder, than had Kraepelin, noting that the course of the disorder was not necessarily progressive (Davison & Neale, 1996). Bleuler also emphasized the primacy of cognitive symptoms, and in particular the loosening of the associations (Wing, 1992).

Relatively minor progress occurred in the classification of schizophrenia for several decades after Bleuler, with most subsequent taxonomies at best described as "neo-Kraepelinian." Two major contributors to the classification of schizophrenia were Kurt Schneider (1959), who introduced the concept of first-rank symptoms, and Crow (1980), who developed the notion of positive and negative symptoms. Schneider grappled with the question that has bedevilled those concerned with the diagnosis of schizophrenia, namely, what symptom or symptoms are essential for a diagnosis of schizophrenia? He was concerned to identify what might be considered the core features of the disorder. Schneider attempted to specify a number of primary or first-rank symptoms of schizophrenia, which he detailed as largely consisting of hallucinations and delusions. In many respects they are similar to the notion of positive symptoms.

Crow (1980) suggested a typology that classifies schizophrenia according to the predominance of either positive or negative symptoms. Positive symptoms involve the presence of abnormal experiences such as auditory hallucinations or delusional beliefs. Negative symptoms refers to the absence of socially expected behavior such as occurs in social withdrawal and poverty of speech. Crow posited two principal subtypes of schizophrenia, one characterized by mostly positive symptoms (Type I), the other by mostly negative symptoms (Type II). According to this theory, Type I schizophrenia is caused by abnormal Dopamine metabolism in the brain, whereas Type II is more related to structural brain abnormalities. While this etiological dichotomy has not received widespread support, the essential distinction between positive and negative symptoms remains a popular and useful organizing principle.

DSM-IV AND SCHIZOPHRENIA

The current diagnostic status of schizophrenia is embodied in the DSM-IV and the ICD-10. The differences between these two nosological systems in classifying schizophrenia has converged noticeably over successive editions, and consequently this discussion will focus on the DSM-IV. The DSM-IV defines schizophrenia as follows: "Schizophrenia is a disturbance that lasts for at least 6 months and includes at least 1 month of active-phase symptoms (i.e., two [or more] of the following: delusions, hallucinations, disorganized speech, grossly disorganized or catatonic behavior, negative symptoms)" (p. 272). The negative symptoms include affective flattening, alogia, and avolition. A number of related but distinct disorders (e.g., schizophreniform, schizoaffective disorder) are also detailed. The DSM-IV states explicitly that "No single symptom is pathognomic of schizophrenia" (p. 274). The distinction between positive and negative symptoms is also outlined. The DSM-IV describes three primary subtypes of schizophrenia: Paranoid, Disorganized, and Catatonic.

To a large extent the DSM-IV has attempted to solve many of the diagnostic problems surrounding schizophrenia (and mental disorder generally) by operationalizing the concept. The provision of clear and explicit diagnostic criteria has neutralized many of the early critics of the diagnosis who had noted that the concept of schizophrenia was often vague, used inconsistently, and low in reliability. However, while the increased specification of schizophrenic symptoms has been a tremendous advantage to researchers, it has also tended to sweep a number of thorny philosophical and scientific issues under the rug.

Perhaps the outstanding theoretical issue for schizophrenia researchers is the heterogeneity problem (Heinrichs, 1993). There is no one symptom that all persons with schizophrenia share. There is no symptom of schizophrenia that does not commonly occur in other disorders such as mania, dementia, or severe head injury. Heinrichs says that "schizophrenia is a heterogeneous illness that, paradoxically, resists subdivision" (p. 221). Thus some uncertainty remains as to whether schizophrenia is most accurately viewed as a single disorder with several subtypes, or as a mixture of different disorders with overlapping symptoms. Heinrichs suggests that it is this heterogeneity problem that accounts for the observation that neuropsychological markers of schizophrenia bear little clear relationship to neurological markers. While acknowledging the difficulties this issue raises for schizophrenia research, we shall put it aside for now. The next issue to consider is the extent to which schizophrenia can be seen to occur across different cultures.

THE PREVALENCE OF
SCHIZOPHRENIA ACROSS CULTURES

Discussion of the frequency of occurrence of psychiatric disorders in different cultures frequently devolves into a debate between the nativist and relativist positions. The nativist argues that core structural features of most major mental disorders are evident in all societies, and that culture accounts chiefly for local variations in symptom formation and presentation. The nativist replies that psychiatrists have begun their crosscultural research studies already convinced of the paramount importance of biology, and that they typically ignore differences while searching for common symptom patterns. However, schizophrenia is one mental disorder for which strong evidence exists for its universality.

This chapter will argue that while important local variations may occur in the presentation of the disorder, and also the prognosis, schizophrenia occurs around the world and at a fairly constant rate (usually of the order of 1%). The strongest support for this notion comes from the results of a series of studies conducted by the World Health Organization (WHO), that began with the International Pilot Study of Schizophrenia in the 1960s (WHO, 1979). Since then, WHO has conducted three major studies examining the incidence of schizophrenia and comparing its outcome across different countries. Tanaka-Matsumi and Draguns (1997) note that the WHO studies have included 20 separate research centers in 17 countries and have involved thousands of patients. The WHO project has also included a prospective epidemiological study that compared the prevalence of schizophrenia crossculturally (Jablensky et al., 1992). This study involved some 1,379 participants who were examined at 12 psychiatric centers across 10 countries. Two major findings to come out of the WHO series of studies have been comparable rates of schizophrenia around the globe, but a markedly different course for the disorder. In particular, outcomes are typically better for those patients from developing countries compared with patients from developed countries. This latter finding has been both consistently reported and a source of controversy as widely varying explanations have been suggested to explain it. The finding that schizophrenia occurs at fairly comparable rates in different countries has, by contrast, been uncontroversial and widely accepted.

THE NEUROPSYCHOLOGY OF SCHIZOPHRENIA

Clinicians have long observed the importance of cognitive problems as an important and debilitating component of schizophrenia. For example, Bleuler's primary symptom was cognitive, namely, a loosening of the associations. However, it was only with the rise of the information processing paradigm in contemporary cognitive psychology, since the late 1950s, that this important aspect of the disorder became a focus for empirical research. Interest in cognitive functioning in schizophrenia grew rapidly in the 1960s and 1970s, although a specifically neuropsychological approach to schizophrenia did not emerge until the early '90s (e.g., David, 1994; Frith, 1992). This approach integrated the cognitive information processing research with findings from new brain imaging techniques and the functional architecture approach of cognitive neuropsychology. The present discussion will now briefly review some of the major findings of the neuropsychology of schizophrenia.

ATTENTION IN SCHIZOPHRENIA

Considerable evidence now exists that a central feature of schizophrenia involves problems with attention. Cohen (1993) categorizes models of attention in schizophrenia into two groups. There are those models that investigate disturbances in information processing and those that focus on disturbances of arousal. Research from an information processing perspective has attempted to explain these attentional difficulties in terms of selective attention, allocation of processing resources, or lowered capacity. A further line of research has compared automatic versus controlled processing and tested the hypothesis that effortful, controlled processing is impaired while automatic processing is not. Perhaps the most prevailing problem for researchers in this area is that schizophrenic participants tend to perform poorly compared to controls, whatever the task. Cohen (1993) comments that "schizophrenic patients show a generalized performance deficit" and that consequently "there are profound problems in the measurement of a specific deficit in schizophrenia" (p. 286).

Research on arousal in people with schizophrenia has tended to concentrate on the orienting response to novel stimuli as measured by skin-conductance changes, and on event-related potentials. One interesting finding from the former line of research is that some 40 to 50 percent of people with schizophrenia fail to demonstrate the skin-conductance orienting response to novel stimuli (Dawson & Nuechterlein, 1984). Cohen (1993) notes that this finding has been replicated in Great Britain, the United States, and Germany, and that it might suggest a severe impairment of passively elicited attention. The other consistent finding from the research on arousal, which is supported by both skin-conductance studies and studies of P3 amplitude, is that schizophrenia is characterized by hyperarousal (Cohen, 1993).

In summary, it is difficult to specify the precise nature of the attentional deficits occurring in schizophrenia, and this picture is further complicated by the presence of a generalized performance deficit. At the same time, the evidence is consistent from information processing studies that schizophrenia is characterized by deficits of attention. Moreover, there is also good evidence from psychophysiological research that schizophrenia is associated with hyperarousal.

EXECUTIVE FUNCTIONING IN SCHIZOPHRENIA

Considerable attention in recent years has been paid to the role of the so-called executive system in schizophrenia. This hypothesized control center for cognitive functioning is widely assumed to be anatomically associated with the prefrontal cortex of the cerebral hemispheres (McCarthy & Warrington, 1990). Interest in the functioning of the prefrontal cortex in schizophrenia arose from the frequent observation that many of the symptoms of lesions of the prefrontal cortex were similar to some of the negative symptoms of schizophrenia (e.g., Frith, 1992; Pantelis & Nelson, 1994). Typical symptoms of frontal lobe lesions may include apathy, impulsiveness, impaired self-monitoring, perseveration, difficulty shifting set, reduced spontaneity, disinhibition, and impaired social behavior (Kolb & Whishaw, 1990; Lezak, 1995). Of course these symptoms do not occur in all instances of frontal damage and the clinical profile varies widely depending on the severity of damage, the site of the lesion, the cause of the lesion, premorbid factors, and so on. However, taken together, these symptoms bear some similarity to the typical negative signs of schizophrenia such as poverty of speech and action, stereotyped actions, social withdrawal, motor retardation, and flattening of affect (Frith, 1992).

The similarity between the symptoms characteristic of frontal lobe damage and of schizophrenia has been further investigated by examining schizophrenic performance on psychometric tests considered sensitive to frontal lobe dysfunction. In particular, researchers have examined performance on the Wisconsin Card-Sorting Test (WCST). The WCST is a test in which satisfactory performance requires abstract concept formation, working memory, and the ability to shift set. There is evidence that performance on this task is frequently impaired in people with schizophrenia (e.g., Nisbet, Siegert, Hunt, & Fairley, 1996; Van der Does & Van den Bosch, 1992).

A further line of evidence for the role of executive systems in the symptoms of schizophrenia has come from functional imaging (PET) studies. Such studies examine blood flow or metabolic processes in the brain, either under resting conditions, or while subjects engage in tasks believed to involve the frontal lobes. Heinrichs (1993) notes that some evidence has emerged for hypofrontality in schizophrenia. This term means that a decreased level of metabolic activity is observed in the dorsolateral prefrontal cortex in some schizophrenic subjects. However, he also comments that this result is not consistently observed in all subjects, and some researchers have not found it at all.

In summary, the evidence for frontal or executive dysfunction in schizophrenia includes similarities observed between schizophrenic symptoms and symptoms characteristic of frontal lesions, the performance of people with schizophrenia on tests of executive functioning, and brain imaging studies. At times, the evidence, especially from brain imaging studies, is inconclusive or even contradictory. However, when the evidence from all three areas is considered together it seems quite convincing that executive functions are impaired in schizophrenia. The precise nature of this impairment remains elusive.

MEMORY IN SCHIZOPHRENIA

A substantial body of evidence exists to demonstrate that schizophrenia is characterized by memory problems, although the exact nature of these problems remains controversial (e.g., Heinrichs, 1993; McKenna, Clare, & Baddeley, 1995). Again, the problem of separating any specific memory deficits from a generalized performance deficit is an issue. Heinrichs (1993) observed that people with schizophrenia typically "learn slowly and inefficiently and utilize ineffective cognitive strategies," and also "perform poorly on many tests of verbal memory" (p. 227). However, he also comments that they perform poorly on a wide range of cognitive tasks compared with healthy controls, and that these memory deficits bear little logical relationship to the known anatomical abnormalities observed in the brains of people with schizophrenia.

Notwithstanding these issues, the evidence is mounting for a more specific pattern of memory deficits in schizophrenia. In a review of the topic, McKenna, Clare, and Baddeley (1995) note that memory impairment in schizophrenia is generally disproportionate to any overall intellectual impairment. They conclude that "the pattern of memory impairment in schizophrenia seems to be one in which short-term memory and at least some aspects of working memory are preserved, this being coupled with a long-term memory impairment which encompasses episodic and semantic memory but which spares procedural and implicit memory" (p. 285).

LANGUAGE IN SCHIZOPHRENIA

Frith (1992) comments that "Language and speech in schizophrenia have been studied more than any other feature" (p. 95). In general, the unusual speech characteristic of schizophrenia is thought to result from deficits at the higher levels of speech production. The severe word-finding difficulties and agrammatical speech characteristic of aphasia after a left frontal stroke, are not typical of schizophrenia. The most bizarre delusion can be expressed in speech that is grammatically and syntactically well formed. The errors are at the level of pragmatics not grammar or syntax.

Andreasen (1979) finds that the most common types of abnormal speech in people with schizophrenia included poverty of speech, poverty of content, tangentiality, derailment, perseveration, loss of goal, and illogicality. Frith (1992) observes that the unusual speech characteristic of schizophrenia is essentially an expressive problem; there is little evidence that schizophrenic people cannot understand what is said to them by others. He suggests that this may arise from two cognitive features of schizophrenia. The first is a poor ability to make inferences about the knowledge and intentions of the listener, or to use the inferences to guide the discussion. The second feature is a deficit in self-monitoring. Frith suggests that such higher order cognitive abilities are likely associated at an anatomical level with the prefrontal cortex.

In summary, much research on speech in schizophrenia has shown characteristic features of abnormal speech, consistent with an expressive difficulty at the higher levels of production (i.e., inferring meaning from the other's speech, organizing and planning a response, mental representations, and self-monitoring). This leads us to so-called mind-reading, another cognitive ability to consider in schizophrenia. It is the ability to form a mental representation of someone else's thoughts, intentions, emotional states, and also their beliefs, desires, wishes, and goals.

REPRESENTATIONAL THINKING IN SCHIZOPHRENIA

The concept of theory of mind and the study of how individuals develop representations of the mental processes of other people has inspired tremendous theoretical and research interest in psychology in recent years. Beginning with Premack and Woodruff's (1978) article "Does the Chimpanzee have a theory of mind?" the concept has generated intense interest in developmental psychology (e.g., Butterworth, Harris, Leslie, & Wellman, 1991; Gopnik & Wellman, 1994), developmental psychopathology (Baron-Cohen, 1995), and cognitive anthropology (Lillard, 1998).

Recently, theory of mind, and the broader issue of how well people with schizophrenia can form valid mental representations of other people's thought processes, have become focuses for researchers interested in schizophrenia. Frith (1992) advances the notion that some of the signs and symptoms of schizophrenia may be explicable in terms of "impairments in processes underlying 'theory of mind' such as the ability to represent beliefs and intentions" (p. 147). Frith suggests that patients with delusions of reference or persecution can form representations of others' beliefs and intentions, and can differentiate these from their own beliefs and intentions, but are poor at inferring their content. He proposes that "certain delusions can be explained as the consequence of losing the ability to 'read' the intentions and beliefs of others" (p. 153).

Frith also speculates that this impairment in the cognitive processes underlying a theory of mind could explain some of the negative symptoms of schizophrenia, such as social withdrawal and avolition. In this case he speculates that people with schizophrenia may have problems representing their own goals, resulting in little spontaneous behavior or perseverative or stimulus driven behavior. Writing in 1992, Frith stated that there were no published studies to date specifically examining theory of mind in schizophrenia. However, since then there has been a flurry of interest in this perspective on cognition in schizophrenia, and evidence is accruing that the ability to make accurate inferences about other people's mental states is diminished in schizophrenia (e.g., Doody, Goetz, Johnstone, Frith, & Cunningham-Owens, 1998; Frith & Corcoran, 1996).

There is a substantial and growing body of research evidence that schizophrenia is characterized by cognitive or neuropsychological deficits. In particular, deficits in attention, executive functioning, memory, language, and representational thinking all have been identified. At the same time, the precise nature of the deficits within some of these cognitive domains remains rather uncertain, and there is certainly no "neuropsychological profile" for schizophrenia. Notwithstanding this muddy picture, the present discussion will next consider the evidence for domains of (normal) cognition that occur in all cultures. One possible argument for a closer integration of these two areas—the neuropsychology of schizophrenia and the cognitive anthropology of mind—with the goal of increasing our understanding of schizophrenia will then be made.

MODULARITY AND DOMAIN
SPECIFICITY IN COGNITION ACROSS CULTURES

Traditional concepts of mind have tended to regard the brain as a general purpose information processing device that is almost infinitely plastic and pliable at the hands of the beast known as culture. The notion that the human mind/brain is a relatively specialized organ comprising a collection of even more specialized subsystems, all operating relatively independently but in a coordinated fashion, is a relatively new idea (or an old idea that is back in fashion). A number of developments in a wide range of disciplines have all contributed to this emerging view of the mind as a highly evolved device containing a number of specialized subsystems, or modules. Three particularly influential developments have been Chomsky's theory of natural language grammar (Chomsky, 1957, 1975), Fodor's concept of the modularity of mind (1983), and the rise of evolutionary psychology (Tooby & Cosmides, 1992).

Undoubtedly, the first major development in reconceptualizing the human mind was Chomsky's revolutionary reappraisal of language and, in particular, psycholinguistics. Chomsky observed that underlying all languages was a deep structure that was effectively the same regardless of the huge differences in the surface structure of languages. He argued also that human infants have an almost effortless ability to acquire their first language and that this ability is both innate and hard wired. Chomsky has proposed that humans are equipped with what he calls a language acquisition device, which is unique to their species. These ideas are sometimes labelled nativist, reflecting their emphasis on innateness and the biological programming of language.

A second major force in the growing interest in domain specificity across cultures arose from Fodor's popularization of the concept of a modular mind (Fodor, 1983). A module, according to Fodor, is an innate and encapsulated subsystem specialized for processing one type of information. There is considerable evidence, for example, that visual perception in the primate nervous system is organized in modular fashion (e.g., Marr, 1982; Zeki, 1993).

A third development in the upsurge of interest in domain specific approaches has been the increasing influence of evolutionary psychology on the study of cognition and cognitive processes (e.g., Pinker, 1997; Tooby & Cosmides, 1992). Evolutionary psychology proponents have argued that the human mind consists of a set of richly structured, content specific, and highly specialized information processing mechanisms that have evolved through natural selection over the millions of years that humans spent as hunter-gatherers on the African savannas (Tooby & Cosmides, 1992). A major implication of the evolutionary psychology manifesto is the idea that cognition itself is a part of the evolutionary process and that natural selection has determined species' cognitive systems just as much as it has determined their wingspan or their temperature regulating mechanisms. The central thesis of this article is that we need to ask the following question before we can begin to understand schizophrenia at a cognitive level: Exactly which cognitive modules or subsystems that have evolved through adaptation by natural selection are not working in people displaying the signs and symptoms of schizophrenia? However, before we can address this question, it is necessary to first define what is meant by the term module, and second, what is meant by the term domain.

Two rather similar and theoretically related constructs that have attracted considerable interest in fields such as cognitive science and cognitive anthropology in recent years are those of modularity and cognitive domains. Both concepts are relevant to the present discussion and so it is important to clarify the distinction between them before proceeding. The contemporary account of modularity began with Chomsky and was both extended and popularized by Fodor. A Fodorian module has a number of characteristics. It is a domain specific subsystem, innately specified, computationally autonomous, and informationally encapsulated. In addition, such modules, according to Fodor, process information quickly and automatically. Variations on this theme now abound and they typically involve harder or softer concepts of modularity.

Modules, then, for the purposes of the present discussion, are cognitive in nature, are located in the brain, and their presence is, presumably, consistent across all humans in all cultures (except of course in some cases of brain damage). For example, there is substantial evidence that a face recognition module exists, and that brain damage can leave some individuals with a specific impairment of this ability, termed prosopagnosia (McCarthy & Warrington, 1990). The ability to recognize human faces seems to be a universal ability among Homo Sapiens, it has obvious biological and adaptive utility, and it can be impaired by cortical damage.

Domains of cognition, by contrast, are those aspects of the environment about which modules receive and process information. Thus domains are thought to represent specific elements or features of an organism's environment, and the brain is considered to be in some way innately prepared for processing such types of information. The exact nature and number of such domains (and modules), is largely a matter of speculation at present. Some examples of cognitive domains have already been mentioned—in particular language and faces. Presumably, the related modules will be some form of language processing module and face perception module.

In general, the notion of modularity has been less controversial for modules that are primarily perceptual in nature. For example, as previously mentioned, there is an abundance of evidence that the visual system is highly modular in organization. However, the notion of modularity is more controversial for other mental processes. Sperber (1994) points out that Fodor's modularity is primarily concerned with "input systems" at the "periphery of the mind," in particular with perception and linguistic decoding. Sperber further notes that "in its centre and bulk, Fodor's mind is decidedly nonmodular" (p. 39). However, proponents of evolutionary psychology have been more enthusiastic about the potential for modularity at higher levels, and have made convincing arguments that such cognitive modules have evolved in much the same way as the opposable thumb and bipedalism. Tooby and Cosmides (1992) argue that it is wrong simply to regard the brain as a general purpose information processing device. Rather, they argue, the brain is inherently good at processing certain types of information, and not other types, and evolution provides the explanation. The next section will consider to what extent specific domains of mind can be observed across diverse cultures, and the implications of this for research on schizophrenia.

The development and growth of cognitive anthropology in recent decades has meant that the traditional focus exclusively on culture in anthropology, in which the mind was seen as of little relevance or importance, has been enhanced by a new perspective that emphasizes the interplay of mind and culture (D'Andrade, 1995; Hirschfeld & Gelman, 1994; Shore, 1996). In fact, the study of mind and culture is one of the richest potential sources of information on the extent to which cognitive domains can be considered universal (Hirschfeld & Gelman, 1994). Moreover, the influence of cognitive science has meant that cognitive anthropologists are now embracing concepts like schema, modularity, mental model, and connectionism in attempting to explain culture (e.g., D'Andrade, 1995; Shore, 1996). Moreover, it is becoming increasingly accepted that cognitive architecture show a degree of modularity in its organization and that this modular structure is reflected across cultures (Hirschfeld & Gelman, 1994). So which domains have been demonstrated to exist across cultures, and which of these domains are the most relevant for understanding the cognitive impairments of schizophrenia?

EVOLUTIONARY PSYCHOLOGY, DOMAIN SPECIFICITY, AND COGNITION IN SCHIZOPHRENIA

Proponents of evolutionary psychology have argued that modularity should not be restricted to just the perceptual or input systems in the brain. Tooby and Cosmides (1992) state that the human mind "consists of a set of evolved information-processing mechanisms instantiated in the human nervous system" that are "richly structured in a content specific way" (p. 24). They also give numerous examples of what such mechanisms might involve. Some of the domains they discuss include mechanisms for "mate selection," language acquisition, family relations, and cooperation" (p. 24), as well as for "a belief-desire folk psychology—a so-called 'theory of mind,'" (p. 90), and "domain-specific reasoning procedures" (p. 92). This is not the full story, however. Witness the following quotation:

Thus, researchers who ask hard questions about how organisms actually solve problems and who focus on the real performance of organisms on natural tasks have had to abandon the idea that the mind is free of content-specialised machinery. Researchers who study colour vision, visual scene analysis, speech perception, conceptual development in children, mental imagery, psychophysics, locomotion, language acquisition, motor control, anticipatory motion computation, face recognition, bio-mechanical motion perception, emotion recognition, social cognition, reasoning, and the perception and representation of motion, for example, cannot account for the psychological phenomena they study by positing computational mechanisms that are solely domain-general and content-independent. . . . In fact, the reality has always been that every field of psychology bristles with observations of content-dependent phenomena. (Tooby & Cosmides, 1992, p. 97)

The important question for the present discussion, given so many possible domains, is exactly which putative domains are most relevant for research on schizophrenia? At this point, our discussion becomes highly speculative. In considering this question the evolutionary psychology perspective is likely to be particularly helpful, in that it indicates how cognition may have evolved within a primate social context, and the types of cognitive mechanisms that are most salient for survival. It is argued that these mechanisms are likely to be among the most productive ones for schizophrenia researchers. For example, the ability to infer another person's motives and to detect deception is one ability that has survival value according to evolutionary psychology. Recent research on theory of mind deficits and causal attributions have suggested the importance of such cognitive abilities in the development of paranoia (Kinderman, Dunbar, & Bentall, 1998).

Another obvious candidate is language. Here the argument for modularity is a strong one. However, as the brief review earlier made it clear, there has already been a great deal of research on language and schizophrenia, and it has been less than enlightening. What has become clear from this research, however, is that language deficits in schizophrenia are primarily expressive in nature, and they involve higher-order cognitive language abilities. Such higher order abilities include self-monitoring and the ability to infer the knowledge and intentions of other speakers. These characteristics of language in schizophrenia are closely related to another important domain demanding further study, namely, representational thinking.

Evolutionary psychology argues that the ability to form a representation of what another human is thinking is an ability that has been acquired and developed through natural selection. The ability to interpret other people's facial expressions, their body language, and their tone of voice, has obvious advantages for survival. In earlier environments, our ancestors had to be able determine who was a friend and who was an enemy, who was a potential mate and who was not. The ability to distinguish between facial expressions associated with suspicion and curiosity, fear and anger, or disgust and sadness, may have been the difference between life and death.

In modern society we also rely on this ability for surviving socially, if not literally. Our ability to accurately express our emotions, to know how and when to express them, to know when to conceal our emotions, and to be able read and interpret the emotions of other people are skills that impact hugely on our ability to form lasting relationships, breed and raise healthy children, and gain high status in our careers. It seems curious, then, that so little research into the mind-reading abilities of people with schizophrenia has taken place until quite recently, especially given the intensity of the interpersonal difficulties that are associated with this disorder. By contrast, such abilities feature prominently in current accounts of autism (Baron-Cohen, 1995). The next section will consider how culture might interact with cognitive domains in the production of schizophrenic symptoms.

DOMAIN SPECIFICITY, CULTURE, AND SYMPTOM FORMATION

The discussion thus far has concentrated on highlighting the importance of considering universal domains of mind and an evolutionary perspective for yielding new insights into schizophrenia. So where does culture fit into all of this, and how do we explain the diversity of symptoms that occur in schizophrenia? For while capacities are inherited, external input or information is necessary to activate any module and to determine its expression. Thus we might expect universally impaired modules related to the symptom form, such as hearing voices or believing that one's thoughts are being tampered with, but the specific nature, content, and meaning of these symptoms will be culturally determined. Thus in one culture paranoid delusions may often focus on the CIA or aliens as persecutory agents, whereas in another culture spirits or dead ancestors may feature more prominently. Moreover, within a single culture the typical symptom motifs may change markedly over time.

For example, Klaf and Hamilton (cited in Tseng & McDermott, 1981) studied over 100 years of hospital records and found that patients in the nineteenth century were characterized by a greater preoccupation with religion and a lesser preoccupation with sex than patients in the twentieth century. Tseng and McDermott (1981) concluded that there are certain core symptoms that are common to schizophrenia in most cultures and that these involve disturbances of perception, thinking, and affect. They go on to say:

Cultural factors, however, operate in the content and expression of delusions and hallucinations. They also influence what we shall call peripheral symptoms and the comparative prominence of symptoms. Whether a patient is more or less withdrawn, more or less violent, the manner in which he detaches himself from society—these are subject to culture. (p. 134)

Al-Issa (1995) reviewed sociocultural factors and hallucinations and concluded that cultures vary in the frequency of different kinds of hallucinations. Al-Issa noted that auditory hallucinations are most common in the West and visual hallucinations less common. In Africa and the Near East, visual hallucinations are more frequently reported, although auditory hallucinations are also common. Al-Issa suggested that "vision may have positive cultural (social and religious) connotations which increase the frequency of visual hallucinations in some non-Western societies" (p. 327). In an earlier article, Al-Issa (1977) speculated that the relative frequencies of hallucinations in different sensory modalities (auditory, visual, olfactory, etc.) reported in Western cultures might even be related to the relative importance of these different sensory channels for interpersonal communication. Thus auditory hallucinations are most common and this may be related to the importance of speech in most interpersonal communication in Western societies. Al-Issa (1977) suggests that "if hallucinations constitute a direct or symbolic expression of the individual's social needs, these needs could be more easily communicated by speech (auditory hallucinations) than by pictures (visual hallucinations)" (p. 581). Al-Issa (1995) also makes the important point that "the study of hallucinations in different cultures would provide an excellent example of how cultural factors intervene between the brain and experience or the brain and behaviour" (p. 372). Thus the issue is not whether symptoms of schizophrenia represent a biological or a social phenomenon, but rather how the biological factors and the social factors interact to result in specific symptoms. Or to put it another way, how the cognitive modules and the social domains interact.

It is not possible to speculate here about how every culture might interact with each one of the rapidly growing number of putative modules that various theorists have suggested exist universally. Consequently, the remainder of this section will focus on the mind-reading module, which has special importance for researchers of schizophrenia. It is hoped that this focus on the theory of mind module will serve as an example of how culture, domain specificity, and symptom formation might interact in the genesis of this disorder. These ideas are unashamedly speculative and intended primarily as signposts for exploratory researchers, rather than as maps of well travelled terrain.

THEORY OF MIND, CULTURE, AND SCHIZOPHRENIA

It should be stated at the outset that a theory of mind approach to schizophrenia is probably most relevant, and may be the only one relevant, for the diagnostic subtype of paranoid schizophrenia. Here the disorder is characterized by delusions and hallucinations of a persecutory or grandiose nature, the defining features are interpersonal in nature, the essential symptoms typically revolving around what the patient believes other people are saying about or doing to him or her. By their very nature, the paranoid symptoms require the patient to make inferences about the mental states of other people and the inferences are that they are threatening. By contrast, the theory of mind (TOM) has no obvious implications for either disorganized or catatonic schizophrenia. With this caveat in mind we can now consider the crosscultural validity of the TOM construct.

Lillard (1998) has recently reviewed the issue of cultural variations of theories of mind. She noted that while this concept typically has been discussed as if it were identical the world over, in fact evidence exists for great variation in folk psychologies around the globe. Yet most discussions of theory of mind assume what Lillard calls the Western American social science model. This model views the mind as contained in the brain, as the seat of mental processes, states, and intentions and indirectly, action, too. It also views our minds and others' minds as private but knowable.

Lillard cites many examples from the anthropological literature that suggest that folk psychologies vary enormously across cultures, and it may be quite inaccurate to assume that the standard TOM is universal. Certainly it seems that the TOM theory cannot universally be applied to different cultural groups without some modifications to take into account cultural differences. Thus a meaningful application of TOM to the understanding of schizophrenia, as a disorder that occurs globally, can only occur if cultural differences in mind-reading are carefully considered. For example, Lillard cites research on the Chewong people of Malaysia as an example of a culture that seems to place very little emphasis on mental explanations for human behavior. According to Howell (cited in Lillard, 1998), they have only about 5 words for naming mental processes and only 23 for emotions and internal bodily states. By comparison, English has over 2000 words alone for emotions.

Similarly, Lillard cites evidence that both the Japanese and Sherpa cultures regard another person's mind as essentially unknowable and, consequently, of limited explanatory utility. Significantly, however, Lillard does not argue that TOM is not a universal phenomenon. Rather, she argues that in some cultures mind is considered less important as an explanation for behavior (being ultimately unknowable) and that in other cultures it is simply not permissible to talk about internal states. She notes that "in cultures in which people do not discuss internal states, people are in a position in which internal states must be conceptualized by each person individually" (Lillard, 1998, p. 13). In short, mind-reading occurs, but it does so individually and privately.

Another important issue Lillard raises is that of ethereal forces. She notes that in many cultures it is accepted that spirits can directly influence the mind and behavior, and that physical or psychological illness is often explained in this way. This raises complex issues for theorists who would readily apply a single, homogeneous TOM model to all cultures, and even more so when considering the phenomenon of auditory hallucinations, which may involve supernatural elements. However, while space precludes a serious consideration of this complex issue, the interested reader would do well to consult Boyer's (1994) fascinating account of Ghosts among the Fang people of Cameroon before concluding that such ethereal phenomena do not fit well into a domain specific cognitive approach. Boyer's analysis illustrates neatly that while the *bekong* (spirits of the dead) possess abilities that defy the laws of physics (e.g., invisibility), their behavior is typically described in terms of a conventional folk psychology.

The preceding discussion has highlighted some of the complexities arising from Lillard's thoughtful article for researchers intent on studying TOM in cultures different from their own. Given that I have already argued from the standpoint of evolutionary psychology that TOM represents one of the most promising avenues for future research on schizophrenia, we must next ask how we can study theory of mind in people with schizophrenia from different cultures? Certainly, if the TOM theory has any special relevance for explaining the disorder at a cognitive level, it should stand up to replication across cultures. Otherwise we have a disorder that occurs universally, and an explanation that is specific to European and American cultures.

There is no ready made or simple answer to the question of how we can study the relationship between schizophrenia and TOM, while also taking culture seriously.

However, those theorists and researchers who are prepared to consider cultural differences in approaching the study of TOM in schizophrenia may at least find fertile ground for developing new theory. For example, if some cultures are very TOM oriented and others less so, then this should be evident in comparing mind-reading abilities in the people with schizophrenia from these cultures. One might also be able to make predictions about the nature of symptoms that should arise. Are paranoid delusions more common in cultures where people typically devote more time and effort to reading other people's intentions, thoughts, and desires? The scope for generating hypotheses that can test both the TOM theory and its relevance for schizophrenia is broad. Ultimately, if schizophrenia is universal, and if TOM is also universal, then deficits in TOM ability should be demonstrable in people with schizophrenia from all cultural backgrounds. Indeed, this might be considered the acid test for both assertions. However, any universal aspects will surely be missed if such research is not conducted with a sophisticated understanding and a degree of respect for cultural differences in theories of mind.

SUMMARY AND CONCLUSION

This chapter has argued that, notwithstanding the difficult diagnostic issues surrounding the disorder of schizophrenia, it is a disorder that occurs globally at quite consistent rates and with known biological and neuropsychological abnormalities. Moreover, there has been growing acceptance in both cognitive science and cognitive anthropology of the existence of specific domains of cognition that are universal. It was argued that a clearer understanding of the cognitive basis of schizophrenia will come from examining the typical cognitive difficulties, with the relevant cognitive domains in mind, and through understanding the likely evolutionary function of these cognitive modules. However, this synthesis can be achieved only by also considering the role of culture in determining how the hypothesized module might interact with the person's social environment. The theory of mind theory was put forward as an example of how modularity, evolution, and culture might be integrated productively to develop more powerful theoretical explanations of disturbed cognition in schizophrenia.

REFERENCES

Al-Issa, I. (1977). Social and cultural aspects of hallucinations. *Psychological Bulletin, 84,* 570–587.

Al-Issa, I. (1995). The illusion of reality or the reality of illusion: Hallucinations and culture. *British Journal of Psychiatry, 166,* 368–373.

American Psychiatric Association (1994). *Diagnostic and statistical manual of mental disorders* (4th ed.). Washington, DC: Author.

Andreasen, N. C. (1979). Thought, language and communication disorders 2: Diagnostic significance. *Archives of General Psychiatry, 36,* 1325–1330.

Baron-Cohen, S. (1995). *Mindblindness: An essay on autism and theory of mind.* London: MIT Press.

Bentall, R. P. (1992). The classification of schizophrenia. In D. J. Kavanagh (Ed.), *Schizophrenia: An overview and practical handbook* (pp. 23–44). London: Chapman & Hall.

Bleuler, E. (1930). *Textbook of Psychiatry.* New York: Macmillan.

Boyer, P. (1994). Cognitive constraints on cultural representations: Natural ontologies and religious ideas. In L. A. Hirschfeld & S. A. Gelman (Eds.), *Mapping the mind: Domain specificity in cognition and culture.* Cambridge, UK: Cambridge University Press.

Butterworth, G., Harris, P. L., Leslie, A. M., & Wellman, H. M. (Eds.). (1991). *Perspectives on the child's theory of mind.* Oxford, UK: Oxford University Press.

Chomsky, N. (1957). *Syntactic structures.* The Hague, Netherlands: Mouton.

Chomsky, N. (1975). *Reflections on language.* New York: Random House.

Chua, S. E., & McKenna, P. J. (1995). Schizophrenia—a brain disease: A critical review of structural and functional cerebral abnormality in the disorder. *British Journal of Psychiatry, 166,* 563–582.

Cohen, R. A. (1993). *The neuropsychology of attention.* New York: Plenum Press.

Crow, T. J. (1980). Molecular pathology of schizophrenia: More than one disease process? *British Medical Journal, 280,* 784–788.

D'Andrade, R. (1995). *The development of cognitive anthropology.* Cambridge, UK: Cambridge University Press.

David, A. S. (1994). The neuropsychological origin of auditory hallucinations. In A. S. David & J. C. Cutting (Eds.), *The neuropsychology of schizophrenia.* London: Lawrence Erlbaum.

Davis, K. L., Kahn, R. S., Ko, G., & Davidson, M. (1991). Dopamine and schizophrenia: A review and reconceptualization. *American Journal of Psychiatry, 148,* 1474–1486.

Davison, G. C., & Neale, J. M. (1996). *Abnormal psychology.* New York: Wiley.

Dawson, M. E., & Nuechterlein, K. H. (1984). Psychophysiological dysfunctions in the developmental course of schizophrenic disorders. *Schizophrenia Bulletin, 10,* 204–232.

Doody, G. A., Goetz, M., Johnstone, E. C., Frith, C. D., & Cunningham-Owens, D. G. (1998). Theory of mind and psychoses. *Psychological Medicine, 28,* 397–405.

Fodor, J. A. (1983). *The modularity of mind.* Cambridge, MA: The MIT Press.

Frith, C. D. (1992). *The cognitive neuropsychology of schizophrenia.* London: Lawrence Erlbaum.

Frith, C. D., & Corcoran, R. (1996). Exploring "theory of mind" in people with schizophrenia. *Psychological Medicine, 26,* 521–530.

Gopnik, A., & Wellman, H. M. (1994). The theory theory. In L. A. Hirschfeld & S. A. Gelman (Eds.), *Mapping the mind: Domain specificity in cognition and culture.* Cambridge, UK: Cambridge University Press.

Gottesman, I., & Shields, J. (1972). *Schizophrenia and genetics: A twin study vantage point.* New York: Academic Press.

Heinrichs, R. W. (1993). Schizophrenia and the brain. *American Psychologist, 48,* 221–233.

Hirschfeld, L. A., & Gelman, S. A., (Eds.) (1994). *Mapping the mind: Domain specificity in cognition and culture.* Cambridge, UK: Cambridge University Press.

Jablensky, A., Sartorious, N., Ernberg, G., Anker, M., Korten, A., Cooper, J. E., Day, R., & Bertelsen, A. (1992). *Schizophrenia: Manifestations, incidence, and course in different cultures.* Psychological Medicine Monograph Supplement 20. Cambridge, UK: Cambridge University Press.

Kinderman, P., Dunbar, R., & Bentall, R. P. (1998). Theory-of-mind deficits and causal attributions. *British Journal of Psychology, 89,* 191–204.

Kolb, B., & Whishaw, I. Q. (1990). *Fundamentals of human neuropsychology.* New York: W. H. Freeman & Co.

Lezak, M. D. (1995). *Neuropsychological assessment.* Oxford, UK: Oxford University Press.

Lillard, A. (1998). Ethnopsychologies: Cultural variations in theories of mind. *Psychological Bulletin, 123,* 3–32.

Marr, D. (1982). *Vision.* New York: W. H. Freeman.

McCarthy, R. A., & Warrington, E. K. (1990). *Cognitive neuropsychology: A clinical introduction.* New York: Academic Press.

McKenna, P., Clare, L., & Baddeley, A. D. (1995). Schizophrenia. In Baddeley, D. A., Wilson, B. A., & Watts, F. N. (Eds.), *Handbook of memory disorders.* New York: Wiley.

Nisbet, H., Siegert, R. J., Hunt, M., & Fairley, N. (1996). Improving schizophrenic inpatient's Wisconsin card-sorting performance. *British Journal of Clinical Psychology, 35,* 631–633.

Pantelis, C., & Nelson, H. (1994). Cognitive functioning and symptomatology in schizophrenia: The role of frontal—subcortical systems. In A. S. David & J. C. Cutting (Eds.), *The neuropsychology of schizophrenia.* London: Lawrence Erlbaum.

Pinker, S. (1997). *How the mind works.* New York: Norton.

Premack, D., & Woodruff, G. (1978). Does the chimpanzee have a theory of mind? *Behavioural and Brain sciences, 4,* 515–526.

Schneider, K. (1959). *Clinical psychopathology.* New York: Grune & Stratton.

Shore, B. (1996). *Culture in mind: Cognition, culture and the problem of meaning.* New York: Oxford University Press.

Sperber, D. (1994). The modularity of thought and the epidemiology of representations. In L. A. Hirschfeld & S. A. Gelman (Eds.), *Mapping the mind: Domain specificity in cognition and culture* (pp. 39–67). Cambridge, UK: Cambridge University Press.

Tanaka-Matsumi, J., & Draguns, J. G. (1997). Culture and psychopathology. In J. W. Berry, M. H. Segall, & Kagitcibasi, C. (Eds.), *Handbook of cross-cultural psychology* (pp. 449–491). Allyn & Bacon.

Tooby, J., & Cosmides, L. (1992). The psychological foundations of culture. In J. H. Barkow, L. Cosmides, & J. Tooby (Eds.), *The adapted mind: Evolutionary psychology and the generation of culture* (pp. 19–136). New York: Oxford University Press.

Tseng, W. S., & McDermott Jr., J. F. (1981). *Culture, mind and therapy: An introduction to cultural psychiatry.* New York: Brunner/Mazel.

Van der Does, A. J. W., & Van den Bosch, R. J. (1992). What determines Wisconsin Card Sorting performance in schizophrenia? *Clinical Psychology Review, 12,* 567– 583.

Wing, J. K. (1992) Differential diagnosis of schizophrenia. In D. J. Kavanagh (Ed.), *Schizophrenia: An overview and practical handbook* (pp. 6–22). London: Chapman & Hall.

World Health Organization. (1979). *Schizophrenia: An international follow-up study.* Geneva, Switzerland: Author

Zeki, S. (1993). *A vision of the brain.* Boston: Blackwell Scientific Publications.

PART III

Applications and Implications

13

Translating Cultural Observations Into Psychotherapy: A Functional Approach

Junko Tanaka-Matsumi,

Douglas Y. Seiden, and Ka Nei Lam

Studies on healing practices across cultures have revealed the close relationship between basic cultural concepts and specific forms of intervention. A shared worldview and shared beliefs by therapist and client concerning the presenting problem are considered universal features of effective therapy in its cultural forms (Frank & Frank, 1991). In his review of variations in psychotherapeutic procedures, Prince (1980) concluded that Western conceptions of psychotherapy must be drastically expanded if one is to understand the therapeutic procedures of other cultures. Recognizing this very broad context of the crosscultural tradition in psychotherapy, we examine the utility of a functional analytic approach to crosscultural clinical assessment. We apply a combined etic–emic perspective (Segall, Dasen, Berry, & Poortinga, 1999) to organize the diverse literature on culture and psychotherapy. The etic position examines universalist features of all forms of psychotherapies (Draguns, 1996a). The emic, or cultural relativist, position helps accommodate culture at the individual level.

   Functional analysis, as will be reviewed in this chapter, is a prominent feature of behavior therapy, which is an empirical approach to clinical case formulation, intervention, and evaluation (Haynes & O'Brien, 1990). Conceptually, a functional analytic approach in behavior therapy has rejected the psychiatric-medical model of abnormal behavior, emphasized ideographic and contextual analysis, and acknowledged sociocultural norms (Ullmann & Krasner, 1975). The relevance of cultural factors in clinical assessment and intervention with culturally diverse populations has been addressed in the literature on cognitive-behavior therapy (e.g., Hayes & Toarmino, 1995; Hays, 1995; Iwamasa, 1997; Matthews, 1997; Tanaka-Matsumi & Higginbotham, 1996; Tanaka-Matsumi, Seiden, & Lam, 1996), multicultural counseling and therapy (Ramirez, 1999; Sue & Sue, 1999), culture and psychopathology (Tanaka-Matsumi & Draguns, 1997), crosscultural psychology (Segall et al., 1999), and cultural psychiatry (Kleinman, 1977). In the last decade we have also witnessed a very rapid increase in publications on the practice of psychotherapy with ethnic minority clients in the United States (see Pedersen, Draguns, Lonner, & Trimble, 1996). These and many other publications have articulated the need for developing culturally sensitive assessment and therapy and for training competent and ethical therapists. However, very limited empirical research on psychotherapy with ethnic minority groups has been conducted, and there has been an even greater paucity of studies on specific conditions that are supposedly crucial for therapeutic effectiveness (Sue, Zane, & Young, 1994).

CULTURAL ACCOMMODATION IN PSYCHOTHERAPY

Culture has been defined in many different ways. Culture is "the man-made part of the environment" (Herskovits, 1948, p. 17). It encompasses "behavioral products of others who preceded us and it contains values, language, and a way of life" (Segall et al., 1999, p. 2). From a semiotic perspective, culture is "an historically transmitted pattern of meanings embodied in symbols" (Geertz, 1973, p. 89). Cultural psychologists emphasize a dynamic interaction of context and person. Effective communication between the therapist and the client in psychotherapy is based on the shared cultural meanings of the concepts and idioms of distress (Mullings, 1984). Pedersen (1997) advocates that all psychotherapies are culture-centered, and that multiculturalism is generic to all counseling relationships. However, the field has yet to develop specific questions to ask during crosscultural clinical assessment in order to guide the clinician's decision making.

The goal of cultural accommodation in psychotherapy is the integration of the cultural context with the design of clinical services. Crosscultural therapists practice cultural accommodation by analyzing the indigenous meanings of deviant behaviors, their perceived causes, and the social reactions they provoke. Kleinman (1978) advocates "therapy as negotiation." He suggests four procedures for negotiating both the meaning of the client-therapist interaction and the cultural meaning of the client's presenting problem. First, the therapist encourages clients to give their own explanation of the presenting problem. Second, the therapist discloses the explanation, or explanatory model, that he or she uses to interpret the problem. Third, the two frameworks are compared for similarities and discrepancies. Finally, the client and clinician translate each explanatory model into mutually acceptable language, so that they may jointly set the content of target behaviors for treatment and outcome criteria.

EMIC AND ETIC ASPECTS IN INDIGENOUS THERAPIES

Indigenous therapies are developed from within a culture to meet the needs of its members in a particular sociocultural context, rather than being transported from the outside. A number of psychotherapy researchers have observed that indigenous therapies have both etic and emic, or cultural, aspects. As a participant observer, Kakar (1982) studied ancient healing practices in India as practiced by shamans and mystics. The success of traditional healing practices in India is attributed to the sharing of the Indian worldview by the healer, the patient, and his or her extended family. The goal of therapy in India is to restore the relational self. Healing practices there often involve the patient's family members, who participate in rituals to expel the bad spirits believed to be the cause of the disorder.

In Africa, strong beliefs in the supernatural causation of disorders have imposed social and cultural limitations on Western psychotherapy (Sow, 1980). In rural Ghana, Field (1960) observed that depressed women would gather in a shrine and participate in time-limited dramatic healing rituals to purge depression, rather than dealing with this distress individually. The cultural practice of healing rituals is reinforced due to their positive effect on depressed women themselves and hence their community. In urban Ghana, Mullings (1984) attributes the success of indigenous therapies such as dramatic rituals to the use of a particular explanatory framework. Here cultural symbols and metaphors are used to explain the nature of illness and the goal of reintegrating the sick person to the lineage and extended family. Csordas & Lewton's (1998) review of the literature on studies of indigenous religious and ritual healing around the world reveals a strong adherence to supernatural worldviews and practices based on cosmic epistemologies. Religious practices, as well as hypnosis, serve to modify and regulate reality of the individual (Prince, 1992; Schumaker, 1995).

Roland (1988), who has practiced psychoanalysis in Japan and India, proposes that the various concepts of psychoanalysis are universal, but that both therapy and therapist training are highly culture specific. He uses the individualism and collectivism dimensions to describe cultural differences in therapist-patient relationships and communication styles. In addition, he discusses the limitation of individual oriented confrontation in therapy in a culture where interdependence has been reinforced to maintain highly ritualized interpersonal relations and social roles. In the Japanese indigenous Morita therapy (Morita, 1928/1998) and Naikan therapy (Tanaka-Matsumi, 1979), an important therapeutic goal is that of social restoration. This is accomplished not by systematic verbal exploration of problems between therapist and client, but rather by initial social isolation from the client's troubling interpersonal networks and by providing a highly structured therapeutic setting and daily schedule to facilitate self-reflection and acceptance of fears and anxieties. Reynolds (1980) calls these Japanese indigenous therapies the quiet therapies due to their emphasis on acceptance of the current plight, structured self-observation, and highly limited and ritualized verbal exchanges between the therapist and the client.

Snacken (1991) distinguishes three models of intervention with non-Western clients: intercultural, bicultural, and polycultural. Intercultural therapy, pioneered in Belgium and France, involves either a single anthropologist-psychologist familiar with the client's language and culture (and sometimes belonging to the client's culture) or two anthropologist-psychologists working in collaboration. Though indigenous terminology may be employed (e.g., *sorcery*), intercultural intervention draws on Western theory (behavioral or analytic systems). What Snacken calls bicultural therapy, as developed by Collomb in Dakar, includes a native healer as member of the treatment team. Although the Western practitioner and traditional healer try to work together, the client consults with each separately and receives both Western and traditional forms of intervention. Snacken's third category, polycultural therapy, best represented by the work of Nathan in France, is an ambitious undertaking in which the client meets at the same time with approximately 15 therapists of diverse national or ethnic backgrounds. In addition, the client is invited to attend with his or her own doctor, psychologist, psychiatrist, or social worker. In polycultural therapy, a multicultural environment is created that transcends the Western–non-Western dichotomy between therapist and client, and in which client's fears of traditional charlatanism or Western "black magic" are allayed.

In sum, psychotherapy is often construed as a social influence process in which both client and therapist variables play important roles in treatment selection and outcome. The context of therapy should be consistent with the beliefs and practices of the client's culture. The goal of cultural accommodation can be enhanced by taking into account the forms and content of indigenous therapies, which reveal culture specific explanatory frameworks for the diagnosis and treatment of abnormal behaviors (Nathan, 1994).

CULTURAL CONSIDERATIONS IN BEHAVIOR THERAPY: A FUNCTIONAL ANALYTIC APPROACH

Crosscultural therapy is broadly defined as an integration of universal principles and culturally distinctive values (Draguns, 1996b). The literature on crosscultural assessment and therapy is in agreement that the therapist must accommodate to the client's unique ethnic and cultural background (Pedersen et al., 1996). Crosscultural therapy occurs when the therapist and the client come from cultures or subcultures with different contingencies of behavior and cultural practices. As cultural and ethnic diversities increase in a given society or a nation, so does the need for extending the application of specific forms of therapy to diverse clients.

Conceptually, the question of cultural differences in behavior therapy has already been addressed (Kanfer & Schefft, 1988; Ullmann & Krasner, 1975). Skinner (1971) emphasized that culture is an integral part of the context of behavior and should be evaluated carefully through functional analysis. He equated culture with the social environment or the evolution of the social contingencies of reinforcement, stating that "individuals shape each other's behavior by arranging contingencies of reinforcement, and what contingencies they arrange and hence what behavior they shape are determined by the evolving social environment, or culture, responsible for their behavior" (Skinner, 1988, p. 48). Contextualists (e.g., Biglan, 1995) emphasize the importance of larger social structures, including societal values and norms that maintain the individual's behavior.

Behavior therapy is founded on the use of empirical single subject designs and assessment of functional relationships between a person's behavior and the environment (Baer, Wolf, & Risley, 1968). This assessment is achieved by means of functional analysis, whose goal is the "identification of important, controllable, causal functional relationships applicable to a specified set of target behaviors for an individual client" (Haynes & O'Brien, 1990, p. 65).

The literature on behavior therapy has always emphasized the close relationship between clinical assessment and treatment. Kanfer and Phillips (1970) stressed that assessment should have "practical clinical utility" (p. 504). They proposed that functional analysis could provide information directly applicable to the formulation of a behavior therapy strategy, and that a functional analysis of behavior was "part and parcel of treatment" (p. 509). As yet, however, there are few practical guidelines for conducting functional analyses with clients whose cultural backgrounds are different from that of the clinician.

At the 1998 World Congress of Cognitive and Behavioral Therapies, Tanaka-Matsumi (1998) presented a symposium on crosscultural functional assessment. The presenters pursued two goals: (1) to examine the influence of cultural variables in behavior therapy case formulation from epistemological, conceptual, and methodological perspectives; and (2) to develop specific recommendations for a culturally sensitive application of behavioral assessment principles. Drawing on an empirical study of behavioral clinicians' cognition, Evans and Paewai (1998) proposed a combined cultural and functional analytic approach to meet the challenge of the bicultural context consisting of white European Pakeha settlers and the indigenous Polynesian people, the Maori, in New Zealand. They outlined a 15-point checklist of quality indicators of culturally sensitive functional analytic procedures for use with the Maori. Included among the 15 checkpoints are an assessment of the client's cultural identity, the use of the client's own idiom (metaphor, symbolism, and language), an assessment of the cultural relevance of certain thoughts that precede the target behavior, and access to culturally relevant social support networks. These cultural considerations greatly expand the scope of behavior therapy, providing a culturally sensitive constructional perspective of clinical assessment (Evans, 1993). The panel agreed that, although the larger cultural and historical context of the client has not been adequately addressed in traditional cognitive behavioral assessment, functional analysis is capable of accommodating cultural variables.

In the remainder of this chapter, we examine both the universal theoretical foundations and the culturally specific requirements of the practice of cognitive-behavior therapy with culturally different clients. We examine how a functional approach and cultural accommodation by the therapist can be put into practice in crosscultural behavior therapy. The eight steps of the Culturally Informed Functional Assessment interview (CIFA; Tanaka-Matsumi, Seiden, & Lam, 1996) are used to illustrate how we can translate cultural observations into cross-cultural cognitive behavioral assessment and treatment planning.

THE CULTURALLY INFORMED FUNCTIONAL ASSESSMENT (CIFA) INTERVIEW: TRANSLATING CULTURAL OBSERVATIONS INTO CASE FORMULATION

How does the behavior therapist conduct a behavioral interview that provides the information needed to formulate culturally sensitive hypotheses regarding problem behaviors, controlling variables, and treatment variables? In principle, we believe that functional analysis can assist behavior therapists in developing culturally effective intervention programs because it identifies the functional relationships between a client's presenting problem(s) and the sociocultural environment.

The CIFA interview (Tanaka-Matsumi et al., 1996) is an instrument designed to (1) increase the accuracy and cultural relevance of case formulation and avoid diagnostic errors, (2) foster the credibility of therapy and prevent early termination, (3) enhance clients' expectation of positive change, and (4) increase clients' active participation in and compliance with treatment.

At each stage of the CIFA interview, the evaluator compares and contrasts the points of view of the client, family, and culture among themselves and with the evaluator's own emerging case formulation. The goal is to define problems accurately, demonstrate respect for the client's culture, and through negotiation arrive at solutions in a manner acceptable to all parties involved. Specifically, the CIFA interview is designed to incorporate the following cultural accommodation criteria in behavior therapy: (1) accepted norms for role behavior; (2) a culture-relevant definition of target behaviors; (3) expectations regarding intervention; and (4) culturally sanctioned change agents (Tanaka-Matsumi & Higginbotham, 1996).

Step 1: Assessment of Cultural Identity and Acculturation

The purpose of the initial stage of the CIFA interview is to assess the cultural identity of the client and the extent of cultural mismatch with the clinician. The sources of information are the client, family or significant others, and the therapist's knowledge of the client's culture.

Marsella and Yamada (in press) regard ethnocultural identity as the extent to which an individual endorses and manifests the cultural traditions and practices of a particular group. Ethnocultural identity is closely related to the development of positive self-identification (Fudge, 1996; Organista & Munoz, 1996; Shiang, Kjellander, Huang, & Bogumill, 1998) and individual's acculturation strategies (Berry & Kim, 1988). The client's acculturation can be assessed empirically using available acculturation scales, such as the Racial Identity Attitude Scale for African Americans (Helms, 1986) and the Suinn-Lew Asian Self-Identity Acculturation Scale (Suinn, Rickard-Figueroa, Lew, & Vigil, 1985) among others. These acculturation scales are designed to assess the client's language(s), social support network, knowledge of cultural practices, participation in certain ethnic and cultural activities, and cultural/ethnic identity.

Berry and Kim (1988) evaluated individual differences in mode of acculturation and found that people with acculturation difficulties reported greater stress and adaptation problems. Information about the client's acculturation gathered at the beginning of the assessment is important with regard to its role as a potential stressor, especially when it is discrepant with that of the family system (Szapocznik & Kurtines, 1993) and, due to its potential influence, via language, with problem expression and therapeutic rapport (Malgady, Rogler, & Costantino, 1987).

Knowledge obtained at this initial stage of the interview can help determine the need for a translator or cultural consultant, though the drawbacks of these options as compared with a clinician/client cultural match must be considered. Ethnic and language match between the therapist and the client have been reported to be important treatment variables for some ethnic groups including Asian Americans and Latino Americans. However, the effect of ethnic match has been found to interact with other variables such as the client's English language proficiency, socioeconomic status (SES), and level of acculturation (Dana, 1993).

Step 2: Presenting Problems

After assessing the client's cultural identity and acculturation, the clinician turns to the presenting problem. The crosscultural therapist evaluates the client's presenting problems with reference to the client's cultural norms in order to avoid misdiagnosis (Evans & Paewai, 1998; Shiang et al., 1998). Whether various aspects of the client's behavior are perceived by the therapist as normal or deviant will influence judgment as to problem type and severity and subsequent treatment decisions.

Clients' self-report of problems is influenced by the cultural context of their learning history. For example, Kleinman (1982) reported that Chinese patients diagnosed with neurasthenia reported predominantly somatic complaints (e.g., dizziness, weakness, chronic pain, and fatigue) and did not verbally express dysphoric mood and other psychological symptoms in a spontaneous manner as is the case with Western depressed clients. However, when he explicitly inquired about certain depressive symptoms according to the DSM-III criteria, they admitted to dysphoric mood, low self-esteem, and trouble concentrating, among other psychological complaints. Kleinman (1982) proposed that neurasthenia in Chinese patients is a cultural idiom for communicating depression with somatization. Draguns (1996b) suggested that somatic symptom presentation is a "culturally shared and context-specific code" (p. 414) among Chinese. Clinicians in Chinese medical settings may reinforce somatization and ignore psychological complaints. Clinicians, as well as patients, are influenced by cultural contingencies.

The therapist interviews family members and cultural informants to actively inquire about the cultural meanings of the presenting problems and the extent to which such behaviors are deviant in terms of excesses and deficits. Further probes by the therapist should determine whether symptoms resembling thought disorder or hallucinations suggestive of psychosis instead may be culturally normative thought processes, idioms of distress, a culture bound syndrome, or perhaps associated symptoms of a nonpsychotic disorder. For example, Whaley (1998) reports that African Americans are generally suspicious of receiving services by whites due to cultural mistrust. African American patients may therefore appear unduly paranoid in psychiatric settings if they are interviewed by white clinicians. In this case, clinician bias would lead to overdiagnosis of paranoid symptoms if the clinician is not familiar with the African Americans' norm of cultural mistrust, which serves as a self-protective function against threats to self-esteem in an interracial social environment.

In the case of a Japanese culture-bound disorder called *Taijin Kyofusho* (Tanaka-Matsumi, 1979), which is translated as anthrophobia, clients fear that their bodily defects (e.g., their gaze, blushing, body odor, or facial expression) offend others. Their complaints are marked by an intense awareness of others, hypersensitivity to the perceived defect, and anxious apprehension. In a collectivistic society that reinforces interdependence and social affiliation, Taijin Kyofusho clients fear that they disturb the interpersonal harmony due to their defect. An American therapist, assessing a Japanese client who reports a fear of displeasing others due to the client's own gaze, might be tempted to call this a delusion, due to the deviancy of this thought and fear from American norms. However, in Japan, fear of eye contact is common even among normal people. Japanese culture reinforces other-oriented concerns, such as "I am offending my colleagues at work due to my eye gaze." The client's fear is an exaggeration of cultural rules regarding eye contact, and a culturally normative concern for how one's behavior affects others (Seiden, Lam, & Tanaka-Matsumi, 1996).

In sum, the therapist has the responsibility of considering the cultural context of the client's presenting problems, and communicating in such a way as to enhance the client's and community's expression of cultural idioms of distress. Familiarity with the crosscultural psychopathology literature can help therapists develop a contextual understanding of both universal and culturally variable aspects of a variety of disorders (Tanaka-Matsumi & Draguns, 1997).

Step 3: Causal Explanatory Model Elicitation

The purpose here is to probe explanatory models of the client's problems and their possible solutions (Higginbotham, West, & Forsyth, 1988; Kleinman, 1978). The therapist gathers contextual data including culture-specific idioms of distress, perceived causes of the problem, and help-seeking behavior. Consistent with steps 1 and 2, the therapist interviews the client, the family, and if necessary, cultural informants. The client's explanations are compared with those of the family and culture so as to avoid (1) pathologization of seemingly unusual but culturally normative responses and (2) minimization of behaviors that may not appear clinically relevant but are, in fact, culturally deviant (López, 1989).

An example of pathologization is when an American school psychologist referred a Japanese child attending an American school to a Japanese therapist because the child was too shy, quiet, and socially "immature" in comparison to American peers. However, the Japanese child said that he had behaved similarly in his former Japanese school where teachers expected students to be obedient, quiet, and conforming. His parents were surprised that the school recommended their child for counseling because they simply considered him to be quiet.

An example of minimization is when a Chinese female student in special education was referred to a Chinese therapist for an evaluation. This student was simply described as "quiet, shy, withdrawn, and fearful" in the school record. However, the Chinese therapist found her to be atypical even using Chinese norms. She had no friends, exhibited extreme social anxiety, had flat affect and no eye contact, could not carry on a conversation in either English or Chinese, and gave irrelevant responses to questions. Her parents told the Chinese therapist that their daughter was "spaced out, does not talk at all at home, just sits and looks at books and is scared to do a lot of things." They considered that "there is something wrong with her brain." Her American teachers may have minimized the severity of the student's dysfunction and assumed that her shyness was explained by cultural differences. These examples underscore the importance of collecting data from the client, family, and the school to contextualize the presenting problems of children.

Perhaps the most telling cultural examples of causal explanatory frameworks are those of culture bound disorders (Prince, 1993). Carr and Vitaliano (1985) propose a culture specific stress response model to assess culture bound disorders, such as *amok* in Malays. Amok is a Malay culture bound disorder believed to be caused by "sickness of liver." Patients are typically young men who have lost something they value (e.g., they have lost property, incurred gambling debts, or have experienced a death in the family). Their extreme frustration and inability to cope with their distress is communicated via anger, violence, excitement, and irritation. Amok has its own culturally approved causal explanation based on social learning practices in the Malay culture of Southeast Asia. Similarly, all culture bound disorders are associated with culturally unique explanations of etiology as well as culturally salient responses by others to the individual manifesting the folk illness.

Step 4: Functional Assessment

The cornerstone of the CIFA interview is the functional assessment. It is the clinician's assessment-derived integration of all the important functional relationships among variables concerning a particular client and involves a process of clinical decision making and problem solving in case formulation (Nezu, Nezu, Friedman, & Haynes, 1997). Functional analysis is conducted after the clinician has become familiar with cultural variables, which provide a normative baseline both for presenting problems and the client's behavior in the interview. The functional analysis identifies antecedent events and consequences of problem behaviors within the client's social network. Cultural factors are viewed as embedded in the client's larger social environment and reinforcement history. Behaviors, cognitions, and emotions that deviate from the client's cultural and/or subcultural norms are probed to determine "important, controllable and causal functional relationships" (Haynes & O'Brien, 1990). This functionalist approach, emphasizing the functions of different behaviors in the individual's environment, stands in contrast to the structuralist approach to analyzing behavior disorders. This latter is exemplified by classification of the form of the behavior, such as by reference to topographic criteria listed in the DSM-IV, which is a standard manual for achieving a syndromal diagnosis without regard to the larger context of the client's difficulties (Thakker & Ward, 1998).

Historically, assessment of antecedents and consequences has evolved from a focus on events in the physical and social environment to recognition of "private events" (Skinner, 1953, p. 257). Kanfer and Saslow (1969) proposed the S-O-R-K-C model, which includes a role for the biological state of the organism ("O") as a mediator of stimulus-response relationships. The notion of biological variables as mediating the environment-behavior link has grown beyond the physiological state to include as mediators (a) temporary somatic (e.g., feeling tired), cognitive (e.g., focusing on past failures), and affective (e.g., feeling happy at a concert) states; and (b) learning history (e.g., a history of reinforcement for assuming a sick role) (Kanfer & Schefft, 1988).

Functional analysis includes the following: (1) identification of problem behaviors that are related to a client's current life circumstances; (2) identification of controlling stimuli, which maintain the problem behaviors, by evaluating both historical and current environmental and organismic events preceding and following those behaviors; (3) selection of target behaviors and intervention techniques; (4) selection of a change agent who is likely to increase the probability of target behavior maintenance and generalization in the naturalistic environment; (5) motivational and developmental factors; and (6) evaluation of process and outcome in terms of behavior change relative to the unique baseline of the individual or group, and through social validation of the target behavior. Various authors of behavioral assessment have articulated and elaborated on these specific goals of functional analysis (e.g., Baer et al., 1968; Haynes & O'Brien, 1990; Kanfer & Saslow, 1969; Nezu et al., 1997).

In addition to the standard questions posed in a behavioral interview, the clinician inquires as to whether the client's reactions to identified controlling variables are similar to or different from typical reactions of their cultural reference group. The clinician seeks to determine whether behavior that differs from the norms of the therapist's culture is normative given the social contingencies of the client's past and/or present psychosocial environment. For example, in Goldstein's (1974) case report of a Navajo child, a counselor attempted to develop the child's attending behavior by selecting eye contact as a target behavior to increase. Eye contact among the Navajos, however, is taken as a stare or "evil eye." The target behavior in this instance was not based on functional analysis, was not culturally acceptable, and attempts at its modification created additional problems for the child. By contrast, a constructivist functional analysis attempts to identify culturally adaptive behaviors that should replace the culturally maladaptive behavior of the client (Evans, 1993).

Sometimes the therapist may find that the client fails to discriminate culture-relevant cues as antecedent stimuli for appropriate social behavior. For example, social contingencies for assertiveness versus conformity may differ in individualistic and collectivistic cultures, and several hypotheses can be advanced to account for cultural sanctions against the display of negative emotions in collectivistic versus individualistic societies (Markus & Kitayama, 1991). Negative emotions indicate disengagement of self from others. A public expression of anger, in particular, disrupts interdependent relationships among ingroup members. Therefore ingroup members learn to be vigilant to cultural antecedents of anger to prevent confrontation. They avoid anger-related antecedents by developing specific role behaviors defined by the status within a social hierarchy.

Focusing on specific behaviors and the context of their occurrences can be useful for individuals who are less ready or have not been reinforced by their social environment to express their emotions. Moreover, the process of identifying the antecedents and consequences of target behaviors helps to uncover both universal and culturally salient functional relationships even when experiences are described and labeled differently in different cultures. Lam (1999) found that, although Chinese children in Hong Kong differed in the extent to which they endorsed sad or angry feelings, their responses to interview questions revealed a differentiation between the experience of sadness and anger. The antecedents of anger (*shengqi* in Chinese) were primarily related to perceived undesirable behaviors of others against the child himself or herself (e.g., teasing, hitting, scolding, or blaming without reason). Anger was rarely perceived by the children as related to their own behavior. Alternatively, antecedents of sadness (*youchou* or *bunkuaile* in Chinese) were more frequently related to the children's own mental state or behaviors (e.g., loneliness, a sense of loss, poor grades, or the perception of having done something wrong). However, it is of note that both the experiences of sadness and anger were associated with interpersonal events. The salience of this interpersonal context of affective experience is consistent with the traditional observation that the self in Chinese culture is defined in relation to others (Gao, Ting-Toomey, & Gudykunst, 1996). On the other hand, the self-deprecation associated with sadness and the sense of injustice associated with anger in Chinese culture have been reported in Western cultures as well (Tanaka-Matsumi, 1995).

In functional assessment, to assess social contingencies of presenting problems the therapist interviews not only the client, but family members as well, and assesses the extent to which the client's problem affects them. Also assessed are factors linking the psychosocial environment with levels of functioning, such as culturally salient social stressors and social support. In addition, the therapist asks how family members respond to the client's problem behavior in everyday situations (Boyd-Franklin, 1989). The therapist should also probe how changing the client's behavior could affect the family in both positive and negative ways.

Crosscultural Reliability of Functional Assessment

Seiden (1999) has recently demonstrated the reliability of crosscultural behavioral case formulation of Chinese neurasthenia using functional assessment. He presented Chinese American and European American clinicians with videotaped behavioral interviews conducted by a Chinese behavior therapist. Patients were four Chinese American immigrants with symptoms of the culture bound syndrome, neurasthenia. On the basis of the video material, each clinician made functional assessment decisions for one of the four videotaped patients (e.g., the problems, their antecedents and consequences, and suggested treatments). Clinical decision content demonstrated majority consensus both within and between clinician cultures on specific crossculturally validated categories. For example, majorities within each clinician culture targeted problems that were somatic; antecedents that were cognitive, somatic, or related to the home/family environment; and consequences that were affective or somatic.

In Seiden's (1999) study, the two clinician groups also demonstrated expected crosscultural differences in their clinical decisions. For example, proportionally more Chinese American than European American clinicians targeted problems involving somatization (e.g., somatization of emotional problems), whereas proportionally more European American than Chinese American clinicians targeted cognitive problems (e.g., intrusive thoughts about adjustment to the United States). In addition, proportionally more Chinese American than European American clinicians targeted stress related antecedents (e.g., stress at work) and social environmental consequences (e.g., extra attention from family members and relief from household responsibilities) as being functionally related to the patients' problems. Although each of the four patients experienced the somatic symptoms associated with neurasthenia, the content of agreed-upon intervention targets and treatments varied from patient to patient. This indicated that neurasthenia is not a unitary phenomenon, and highlighted the usefulness of functional assessment in generating context-rich data necessary for individualized treatment planning. In the CIFA interview, the functional analysis, together with information previously gathered regarding cultural identity, acculturation, presenting problems, and causal explanatory models, forms the basis for the clinician's own explanatory model and case formulation of the client's problem.

Step 5: Causal Explanatory Model Comparison and Negotiation

Having arrived at a case formulation, the clinician proceeds to compare this clinical causal explanatory model with that of the client. Increasing the agreement between the explanatory models of client and clinician has been proposed as a means of improving communication, increasing satisfaction and compliance, and decreasing frustration and management problems. At this stage, the clinician, client, and/or family compare and contrast elements of their respective explanations for the problem and attempt to resolve discrepancies. Specifically, negotiating explanatory models may involve agreeing on (a) definitions of terminology, (b) causation, and/or (c) whether or not to apply a specific label to a problem. For example, Jenkins (1988) reported that the majority of the relatives of Mexican American psychiatric patients who had a hospital diagnosis of schizophrenia said that the problem was one of *nervios* (nerves), which is a familiar and less stigmatizing illness label among Mexican Americans.

Even when the clinician and client or family do not share similar values or agree on the meanings of certain behaviors, incorporating the client's or family's opinions into the case formulation should enhance the likelihood of agreement on target behaviors and treatment goals. For example, during a diagnostic interview in Hong Kong with the third author, a Chinese boy, who had recently immigrated to Hong Kong from Mainland China, admitted social phobic experiences. These included fear and avoidance of speaking in class or participating in social activities, failure to make direct eye contact, and feelings of isolation and anger as a result of rejection and teasing by peers. Although the child's parents readily perceived their son's behavior as problematic, they framed the problem more in terms of his possible difficulty in getting a future job than in terms of his current subjective distress in school, dissatisfaction with interpersonal relationships, or level of assertiveness, these latter problems likely being the focus of Western individual therapy. They acknowledged the practical value of participating in social activities more readily than the associated personal enjoyment as a goal of therapy in and of itself. The Western-trained Chinese therapist was able to increase the parents' willingness to agree to a social skills intervention by taking into account their frame of reference rather than trying to convince them of the values and goals implicit in Western psychotherapy.

Step 6: Treatment Variables

This step involves the generation, comparison, and negotiation of explanatory models relating to treatment variables. These include culturally acceptable treatment goals, target behaviors, change agents, and techniques. Behavior therapy actively seeks and trains specific individuals such as parents and teachers, who can reinforce clients in the naturalistic environment to be part of the intervention. The use of behavior change agents selected from the client's own environment should increase the probability of the target behavior's maintenance and generalization in the naturalistic environment. Numerous authors have also noted the success of therapeutic procedures that rely on the ability of social networks to influence the identified client (e.g., Boyd-Franklin, 1989; Leung & Lee, 1996; Shiang et al., 1998). Since one major goal of any psychotherapy is the reintegration of the client into the appropriate social network, behavior therapy's functional approach to identifying effective change agents is consistent with its contextual emphasis.

The therapist should acknowledge culturally salient help-seeking preferences of the client in order to facilitate negotiation of acceptable settings and treatment strategies, and to increase compliance. The therapist should ask the client and/or family about prior help-seeking experiences, their own preferences concerning treatment, and the acceptability and perceived consequences of the clinician's treatment proposals. The therapist should also inquire about culture specific treatment modalities. Finally, modifications are discussed in an attempt to arrive at a mutually acceptable treatment plan.

Techniques of therapeutic changes are numerous, diverse, and generic (Bandura, 1969; Frank & Frank, 1991). For example, De Silva (1988) identified 14 techniques of behavior change in the literature of the early Buddhism practiced in Sri Lanka and other parts of Asia. The Buddhist techniques focus on training in mindfulness and meditation, and also include (1) fear reduction through graded exposure, (2) use of rewards to increase desirable behavior, (3) use of modeling, (4) stimulus control, (5) aversion techniques to eliminate undesirable behavior, (6) social skills training, (7) self-monitoring, (8) control of intrusive thoughts, (9) intense exposure to unwanted thoughts to reduce attachments to them, (10) a graduated approach to develop positive feelings toward others, (11) using discriminative cues to control behavior, (12) use of response cost to reduce undesirable behavior, (13) use of family members as behavior change agents, and (14) behavioral methods. Although these techniques are embedded within the Buddhist cultural and religious context, they are consistent with the techniques used in modern behavior therapy. Therefore, behavior therapy procedures should appeal to Buddhist client groups wishing to develop self-control, if it was used in a culturally appropriate context (De Silva, 1988).

Step 7: Data Collection

In this phase of the CIFA interview, the clinician explores the acceptability and consequences of data collection to the client and family and how they may be looked on by the cultural reference group. Central to behavior therapy is the ongoing assessment of treatment targets and/or behaviors under consideration for eventual intervention. However, clients may not expect to be asked to monitor their target behavior. Therapists should clearly explain what it is that they want clients to do, and they should model self-monitoring procedures in the session. They may fill out some hypothetical data together with the client to illustrate the steps. For example, the first author has trained parents of Japanese children with vocal and motor tic disorders to record the severity of tics each day and to note any significant events of the day. By so doing, parents gradually learn the association between the fluctuating intensity and frequency of tics and life events in the child's environment. Parents can then take an active part in their child's therapy and cooperate in the implementation of behavior change techniques at home. With individual clients, therapists should start with a simple procedure to develop clients' skills in self-monitoring and review the data in the session to demonstrate the benefit of data collection for the client. Data-based therapy procedures set specific goals for therapy and therefore clients are likely to develop more awareness of their own target behaviors.

Step 8: Other Treatment Concerns

Following agreement on treatment and data collection modalities, the final step of the CIFA interview is a discussion of treatment duration, treatment course, and expected outcome. The concerns of the client and family are addressed, including issues related to financing, scheduling, transportation, and confidentiality. The interview may be considered complete if the clinician is of the opinion that the interview process has resulted in agreement on a course of action acceptable both from a therapeutic and ethical standpoint. If agreement has not been reached and the clinician is pessimistic as to the likelihood of success, an appropriate referral can be made to other helpers with approaches coinciding more closely with the client's or family's preferences.

CONCLUSION

Crosscultural therapy involves the practice of assessment and therapy by a therapist whose cultural background differs from that of the client. The literature on culture and psychopathology and guidelines for functional analytic case formulation converge in their emphasis on the contextual nature of human suffering. Recognizing this, we have formulated specific functional approaches to crosscultural therapy, with a focus on behavioral assessment and therapy in a crosscultural context. It is important to note that functionalist approaches can be applied to a diversity of therapeutic practices. To this end, we have included many examples from different therapies to illustrate the importance of understanding the cultural context of therapeutic practices. The future of crosscultural psychotherapy depends on our ability to gather and learn from empirical data on the effectiveness of traditional and innovative therapies as practiced in the crosscultural therapist-client context.

REFERENCES

Baer, D. M., Wolf, M. M., & Risley, T. R. (1968). Some current dimensions of applied behavior analysis. *Journal of Applied Behavior Analysis, 1,* 91–97.

Bandura, A. (1969). *Principles of behavior modification.* New York: Holt, Rinehart & Winston.

Berry, J. W., & Kim, U. (1988). Acculturation and mental health. In P. R. Dasen, J. W. Berry, & N. Sartorius (Eds.), *Health and cross-cultural psychology: Towards applications* (pp. 207–236). Newbury Park, CA: Sage.

Biglan, A. (1995). *Changing cultural practices.* Reno, NV: Context Press.

Boyd-Franklin, N. (1989). *Black families in therapy: A multisystem approach.* New York: Guilford Press.

Carr, J. E., & Vitaliano, P. P. (1985). The theoretical implications of converging research on depression and the culture-bound syndromes. In A. Kleinman & B. Good (Eds.), *Culture and depression* (pp. 244–266). Berkeley, CA: University of California Press.

Csordas, T. J., & Lewton, E. (1998). Practice, performance, and experience in ritual healing. *Transcultural Psychiatry, 35,* 435–512.

Dana, R. H. (1993). *Multicultural assessment perspectives for professional psychology.* Boston: Allyn & Bacon.

De Silva, P. (1988). Buddhist psychology: A therapeutic perspective. In U. Kim & J. W. Berry (Eds.), *Indigenous psychologies: Research and experience in cultural context* (pp. 221–239). Newbury Park, CA: Sage.

Draguns, J. G. (1996a). Humanly universal and culturally distinctive: Charting the course of cultural counseling. In P. B. Pedersen, J. G. Draguns, W. J. Lonner, & J. E. Trimble (Eds.), *Counseling across cultures* (pp. 1–20). Thousand Oaks, CA: Sage.

Draguns, J. G. (1996b). Abnormal behavior in Chinese societies: Clinical, epidemiological, and comparative studies. In M H. Bond (Ed.), *The psychology of Chinese people* (pp. 171–212). Hong Kong: Oxford University Press.

Evans, I. M. (1993). Constructional perspectives in clinical assessment. *Psychological Assessment, 5,* 264–272.

Evans, I. M., & Paewai, M. K. (1998, July). Functional analysis in a bi-cultural context. In J. Tanaka-Matsumi (Chair), *Cross-cultural functional assessment.* Symposium conducted at the World Congress of Behavioral and Cognitive Therapies, Acapulco, Mexico.

Field, M. J. (1960). *Search for security: An ethnopsychiatric study of rural Ghana.* Evanston, IL: Northwestern University Press.

Frank, J. D., & Frank, J. B. (1991). *Persuasion and healing.* Baltimore, MD Johns Hopkins University Press.

Fudge, R. (1996). The use of behavior therapy in the development of ethnic consciousness: A treatment model. *Cognitive and Behavioral Practice, 3,* 317–336.

Gao, G., Ting-Toomey, S., & Gudykunst, W. (1996). Chinese communication processes. In M. H. Bond (Ed.), *The psychology of Chinese people* (pp. 280–293). Hong Kong: Oxford University Press.

Geertz, C. (1973). *The interpretation of cultures.* New York: Basic Books.

Goldstein, G. S. (1974). Behavior modification: Some cultural factors. *Psychological Record, 24,* 89–91.

Hayes, S. C., & Toarmino, D. (1995). If behavioral principles are generally applicable, why is it necessary to understand cultural diversity? *The Behavior Therapist, 18,* 21–23.

Haynes, S. N., & O'Brien W. H. (1990). Functional analysis in behavior therapy. *Clinical Psychology Review, 10,* 649–668.

Hays, P. A. (1995). Multicultural applications of cognitive-behavior therapy. *Professional Psychology Research and Practice, 26,* 309–315.

Helms, J. E. (1986). Expanding racial identity theory to cover the counseling process. *Journal of Counseling Psychology, 33,* 62–64.

Herskovits, M. J. (1948). *Man and his works: The science of cultural anthropology.* New York: Knopf.

Higginbotham, H. N., West, S., & Forsyth, D. (1988). *Psychotherapy and behavior change: Social, cultural and methodological perspectives.* New York: Pergamon.

Iwamasa, G. Y. (1997). Behavior therapy and culturally diverse society: Forging an alliance. *Behavior Therapy, 28,* 347–358.

Jenkins, J. H. (1988). Conceptions of schizophrenia as a problem of nerves: A cross-cultural comparison of Mexican-Americans and Anglo-Americans. *Social Science and Medicine, 26,* 1233–1243.

Kakar, S. (1982). *Sharmans, mystics and doctors.* New York: Knopf.

Kanfer, F. H., & Phillips, J. S. (1970). *Learning foundations of behavior therapy.* New York: John Wiley & Sons.

Kanfer, F. H., & Saslow, G. (1969). Behavioral diagnosis. In C. Franks (Ed.), *Behavior Therapy: Appraisal and status* (pp. 417–444). New York: McGraw-Hill.

Kanfer, F. H., & Schefft, B. K. (1988). *Guiding the process of therapeutic change.* Champaign, IL: Research Press.

Kleinman, A. (1977). Depression, somatization, and the "new cross-cultural psychiatry." *Social Science and Medicine, 11,* 3–9.

Kleinman, A. (1978). Clinical relevance of anthropological and cross-cultural research: Concepts and strategies. *American Journal of Psychiatry, 135,* 427–431.

Kleinman, A. (1982). Neurasthenia and depression: A study of somatization and culture in China. *Culture, Medicine and Psychiatry, 6,* 117–190.

Lam, K. (1999). *An emic-etic approach to the study of childhood depression among Hong Kong children.* Unpublished manuscript. Hofstra University, Hempstead, NY.

Leung, P. K., & Lee, P. W. (1996). Psychotherapy with Chinese. In M. H. Bond (Ed.), *The handbook of Chinese psychology* (pp. 441–456). Hong Kong: Oxford University Press.

López, S. R. (1989). Patient variable biases in clinical judgment: Conceptual overview and methodological considerations. *Psychological Bulletin, 106,* 184–204.

Malgady, R. G., Rogler, L. H., & Costantino, G. (1987). Ethnocultural and linguistic bias in mental health evaluation of Hispanics. *American Psychologist, 42,* 228–234.

Markus, H. R., & Kitayama, S. (1991). Culture and the self: Implications for cognition, emotion, and motivation. *Psychological Review, 98,* 224–253.

Marsella, A. J., & Yamada, A. M. (in press). Culture and mental health: An introduction and overview of foundations, concepts, and issues. In I. Cuellar & F. Paniagua (Eds.), *The handbook of multicultural mental health: Assessment and treatment of diverse populations.* New York: Academic Press.

Matthews, A. K. (1997). A guide to case conceptualization and treatment planning with minority group patients. *The Behavior Therapist, 20,* 35–39.

Morita, S. (1998). *Morita therapy and the true nature of anxiety-based disorders (Shinkeishitsu)* (A. Kondo, Trans.). Albany, NY: State University of New York Press. (Original work published 1928.)

Mullings, L. (1984). *Therapy, ideology and social change: Mental healing in urban Ghana.* Berkeley, CA: University of California Press.

Nathan, T. (1994). *L'influence qui guerit.* Paris: Editions Odile Jacob.

Nezu, A. M., Nezu, A., Friedman, S. H., & Haynes, S. N. (1997). Case formulation in behavior therapy: Problem solving and functional analytic strategies. In T. D. Eells (Ed.), *Handbook of psychotherapy case formulation* (pp. 368–401). New York: Guilford.

Organista, K. C., & Munoz, R. (1996). Cognitive behavioral therapy with Latinos. *Cognitive and Behavioral Practice, 3,* 255–270.

Pedersen, P. B. (1997). *Culture-centered counseling interventions: Striving for accuracy.* Thousand Oaks, CA: Sage.

Pedersen, P. B., Draguns, J. G., Lonner, W. J., & Trimble, J. E. (Eds.). (1996). *Counseling across cultures* (4th ed.). Thousand Oaks, CA: Sage.

Prince, R. H. (1980). Variations in psychotherapeutic procedures. In H. C. Triandis & J. G. Draguns (Eds.), *Handbook of cross-cultural psychology: Vol. 6. Psychopathology* (pp. 291–350). Boston: Allyn & Bacon.

Prince, R. (1992). Religious experience and psychopathology: Cross-cultural perspectives. In J. F. Schumaker (Ed.), *Religion and mental health* (pp. 281–290). New York: Oxford University Press.

Prince, R. H. (1993). Culture-bound syndromes: The example of social phobias. In A. M. A. Ghadirian, & H. E. Lehmann (Eds.), *Environment and psychopathology* (pp. 550–572). New York: Springer.

Ramirez, M. (1999). *Multicultural psychotherapy: An approach to individual and cultural differences* (2nd ed.). Boston: Allyn & Bacon.

Reynolds, D. K. (1980). *The quiet therapies: Japanese pathways to personal growth.* Honolulu: University Press of Hawaii.

Roland, A. (1988). *In search of self in India and Japan: Toward a cross-cultural psychology.* Princeton, NJ: Princeton University Press.

Schumaker, J. F. (1995). *The corruption of reality: A unified theory of religion, hypnosis and psychotherapy.* Amherst, NY: Prometheus Books.

Segall, M. H., Dasen, P. R., Berry, J. W., & Poortinga, Y. H. (1999). *Human behavior in global perspective: An introduction to cross-cultural psychology* (2nd ed.). Boston: Allyn & Bacon.

Seiden, D. Y. (1999). *Cross-cultural behavioral case formulation with Chinese neurasthenia patients.* Unpublished Doctoral Dissertation, Hofstra University, Hempstead, NY.

Seiden, D. Y., Lam, K. N., & Tanaka-Matsumi, J. (1996, February). Taijin Kyofusho: Cultural context of social phobias in Japan. In J. G. Draguns (Chair), *Social phobia, Taijin Kyofusho, and anthropophobia: Three disorders or one? Observations in China, Japan, and the United States.* Symposium conducted at the annual meeting of the Society for Cross-Cultural Research, PA.

Shiang, J., Kjellander, C., Huang, K., & Bogumill, S. (1998). Developing cultural competency in clinical practice: Treatment considerations for Chinese cultural groups in the United States. *Clinical Psychology: Science and Practice, 5,* 182–210.

Skinner, B. F. (1953). *Science and human behavior.* New York: Macmillan.

Skinner, B. F. (1971). *Beyond freedom and control.* New York: Bantam.

Skinner, B. F. (1988). Selection by consequences. Commentaries and responses. In A. C. Catania & S. Harnad (Eds.), *The selection of behavior: The operant behaviorism of B. F. Skinner* (pp. 11–76). New York: Cambridge University Press.

Snacken, J. (1991). Guide de le pratique dans un contexte multiculturel et interdisciplinaire. In J. Leman & A. Gailly (Eds.), *Therapies interculturelles* (pp. 135–140). Bruxelles, Belgium: Editions Universitaires, De Boeck Université.

Sow, I. (1980). *Anthropological structures of madness in Black Africa.* New York: International Universities Press.

Sue, D. W., & Sue, D. (1999). *Counseling the culturally different: Theory and practice* (3rd ed.). New York: John Wiley.

Sue, S., Zane, N., & Young, K. (1994). Research on psychotherapy with culturally diverse populations. In A. E. Bergin & S. L. Garfield (Eds.), *Handbook of psychotherapy and behavior change* (4th ed.) (pp. 783–817). New York: John Wiley.

Suinn, R. M., Rickard-Figueroa, K., Lew, S., & Vigil, P. (1985). Career decisions and an Asian acculturation scale. *Journal of the Asian American Psychological Association, 10,* 20–28.

Szapocznik, J., & Kurtines, W. M. (1993). Family psychology and cultural diversity. Opportunity for therapy, research and application. *American Psychologist, 48,* 400–407.

Tanaka-Matsumi, J. (1979). Taijin Kyofusho: Diagnostic and cultural issues in Japanese psychiatry. *Culture, Medicine and Psychiatry, 3,* 231–245.

Tanaka-Matsumi, J. (1995). Cross-cultural perspectives on anger. In H. Kassinove (Ed.), *Anger disorders: Definition, diagnosis and treatment* (pp. 81–90). Washington, DC: Taylor & Francis.

Tanaka-Matsumi, J. (1998, July). *Cross-cultural functional assessment.* Symposium conducted at the World Congress of Behavioral and Cognitive Therapies, Acapulco, Mexico.

Tanaka-Matsumi, J., & Draguns, J. G. (1997). Culture and psychopathology. In J. W. Berry, M. H. Segall, & C. Kâgitçibasi (Eds.), *Handbook of cross-cultural psychology: Vol. 3. Social psychology, personality and psychopathology* (2nd ed.)(pp. 449–491). Boston: Allyn & Bacon.

Tanaka-Matsumi, J., & Higginbotham, H. N. (1996). Behavioral approaches to counseling across cultures. In P. B. Pedersen, J. G. Draguns, W. J. Lonner, & J. E. Trimble (Eds.), *Counseling across cultures* (pp. 266–292). Thousand Oaks, CA: Sage.

Tanaka-Matsumi, J., Seiden, D.Y., & Lam. K. (1996). The culturally informed functional assessment (CIFA) interview: A strategy for cross-cultural behavioral practice. *Cognitive and Behavioral Practice, 3,* 215–233.

Thakker, J., & Ward, T. (1998). Culture and classification: The cross-cultural application of the DSM-IV. *Clinical Psychology Review, 18,* 501–529.

Ullmann, L. P., & Krasner, L. (1975). *A psychological approach to abnormal behavior* (2nd ed.). Englewood Cliffs, NJ: Prentice-Hall.

Whaley, A. L. (1998). Ethnicity/race, paranoia, and psychiatric diagnoses: Clinician bias versus sociocultural differences. *Journal of Psychopathology and Behavioral Assessment, 19,* 1–20.

14

Culture and Cognitive Theory: Toward a Reformulation

Jo Thakker and Russil Durrant

In a provocative and important recent article Anthony Marsella (1998) makes an eloquent plea for the forging of a new metadiscipline of psychology that he labels global-community psychology. Marsella argues that we need a radical rethinking of the fundamental premises of psychology, rooted as they are in Western cultural traditions. Features of an emergent global-community psychology include an emphasis on multicultural and multidisciplinary approaches to human behavior that draw attention to the importance of context and meaning in human lives. Marsella's call for a global-community psychology reflects, in part, a growing body of literature that demonstrates the importance of cultural factors in a diversity of psychological domains such as cognition, emotion, social behavior, and psychopathology.

The relationship between culture and cognition, for example, has been explored in some detail by both psychologists (e.g., Semin & Zweir, 1997; Serpell & Boykin, 1994), and anthropologists (e.g., Bloch, 1998; D'Andrade, 1995). Bartlett's (1932) seminal work on the nature of human memory demonstrated the ways in which cultural knowledge, embodied in schemas, can affect the pattern and process of memory reconstruction. More contemporary research attests to the way cultural factors can impinge on various aspects of cognition, including memory and reasoning (D'Andrade, 1995), attribution style (Morris & Peng, 1994; Semin & Zweir, 1997; Triandis, 1989), knowledge structures, (Serpell & Boykin, 1994), and value hierarchies (Smith & Schwartz, 1997).

The importance of attending to cultural variables in understanding the nature of mental disorders is also becoming increasingly apparent (Tanaka-Matsumi & Draguns, 1997; Thakker & Ward, 1998). For example, the underlying philosophy of the universalist approach to the classification of psychopathology offered by the DSM-IV has been called into question. More specifically, the view entrenched in the biomedical model, that mental disorders are the same across cultures, cannot be sustained (Thakker & Ward, 1998). Presentation of major disorders such as depression and schizophrenia have been shown to vary significantly across cultures (see for example, Draguns, 1995; Kleinman, 1988; Westermeyer, 1989). Furthermore, the existence of a range of culture bound disorders (although diagnostically somewhat controversial), suggests that a satisfactory understanding of mental disorder must take into account the significance of cultural particulars (Kirmayer, 1991). Because cognitive factors often are viewed as central to the understanding of the diagnosis, etiology, and treatment of many mental disorders (e.g., Teasdale & Barnard, 1993; Williams, Watts, MacLeod, & Matthews, 1997), there is much scope for an exploration of the various relations that occur between culture, cognition, and psychopathology, as contributors to this volume demonstrate.

In this chapter, we aim to draw on and extend the implications of the body of research, briefly outlined above, in the context of a dynamic model of mental disorder; one that attempts to do justice to the rich interplay between cognitive, cultural, and biological variables. First, we outline a theoretical perspective of the relations between culture, cognition, and biology presented in the context of a domain specific view of human cognitive architecture. Second, we illustrate the relationship between culture, cognition, and biology in the domain of psychopathology, drawing on the example of anxiety disorder. Third, we present a model of mental disorder developed by Thakker, Ward, & Strongman (in press) that addresses the relationships between culture, cognition, and biology in the context of psychopathology. We conclude with some thoughts on the role of interdisciplinary integration in the domain of psychopathology.

THE RELATIONSHIPS BETWEEN
CULTURE, COGNITION, AND BIOLOGY

"*What we are* is very much a matter of what culture has made us" suggests the philosopher Daniel Dennett (1995, p. 340) in his recent book *Darwin's Dangerous Idea*. It is clear, as Dennett indicates, that people are influenced in a myriad of ways by the culture in which they are embedded. Belief systems or worldviews vary considerably across cultures, with potentially profound implications for human thought and behavior. The striking pattern of within-culture similarities and between-culture differences in human behavior is testimony to the role of culturally acquired patterns of beliefs, desires, and values. However, it is also clear that there are substantial degrees of similarity between peoples of different cultures, regardless of the specific patterns of beliefs and values that occur. Indeed, it has been argued that anthropologists and crosscultural psychologists have focused predominantly on patterns of differences between cultures while neglecting relevant underlying similarities (Brown, 1991).

The question of the nature and degree of crosscultural differences and, more generally, the extent or role that culture plays in human development, have been perennial themes in psychology, anthropology, and sociology. The well-worn distinctions between universalism and relativism and between culture and nature reflect this enduring interest. Focusing more specifically on the relations between culture and cognition we can make a distinction between weak and strong formulations of cultural cognition. The weak version of the relationship between culture and cognition concedes that the contents of cognition are often highly variable across different cultures, however, the processes that underlie these variations are themselves crossculturally invariant.

Thus, for example, although language varies in its surface features in different cultures, this variety is underpinned by universal psychological mechanisms that generate universal grammars (Chomsky, 1975; Pinker, 1994). Empirical support for this weak version of cultural cognition is provided by various lines of research. For example, living-kind classification, the natural taxonomies of flora and fauna, shows strong commonalties across all cultures although the specific contents of the classification scheme are naturally variable (Berlin, 1978; Atran, 1990). Specifically, there is a crosscultural tendency to classify living-kind entities in a hierarchical fashion and to treat biological species in essentialist terms. Of course, the specific animals and plants that people in different cultures treat in such fashions will be determined by local biogeographical features.

In contrast to the weak version of cultural cognition, advocates of the strong version maintain that not only does the content of cognition vary across cultures, but so too does the very nature of cognitive processes. Culture here can be seen to radically affect the basic nature of cognitive and neural architecture. As the psychologist Merlin Donald (1991, p. 14) suggests, "Cultures restructure the human mind, not only in terms of its specific contents, which are obviously culture bound, but also in terms of its fundamental neurological organization." An example of such culture-based effects on neural organization is provided by Jovanovski (1995). According to Jovanovski, people raised in urban areas respond differently to visual tests than people who have grown up in rural areas. The former respond more readily to angular and structured stimuli whereas the latter show more sensitivity to less regular and perhaps more natural configurations. This finding is explained as the result of differential deterioration of specific clusters of cells in the neural cortex during development. Jovanovski (1995) concludes on the basis of this research that " if cultural standards, impressions, and experiences can influence no less than our visual tendencies, then, indeed, we could hardly convincingly deny that those same social characteristics can and do give rise to context-identifiable ideas, interpretations, worries, phobias and obsessions" (p. 295).

How are we to reconcile these two versions of cultural cognition? Should we accept the idea that cultures have the power to radically restructure the fundamental organization of the human mind, or is the influence of culture on cognition a more moderate one? This issue is crucial in the present context, for it lies at the heart of understanding how we should adequately conceptualize the importance of cultural factors in understanding the nature of mental disorder. We will argue that a richer understanding of the relationship between culture and cognition can be fruitfully obtained by adopting a domain specific or modular view of human cognition. Moreover, we argue that a consideration of biological factors, specifically evolutionary considerations, can further our understanding of the culture-cognition interface. Finally, we suggest that we must adopt an approach to human cognition that fully realizes the dynamic reciprocal relationship between mind and world. These three themes reflect important general trends in cognitive theory. In what follows we address each of these points in turn, before combining the central ideas in a way that helps us further our understanding of both cognitive universality and cultural diversity.

THE DECLINE OF INDIVIDUALISM IN PSYCHOLOGY

In a comprehensive review of historical developments in cognitive theory, Bechtel, Abrahamsen, and Graham (1998), note an increasing shift away from approaches to cognition that limit themselves to addressing information processing within the mind, toward a recognition of the importance of the environmental embeddedness of human cognitive systems. For a considerable period of time, mainstream cognitive psychologists have directed their intellectual labors toward elucidating the internal systems of information processing within the human mind via often highly artificial experimental protocols. This approach, by itself, however, has led to an impoverished view of the human mind; one that has failed to do full justice to the real-world nature of human cognition.

This individualist research program in cognitive psychology, which has been labeled methodological solipsism by the philosopher Jerry Fodor (1980), has drawn a variety of criticisms from a diverse range of sources. Philosophers of various theoretical persuasions (e.g., Burge, 1986; Kitcher, 1985; Millikan, 1993) have convincingly argued that the nature of mental states can only be fully understood by reference to the external environment. In a similar vein, researchers in cognitive psychology and artificial intelligence have begun to direct their attention to the situated nature of human cognition (e.g., Clark, 1997) as it occurs in real-world environments (see Hutchins, 1995).

Cognitive anthropologists (e.g., D'Andrade, 1995) have also drawn attention to the way in which environmental factors, specifically those related to the cultural environment, can exert important influences on the nature of cognition. D'Andrade (1995) emphasizes that we should conceptualize the relationship between culture and cognition as essentially reciprocal in nature: the psyche is influenced by cultural representations, which themselves are selected and modified in terms of the capacities of the human cognitive system.

THE MODULARITY OF MIND

Another important development in cognitive theory is the growing acceptance of some version of the modularity thesis of human cognitive architecture (Appelbaum, 1998). Made popular in part by Fodor (1983), proponents of the modularity thesis argue that human cognition can be best characterized as containing many distinct subsystems that are dedicated to specific functions. Modular, or domain specific, approaches to the mind reject the view that knowledge acquisition is driven by a few content-independent domain general processes. Instead, the human mind is replete with a multiplicity of content specific mechanisms dedicated to processing specific classes of information.

The modularity thesis has received a growing body of empirical support. Specifically, there is evidence for modular mechanisms dedicated to various cognitive domains such as language (Chomsky, 1975; Pinker, 1994), biological classification (Atran, 1990; Berlin, 1978), mental state attribution (Baron-Cohen, 1995; Leslie, 1987), object perception (Spelke, 1988), and numeracy (Wynn, 1992), among others (see Hirschfeld & Gelman, 1994, for a good review). However, there still remains considerable debate over many aspects of modularity. It is unclear just how many modules humans possess, how best to characterize them, what their relationships are to one another, and so forth (see Karmiloff-Smith, 1992, and Samuels, 1998, for interesting alternatives). We will not address these issues here. However, it is likely that the range of domain specific mechanisms that humans possess is likely to be supplemented by some more domain general processes, and that there are rich connections between different modules (conceptual ones at least) that give rise to the creative and flexible nature of human cognition.

THE ROLE OF EVOLUTIONARY THEORY

The importance of evolutionary theory for understanding the nature of human mentation and behavior has also received renewed interest in recent times (e.g., Barkow, Cosmides, & Tooby, 1992; Buss, 1995; Pinker, 1997). Evolutionary psychologists argue that to understand how the mind works we must pay due attention to the problems that the mind has been designed to solve. The mind, it is suggested, is as much a product of evolution as is the body, and should be studied using similar methods. Although we reject the claim that evolutionary psychology provides a revolutionary new paradigm for psychological science (e.g., Buss, 1995), we would argue that questions of evolutionary origin are certainly relevant to our understanding of human cognition and its relation to culture.

An evolutionary approach naturally meshes with both a domain specific view of mind and an anti-individualist approach to human cognition. Evolutionary psychologists (e.g., Cosmides & Tooby, 1994; Pinker, 1997) argue that cognitive modules are best characterized as evolved mechanisms with distinct phylogenetic histories. A general purpose view of cognition, it is argued, is biologically unfeasible, because what counts as adaptive behavior differs significantly across different domains. Moreover, there must be some way in which learning is framed, or constrained, in order to direct the organism toward the narrow envelope of contextually relevant behavior. Furthermore, from an evolutionary point of view, cognition must be embedded in the real world. That is, for adaptive behavior to be generated there must be rich, reciprocal relations between the mind and the environment, including the social environment.

EXPLAINING CULTURAL DIVERSITY

At first glance, a modular theory of mind, coupled with an evolutionary perspective, may seem unable to do justice to an understanding of the role of culture in cognition, and the generation of cultural diversity. However, if we accept the thoroughly epigenetic character of human cognitive development, cultural diversity can be viewed as a natural consequence of an evolved, domain specific mind embedded in a rich social and cultural environment. Cultural learning, according to this perspective, is not a passive domain general affair (cultures do not entirely determine the nature of thought), but rather is best thought of as active, directed, and domain specific in character. The view we adopt here is nicely summarized by E. O. Wilson (1998) in his recent book *Consilience*:

Culture is created by the communal mind, and each mind in turn is the product of the genetically structured human brain. Genes and culture are therefore inseverably linked. But the linkage is flexible, to a degree still mostly unmeasured. The linkage is also tortuous: Genes prescribe epigenetic rules, which are the neural pathways and regularities in cognitive development by which the individual mind assembles itself. The mind grows from birth to death by absorbing parts of the existing culture available to it, with selections guided through the epigenetic rules inherited by the individual brain. (p. 127)

To understand how cultural diversity is generated from this perspective, it is useful to consider the important distinctions made by the cognitive anthropologist Dan Sperber (1996) between proper and actual domains. The proper domain of some conceptual module is all the information in the organism's environment that it is the module's biological function to process; the actual domain is all the information that satisfies the module's input conditions. For example, the living-kind module alluded to earlier has been designed to process information about biological species that one encounters in the environment. However, the actual domain of this module will include information about all sorts of other entities such as dinosaurs and dragons, which we have had no direct experience with at all. In a similar fashion, our theory-of-mind module, designed to generate causal explanations of human behavior in terms of intentional states (beliefs, desires, and so forth), is employed to explain the behavior of other animals, and even nonbiological entities such as weather systems and automobiles. In these cases, what remains invariant across individuals are the underlying cognitive operations, while content is free to change depending on specific local details.

Cultural cognition, therefore, can be seen to be generated from an active process of domain specific learning across varying cultural contexts. Although innate knowledge structures guide the organisms to certain classes of information in the environment, culture strongly influences the subsequent form that the acquired knowledge will take. As Gardner (1983, 1985) has argued, modules undergo lengthy developmental constructions and thus are open to potentially strong influences from social and cultural factors.

The perspective on the human mind we have presented in this section thus far suggests that the weak version of the cultural cognition hypothesis is both true and potentially highly relevant in understanding human behavior. Although learning, including cultural learning, is likely to some extent to be constrained along domain specific lines, there are substantial degrees of freedom available for the generation of culturally unique patterns of representations. Moreover, the way various systems of information are integrated in the mind provides further avenues for cultural differentiation. We remain agnostic, however, on the strong version of cultural cognition. Although it is unlikely that cultures radically alter fundamental cognitive processes within domains, there is still room for substantial cognitive reorganization on the basis of specific patterns of development. In evaluating the plausibility of the strong hypothesis on cultural cognition, it is best to proceed on a case-by-case basis.

In the next section we explore some of the implications of the framework presented above in the context of psychopathology. More specifically, we demonstrate the interplay of cognitive, cultural, and biological variables in the context of anxiety disorders.

CULTURE AND COGNITION IN THE CONTEXT OF PSYCHOPATHOLOGY: ANXIETY DISORDERS

Anxiety disorders provide a potentially fruitful example for illustrating the interrelationships that occur between cognitive, cultural, and evolutionary factors in the context of mental disorder. Research on anxiety disorders has often directed attention to the role of cognitive processing mechanisms (e.g., Beck & Emery, 1985; Eysenck, 1997; Mathews & MacLeod, 1994; Williams et al., 1997) as well as invoking the potentially functional or adaptive role that anxiety has to play (e.g., Beck & Emery, 1985; Marks, 1987; Marks & Nesse, 1994). Crosscultural investigations have also revealed considerable cultural patterning in the manifestation of anxiety disorders, as well as the occurrence of specific culture bound instances of anxiety related disturbances (e.g., Al-Issa & Oudji, 1998; Kirmayer, 1991; Levine & Gaw, 1995).

Many important approaches to anxiety have adopted a cognitive perspective. For example, Beck and Emery (1985) have argued that cognitive factors are central to the etiology and maintenance of a wide range of anxiety disorders. Beck and Emery emphasize the role that schemata—cognitive structures that influence a person's appraisals and interpretations of experiences—have to play in relevant information processing tasks. Schemata direct processing resources toward certain aspects of the situation that they are congruent with. The schemata of anxious individuals are characterized by themes of danger, vulnerability, and threat. Thus a range of cognitive distortions and biases are generated in anxious individuals that influence how they experience events and that feed back into their cognitive and emotional states.

Other important theoretical approaches to anxiety (e.g., Eysenck, 1997; Williams et al., 1997) have also adopted a cognitive perspective. Although to some extent similar to the approach pursued by Beck and Emery (1985), both Eysenck and Williams et al. have extended the work of Beck and Emery by highlighting the importance of attending to multiple levels of processing in the context of anxiety disorders. The distinction between perceptual and conceptual processing favored by Williams et al. (1997), for example, is helpful in understanding the nature of unconscious attentional mechanisms that appear to be relevant in the generation of anxiety states. What all the cognitive approaches to anxiety disorders emphasize, however, is the importance of examining the nature of specific attentional and interpretive biases.

The occurrence of such processing biases in anxious individuals has received considerable empirical support from a diverse range of experimental studies (for reviews see Mathews & MacLeod, 1994; Mineka & Gilboa, 1998; Mineka & Sutton, 1992). The general finding from this body of literature is that anxiety is closely associated with typically automatic preconscious biases for threatening information. Some kind of attentional biases seem to exist in all anxiety disorders. Cognitive biases and distortions have been found in patients with social phobia (Foa, Franklin, Perry & Herbert, 1996; Wells & Clark, 1997), panic disorder (Khawaja & Oei, 1998), post-traumatic stress disorder (Cassidy, McNally & Zeitlin, 1992), and specific phobias (Watts, McKenna, Sharrock & Trezise, 1986). Such biases have been shown to occur entirely unconsciously (e.g., Ohman & Soares, 1994), although for some anxiety disorders, such as social phobia, conscious cognitive distortions are also implicated (Wells & Clark, 1997).

The specific pattern of attentional and interpretative biases found in anxiety disorders, along with the nature of the stimuli that elicit them, has led a number of researchers to adopt an evolutionary framework (e.g., Baumeister & Tice, 1990; Beck & Emery, 1985; Marks, 1987; Marks & Nesse, 1994). Broadly speaking, advocates of evolutionary approaches suggest that anxiety in general is adaptive, because it directs cognitive resources and motivates behavior in a manner that is likely to reduce the possibility of harm and hence increase reproductive success. Anxiety disorders, from this perspective, simply reflect exaggerations of various subtypes of normal anxiety (Marks & Nesse, 1994). Marks and Nesse stress the relative domain specificity of anxiety responses; subtypes of anxiety evolved to give selective advantages to particular kinds of danger. These subtypes, however, are only partly differentiated because different threats often co-occur, and similar responses to diverse stimuli are sometimes indicated.

The early work of Marks (1969) and Seligman (1970) on the development of phobias had implicated the role of evolutionarily prepared biases in both attention and learning. Marks argued that humans are more likely to attend to phylogenetically relevant stimuli in the world, a phenomenon he labeled prepotency. In a similar fashion, Seligman argued that humans are more likely to learn fear associations to some classes of stimuli but not to others; that is, humans are prepared to develop fears to objects and events in the world that have important consequences for survival and reproduction. This approach to the development of fears and phobias helps to explain the nonrandom distribution of such fears. As Marks (1987) suggests, humans are more likely to develop phobias to objects and events that would have posed specific threats to reproductive success in ancestral environments. Thus fear of spiders, snakes, heights, social situations, enclosed spaces, and so forth are more prevalent than are fears of dangerous but novel stimuli such as cars and electric outlets. An evolutionary approach also helps to explain the ontogenetic development of such fears and phobias. For example, a fear of heights appears in infants immediately prior to the average age that they begin crawling and intensifies with crawling experience. Similarly, a fear of animals emerges at about age two—an age when infants begin to explore further afield (see Ost, 1987, for details of the ages when different phobias typically emerge). To summarize, evolutionary approaches to anxiety disorders emphasize the role of innate domain specific mechanisms that direct attention (often preconsciously—see Ohman, 1997) toward certain kinds of stimuli in the world: ones that have phylogenetic relevance.

Evolutionary approaches to anxiety disorders, however, have not gone without criticism (e.g., Davey, 1995; McNally, 1987; Merckelbach & de Jong, 1997). Questions have been asked regarding the putative adaptive advantages of specific phobias, such as blood injury phobia (Page, 1994), and their have been critiques of more general approaches such as Seligman's preparedness theory (McNally, 1987; Davey, 1995). The details of these criticisms will not concern us here, however. What emerges as prominent in the challenges to evolutionary approaches is the role that cultural factors have to play in the nature of anxiety disorders. Both Davey (1995) and Merckelbach and de Jong (1997) argue that variations in social taboos, culturally variable patterns of beliefs, locally relevant information about potential dangers, and so forth, exert potentially powerful effects on the development of specific fears. Cultural schemata are conceptualized as providing strong top-down influences on the cognitive mechanisms that direct attention toward relevant stimuli in the environment. Hence it is suggested that it may be cultural, rather than evolutionary, factors that generate expectancy biases regarding the sorts of objects and situations toward which people develop fears and phobias.

Crosscultural approaches to anxiety disorders suggest that they are a universal phenomenon. However, the events that precipitate anxiety are strongly influenced by a diverse range of cultural factors (Aderibigbe & Pandurangi, 1995; Al-Issa & Oudji, 1998; Levine & Gaw, 1995). Al-Issa and Oudji (1998, p. 144), for example, in a recent review of culture and anxiety, conclude: "Epidemiological data suggests [sic] that anxiety disorders are universal. However, the meaning of the concept of anxiety and of its manifestations seem[s] to vary from one culture to another." The existence of a number of culture bound anxiety syndromes serves to underscore this conclusion. Some examples of such culture bound disorders include ataque de nervios, dhat, kayak angst, brain fog, koro, and taijin kyofusho (Levine & Gaw, 1995).

Koro, to take one example, provides an instructive illustration of the role that cultural beliefs have to play in the manifestation of anxiety. Koro occurs in a diverse range of cultures but is most prominent in India, Southeast Asia, and China (Aderibigbe & Pandurangi, 1995). Koro is characterized by an extreme fear that the penis is retracting into the abdomen and will eventually cause death. Individuals with this fear experience extreme panic and terror, often accompanied with heart palpitations, outbursts of sweating, and catastrophic cognitions relating to sexual functioning and the sexual organs (Levine & Gaw, 1995). Koro appears to be associated with a specific pattern of beliefs regarding the existence of koro itself, as well as more general beliefs and values centered on micturation, masturbation, and sexual functioning. The role of beliefs in koro itself in the etiology of this disorder is clearly illustrated in the incidence of koro epidemics, such as the one that occurred in Guangdong, China (Tseng, Mo, Jing, Li, Ou, Chen & Jiang, 1988). Koro has, however, been reported in individuals with no prior knowledge of the disorder. For example, Chowdhury & Rajbhandri (1995) report a case of koro in a Nepali patient, which in the absence of any preexisting beliefs about koro, seemed to be related to more specific beliefs about the fear of semen depletion and guilt associated with masturbation. A general model of koro proposed by Simons (1985) suggests that endemic beliefs about koro (and general beliefs about sexual functions, seminal fluid, and so forth) lead to a greater monitoring and awareness of penile states, which leads in turn to anxiety if the penis appears to be smaller than usual. This anxiety, by reducing blood flow to the penis, increases penile shrinkage, leading to a feedback loop of mounting anxiety. This feedback loop is exacerbated when a koro epidemic is believed to be occurring.

The example of koro and other such culture bound disorders seems to be problematic from an evolutionary perspective. It is hard to see how catastrophic cognitions and attentional biases directed at penile states is likely to further reproductive goals (although no doubt some such story could be concocted). Moreover, the culture specific nature of koro seems to implicate the role of more general and culturally idiosyncratic patterns of belief. However, we argue that the adaptive nature of anxiety has both more general and specific characteristics (see Marks & Nesse, 1994, for a similar perspective), and nicely illustrates the complementary role of evolutionary and cultural factors. Because what is harmful and threatening in the environment is, in some cases, specific to given times and locations, some learning mechanisms implicated in the development of fears are relatively content free. That is, the learning mechanisms are directed toward what other individuals in the community find aversive or threatening; subsequently, some fears will be idiosyncratic to particular cultural or historical contexts. In addition, other kinds of threats are likely to have been more enduring in nature. Thus fears of social exclusion, certain kinds of animals, heights, strangers, and so forth are representative of recurrent threats to survival and reproductive success. More domain specific mechanisms are implicated in the generation of fears in such contexts. Of course, such specific fears can still be exacerbated, attenuated, or altered in various ways depending on specific cultural and developmental contexts. Thus the attentional and interpretive biases found in the context of anxiety disorders reflects both phylogenetically and ontogenetically mediated influences that are directed toward specific objects and events in the physical and cultural environment.

The dynamic, interactive, role that biological and cultural factors have to play in the context of anxiety disorders is nicely illustrated in the case of social phobias. With a lifetime prevalence of eleven and fifteen percent for men and women, respectively, social phobias are one of the more common anxiety disorders that clinicians are presented with (Kessler, McGonagle, Shanyang, Nelson, Hughes, Eshleman, Wittchen, & Kendler, 1994). Cognitive approaches to social phobia (e.g., Wells & Clark, 1997) stress the important role that various cognitive distortions, especially pertaining to the self, have to play in the etiology and maintenance of this disorder. Various lines of research indicate that socially anxious individuals engage in excessive degrees of self-focused processing in social situations (e.g., Hartman, 1983; Hope, Rapee, Heimberg, & Dombeck, 1990). Social phobics are also more likely to choose negative interpretations of ambiguous social situations (Stopa & Clark, 1993) and overestimate the probability that negative social events are likely to occur (Foa et al., 1996). These distortions tend to be domain specific in character, only occurring in the context of social situations.

Fear of social exclusion, argues Baumeister and Tice (1990), is one of the major causes of anxiety and is the essential factor underlying the fears exhibited in social phobics. It is suggested that the desire for interpersonal belongingness is a fundamental human motive (Baumeister & Leary, 1995), one that reflects an evolutionary history of adaptation to social life. Threats of social exclusion generate anxiety, as such indications may be symptomatic of rejection from one's group, which in ancestral environments would have entailed substantial costs in fitness. Baumeister and Tice (1990) indicate that such threats of social exclusion are perceived as threats to the self. The self has the important function of relating a person to their social group. Self-esteem, therefore, may function as a proxy measure of one's interpersonal status (Leary, Tambor, Terdal, & Downs, 1995). Individuals with social phobia represent cases where a concern for social inclusion, coupled with relatively low self-esteem, generates an excessive monitoring of one's behavior in social contexts, leading to negative evaluations of social performance and the various symptom patterns characteristic of social phobia.

The important role of the self in the generation of social anxiety suggests that social phobias should manifest in different ways across cultures. This follows from a consideration of the way that the construction of the self varies depending on the specific cultural contexts (Markus & Kitayama, 1991; Markus, Mullaly, & Kitayama, 1997; Triandis, 1989). Specifically, whereas in Western cultures the self is conceptualized as an independent entity, in other collectivist cultures, such as Japan, the self is an interdependent construct, one that draws its meaning from the context of specific, often highly homogenous social groups. These differences imply different pathways for the generation of self-esteem. As Baumeister and Tice (1990, p. 178) suggest: " . . . high self-esteem arises from believing that one possesses the traits that should maximize one's chances for being included in social groups."

In the context of Western culture the characteristics indicative of high self-esteem and social inclusion include the maintenance of independence, material success, and self-enhancement. By contrast, collectivist cultures emphasize that a positive view of self is intimately linked to the appropriate adjustment of oneself so as to fit in with others in interpersonal situations. These crosscultural differences in the construction of self and corresponding differences in the values associated with social inclusion, should generate variations in the contexts that generate social anxiety. Specifically, in individualistic Western cultures, fear of being negatively evaluated by others should be a primary social concern, whereas in collectivist cultures, fear of not "fitting in" or of giving offense should be relativity more important in social situations.

The existence of the culture bound syndrome taijin kyofusho and the way it contrasts with social phobia as it is manifest in Western cultures is an instructive illustration of some of the differences outlined above. Taijin kyofusho is a common disorder in Japan and is characterized by an excessive concern with offending others by inappropriate social behavior. Typical concerns include fear of embarrassing others by blushing, generating offensive body odors, or having unpleasant facial expressions (Kirmayer, 1991). The unique pattern of symptoms found in taijin kyofusho are linked to the importance of certain values in Japanese culture such as those related to the importance of acting appropriately in front of other individuals. The complex demands of intricately structured status hierarchies in Japan further contribute to the etiology and maintenance of this disorder (Kirmayer, 1991). The development of an interdependent view of self in Japan brings to the fore concerns related to maintaining the appropriate pattern of social behavior in interpersonal contexts.

In summary, universal concern with social inclusion and belongingness to one's social group leads, in some individuals, to social anxiety when such inclusion is perceived to be threatened. The mechanisms that are implicated in the evaluation of one's social acceptance are intricately linked to the construction of self. Following Baumeister and Tice (1990), we suggest that the self can be viewed as an adaptation to social life that functions to provide information regarding one's relative position within the social group. Because the nature of the self varies across cultures, the sorts of situations that generate threats to the self will also manifest cultural variability. These differences will generate variations in the etiology and symptomology of socially related anxiety disorders.

Thus innately prepared, domain specific fears can generate cultural diversity in the manifestation of specific disorders, depending on specific developmental pathways. In accordance with this view, a disorder such as taijin kyofusho can be conceptualized as being bioculturally constructed. More generally, a view of cognition (itself central to an understanding of a diverse range of mental disorders) that emphasizes the centrality of context, evolutionary forces, and domain specificity can help us understand both the ubiquity of anxiety disorders as well as the specific patterns of cultural differences that are found. The relative explanatory role that evolutionary or cultural factors may play in the context of anxiety disorders can be assessed only on a case-by-case basis. However, we wish to highlight here that our understanding of anxiety disorders, and indeed mental disorders in general, is advanced by considering the interplay of multiple factors, including those of a cognitive, cultural, and biological nature. A model of mental disorder, which aims to capture this interplay, is presented in the following section.

Cognitive Theory in Context:
A Model of Mental Disorder

The examples presented above suggest that in the context of psychopathology there are particular aspects of cognition that vary across cultures. Cognitive variability is linked on the one hand to specific biological aspects of cognitive development, and on the other to patterns of cultural diversity. In order to fully understand the relationship between culture and cognition in the context of psychopathology, it is useful to develop a visual conceptualization of the interrelationships between these variables. Figure 14.1 depicts a model that has been used elsewhere to define mental disorder (Thakker, Ward, & Strongman, in press). However, it is equally useful as a means for conceptualizing the nature of cognition and the connection between cognition and other variables that are relevant to psychopathology. Arguably, an adequate theory of cognition must look not only at "core" cognitive components, but also at the forces that act on those components, such as sociocultural and biological factors. Also relevant are factors that are unique to the individual, who may be referred to as the "self."

According to this view, then, cognition is part of a system that has four main components: (1) psychological components, which are the mental processes that are seen as central to cognition, and in relation to which cognition is typically defined; (2) biological components, which are the "hardware" underlying the mental processes; biological components can also be thought of in ultimate terms in respect to evolutionary adaptation and phylogenetic history; (3) sociocultural variables, which constitute the social environment in which the person exists; and (4) the self, which is the individual element or, more precisely, the unique

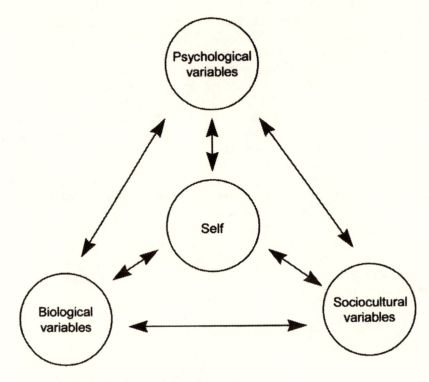

Figure 14.1. A model of mental disorder.

confluence of all the components. The placing of the self in the center of the model emphasizes the very significant and dynamic impact that the self has on all other factors. As indicated by the arrows in the representation, all the variables interact, sometimes directly and sometimes via the self. However, the self as an active purveyor and processor of meaning is seen as critical in the manifestation of mental disorder.

While, as mentioned, this model was previously presented simply as a definition of mental disorder, it is wholly pertinent to the present discussion insofar as it provides a formulation of the relationship between culture and cognition in the context of psychopathology. In terms of understanding mental disorders—especially their etiologies and crosscultural determinants—it is advantageous to analyze cognition in relation to other significant variables with which cognition interacts. However, although this model has four components, each of which is proposed to be essential to understanding psychopathology, it is theorized (Thakker, Ward, & Strongman, in press) that the extent of involvement of each component may vary across disorders. What is suggested, then, is that some disorders may have a strong biological component, whereas others may have a stronger cultural component. The key point is that different disorders are seen as having different etiological pathways, not simply in terms of the precise cause but also in terms of the general type of cause.

A useful distinction to employ in this context is the one drawn by the philosopher Peter Railton (1981) between relevance and salience. Railton argues that we should be striving for ideally complete explanations in science, ones that can elaborate the full panoply of causal (and noncausal) connections that obtain between phenomena. Such an explanation, however, is unlikely to be forthcoming. Individual scientists labor, instead, on illuminating specific aspects of the ideal causal story, and are strongly influenced by pragmatic concerns. The complete causal story determines what is relevant in a particular case, while salience is determined on a more individual basis. Thus in the context of mental disorder, aspects of biology, cognition, culture, and self are all relevant in furthering our understanding of all mental disorders. However, some kinds of variables will be more salient, depending on the disorder under consideration.

For example, in the case of a disorder such as dementia, although it may have important cognitive and cultural aspects, biological variables are probably most salient, in terms of specific patterns of neural degeneration in the brain. Autism, on the other hand, is perhaps most saliently conceptualized as a cognitive disorder, one that results as the malfunction to the "theory-of-mind module" (Baron-Cohen, 1995). In contrast, the Japanese culture bound syndrome of taijin kyofusho (Kirmayer, 1991) suggests the salience of variables that focus on the relationship between culture and the self. Patients with taijin kyofusho, as outlined earlier, demonstrate an extreme form of social phobia characterized by an excessive concern with offending others by inappropriate social behavior. It is likely that cultural variables relating to the inappropriateness of emotional display and the interdependence of self, characteristic of collectivist cultures such as Japan, are predominantly responsible for the specific nature of this disorder. Of course the more general fear of social exclusion is probably universal in nature and may reflect the presence of mechanisms that have evolved to respond to more enduring and ubiquitous threats to survival; so other sorts of variables are relevant in this context, but are arguably not as salient.

One important aspect of the model presented here is that it views psychopathology as occurring within a context. Behavior is mediated by beliefs and values (that is, psychological or cognitive variables) that are influenced to various degrees by cultural circumstances, depending on the specific psychological domain in question. The breakdown of behavior also has similar constraints. These constraints work in two ways. First, behavior is influenced by implicit rules governing that which is considered normal; even when people are mentally unwell they still will attempt to conform to the expectations of those around them. Second, behavior is influenced by folk conceptions and folk categories of mental disorder; people who are mentally ill will be affected by their own ideas of mental illness and by what they believe is typical of people who are "mad" or who have "lost their minds." The impact of cultural beliefs and values on the nature of mental disorders can be assessed only on a case-by-case basis, and will depend in part on the cognitive domains under consideration. It is clear, however, that any fully realized theory of mental disorder must pay due attention to the influence of cultural factors on cognition, biology, and the self.

CONCLUSION

In this chapter we have considered the importance of cognitive theory for understanding the way that cultural variables impact on the nature of psychopathology. We suggest that a view of cognition informed by a domain specific evolutionary approach can prove fruitful in understanding the relationships that exist between culture and cognition and thus between culture and mental disorder. Because, regardless of domain specific constraints, cognitive development is thoroughly epigenetic in nature, there is substantial room for the generation of cultural diversity at the cognitive level, which has important implications for the nature of self and the etiology and presentation of psychiatric disorders.

Marsella (1998), in his plea for a global-community psychology, embraces the values of theoretical pluralism, cultural diversity, and interdisciplinary intellectual endeavor. We concur with these values and suggest that the plenitude of theories of mental disorder pitched at multiple levels of analysis needs to develop in a way that fosters mutual coherence between theories. Thus our best cognitive theories of mental disorder should be consistent with and informed by our best biological and cultural theories, and vice versa. Furthermore, our efforts at theory construction in the field of mental disorder should be informed by the efforts of mainstream psychologists working in a variety of domains. Shweder and Sullivan (1993, p. 517) in their review of cultural psychology conclude by suggesting that "The 1990's is the decade of ethnicity. It should also be the decade when anthropologists and psychologists (and linguists and philosophers) unite to deepen our understanding of the varieties of normal consciousness." We endorse these general ideas, but would add (now that the decade has drawn to an end), that a richer understanding of *abnormal* psychological processes is similarly advanced by considered crossdisciplinary investigations.

REFERENCES

Aderibigbe, Y. A., & Pandurangi, A. K. (1995). The neglect of culture in psychiatric nosology: The case of culture bound syndromes. *International Journal of Social Psychiatry, 41,* 235–241.

Al-Issa, I., & Oudji, S. (1998). Culture and anxiety disorders. In S. S. Kazarian and D. R. Evans (Eds.). *Cultural clinical psychology: Theory, research, and practice.* (pp. 127–152). New York: Oxford University Press.

Appelbaum, I. (1998). Modularity. In W. Bechtel & G. Graham (Eds.), *A companion to cognitive science* (pp. 625–636). Oxford: Basil Blackwell

Atran, S. (1990). *Cognitive foundations of natural history: Towards an anthropology of science.* Cambridge, UK: Cambridge University Press.

Barkow, J., Cosmides, L., & Tooby, J. (Eds.). (1992). *The adapted mind: Evolutionary psychology and the generation of culture.* New York: Oxford University Press.

Baron-Cohen, S. (1995). *Mindblindness: An essay on autism and theory of mind.* Cambridge, MA: MIT press.

Bartlett, F. C. (1932). *Remembering: A study in experimental and social psychology.* Cambridge, UK: Cambridge University Press.

Baumeister, R. F., & Leary, M. R. (1995). The need to belong: Desire for interpersonal attachments as a fundamental human motivation. *Psychological Bulletin, 117,* 497–529.

Baumeister, R. F., & Tice, D. M. (1990). Anxiety and social exclusion. *Journal of Social and Clinical Psychology, 9,* 165–195.

Bechtel, W., Abrahamsen, A., & Graham, G. (1998). The life of cognitive science. In W. Bechtel & G. Graham (Eds.), *A companion to cognitive science* (pp. 1–105). Oxford: Basil Blackwell.

Beck, A. T., & Emery, G. (1985). *Anxiety disorders and phobias: A cognitive perspective.* New York: Basic books.

Berlin, B. (1978). Ethnobiological classification. In E. Rosch & B. Lloyd (Eds.), *Cognition and categorization* (pp. 9–26). Hillsdale, NJ: Lawrence Erlbaum Associates.

Bloch, M. E. F. (1998). *How we think they think: Anthropological approaches to cognition, memory, and literacy.* Boulder, CO: Westview Press.

Brown, D. E. (1991). *Human universals.* New York: McGraw–Hill.

Burge, T. (1986). Individualism and psychology. *The Philosophical Review, 95,* 3–46.

Buss, D. M. (1995). Evolutionary psychology: A new paradigm for psychological science. *Psychological Inquiry, 6,* 1–30.

Cassiday, K. L., McNally, R. J., & Zeitlin, S. B. (1992). Cognitive processing of trauma cues in rape victims with post-traumatic stress disorder. *Cognitive Therapy and Research, 16,* 283–295.

Chomsky, N. (1975). *Reflections on language.* London: Pantheon.

Chowdhury, A. N., & Rajbhandri, K. C. (1995). Koro with depression in Nepal. *Transcultural Psychiatric Research Review, 32,* 87–90.

Clark, A. (1997). *Being there: Putting brain, body and world together again.* Cambridge, MA: MIT Press.

Cosmides, L., & Tooby, J. (1994). Origins of domain specificity: The evolution of functional organization. In L. A. Hirschfeld, & S. A. Gelman (Eds.), *Mapping the mind: Domain specificity in cognition and culture* (pp. 85–116). Cambridge, UK: Cambridge University Press.

D'Andrade, R. (1995). *The development of cognitive anthropology.* Cambridge, UK: Cambridge University Press.

Davey, G. C. L. (1995). Preparedness and phobias: Specific evolved associations or a generalized expectancy bias? *Behavioral and Brain Sciences, 18,* 289–325.

Dennett, D. C. (1995). *Darwin's dangerous idea: Evolution and the meanings of life.* New York: Simon & Schuster.

Donald, M. (1991). *Origins of the modern mind: Three stages in the evolution of culture and cognition.* Cambridge, MA: Harvard University Press.

Draguns, J. G. (1995). Cultural influences upon psychopathology: Clinical and practical implications. In A. Bergman & J. Fish (Eds.), *Special issue: Multicultural influences on mental illness, Journal of Social Distress and the Homeless, 4,* 89–114.

Eysenck, M. W. (1997). *Anxiety and Cognition: A unified theory.* Hove: Psychology Press.

Foa, E. B., Franklin, M. E., Perry, K. J., & Herbert, J. D. (1996). Cognitive biases in generalized social phobia. *Journal of Abnormal Psychology, 105,* 433–439.

Fodor, J. (1980). Methodological solipsism considered as a research strategy in cognitive psychology. *Behavioral and Brain Sciences, 3,* 63–73.

Fodor, J. (1983). *The modularity of mind.* Cambridge, MA: MIT Press.

Gardner, H. (1983). *Frames of mind: The theory of multiple intelligences.* New York: Basic Books.

Gardner, H. (1985). The centrality of modules. *Behavioral and Brain Sciences, 8,* 11–12.

Hartman, L. M. (1983). A meta-cognitive model of social anxiety: Implications for treatment. *Clinical Psychology Review, 3,* 433–456.

Hirschfeld, L. A., & Gelman, S. A. (Eds.). (1994). *Mapping the mind: Domain specificity in cognition and culture.* Cambridge, UK: Cambridge University Press.

Hope, D. A., Rapee, R. N., Heimberg, R. G., & Dombeck, N. J. (1990). Representations of the self in social phobia: Vulnerability to social threat. *Cognitive Therapy and Research, 14,* 177–189.

Hutchins, E. (1995). *Cognition in the wild.* Cambridge, MA: MIT Press.

Jovanovski, T. (1995). The cultural approach of ethnopsychiatry: A review and critique. *New Ideas in Psychology, 13,* 281–297.

Karmiloff-Smith, A. (1992). *Beyond modularity: A developmental perspective on cognitive science.* Cambridge, MA: MIT Press.

Kessler, R. C., McGonagle, K. A., Shanyang, Z., Nelson, C. B., Hughes, M., Eshleman, S., Wittchen, H. U., & Kendler, K. (1994). Lifetime and 12-month prevalence of DSM-III-R psychiatric disorders in the United States. *Archives of General Psychiatry, 51,* 8–19.

Khawaja, N. G., & Oei, T. P. S. (1998). Catastrophic cognitions in panic disorder with and without agoraphobia. *Clinical Psychology Review, 18,* 341–365.

Kirmayer, L. J. (1991). The place of culture in psychiatric nosology: Taijin Kyofusho and DSM-III-R. *Journal of Nervous and Mental Disorder, 179,* 19–28.

Kitcher, P. (1985). Narrow taxonomy and wide functionalism. *Philosophy of Science, 52,* 78–97.

Kleinman, A. (1988). *Rethinking psychiatry: From cultural category to personal experience.* New York: The Free Press.

Leary, M. R., Tambor, E. S., Terdal, S. K., & Downs, D. L. (1995). Self-esteem as an interpersonal monitor: The sociometer hypothesis. *Journal of Personality and Social Psychology, 68,* 518–530.

Leslie, A. (1987). Pretence and representation: The origins of "theory of mind." *Psychological Review, 94,* 412–426.

Levine, R. E., & Gaw, A. C. (1995). Culture bound syndromes. *The psychiatric clinics of North America, 18,* 523–537.

Marks, I. M. (1969). *Fears and phobias.* New York: Academic Press.

Marks, I. M. (1987). *Fears, phobias and rituals.* New York: Oxford University Press.

Marks, I. M., & Nesse, R. M. (1994). Fear and fitness: an evolutionary analysis of anxiety disorders. *Ethology and Sociobiology, 15,* 247–261.

Markus, H. R. & Kitayama, S. (1991). Culture and the self: Implications for cognition, emotion, and motivation. *Psychological Review, 98,* 224–253.

Markus, H. R., Mullaly, P. R., & Kitayama, S. (1997). Selfways: Diversity in modes of cultural participation. In U. Neisser & D. A. Jopling (Eds.), *The conceptual self in context: Culture, experience, self-understanding* (pp. 13–62). Cambridge, UK: Cambridge University Press.

Marsella, A. J. (1998). Toward a "global community psychology": Meeting the needs of a changing world. *American Psychologist, 53,* 1282–1291.

Mathews, A., & MacLeod, C. (1994). Cognitive approaches to emotion and emotional disorders. *Annual Review of Psychology, 45,* 25–50.

McNally, R. J. (1987). Preparedness and phobias: A review. *Psychological Bulletin, 101,* 283–303.

Merckelbach, H., & de Jong, P. J. (1997). Evolutionary models of phobia. In G. C. L. Davey (Ed.), *Phobias: A handbook of theory, research and treatment* (pp. 323–349). Chichester: John Wiley & Sons.

Millikan, R. G. (1993). *White queen psychology and other essays for Alice.* Cambridge, MA: MIT Press.

Mineka, S., & Gilboa, E. (1998). Cognitive biases in anxiety and depression. In W. F. Flack, Jr., & J. D. Laird (Eds.), *Emotions in psychopathology: Theory and research.* New York: Oxford University Press.

Mineka, S., & Sutton, S. K. (1992). Cognitive biases and the emotional disorders. *Psychological Science, 3,* 65–69.

Morris, M. W., & Peng, K. (1994). Culture and cause: American and Chinese attributions for social and physical events. *Journal of Personality and Social Psychology, 67,* 949–971.

Ohman, A. (1997). Unconscious pre-attentive mechanisms in the activation of phobic fear. In G. C. L. Davey (Ed.), *Phobias: A handbook of theory, research, and treatment* (pp. 349–375). Chichester: John Wiley & Sons.

Ohman, A., & Soares, J. J. F. (1994). "Unconscious anxiety": Phobic responses to masked stimuli. *Journal of Abnormal Psychology, 103,* 231–240.

Ost, L. G. (1987). Age of onset in different phobias. *Journal of Abnormal Psychology, 96,* 223–229.

Page, A. C. (1994). Blood-injury phobia. *Clinical Psychology Review, 14,* 443–461.

Pinker, S. (1994). *The language instinct.* London: Penguin.

Pinker, S. (1997). *How the mind works.* London: Allen Lane, the Penguin Press.

Railton, P. (1981). Probability, explanation, and information. *Synthese, 48,* 233–256.

Samuels, R. (1998). Evolutionary psychology and the massive modularity hypothesis. *British Journal of Philosophy of Science, 49,* 575–602.

Seligman, M. E. P., (1970). On the generality of laws of learning. *Psychological Review, 77,* 406–418.

Semin, G., & Zweir, S. (1997). Social cogntion. In J. W. Berry, M. H. Segall, & C. Kagitcibasi (Eds.), *Handbook of cross-cultural psychology: Vol. 3. Social behavior and applications* (pp. 51–77). Boston: Allyn & Bacon.

Serpell, R., & Boykin, A. W. (1994). Cultural dimensions of cognition: A multiplex, dynamic system of constraints and possibilities. In R. J. Sternberg (Ed.), *Thinking and problem solving* (pp. 235–258). San Diego, CA: Academic Press.

Shweder, R. A., & Sullivan, M. A. (1993). Cultural psychology: Who needs it? *Annual Review of Psychology, 44,* 497–523.

Simons, R. C. (1985). Introduction. The genital retraction taxon. In R. C. Simons & C. C. Hughes (Eds.), *The culture-bound syndromes: Folk illnesses of psychiatric and anthropological interest* (pp. 151–155). Dordrecht, the Netherlands: D. Reidel Publishing Company.

Smith, P. B., & Schwartz, S. (1997). Values. In J. W. Berry, M. H. Segall, & C. Kagitcibasi (Eds.), *Handbook of cross-cultural psychology: Vol. 3. Social behavior and applications* (pp. 77–119). Boston: Allyn & Bacon.

Spelke, E. (1988). The origins of physical knowledge. In L. Weiskrantz (Ed.), *Thought without language* (pp. 168–184.) Oxford: Clarendon Press.

Sperber, D. (1996). *Explaining culture: A naturalistic approach.* London: Blackwell Publishers.

Stopa, L., & Clark, D. M. (1993). Cognitive processes in social phobia. *Behaviour Research and Therapy, 31,* 255–267.

Tanaka-Matsumi, J., & Draguns, J. (1997). Culture and psychopathology. In J. W. Berry, M. H. Segall, & C. Kagitcibasi (Eds.), *Handbook of cross-cultural psychology: Vol. 3. Social behavior and applications* (pp. 449–493). Boston: Allyn & Bacon.

Teasdale, J. D., & Barnard, P. J. (1993). *Affect, cognition, and change: Re-modelling depressive thought.* Hove, UK: Lawrence Erlbaum Associates.

Thakker, J. & Ward, T. (1998). Mental disorder and cross-cultural psychology: A constructivist perspective. *Clinical Psychology Review, 18,* 501–529.

Thakker, J., Ward, T., & Strongman, K. T. (in press). Mental disorder and cross-cultural psychology: A constructivist perspective. *Clinical Psychology Review.*

Triandis, H. C. (1989). The self and social behavior in differing cultural contexts. *Psychological Review, 96,* 506–520.

Tseng, W. S., Mo, G. M., Jing, H., Li, L. S., Ou, L. W., Chen, G. Q., & Jiang, D. W. (1988). A sociocultural and clinical study of a Koro (genital retraction panic disorder) epidemic in Guangdong, China. *American Journal of Psychiatry, 145,* 1538–1543.

Watts, F. N., McKenna, F. P., Sharrock, R., & Trezise, L. (1986). Colour naming of phobia related words. *British Journal of Psychology, 77,* 97–108.

Wells, A., & Clark, D. M. (1997). Social phobia: A cognitive approach. In G. C. L. Davey (Ed.), *Phobias: A handbook of theory, research and treatment* (pp. 3–27). Chichester, UK: John Wiley & Sons.

Westermeyer, J. (1989). *Mental health for refugees and other immigrants: Social and preventative approaches.* Springfield, IL: Thomas.

Williams, J. M. G., Watts, F. N., MacLeod, C., & Mathews, A. (1997). *Cognitive psychology and emotional disorders (2nd ed.).* Chichester, UK: John Wiley & Sons.

Wilson, E. O. (1998). *Consilience: The unity of knowledge.* New York: Alfred A. Knopf.

Wynn, K. (1992). Addition and subtraction by human infants. *Nature, 358,* 749.

15

Toward a New Model of Symptom Formation: Implicit Theories and Sexual Offending

Tony Ward and Thomas Keenan

There appears to be little doubt that child molesters think about their victims in a self-serving and distorted manner (Marshall, 1996; Ward, Hudson, Johnston, & Marshall, 1997). For example, children may be depicted by the offender as being sexually provocative and as having benefited from the experience of sexual abuse (Hayashino, Wurtele, & Klebe, 1995; Stermac & Segal, 1989). Much of the empirical and theoretical work in the area of cognitive distortions has examined cognitive content, that is, examined the meaning of offenders' beliefs and attitudes (e.g., Abel, Becker, & Cunningham-Rathner 1984; Abel, Gore, Holland, Camp, Becker, & Rathner, 1989). This work indicates that child molesters have beliefs that legitimize sexual involvement with children and that function to maintain offending. For example, child molesters, most particularly those men offending against someone other than a family member, see children in sexual terms, as wanting sex, as not being harmed by sexual contact with an adult, and view themselves as not really being responsible.

In this chapter we argue that sexual offenders' cognitive distortions emerge from underlying causal theories about the nature of their victims. These implicit theories function like scientific theories in so much as they are used to explain empirical regularities (e.g., other people's actions) and to make predictions about future states of the world. They are relatively coherent and are constituted by a number of interlocking beliefs and their component concepts and categories. The relationship of these beliefs and categories to one another gives each theory its unique explanatory power and form. Thus categories are theory impregnated and can only really be understood via their relationships to other concepts within a theory's network of constructs.

In this chapter we explore the application of the idea that sexual offenders' cognitive distortions can be profitably characterized as theories. The central thesis of this chapter, that maladaptive behavior and symptoms emerge from underlying implicit theories, could just as easily be applied to many forms of psychopathology. For example, in Beck's (1996) cognitive theory of depression, underlying maladaptive assumptions acquired during childhood are hypothesized to cause a person to interpret critical interpersonal events in a distorted and negative manner. The resulting self-statements may contain excessively critical and negative reflections on the self, the world, and the future, and result in persistent low mood, loss of motivation, and other symptoms of depression. In a recent book, Alford and Beck (1997) have described these assumptions as personal theories that directly influence the way individuals ascribe meaning to events and phenomena. The content of such implicit theories is strongly influenced by the broader cultural context within which such individuals function. Western societies tend to be individualistic and therefore the content of depressive beliefs often tends to reflect themes of personal failure and inadequacy (Beck, 1996).

Implicit theories are formed in specific cultural contexts and represent offenders' interpretations evoked by individuals or events at a specific time (Strauss & Quinn, 1997). Along with Sperber (1996) and Strauss and Quinn (1997), we assume that cultural factors exert their influence through individual knowledge structures. That is, in order to explain cultural phenomena, it is necessary to invoke psychological processes as well as broader macro-level phenomena such as cultural institutions. Such lay or implicit theories have also been called folk psychological knowledge and represent everyday understandings of close relationships, other peoples' actions, the structure of the natural world, and the nature of mental states. This knowledge is clearly influenced by culturally derived beliefs, values, and norms (D'Andrade, 1995). A variety of terms have been used to refer to this knowledge, for example, implicit theories, commonsense theories, folk psychological theories, lay theories, or intuitive theories. We will use the term implicit theory to cover all these uses. Such theories are called *implicit* as they are rarely articulated in a formal sense and may not easily be expressed by an individual.

In this chapter we aim to specify in detail the possible content of implicit theories in child molesters. First, we will briefly describe the nature of implicit theories in psychology and then consider the application of this construct to child molesters. Next, based on a review of the scales used to measure cognitive distortions in offenders, we will elaborate a number of the most common implicit theories that describe the thinking of child molesters. Finally, we will consider some research and clinical implications of the implicit theory perspective.

IMPLICIT THEORIES IN PSYCHOLOGY

In recent years a number of researchers in developmental (e.g., Gopnik & Meltzoff, 1997; Wellman, 1990), cognitive (e.g., Keil, 1991; Kuhn, 1989), and personality (e.g., Dweck, Chiu, & Hong, 1995) psychology have argued that understanding and explanation is underpinned by implicit or lay theories. This research suggests that from an early age knowledge is organized into theories that facilitate understanding of the world. Such theories enable individuals to explain and understand aspects of their social environment or their own behavior and cognition, and therefore to make predictions about future events. These predictions typically take the form of expectations and help people control their lives. Theories also constrain the kind of inferences individuals make about unseen or underlying states. For example, inferring that a partner is angry or upset will be based on knowledge of the relationship between certain mental states, conditions, and behavior. Forgetting a birthday (condition), and noting that a partner refuses to converse (behavior), will typically result in a causal inference that he or she is angry (mental state) about the failure to acknowledge his or her birthday. Knowledge of the form of implicit theories concerning mental states (i.e., what mental states are, how they are expressed, how they interact), their relationship to social conditions, and their expression in behavior, enables individuals to make inferences about what another person probably is experiencing and to predict his or her future actions. An individual's cultural understanding partially determines the content of these theories as well as the structure and content of the events that confront him. For example, the relationship between mental state terms, social practices (e.g., birthdays), and subsequent behavior is specified by a culture.

Thus a good deal of our knowledge is thought to be theory-like in some respects (Keenan & Ward, in press). First, many implicit theories contain assumptions that specify an ontology, that is, describe the basic nature of human beings in terms of core (culturally derived) psychological structures and processes. Second, these constructs and their relationships are used to explain human actions in different contexts, and like theoretical terms in a scientific theory, refer to unobservable mechanisms or psychological states. For example, socially avoidant behavior might be explained by reference to fears of rejection, or doubts about the trustworthiness of potential partners. Third, implicit theories are relatively coherent and contain a number of beliefs and concepts that are interconnected.

A final feature in common with scientific theories is that implicit theories produce interpretations of evidence, as opposed to theory neutral descriptions of evidence. In other words, observations are theory-laden. What counts as evidence or information bearing on a theory's truth or falsity depends on its constructs. For example, if a sexual offender believes that children are inherently sexual, he is likely to interpret a child's asking to sit on his lap in sexual terms, rather than as indicating friendliness. Similarly, in Western societies rapists are more likely to interpret a woman's friendly behavior in a suspicious and possibly sexual way (Malamuth & Brown, 1994).

The basic conception of psychological functioning endorsed by implicit theory researchers is a *belief-desire* one. Both beliefs and desires refer to associated groups of mental states, with beliefs to be understood broadly as including knowledge, convictions, suppositions, ideas, and opinions, and desires to be understood broadly as including all pro and con attitudes such as lusts, wants, wishes, preferences, goals, obligations, and values (Wellman, 1990). Together, beliefs and desires lead to action and form the framework within which other peoples' behavior is interpreted (Wellman, 1990). Different cultures and subcultures may vary in terms of the role they ascribe to mental states in generating actions and in the type of mental states favored in certain contexts or domains. For example, it is arguable that Western cultures tend to sexualize children and women and overly emphasize the role of sexual motives in interpersonal interactions.

Individuals learn that the mind interprets situations and that people may represent the same event differently. That is, the mind actively construes and interprets information rather than passively copying events in the world. Therefore, people do not have direct access to reality but rather construct the world mentally. It is this construction that guides their actions and interpretations of others' actions. This is the case even when reality is misrepresented. Chandler has consistently argued in recent years (e.g., Carpendale & Chandler, 1996) that children develop an understanding of false beliefs well before they develop a truly interpretative theory of mind. His theory hinges on the appreciation that people who are exposed to the same information may legitimately come to different beliefs about the situation or person.

As a final point, it is helpful to briefly consider the relationship between early experiences and the development of a theory of mind in children. Children's developing theories are malleable and are clearly affected by their experiences. Keenan and Ward (in press) suggest that there are a number of ways in which the child's development of implicit theories may impact on the development behavior problems. One is that children may develop *deviant theories*, theories that reflect an undue emphasis on content such as aggression or sexuality. For example, Happé and Frith (1996) have argued that children exposed to a history of aggression and violence in the home during the formative years for a theory of mind may develop a "theory of nasty mind," that is, a theory that includes a prominent role for aggressive interactions. Keenan & Ward also suggest that delays in the acquisition of a theory of mind may act as a risk factor for entrance to a developmental pathway that leads to the development of serious problems in peer interaction. Research on individual differences in the development of a theory of mind has begun to show that differences in early factors such as the security of attachment between infant and caregiver are associated with the rate of theory-of-mind acquisition (Meins, Fernyhough, Russell, & Clark-Carter, 1998). Meins et al. (1998) have shown that security of attachment in infancy predicts age differences in performance on theory-of-mind tasks in the preschool years (see also Fonagy, Redfern, & Charman, 1997).

Given the fact that many sexual offenders come from disturbed family backgrounds and are known to show high rates of insecure attachment (Ward, Hudson, & Marshall, 1996), the argument that many offenders would have developed deviant theories of mind and/or experienced delays in the acquisition of a theory of mind is very plausible. Deviant theories and delays in acquisition may result in difficulty understanding other peoples' actions and therefore in a failure to respond appropriately in different social situations. In turn, the offender could experience high levels of interpersonal stress and possibly increased social rejection. In essence, the experience of poor quality early relationships may impact on the development of adaptive implicit theories and ultimately may aid ongoing social alienation and distress. Different cultural models and social norms can impact on children's early learning environments and influence the way they interpret and understand their world. As Bronfenbrenner (1979, 1986) suggests, cultural influences may act on children at many levels, from family-level influences to cultural influences, as transmitted through the media and other institutions. On our analysis, a history of violence has the potential to result in the development of skewed theories about other people (e.g., other people always try to hurt you) and therefore makes it harder to understand and explain their actions.

In this chapter the general theoretical framework referred to above is fleshed out, and detailed examples of implicit theories hypothesized to generate cognitive distortions in child molesters are described. In order to develop these implicit theories a number of recent measures of cognitive distortions and research articles were consulted. The measures include Bumby's (1996) MOLEST Scale, Abel and Becker's Cognitions Scale (Abel, et al., 1984), and the Hanson Sex Attitude Questionnaire (Hanson, Gizzarelli, & Scott, 1994). In addition, a number of empirical studies based on interviews with child molesters and a recent review paper were examined with a view to identifying examples of cognitive distortions (e.g., Neidigh & Krop, 1992; Ward, Fon, Hudson, & McCormack, 1998; Ward et al., 1997). These items helped to constrain the development of the implicit theories listed below, and were also used to check the scope of each implicit theory.

SEXUAL OFFENDERS' IMPLICIT THEORIES

As stated earlier, current research in personality, cognitive, and developmental psychology presents a convincing case for the idea that individuals construct theories about aspects of their world in order to understand, explain, and control it. Drawing on this research, we suggest that sexual offenders' implicit theories about their victims are structured around two core sets of mental constructs: beliefs and desires. These theories contain a number of distinct ideas and mental constructs, including propositions about their victims' desires (wants, wishes, preferences) and their beliefs. These ideas are organized in the form of implicit theories in which basic entities (e.g., women or children) and their relationships and properties are represented. For example, women (entity) may be viewed as untrustworthy, sexually promiscuous (property) individuals who are intent on manipulating (relationship) and sexually enticing (relationship) men (entity). It is plausible to view these types of implicit theories in part, at least, as cultural representations that provide a backdrop against which individual learning experiences operate to strengthen or weaken their influence. Sexual offenders' implicit theories emerge as they attempt to understand the meaning of other peoples' abusive behavior and/or inappropriate cultural messages in various media. Frequently these two factors are associated and may function to strengthen each other's influence, as when a father shows his child pornography at a very early age.

Thus an offender's theory or model of a victim contains a representation of the victim's desires (needs, wants, preferences), beliefs, and attitudes. These implicit theories guide the processing of information, or evidence, that is relevant to the theory's truth or falsity. Evidence that does not fit the theory's basic assumptions and predictions is rejected or interpreted in light of these core assumptions. The offender draws on his implicit theories about victims and infers their mental states, interprets their behavior, and makes predictions about their future actions and mental states.

Implicit theories contain different levels of beliefs or ideas starting with the most general and, at the lower level, referring to particular victims. We hypothesize that offenders' maladaptive implicit theories include general assumptions about the nature of people and the world (e.g., mental states and their relationships to each other and behavior), middle level beliefs dealing with categories of entities, such as women and children, and finally beliefs attributed to a particular victim. The key beliefs are those at the general and middle level; they persist and constitute the conceptual foundation of offenders' interpretations and explanations of victims' actions and mental states.

Thus an offender's implicit theory about a victim or victims is a composite of these different kinds of constructs, beliefs, and ideas. A particular theory will contain relatively abstract assumptions about the nature of the victim and specify the kinds of general capabilities a victim has (e.g., is able to identify needs and to make his/her own decisions), describe the types of beliefs and desires typically found in entities of that kind (e.g., preferences in children), and outline the specific features of his past or current victims.

Implicit theories dictate what counts as evidence and how it is to be interpreted. If there is a discrepancy between an offender's implicit theory and evidence, the evidence may be reinterpreted, rejected, or rarely, the theory may be modified. For example, a child's friendly behavior toward an offender could be interpreted to mean that she wants sex or that she is simply being affectionate. We suggest that a child molester is likely to interpret this behavior (i.e., evidence) in sexual terms. Even in situations where there is no inference to sexual motives on behalf of the child, the offender's implicit theory is unlikely to be substantially altered. It takes consistently contradictory evidence for an implicit theory to be replaced or restructured. Occasional anomalous observations can be accounted for by minor adjustments, such as, "This child is different from most other children" or "She may not want sex on this occasion, but usually when she is behaving in this way, she does." Thus any revisions are likely to be comprised initially of ad hoc hypotheses and only result in a replacement of the original theory when the weight of the counterevidence is too hard to ignore (Gopnik & Meltzoff, 1997; Gopnik & Wellman, 1994). Offenders also select environments (e.g., other child molesters, men with similar attitudes and beliefs) that support their lifestyles and implicit theories. Those who lack well-integrated offense supportive implicit theories, for example, some incest offenders, may primarily exhibit process related distortions, where the aim is to discredit or ignore evidence that they have behaved in an abusive manner. Alternatively, their offending may be a function of state factors, such as being under extreme stress or taking drugs. In these situations, the offender is hypothesized to fail to utilize his adaptive implicit theories (i.e., knowledge) and as a consequence behave in a disinhibited, sexually abusive manner (Keenan & Ward, in press; Ward, Hudson & Keenan, 1998). For example, an individual might believe that children are not capable of making reasoned decisions about sexual activity with adults, but when intoxicated he might not draw on this knowledge and instead make erroneous causal inferences about a child's underlying needs and desires.

EXAMPLES OF IMPLICIT THEORIES IN SEXUAL OFFENDERS

In this section, based on a review of the scales used to measure cognitive distortions in sexual offenders, we elaborate a number of the most common implicit theories that describe the thinking of sexual offenders. Reviewing this material we have identified five implicit theories that collectively are able to account for the majority of specific distortions contained in the above measures and research papers. These are children as sexual objects, entitlement, nature of harm, dangerous world, and uncontrollability.

Children as Sexual Objects

The general assumptions and beliefs associated with this implicit theory revolve around the construal of people as sexual beings, and related to this central characteristic, the suggestion that people are primarily motivated by a desire for pleasure. Children are thought to share this feature and be capable of enjoying and desiring sex. Therefore beliefs about how their sexual needs might be met, in conjunction with the existence of sexual desires, result in sexualized behavior. Thus the claim that "children often initiate sex and know what they want" assumes that they have sexual feelings and preferences and that the expression of these desires is legitimate and even beneficial. Additionally, children are thought to possess the capacity to identify practices and behaviors that satisfy them and to make decisions about when, with whom, and how their sexual needs will be fulfilled. This implicit theory conceptualizes children as possessing certain beliefs, *and* specific desires or wants, and preferences: They possess the knowledge to be able make informed decisions about sexual activity with adults, and are able to develop strategies designed to achieve sexual goals. This implicit theory can lead to an interpretation of children's everyday behavior as revealing sexual preferences and intent, for example, sitting on an adult's lap, exposing their pants while playing, or hugging the offender. Because the existence of sexual desires is viewed as natural, and an intrinsic part of children's nature, sexual experience is viewed as benign and harmless (see below). Therefore any sexual experiences with an adult are unlikely to be harmful, and in fact more likely to have a beneficial effect on a child.

An implication of this implicit theory is that individuals have the right to express their sexual needs. If (early) strong sexual needs are part of our basic nature, then it would be (according to this theory) wrong to deny or distort their expression. Failure to express sexual desires and urges might cause harm and unduly distort or frustrate a person's functioning. Therefore, according to this implicit theory, it is natural to permit the free expression of human sexuality. Because sex is viewed as a defining feature of human beings, it has an almost sacred or cleansing quality. Sex permits us to express love and affection to others, and by virtue of its power can leave people feeling secure and loved. Any sexual behavior is therefore benign and life enriching, and only harmful in extraordinary circumstances.

An associated general belief that underpins the above implicit theory is that human beings are capable of identifying their own needs and making their own decisions. In a sense they are autonomous decision makers and do not require the assistance of others to establish priorities and to formulate plans to accomplish these goals. Children are viewed as possessing the cognitive capabilities to identify their needs and preferences, evaluate how they might best be satisfied, set sexually related goals, and develop a plan to achieve them.

Ironically, the knowledge of cultural differences in sexual behavior and practice may play a role in the offender's beliefs about the legitimacy of their behavior, serving to maintain a belief in the acceptability of their offenses. Cultural differences may be invoked by child molesters as a way of justifying their behaviors, for example, pointing to the practices of the ancient Greeks or of cultures in which children marry at an early age. In these cases, the offender may use cultural differences in sexual practice to attempt to cast the beliefs of their own society as simply another "orientation," which should be recognized as no more legitimate than their own.

Entitlement

This implicit theory is based on the core idea that some people are superior to and more important than others. Because of their superior status such individuals have the right to assert their needs above others', and to expect that this will be acknowledged and agreed to by those who are judged to be less important. The source of this legitimacy might be based on gender, class, or some other factor such as culture. Baumeister and Heatherton (1996) argue that cultural contexts may lead to the development of conditions that legitimize sexually aggressive behavior. Cultures that emphasize individualism may implicitly view the fulfilment of one's own needs at the expense of others' as an acceptable position to hold. For example, men might be viewed as more powerful and important than children and women, and therefore as having the right to have their sexual needs met when they want, and with whom they want. Offenders are hypothesized to believe that they are entitled to special consideration and that victims are likely to feel secure and enjoy the fact that their basic function is to satisfy the offender's sexual and emotional needs. In this implicit theory the desires and beliefs of the offender are paramount and those of the victim ignored or viewed as only of secondary importance.

An implication of the belief that some people are more valuable and important than others is that for such individuals there are no binding universal moral truths or rules. Whatever it is possible to get away with is legitimate and acceptable. High status or privileged individuals' desires and needs are the only arbitrators of what is acceptable, and the expression of these needs is natural and right. Because men (the offender) are of greater importance than children, they have the right to have sex whenever they want to, and the child is expected to permit this, and to, perversely, enjoy the experience of being dominated and controlled. Russell (1995) makes this same point regarding incest offenders, specifically men who offend against their female children. She argues that the male sense of entitlement, derived from their position in a society that fosters the belief that women are responsible for servicing their husband's needs, allows the male to hold the belief that if his wife is not providing for his sexual needs, then his daughter is an acceptable substitute.

Dangerous World

This implicit theory is based on the core belief that the world is a dangerous place and that other people are likely to behave in an abusive and rejecting manner in order to promote their own interests. There are two variations of this implicit theory. The first stipulates that it is necessary to fight back and achieve dominance and control over other people. This involves punishing individuals who appear to inflict harm on the offender and, especially, to ensure that his own position is strengthened. Therefore if children and/or women are perceived as threats and in need of retribution, they may become victims of sexual abuse. The beliefs and desires of other people are a focus of this implicit theory, particularly those signifying malevolent intentions. Therefore the content of this theory refers to the desires of other people to dominate or hurt the offender and the beliefs associated with mental states. In addition, the offender views himself as capable of retaliation and asserting his dominance over others.

The second strand is conceptually related to the perception of the world as threatening, but in this form the major focus is on the unreliability of adults and the dependability of children. The core belief is that many people are untrustworthy, rejecting, and will take unfair advantage of (blameless) men. This is particularly evident with adults; children are thought to be more reliable, accepting, and able to be trusted. They can provide offenders with love and caring and will put the offenders' needs before their own. Therefore the expectation is that offenders' needs to be loved and cared for can be met by children and that they will never exploit or reject them. Children understand the offender's sexual desires and are happy to satisfy him. The content of this implicit theory will contain assumptions about the desires and beliefs of malevolent adults and (potentially) caring children. In contrast to the above variant, the offender believes that he is incapable of direct retaliation or dominance over other adults.

Uncontrollable

The key assumption in this implicit theory is that the world is essentially uncontrollable and inexorable in its actions. Human beings are constituted out of structures and processes that cannot be substantially altered or managed; emotions, sexual feelings, and events all just happen to people, and those people are unable to exert any major personal influence on the world. The basic psychological nature of human beings is thought to be determined during early life by powerful learning experiences and/or biological causes. In some variants of this implicit theory, powerful religious or spiritual forces are construed as causing a person to behave in certain ways, for example, being told "It was a sin, the devil made me do it." Pertinent early learning experiences include being sexually abused as a child, or being exposed to a traumatic event such as the loss of a parent. These uncontrollable factors are thought to leave the offender with deviant preferences that he is unable to suppress or manage. Because (according to this theory) it is not possible to control sexual urges, the only thing a man can do is permit their expression. In a sense, sexual desires are viewed as external to the offender and therefore offenders are not responsible for their sexually abusive behavior. In fact, blame may be directed at those who are viewed as responsible for the experience of deviant sexual desires (e.g., the victim), and an offender may feel blameless, a victim of factors beyond his control.

Additional causal factors may be the experience of stress and alcohol or drug intoxication. The lack of control in such situations may be attributed to earlier experiences that are thought to have caused the person to drink or take drugs, or that caused him to make poor vocational and relationship choices. The key point is that in this implicit theory there are hypothesized to be factors beyond an offender's control that underlie his sexually abusive behavior. The content of this implicit theory is concerned with the belief that mental states are uncontrollable and that desires and needs compel the offender to seek their satisfaction.

Nature of Harm

This implicit theory is concerned with the nature of harm and is based on two general beliefs (a) there are degrees of harm and (b) sexual activity in itself is beneficial and unlikely to harm a person. The first assumption conveys the plausible idea that harm spans a dimension ranging from little or no distressing consequences at one end of the dimension, to extreme damage at the other. The possibility of adverse consequences is moderated by several factors such as the degree of force used, the victim's awareness of the abuse, and its social meaning. One the one hand, a victim who was physically assaulted, was conscious throughout the experience, and where the person inflicting the abuse was in a position of trust and responsibility, is likely to suffer considerable distress. On the other hand, if the victim was not physically harmed, asleep at the time, and was victimized by a stranger, they will (according to the theory) be less seriously affected. Relatedly, if a sexual offense could have been more harmful (i.e., more intrusive, etc.), then any lesser act is viewed as more acceptable, and the offender less culpable. Thus according to this implicit theory, because the victim could have been harmed more, and the offender chose not to do this, he is viewed as having due regard for the victim's well-being and should not be judged too harshly.

The second belief concerns the nature of sexual experience and is essentially based around the idea that sex is inherently a beneficial experience (see "Children as sexual objects" implicit theory). Therefore any distressing effects of sex are thought to be a function of the moderators described above (e.g., society's reaction to it) rather than from the sexual experience itself. As stated above, this is due to the assumption that human beings are essentially sexual in nature and therefore any expression of this fundamental need is natural and good. Thus these two assumptions can lead to a judgement that children are unlikely to be harmed by sex with an adult, and any distress evident is most probably a function of additional violence, or the way people respond to the child's experience, rather than by the sexual abuse itself. This theory is more a secondary one and we suggest it is typically utilized in association with one of the other implicit theories outlined above.

IMPLICATIONS

The content of the implicit theories described above is critical in determining how certain kinds of evidence are to be interpreted and what meaning they might hold for the individual. For example, apparent counterevidence to the theory that sex is beneficial, such as hearing the child cry or decline any sexual advances, can be explained away as either indicating a disguised desire for sex, or being an isolated, and therefore misleading, piece of data. A child's request to sit on an offender's knee could be interpreted as an indictor of sexual interests, or as the child's wanting reassurance or affection. We suggest that a child molester is likely to interpret this behavior in a sexual way because of an underlying implicit theory that children are sexual objects. The content of an implicit theory will cause an offender to disregard or ignore alternative interpretations of offense-related cues and result in subsequent selective information processing. In addition, theories also constrain the kind of inferences individuals make about unseen or underlying states. The actions of a victim (or potential victim) will lead to the activation of an implicit theory and favor the interpretation of this data in a maladaptive manner. In turn, the offender will make inferences about the victim's needs, desires, beliefs, and motives based on this information, and act toward them accordingly. Thus knowledge in the form of implicit theories enables individuals to make inferences about what another person is probably experiencing, and to predict his or her future actions.

The above implicit theories can be organized depending on the degree to which they primarily focus on the offender (entitlement, and uncontrollable implicit theories), the victim (sexual objects and nature of harm implicit theories), or the world (dangerous world implicit theory)—although, it needs to be emphasized that each implicit theory has clear implications for all three of these categories. For example, the assumption that children are sexual beings suggests that the offender is also inherently sexual. Or, the belief that the offender is a special person and therefore entitled to preferential treatment implies that the victim should respect and acknowledge this "fact." Again, the theory that the world is full of untrustworthy and rejecting individuals indicates that the offender should prefer those individuals whom he believes are an exception to this general rule, for example, children.

As described in the section on the nature of implicit theories, each of the above theories contains beliefs about the world, victims in general, and the particular victim or victims in question. As stated above, the content of these theories is hypothesized to be derived from the prevailing cultural backdrop and offenders' specific learning experiences. Therefore a child molester will draw on his knowledge about particular situations and victims (or categories of people such as children), and develop a specific model to account for the actions of his victim and the particular circumstances he finds himself in. This specific theory will enable him to understand and interpret his victims' behavior and make predictions about their future actions. This knowledge will guide his planning and or underpin all his offense-related behaviors.

In the same way that an implicit theory helps an offender to understand and predict another's behavior, so too does knowledge of his implicit theories help the clinician. As we have outlined above, the range of theories that sexual offenders may hold forms a reasonably large set. Moreover, these theories have differing implications for the offender's beliefs and behavior and very likely differ in their specific etiologies. In our view, a clinician could profitably use information about the nature of these specific theories to make inferences about the kinds of judgements and evaluations of sexual content a sexually abusive individual might make/hold. Knowledge of the offender's cognitive structures and typical

ways of processing the world would potentially allow the clinician to more accurately infer how he would see a given situation. Finally, knowing the nature of
such implicit theories could help the clinician to appropriately challenge the
offender's beliefs by structuring evidence (in the course of therapy) that directly
challenges the validity of his theories. This may force the offender to restructure
his views and ultimately push the therapeutic process forwards.

It is possible for child molesters to hold many or just one or two of the above
implicit theories, although they do appear to cluster into distinct content areas.
An individual who believed that children were essentially sexual objects may
also view himself as entitled to assert his needs over those of other people.
However, it is unlikely that he would also view the world as dangerous and
unpredictable. If all human beings are viewed as essentially motivated by a
desire for sex, then the power and control issues evident in the latter theory are
somewhat inconsistent with these concerns. However, it is plausible that an individual might conceive of the world as uncontrollable and also view himself as a
victim of powerful and unmanageable forces.

Related to this possibility, different subtypes of sexual offenders may hold different implicit theories or subtypes of a theory, that is, they could be differentiated according to the diverse content of the beliefs and constructs comprising
their theories. For example, one molester's implicit theory might stress the sexual nature of children, while another might portray them as sources primarily of
emotional support and love in a hostile world. Similarly, an offender might conceptualize children as seductive and as desiring sexual contact with adults, while
another might believe that he is entitled to have sex with whom he wants. The
latter individual's implicit theory is designed to legitimize his perceived importance and right to dominate others.

There is also the related question concerning the differences between child
molesters' implicit theories and those of nonoffenders. The theory presented in
this chapter is a single factor or level II theory (Ward & Hudson, 1998) and is not
intended to be a comprehensive account of sexual offending. The focus is on cognitive distortions and the underlying mechanisms hypothesized to generate them.
We have suggested that maladaptive implicit theories could underpin child
molesters' distorted perceptions of their victims and themselves. It is possible
that nonoffenders also share some of these implicit theories, but unlike offenders, never attempt to sexually abuse children. If this is the case, then maladaptive
implicit theories might be necessary for sexual abuse to occur, but not sufficient.
We have argued elsewhere (Keenan & Ward, in press; Ward et al., 1998) that cognitive distortions interact with other predisposing factors such as failures of self-
regulation. In addition, other factors such as deviant sexual preferences, insecure
attachment, and a lack of social competency could be additional, crucial components in the genesis of such crimes. However, it is our contention that because
implicit theories determine the interpretation of other peoples' actions and therefore constrain the kind of causal inferences that are drawn concerning their
needs, desires, and beliefs, they will have a major role in the development of

maladaptive interpersonal strategies and goals. If a person has a faulty or skewed theory about women or children, he is likely to fail to develop effective intimacy and social skills, and may struggle to understand the way other people function. In other words, his dysfunctional implicit theories cause him to see the world in an offense supportive manner.

CONCLUSIONS

In this chapter we have suggested that child molesters' cognitive distortions are generated by maladaptive implicit theories concerning the nature of victims, the offender, and the world. An examination of a number of scales used to measure distortions, and several papers describing offenders' cognitive distortions, resulted in the formulation of five implicit theories, each capable of generating a number of maladaptive thoughts. Implicit theories are used to explain, understand, and predict the behavior of victims and aid in the planning and execution of sexual offenses. They are typically not consciously articulated and facilitate the processing of offense-related information.

An interesting question concerns the origins of maladaptive implicit theories in sexual offenders. In a recent paper, Ward (in press) argued that they are the result of early developmental experiences and provide children with a way of understanding their interpersonal world. Researchers have identified a number of implicit theories that appear to account for individual differences in children's conceptions of abilities and mental states (e.g., Dweck et al., 1995; Gopnik & Wellman, 1994). The content of these theories appears to be related to differential learning experiences. For example, a greater exposure to critical, demanding parents is likely to result in a child viewing intelligence as fixed and unchangeable (Dweck et al., 1995). Similarly, if a child is confronted with abusive, violent behavior on the part of a parent, he or she is more inclined to interpret other children's benign actions in a hostile and aggressive manner (Ward, Keenan, & Hudson, in press). Clearly the values and content of practices that contribute to the formation of offenders' implicit theories are associated with broader cultural norms and beliefs. A child might witness a physical assault on his mother and conclude that women are inferior to men and should be treated violently. This belief might contribute to the formation of additional dysfunctional attitudes and beliefs about women and subsequent sexually aggressive behavior.

In view of the fact that sexual offenders' early experiences are frequently associated with sexual and physical abuse (Ward et al., in press) it is plausible to assume that their early theories will focus on explaining and understanding the nature of these problems. Premature exposure to sexual activity could leave a child believing that it is normal for adults and children to engage in sex with each other. The extrapolation to sex as the primary or key characteristic of human beings is a plausible extension of such a theory. Each of the above implicit theories could emerge from particular kinds of interpersonal experience and/or modeling by siblings, peers, or parents. For example, consistently rejecting and indifferent parenting may result in the acquisition of a dismissive attachment style and an associated internal working model stressing the importance of personal independence and an avoidance of emotions (Ward, Hudson, Marshall, & Siegert, 1995). Such individuals may develop an exaggerated sense of self-entitlement and find it difficult to appreciate other peoples' point of view. Some maladaptive beliefs may be culturally entrenched and their manifestation in cultural products such as films, television shows, and books provide an alternative source of information concerning the role of deviant sexual preferences in human activities (Marshall, 1996). Arguably, patriarchal societies legitimate male dominance over females and children and therefore provide reinforcement for implicit theories that stress male entitlement (Marshall & Barbaree, 1990). In our view there is an intimate relationship between different cultural values and practices and the kind of learning experiences children are exposed to.

From a clinical perspective, the existence of implicit theories means that a comparatively few integrated beliefs and concepts will generate a great number of cognitive distortions. These influence the way evidence bearing on a theory's truth or falsity is evaluated, and how an offender approaches treatment. Therefore, it is crucially important that therapists identify the core implicit theories associated with a child molester's offense process rather than focus entirely on individual statements. Effective treatment is likely to require the challenging and restructuring of these core theories. Just as cognitive therapy for depression requires the replacement of core maladaptive beliefs in addition to the challenging of automatic thoughts (Beck, 1996), so (we argue) does effective cognitive restructuring with child molesters require the development of more adaptive implicit theories. One goal of therapy, then, is to replace the implicitly held theories with more socially acceptable explicit alternative beliefs, for example, understanding that children are not capable of making reasoned decisions concerning sexual relationships with adults, or that it is a mistake to suggest that children are driven by sexual desires in the way some adults are.

On a final note, we argue in this chapter that it is possible to develop an integrated account of child molesters' cognitive distortions by focusing on the role of implicit theories in offense-related behavior. This perspective links research and theory in a number of diverse areas of psychology and attempts to create a common framework for understanding the relationship between cognition and behavior. It is able to explain the link between culturally entrenched values and beliefs and sexually abusive behavior; implicit theories are formed through a combination of specific learning experiences and are then exposed to cultural practices, values, and beliefs. Arguably, child molesters share with other individuals a need to understand and explain interpersonal regularities and traumatic events. They fashion theories in an attempt to provide this understanding and to help themselves make predictions about future events. Unfortunately, the relative coherence of these implicit theories, their maladaptive content, and the tendency for evidence to be interpreted in a manner consistent with a theory's core assumptions mean that therapeutic change occurs slowly and imperfectly. It is important to investigate the nature of sexual offenders' beliefs about their victims, and people in general, and to develop detailed descriptions of their core ideas. We suggest that an implicit theory perspective can provide us with a useful framework within which to approach the complex problems of child sexual abuse and offender treatment.

REFERENCES

Abel, G. G., Becker, J. V., & Cunningham-Rathner, J. (1984). Complications, consent and cognitions in sex between children and adults. *International Journal of Law and Psychiatry, 7,* 89–103.

Abel, G. G., Gore, D. K., Holland, C. L., Camp, N., Becker, J. V., & Rathner, J. (1989). The measurement of cognitive distortions of child molesters. *Annals of Sex Research, 2,* 135–152.

Alford, B. A., & Beck, A. I. (1997). *The integrative power of cognitive therapy.* New York: Guilford.

Baumeister, R. E., & Heatherton, T. F. (1996). Self-regulation failure: An overview. *Psychological Inquiry, 7,* 1–15.

Beck, A. T. (1996). Beyond belief: A theory of modes, personality, and psychopathology. In P. M. Salkovskis (Ed.), *Frontiers of cognitive therapy* (pp. 1–25). New York: Guilford.

Bronfenbrenner, U. (1979). Contexts of child rearing: Problems and prospects. *American Psychologist, 34,* 844–850.

Bronfenbrenner, U. (1986). Ecology of the family as a context for human development: Research perspectives. *Developmental Psychology, 22,* 723–742.

Bumby, K. M. (1996). Assessing the cognitive distortions of child molesters and rapists: Development and validation of the MOLEST and RAPE scales. *Sexual Abuse: A Journal of Research and Treatment, 8,* 37–54.

Carpendale, J. I., & Chandler, M. J. (1996). On the distinction between false belief understanding and subscribing to an interpretative theory of mind. *Child Development, 67,* 1686–1706.

D'Andrade, R. (1995). *The development of cognitive anthropology.* Cambridge, UK: Cambridge University Press.

Dweck, C. S., Chiu, C., & Hong, Y. (1995). Implicit theories and their role in judgements and reactions: A world from two perspectives. *Psychological Inquiry, 6,* 267–285.

Fonagy, P., Redfern, S., & Charman, T. (1997). The relationship between belief-desire reasoning and a projective measure of attachment security (SAT). *British Journal of Developmental Psychology, 15,* 51–61.

Gopnik, A., & Meltzoff, A. N. (1997). *Words, thoughts, and theories.* Cambridge, MA: MIT Press.

Gopnik, A., & Wellman, H. M. (1994). The theory theory. In L. A. Hirschfeld & S. A. Gelman (Eds.), *Mapping the mind: Domain specificity in cognition and culture* (pp. 257–293). New York: Cambridge University Press.

Hanson, R. K., Gizzarelli, R., & Scott, H. (1994). The attitudes of incest offenders: Sexual entitlement and acceptance of sex with children. *Criminal Justice and Behavior, 21,* 187–202.

Happé, F., & Frith, U. (1996). Theory of mind and social impairment in children with conduct disorder. *British Journal of Developmental Psychology, 14,* 385–398.

Hayashino, D. S., Wurtele, S. K., & Klebe, K. J. (1995). Child molesters: An examination of cognitive factors. *Journal of Interpersonal Violence, 10,* 106–116.

Keenan, T., & Ward. T. (in press). A theory of mind perspective on cognitive, affective, and intimacy deficits in child sex offenders. *Sexual Abuse: A Journal of Research and Treatment.*

Keil, F. (1991). The emergence of theoretical beliefs as constraints on concepts. In S. Carey & R. Gelman (Eds.), *The epigenesis of mind: Essays on biology and cognition* (pp. 237–256). Hillsdale, NJ: Erlbaum.

Kuhn, D. (1989). Children and adults as intuitive scientists. *Psychological Bulletin, 96,* 674–689.

Malamuth, N. M., & Brown, L. M. (1994). Sexually aggressive men's perceptions of women's communications: Testing three explanations. *Journal of Personality and Social Psychology, 67,* 699–712.

Marshall, W. L. (1996). Assessment, treatment, and theorizing about sex offenders: Developments over the past 20 years and future directions. *Criminal Justice and Behavior, 23,* 162–199.

Marshall, W. L., & Barbaree, H. E. (1990). An integrated theory of the etiology of sexual offending. In W. L. Marshall, D. R. Laws, & H. E. Barbaree (Eds.), *Handbook of sexual assault: Issues, theories, and treatment of the offender* (pp. 257–275). New York: Plenum Press.

Meins, E., Fernyhough, C., Russell, J., & Clark-Carter, D. (1998). Security of attachment as a predictor of mentalizing abilities: A longitudinal study. *Social Development, 7,* 1–24.

Neidigh, L., & Krop, H. (1992). Cognitive distortions among child sexual offenders. *Journal of Sex Education and Therapy, 18,* 208–215.

Russell, D. E. H. (1995). The prevalence, trauma, and sociocultural causes of incestuous abuse of females: A human rights issue. In R. J. Klerer, C. R. Figley & B. P. Gersons (Eds.), *Beyond trauma: Cultural and societal dynamics.* New York: Plenum.

Sperber, D. (1996). *Explaining culture: A naturalistic approach.* London: Blackwell.

Strauss, C., & Quinn, N. (1997). *A cognitive theory of cultural meaning.* Cambridge, UK: Cambridge University Press.

Stermac, L. E., & Segal, Z. V. (1989). Adult sexual contact with children: An examination of the cognitive factors. *Behavior Therapy, 20,* 573–584.

Ward, T. (in press). Sexual offenders' cognitive distortions as implicit theories. *Aggression and Violent Behavior.*

Ward, T., Fon, C., Hudson, S. M., & McCormack, J. (1998). A descriptive model of dysfunctional cognitions in child molesters. *Journal of Interpersonal Violence, 13,* 129–155.

Ward, T., & Hudson, S. M. (1998). The construction and development of theory in the sexual offending area: A metatheoretical framework. *Sexual Abuse: A Journal of Research and Treatment, 10,* 47–63.

Ward, T., Hudson, S. M., Johnston, L., & Marshall, W. L. (1997). Cognitive distortions in sex offenders: An integrative review. *Clinical Psychology Review, 17,* 479–507.

Ward, T., Hudson, S. M., & Keenan, T. (1998). A self-regulation model of the sexual offense process. *Sexual Abuse: A Journal of Research and Treatment, 10,* 141–158.

Ward, T., Hudson, S. M., & Marshall, W. L. (1996). Attachment style in sex offenders: A preliminary study. *Journal of Sex Research, 33,* 17–26.

Ward, T., Hudson, S. M., Marshall, W. L., & Siegert, R. J. (1995). Attachment style and intimacy deficits in sexual offenders. *Sexual Abuse: A Journal of Research and Treatment, 7*, 317–335.

Ward, T., Keenan, T., & Hudson, S. M. (in press). Understanding cognitive, affective, and intimacy deficits in sexual offenders: A developmental perspective. *Aggression and Violent Behavior.*

Wellman, H. M. (1990). *The child's theory of mind.* Cambridge, MA: MIT Press.

16

Cultural Assumptions, Social Justice, and Mental Health: Challenging the Status Quo

Isaac Prilleltensky

While transnational corporations and powerful governments glorify the accomplishments of capitalism toward the end of the millennium (Dobbin, 1998), an ever increasing mass of people continues to suffer from injustice (Ransom, 1999) and mental health problems (Kramer, 1992). While public relations firms assist financial empires and world leaders to solidify their domination over most of the world's resources (Stauber & Rampton, 1995), suffering and disease proliferate because of lack of access to basic needs such as food, clothing, shelter, and medicine (Korten, 1995). While a few people become richer every year, more and more people become poorer and live in abject poverty (Ransom, 1999).

The architects of public opinion and the guardians of the status quo rely heavily on the creation and procreation of cultural assumptions that secure the hegemonic domination of power elites over most of the unsuspecting public (Rose, 1999). The public has come to accept the ideology of individualism, the invisible hand of the market, and the philosophy of competition as the new mantras of the twentieth century (Saul, 1995). Certain cultural assumptions about the good life and the good society and about social problems and solutions circumscribe the horizon of possibilities concerning what type of society we have, and what type of community we could devise for ourselves. Hegemonic notions regarding the "nature" of human beings limit our ability to imagine how societies might be improved.

This chapter is concerned with the role of certain cultural assumptions in mental health and social justice. The chapter has two main objectives, a descriptive and a prescriptive one. The first objective is to describe a model that explains the influence of cultural assumptions on distributive justice and mental health. The second aim is to prescribe certain steps for challenging cultural presuppositions that undermine both social justice and mental health. First, I present an overview of the model. Following that, I apply the model to the current state of affairs in Western societies. The third and final section offers ways of challenging the status quo.

OVERVIEW OF THE MODEL

The model consists of four main modules: cultural assumptions, social justice, resources, and mental health. As can be seen in Figure 16.1, cultural assumptions influence mental health directly and indirectly. I will claim below that cultural assumptions exert a direct influence on mental health via societal and psychological discourses, and an indirect influence via conceptions of social justice. Notions of social justice have an impact on the allocation of resources in society, a phenomenon with notable consequences for the mental health of the population. In short, certain cultural norms and discourses have a negative impact on the mental health of the population. These norms affect also the predominant conceptions of social justice, which, in turn, determine the distribution of resources in society, a key factor in the promotion of mental health. I explain below the different components of the model and how they interact with each other.

Cultural Assumptions

Cultural assumptions are the predominant conceptions about individuals and society that are almost taken for granted in a particular context. These are largely unquestioned presuppositions about what is proper, what is desirable, what the nature of human beings is, what a problem is, and what is possible in society. Cultural assumptions create and limit discourses about how human beings should interact with each other, how they should make a living, and about welfare, dependency, health, and safety. These assumptions penetrate daily conversations through newspaper reports, speeches by politicians, commentators, movies, and television.

Cultural assumptions respond to group interests; they are not formed in a vacuum. They serve the needs of those invested in perpetuating the societal status quo (Macedo, 1994). My usage of cultural assumptions here is reminiscent of Gramsci's concept of hegemony. The phenomenon of consent and conformity achieved by persuasion and cultural assumptions rather than force is what Gramsci (1971) called cultural hegemony. This concept is well summarized by Boggs (1976): "By hegemony Gramsci meant the permeation throughout civil society of an entire system of values, attitudes, beliefs, morality, etc., that is in one way or another supportive of the established order and the class interests that

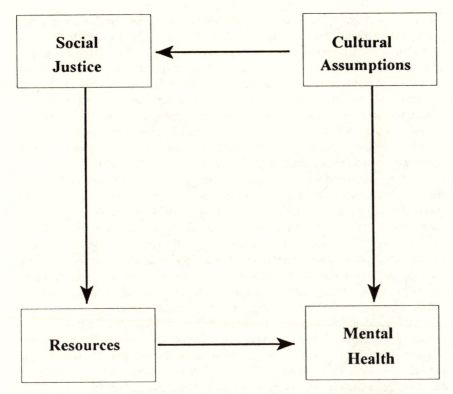

Figure 16.1. The direct and indirect impact of cultural assumptions on mental health.

dominate it" (p. 39). So successful is the hegemonic project in many societies that individuals need not be externally controlled to fit into the prescribed mold; they regulate themselves. As Rose (1999) put it:

Disciplinary techniques and moralizing injunctions as to health, hygiene and civility are no longer required; the project of responsible citizenship has been fused with individuals' projects for themselves. What began as a social norm here ends as a personal desire. Individuals act upon themselves and their families in terms of the languages, values and techniques made available to them by professions, disseminated through the apparatuses of the mass media (p. 88).

Cultural assumptions supportive of the societal status quo are spread through-out society in multiple ways. In this chapter I am concerned primarily with dissemination of hegemonic notions through societal and psychological discourses.

Societal Discourses. Cultural assumptions and hegemonic notions shape the contours of societal discourse about the good life and the good society. I use these two terms here because they embody many assumptions about popular conceptions of psychology, politics, sociology, and mental health. People hold implicit or explicit versions of the good life. Is the good life fostered by the accumulation of material possessions or by an ascetic life style? Do we find meaning in the spiritual enrichment found in close friendships or in incessant work? Do we value individualism and competition or sharing and collectivism? Each society prescribes and proscribes certain modes of thought and conduct through the media, and an ever increasing and sophisticated army of opinion makers helps in the process. As we shall see below, prevalent conceptions of the good society and the good life have serious and rather deleterious effects on the mental health of the powerless and the oppressed (Prilleltensky & Gonick, 1996).

Psychological Discourses. Without a doubt psychological discourse has penetrated almost every facet of life: the bedroom, the school, the hospital, the workplace, the family, the government (Prilleltensky, 1994). Psychological advice is sought to solve innumerable problems and psychologists dutifully respond to the call. But psychologists do not just answer the call to solve problems created by others. They themselves contribute to the very creation of social problems through an extensive lexicon of assessment, diagnosis, classification, treatment, rehabilitation, normalcy, deviancy, adjustment, and the like. The tools used by psychologists to define and solve problems contribute to cultural assumptions about the good and normal life. Melucci (1996) points out that the professionals entrusted with helping others activate a "chain reaction of diagnosis-therapy-new diagnosis which perpetuates our dependence on the experts. These processes tend to generate a widespread self-labelling process through which we internalize the criteria used in the external definition of our condition" (p. 85).

Societal discourses concerning the good life and the good society, as much as psychological discourses regarding problem definition and problem solutions, convey cultural assumptions about what is acceptable and unacceptable in society. In combination, they exert a powerful impact on mental health and social justice. If our prevalent notion of the good life is a life of competition and personal achievement, we should not be surprised that alienation, isolation, mindless consumerism, and lack of compassion characterize the social condition (Kohn, 1986; Sloan, 1996).

Distributive Justice

The way we define problems dictates the way we solve them. If we define justice as giving people what they deserve based on their merit, and if merit derives from education and opportunities in life, then we reward only those who had a chance to advance themselves.

Concepts of social justice include procedural, retributive, and distributive justice (Tyler, Boeckman, Smith, & Huo, 1997). Here I concentrate on distributive justice because it has direct implications for the allocation of resources in society, a phenomenon with multiple consequences for mental health (Zill, Moore, Wolpow Smith, Stief, & Coiro, 1995).

Distributive justice may be defined as the fair and equitable allocation of bargaining powers, resources, and obligations in society (Miller, 1978). Resources can be distributed according to various criteria, such as need, merit, or equality. It can be argued that under conditions of equality of opportunity, the principle of merit may apply. But an argument can be made that, under conditions of inequality, need is the more appropriate criterion. In other words, the social context determines to a large extent the most appropriate criterion. In a case where there are jobs for everyone, and all persons have adequate training to perform these jobs, it can be argued that people who work harder or who contribute more to the common good may be rewarded more than others. But if we live in a society where there are not enough jobs, and the jobs available are only for those who have a certain training, there are many people who remain unemployed despite their intentions to join the labor force. In such a case, it would be more adequate to distribute societal resources according to need in order to procure basic necessities for those who cannot provide for themselves.

Many societies adopt a mixed model of individual and social responsibility (Eichler, 1997). However, in many others, injustice is perpetuated by distributing resources almost exclusively according to merit, in gross disregard for the social needs of marginalized groups (George & Wilding, 1976; Miller, 1978). Distributive justice calls for the re-allocation of resources in order to attain a balance between the goods and opportunities of all social groups. Without an even distribution of social goods, other basic needs and rights such as health and self-determination cannot be fulfilled.

Notions of the good life and the good society, as well as definitions of personal problems, impinge on our conceptions of social justice. Our conceptions of distributive justice contribute, in turn, to the allocation of resources in society, a key determinant of mental health.

Resources

Resources can be material or psychological aids in the procurement of physical and emotional wellness. Material resources include food, clothing, shelter, and health care. Psychological resources include a secure attachment, social support, self-efficacy, nurturing relationships, social skills, and the like. Research has shown that access to both material and psychological resources can contribute significantly to the promotion of mental health (Prilleltensky, Nelson, & Peirson, 1999).

Access to resources is determined, to a large extent, by the model of justice employed in society. More and more Western societies are shying away from models of social responsibility that call upon the state to provide welfare for those who cannot provide for themselves (Griffin Cohen, 1997). Models of social or individual responsibility are dictated, in turn, by predominant cultural assumptions about the good life and the good society, about the worthy and unworthy citizen. These conceptions have an ultimate impact on mental health.

Mental Health

Mental health can be defined as a state of psychological wellness characterized by the satisfactory fulfilment of basic human needs (Prilleltensky, Nelson, & Peirson, 1999). Some of the basic needs for mental health include a sense of mastery, control, and self-efficacy; emotional support and secure attachment; cognitive stimulation; sense of community and belonging; respect for personal identity and dignity; and others (Basic Behavioral Science Task Force, 1996a, 1996b).

Individuals experience mental health and the fulfilment of basic needs depending on the resources available to families and communities (McLoyd, 1998). For some families, lack of food and money to pay the rent are major sources of stress. For others, this is not a problem at all. For those who lack basic resources, society's cultural assumptions about the poor are very important because these ideas can determine to what extent governments will supply basic necessities for the needy.

In summary, cultural assumptions exert a direct influence on mental health through definitions of the good life and the good society and through psychological definitions and solutions to problems. Notions of the good life derived from competition and individualism lead to social isolation and psychological stress. When these problems are defined in individualistic terms, the person is viewed as responsible for her or his suffering. But cultural assumptions also exert an indirect influence on mental health via society's definitions of social justice. The way we frame justice determines how we allocate resources, and the way we allocate resources has a direct impact on the mental health of the poor and the vulnerable (McLoyd, 1998). We turn now to an examination of how the model explains the actual state of affairs with regard to mental health and social justice.

ACTUAL STATE OF AFFAIRS

In this section, I will describe the current relationship between cultural assumptions, social justice, resources, and mental health in Western societies. I am most familiar with the North American context, but from readings and personal research I know that the situation is somewhat similar in other industrialized countries as well (Prilleltensky, Laurendeau, Chamberland, & Peirson, 1999). I will analyze now the state of affairs with regard to each one of the factors involved in the model. Following that I will show how they interact to produce powerful effects on the mental health of the population.

Cultural Assumptions

As noted in the overview of the model, cultural assumptions about what is acceptable and unacceptable in society are both created and promulgated by societal and psychological discourses. I will examine each one of these discourses in turn.

Societal Discourses. Predominant notions of what is the good life and the good society are enormously influenced by the culture of consumerism, hedonism, and individualism. It is no exaggeration to claim that advertising serves as the main guide of behavior for vast numbers of consumers who direct their lives according to the latest fashions and corporate dictates (Sloan, 1996). What to wear, where to dine, what car to drive, what credit card to use, what movie star to emulate, what politician to gossip about; all these aspects of life are managed by public relations firms specializing in impression management and marketing of artificially created needs (Stauber & Rampton, 1995).

For products to sell, producers need consumers who worry about how they look, what they drive, and where they shop. In short, they need people who adulate themselves. They need a culture of individualism where the self becomes the main preoccupation of consumers. Rather than citizens, they need consumers (Rose, 1999). The ideology of consumerism goes hand in hand with individualism. The person is the center of the world.

But the cultural assumptions of the market assault us in other ways as well. The marketers bombard the market with unhealthy products that distort our sense of well-being and that produce addictive behaviors. Under the banner of personal choice and responsible consumption, corporations invade our public space with images of violence, drugs for hyperactive children, and with a diet industry that leads to eating disorders. The cultural assumption that consumers are adults who can choose to watch or consume whatever they like provides a rationale for selling bogus diet products, tobacco, and for broadcasting thousands of scenes of violence and rape on television.

The ideological creation of the self-contained individual serves not only economic but political purposes as well (Cushman, 1990). From an economic point of view, the person as consumer is the fuel that drives the capitalist engine. From a political point of view, the individual is constructed as the source of both self-fulfilment and suffering. Success is attributed to personal merit, and misery to personal failure (Sarason, 1981). When problems befall individuals, it is primarily their personal responsibility to survive. They are on their own. The dominant cultural assumptions are that people are to help themselves, as if we are all the product of "personal" merit, disconnected from the help of others, or unaffected by opportunities (or lack thereof) afforded us by privilege or deprivation. Hence when suffering occurs, it is not at the political system that we turn our gaze, but rather inward, toward an exploration of personal deficits. Thus the culture of individualism does not only create suffering by fomenting fragmentation and competition, but it also leaves individuals to their own devices to overcome stress and pain.

Psychological Discourses. Mainstream psychology's view of the good life is also based on individualism and tacit acceptance, if not outright promotion, of the consuming citizen (Sampson, 1983; Sarason, 1981). Mainstream psychology successfully looks for and locates pathology within the individual or within the family (Cohen, 1990, 1994; Pilgrim, 1992). The search for personal deficits culminates, naturally, in person-centered interventions devoid of attention to power structures. These strategies lead, in turn, to victim-blaming definitions (Prilleltensky, 1994). Psychological problems tend to be reified into categories such as personality disorders, character flaws, or thought disturbances (Cohen, 1990, 1994). However prevalent mental health problems might be, they do not exist on their own, nor do they come out of thin air. Instead, they are connected to people's social support, employment status, housing conditions, history of discrimination, and overall personal and political power (Cohen, 1993, 1997; Mack, 1994; Prilleltensky, 1999a).

Working for social justice is the most foreign concept for mental health professionals (Albee, 1986; Cohen, 1997; Mack, 1994). Most of them can see how to advance autonomy and caring, even some measure of collaboration, but when it comes to social justice, mental health workers are at a loss. This is not because of lack of models, but rather because of a perennial, pervasive, and unjustified separation between their role as citizens and their role as professionals. Social justice, we are told, belongs in the private life of the psychiatrist or the psychologist, not in their professional role. In the end, psychologists adopt and propagate a discourse that locates pathology within individuals, that produces victim blaming, and that diverts attention from issues of social justice because it reduces social problems to issues of personal struggle (Fox, 1997).

In combination, societal and psychological discourses strengthen cultural assumptions regarding individualism, consumerism, and political illiteracy. Cultural assumptions regarding the good society revolve around individuals, not collectives. Thus we lack a discourse that examines social dilemmas in communitarian terms. It all starts and ends with atomized individuals removed from social contexts (Cushman, 1990; Sampson, 1999).

Distributive Justice

The spin doctors of globalization seem to have successfully erased the language of social justice from popular vocabulary (Leonard, 1997). Enormous and unprecedented gaps between the rich and the poor are described in technical, economic, and bureaucratic terms completely devoid of political connotations (Allahar & Côté, 1998). Somehow we have lost the language of social justice. Instead, we have gained the idolatry of econometrics and the consensual discourse of globalization. Words like exploitation, domination, and oppression are nowhere to be found in popular media, as if they vanished with the Berlin wall. Problems of profound injustice that are quintessentially the subject of politics and exploitation are transformed into technical problems to be fixed with better management of resources and more fiscal responsibility. Social justice is a nonissue in the mainstream media. It is only resistance groups that still use the language of justice. Unfortunately, their voice is inaudible amidst the cheer of system apologists.

Resources

The allocation of resources in society is tied to the concept of social justice. The predominant philosophy of individualism, self-interest, and survival of the fittest leads to a model of personal responsibility (Eichler, 1997). Society is not to blame for personal misfortune, which means that insufficient resources are a private matter. This model of individual responsibility has led many countries in the West to dismantle the welfare state. As a consequence, the poor and the disadvantaged have less access to basic necessities such as decent housing and proper medical care (Griffin Cohen, 1997).

A model of social responsibility would uphold the values of social justice, collectivism, cooperation, and solidarity. Under such philosophy, resources would be allocated according to need, but the reality is that many Western nations are retreating from this model. Some European countries like Denmark, Sweden, and Holland have retained this philosophy of social responsibility, thus ensuring the provision of adequate resources for the poor (Prilleltensky, Nelson, & Peirson, 1999).

Mental Health

The moment we define mental health as a state of affairs in which certain basic needs are met, it becomes clear that mental health is connected to resources. When psychological and material resources are present, chances are that mental health will ensue. When resources of either kind are scarce, chances are mental health will be poor. The ability of parents to satisfy children's need for love, secure attachments, empathy, and stimulation, is related to parents' mental health and levels of stress. Parents' mental health, in turn, is related to socioeconomic status and educational opportunities. In other words, parental and family wellness is related to community wellness, which includes elements such as safety, formal and informal supports, solidarity, cohesion, social services, and recreational facilities. Community wellness, in turn, depends on societal wellness, which is characterized by conditions of employment and economic security, decent housing, health insurance, democratic institutions, and a culture of peace (McLoyd, 1998; Prilleltensky, Nelson, & Peirson, 1999).

The problem with current definitions of mental health is that they concentrate on the person and neglect to take into account the interdependence of personal wellness with parental, family, community, and societal wellness. As a result of narrow definitions of mental health, we see an ever increasing number of people suffering from psychological problems. In Canada, for instance, which has been voted six years in a row by the United Nations as the best country in the world, it is estimated that 26 percent of children experience behavioral, learning, emotional, or social problems (Offord, Boyle, & Szatmari, 1987). In the province of Ontario, research has found that:

31% of men and 21.1% of women reported having been abused while growing up. Childhood sexual abuse was reported by 12.8% of women and 4.3% of men. Severe abuse was reported by 10.7% of men and 9.2% of women, and severe sexual abuse was reported by 11.1% of women and 3.9% of men (Brown, 1997, p. 867).

In the early '90s, Kramer (1992) documented what he called the pandemic of mental and emotional disorders, claiming that current global trends in poverty and family breakdown will result in unprecedented numbers of children and adults suffering from psychological problems. Using a rather conservative estimate of prevalence rate of 12 percent for mental, behavioral, and developmental disorders in children around the world, Kramer reported that:

the total number of cases of mental disorders in children under 18 years of age would increase from 237.8 million in 1990 to 261.5 in the year 2000, an increase of 10%. In the more developed regions the number of cases would increase from 37.8 million to 38.2 million (Kramer, 1992, p. 15).

According to the U.S. Institute of Medicine (1994), at least 12 percent of children "suffer from one or more mental disorders, including autism, attention deficit hyperactivity disorders, severe conduct disorder, depression, and alcohol and psychoactive substance abuse and dependence" (p. 487). The same source indicates that 20 percent of adults in the United States currently suffer from a psychiatric impairment, and 32 percent can be expected to develop such an illness during their lifetime.

These are alarming figures that call for a dramatic change in the way we deal with psychological problems. As I shall suggest below, two major changes that are required have to do with shifting the emphasis from treatment to prevention, and expanding the scope of care from the individual to the family, the community, and society as a whole. But for these transformations to take effect, the cultural assumptions that locate pathology strictly within the individual must be challenged.

CHALLENGING THE STATUS QUO

A philosophy of individualism rests at the core of many Western cultures. This credo has an impact on the mental health of the population by eroding a vital sense of community, fostering isolation, and limiting treatment to person centered approaches that obviate the need for social interventions. In addition, an individualistic mentality permeates constructions of social justice, leading to distributions of rewards based on personal merit alone, dismissing the value of other criteria such as need, inequality of opportunity, and disadvantage. In the absence of these criteria, and with an exclusive focus on personal merit, those who lack access to resources are blamed for their condition. Thus the poor and the oppressed suffer not only from lack of resources, but also from social accusations of laziness, incompetence, and exploitation of the system (Leonard, 1997; Rose, 1999; Wilson, 1996). Under these conditions of deprivation and stress, few people can escape negative mental health outcomes (Zill et al., 1995). In this section I challenge cultural assumptions of individualism, prevailing concepts of social justice, current allocations of resources, and, ultimately, the way we define and treat mental health problems.

Cultural Assumptions

Predominant conceptions of the good, the bad, and the unworthy are created in many cultural sites (Rose, 1999). As we have seen, two vehicles for the creation and proliferation of unquestioned cultural assumptions are societal and psychological discourses. I challenge each one in turn.

Societal Discourses. I have claimed elsewhere that bogus dichotomies between the needs of the individual and the needs of the community are pernicious to the mental health of the population (Prilleltensky, 1997). Philosophical schools of thought oppose liberalism, with its emphasis on the needs of the individual for freedom and choice, with communitarianism, which focuses on responsibility toward the common good. These binary classifications are abstractions that do not represent the actual needs of individuals in communities. In actuality, people require both rights and responsibilities to survive and coexist. A supreme obsession with personal gain leads to a distortion of self-determination into self-preoccupation, whereas relentless sacrifice for the good of the community leads to neglect of personal needs. In societies that exalt individualism we observe an erosion in the sense of community, whereas in communities that demand personal abnegation we notice a craving for individual liberties (Prilleltensky, 1997). This is an indication that what we need is a balance between values that uphold personal rights and needs, and values that protect the integrity of vital community structures (Prilleltensky, Laurendeau, Chamberland, & Peirson, 1999).

Whether we like it or not, our personal fate is linked to the fate of the common good. For instance, personal health depends on rules for environmental protection and on adequate budgets for national health insurance. The tenet that personal effort alone can lead to happiness is unfounded (Sampson, 1999). We all depend on others and on community structures like schools, sanitation systems, hospitals, housing standards, and civil society for survival and progress. The problem in many Western societies is that those who achieve success are invested in defining health as a personal matter, thereby absolving themselves of the need to pay taxes or contribute to the common good. Entire ideologies are built to justify the status quo, and individualism is at the root of most of them. For as long as neoliberal philosophies obscure the need for more communitarian social policies, we can expect a perpetuation of the dominant model of personal responsibility. The time has come to ask whose interests are protected and whose needs are neglected by the current neoliberal philosophies (O'Neill, 1994).

Psychological Discourses. Psychology has traditionally operated from an individualistic paradigm that defined and treated problems as atomized events inside people's minds. Even community psychology interventions, which are supposed to enlarge the scope of solutions, are primarily limited to person centered coping skills (Prilleltensky & Nelson, 1997). The dilemma resides in trying to frame human problems in interdisciplinary terms, but without giving up the allegiance to the mother discipline of psychology, which is ultimately very limiting in scope (Sampson, 1999; Sloan, 1996). New developments in critical psychology offer praxis frameworks for overcoming parochial epistemological and action approaches (Prilleltensky, 1999a).

There is a need to turn the gaze of psychology from the victim and the oppressed to the oppressor. Well-meaning professionals concentrate on the needs of the disadvantaged, and for good and valid reasons. But we also need to examine what the motivations are that lead so many people to exploit others economically and psychologically with impunity. Surely we need to empower the weak and the oppressed, but we equally need to depower the rich and the exploitive. Psychology should turn its gaze and explore not only "what is wrong" with the poor, but also "what is wrong" with the rich and the greedy and the oppressive. After all, many of these people are the guardians of injustice.

Social Justice

Challenging the status quo means reclaiming the language of social justice. A major victory for the apologists of globalization and capitalism must be the eradication of the term from social debate altogether. Instead, social ills are defined in terms of uncontrollable and unexpected economic turns, devoid of any political connotations or relation to structures of social injustice (Allahar & Côté, 1998). Unless we reintroduce the language of social justice in the public domain, and unless we challenge narrow conceptions of social justice based on merit, chances are psychological problems tied to disadvantage will deepen.

What we need is a process of conscientization. This concept, developed by the Brazilian educator Paulo Freire (1994), refers to the process whereby people attain an insightful awareness of socioeconomic, cultural, psychological, and political circumstances affecting their lives, and of their potential to transform that reality. Conscientization is achieved by the concurrent implementation of two tasks, namely denunciation and annunciation. While the former deconstructs ideological messages that distort people's awareness of oppressive conditions, the latter elaborates means of advancing emancipation and liberation.

Resources

Neoliberal and neoconservative governments alike have coopted the language of community development and have used it to reduce resources. Under the pretence that "empowered" communities can deal with their own problems, many governments gradually withdraw or privatize essential services such as health (Leonard, 1997). If the poor and the oppressed are to be protected from severe reductions in resources, governments must be challenged to retain essential services and restore those that have already been cut. Without vital resources, we cannot expect the mental health of the disadvantaged to improve.

Mental Health

Two challenges in promoting wellness and improving mental health are (1) to expand the definition and scope of interventions from the individual to community and societal levels of analysis, and (2) to shift the emphasis from treatment to prevention (Albee, 1986). The individualistic and reactive nature of psychological treatments is rooted in the cultural model of personal responsibility. Psychology is not and cannot be detached from the predominant values and cultural assumptions of our time. Although some researchers wish psychology could render "neutral empirical and theoretical truth" (Kendler, 1993, p. 1046), such an ideal is unattainable.

In critical psychology, mental health problems are framed in holistic terms that take into account the psychological, social, and economic circumstances surrounding a person's life (Prilleltensky, 1999b). Mental health problems are examined in light of social and interpersonal factors oppressing and disempowering the individual. Critical psychology interventions strive to equalize power in a person's life and in society as a whole. Psychology must pursue justice in a person's life and in societal structures at the same time (Fox & Prilleltensky, 1997; Prilleltensky, 1999a). Only then can we hope to challenge cultural assumptions that are inimical to mental health and social justice.

REFERENCES

Albee, G. W. (1986). Toward a just society: Lessons from observations on the primary prevention of psychopathology. *American Psychologist, 41,* 891–898.

Allahar, A. L., & Côté, J. E. (1998). *Richer and poorer.* Toronto, Canada: Lorimer.

Basic Behavioral Science Task Force of the National Advisory Mental Health Council. (1996a). Basic behavioral science research for mental health: Family processes and social networks. *American Psychologist, 51,* 622–630.

Basic Behavioral Science Task Force of the National Advisory Mental Health Council. (1996b). Basic behavioral science research for mental health: Vulnerability and resilience. *American Psychologist, 51,* 22–28.

Boggs, C. (1976). *Gramsci's Marxism.* London: Pluto Press.

Brown, C. (1997). Child abuse survey stuns Ontarians. *Canadian Medical Association Journal, 157,* 867.

Cohen, D. (Ed.). (1990). Challenging the therapeutic state: Critical perspectives on psychiatry and the mental health system. [Special issue]. *Journal of Mind and Behavior, 11*(3/4).

Cohen, C. (1993). Poverty and the course of schizophrenia: Implications for research and policy. *Hospital and Community Psychiatry, 44,* 951–958.

Cohen, D. (Ed.). (1994). Challenging the therapeutic state, part two: Further disquisitions on the mental health system. [Special issue]. *Journal of Mind and Behavior, 15*(1/2).

Cohen, C. (1997). The political and moral economy of mental health. *Psychiatric Services, 48,* 768–774.

Cushman, P. (1990). Why the self is empty: Toward a historically situated psychology. *American Psychologist, 45,* 599–611.

Dobbin, M. (1998). *The myth of the good corporate citizen: Democracy under the rule of big business.* Toronto, Canada: Stoddart.

Eichler, M. (1997). *Family shifts: Families, policies, and gender equality.* Toronto, Canada: Oxford University Press.

Fox, D. (1997). Psychology and law: Justice diverted. In D. Fox & I. Prilleltensky (Eds.), *Critical psychology: An introduction* (pp. 217–232). London: Sage.

Fox, D., & Prilleltensky, I. (Eds.). (1997). *Critical psychology: An introduction.* London: Sage.

Freire, P. (1994). *Pedagogy of the oppressed* (Rev. ed.). New York: Continuum.

George, V., & Wilding, P. (1976). *Ideology and social welfare.* Boston, MA: Routledge & Kegan Paul.

Gramsci, A. (1971). *Selections from the prison notebooks.* London: Lawrence & Wishart.

Griffin Cohen, M. (1997). From the welfare state to vampire capitalism. In P. M. Evans & G. R. Wekerle (Eds.), *Women and the Canadian welfare state* (pp. 28–67). Toronto, Canada: University of Toronto Press.

Kendler, H. H. (1993). Psychology and the ethics of social policy. *American Psychologist, 48,* 1046–1053.

Kohn, A. (1986). *No contest: The case against competition.* Boston: Houghton Mifflin.

Korten, D. (1995). *When corporations rule the world.* San Francisco: Berrett-Koheler.

Kramer, M. (1992). Barriers to the primary prevention of mental, neurological, and psychological disorders of children: A global perspective. In G. W. Albee, L. A. Bond, & T. V. Cook Monsey (Eds.), *Improving children's lives: Global perspectives on prevention* (pp. 3–36). Hanover, NH: University Press of New England.

Leonard, P. (1997). *Postmodern welfare: Reconstructing an emancipatory project.* London: Sage.

Macedo, D. (1994). *Literacies of power.* Boulder, CO: Westview.

Mack, J. E. (1994). Power, powerlessness, and empowerment in psychotherapy. *Psychiatry, 57,* 178–198.

McLoyd, V. C. (1998). Socioeconomic disadvantage and child development. *American Psychologist, 53,* 185–204.

Melucci, A. (1996). *The playing self: Person and meaning in the planetary society.* New York: Cambridge University Press.

Miller, D. (1978). *Social justice.* Oxford, UK: Clarendon.

Offord, D., Boyle, M., & Szatmari, P. (1987). Ontario Child Health Study, II: Six month prevalence of disorder and rates of service utilization. *Archives of General Psychiatry, 44,* 832–836.

O'Neill, J. (1994). *The missing child in liberal theory.* Toronto, Canada: University of Toronto Press.

Pilgrim, D. (1992). Psychotherapy and political evasions. In W. Dryden & C. Feltham (Eds.), *Psychotherapy and its discontents* (pp. 225–242). Bristol, PA: Open University Press.

Prilleltensky, I. (1994). *The morals and politics of psychology: Psychological discourse and the status quo.* Albany, NY: State University of New York Press.

Prilleltensky, I. (1997). Values, assumptions, and practices: Assessing the moral implications of psychological discourse and action. *American Psychologist, 47,* 517–535.

Prilleltensky, I. (1999a). Critical psychology praxis. In M. Montero (Ed.), *La Psicologia al fin del siglo [Psychology at the end of the century]* (pp. 279–304). Caracas, Venezuela: Sociedad Interamericana de Psicologia.

Prilleltensky, I. (1999b). Critical psychology foundations for the promotion of mental health. *Annual Review of Critical Psychology, 1,* 95–110.

Prilleltensky, I., & Gonick, L. (1996). Polities change, oppression remains: On the psychology and politics of oppression. *Political Psychology, 17,* 127–147.

Prilleltensky, I., Laurendeau, M.C., Chamberland, C., & Peirson, L. (1999). Vision and values for child and family wellness. In I. Prilleltensky, G. Nelson, & L. Peirson (Eds.), *Promoting family wellness and preventing child maltreatment: Fundamentals for thinking and action.* Book submitted for publication.

Prilleltensky, I., & Nelson, G. (1997). Community psychology: Reclaiming social justice. In D. Fox & I. Prilleltensky (Eds.), *Critical psychology: An introduction* (pp. 166–184). London: Sage.

Prilleltensky, I., Nelson, G., & Peirson, L. (Eds.). (1999). *Promoting family wellness and preventing child maltreatment.* Book submitted for publication.

Ransom, D. (1999, May). The dictatorship of debt. *New Internationalist, 312,* 7–10.

Rose, N. (1999). *Powers of freedom.* New York: Cambridge University Press.

Sampson, E. E. (1983). *Justice and the critique of pure psychology.* New York: Plenum.

Sampson, E. E. (1999). Liberating psychology. In M. Montero (Ed.), *La Psicologia al fin del siglo [Psychology at the end of the century]* (pp. 305–322). Caracas: Sociedad Interamericana de Psicologia.

Sarason, S. B. (1981). *Psychology misdirected.* New York: Free Press.

Saul, J. R. (1995). *The unconscious civilization.* Concord, Ontario, Canada: Anansi.

Sloan, T. (1996). *Damaged life: The crisis of the modern psyche.* London: Routledge.

Stauber, J., & Rampton, S. (1995). *Toxic sludge is good for you.* Monroe, ME: Common Courage Press.

Tyler, T. R., Boeckman, R. J., Smith, H. J., & Huo, Y. J. (1997). *Social justice in a diverse society.* Boulder, CO: Westview Press.

U. S. Institute of Medicine (1994). *Reducing risks for mental disorders: Frontiers for preventive intervention research.* Washington, DC: National Academy of Science.

Wilson, M. (1996). Citizenship and welfare. In M. Lavalette & A. Pratt (Eds.), *Social policy* (pp. 182–195). London: Sage.

Zill, N., Moore, K. A., Wolpow Smith, E., Stief, T., & Coiro, M. J. (1995). The life circumstances of children in welfare families: A profile based on national survey data. In P. L. Chase Landsdale & J. Brooks-Gunn (Eds.), *Escape from poverty: What makes a difference for children?* (pp. 38–59). New York: Cambridge University Press.

Index

Acculturation, 91, 96, 164, 199, 205
Action research, 13
Acute stress disorder, 67
Alcohol abuse, 72, 81–94, 260
Alcoholics Anonymous, 8–10
Alexithymia: culture and, 69–70, 77
Alienation, 63, 254, 258
Alogia, 173
Altered states of consciousness, 73
Ambition, 45
American society, 22, 45–46
Amnesia, 158, 162
Amok, 69, 201–2
Anger, 55–56, 109, 164, 183, 201, 203–5;
    depression and, 55–56
Angst, 63, 68, 222
Anomie, 152
Anorexia nervosa, 95–105
Anthropological theory, 21–22
Antidepressant medication, 53
Antisocial personality disorder, 26–28,
    44–45, 148–9, 151
Anxiety, 11–12, 54, 61, 67–79, 131, 138,
    151, 200, 214; cognitive theory and,
    225–8; cultural cognition and,
    219–25; social, 145; substance abuse
    and, 67
Apathy, 176

Aphasia, 177
Art, 12, 77
Artificial intelligence, 20, 216
Asceticism: eating disorders and, 102
Assessment techniques, 6, 10–11
Astrological therapies, 137–138
Ataque de nervios, 222
Attention biases, 19
Attention-seeking, 45
Attributions: illness and, 63–64
Autism, 183
Avolition: schizophrenia and, 173, 179
Ayurveda therapies, 138

Behavior therapy, 76–77; cultural consid-
    erations in, 196–8
Biological determinism, 46
Biomedical disorders, 12
Bipolar disorder, 68
Borderline personality disorder, 44–45,
    148–9, 151
Brain fog, 222
Bulimia nervosa, 95–105

Capitalism, 124, 251, 257
Capitalist society, 40
Caste-contamination, 124
Catastrophic ideation, 11–12

Catatonia, 171, 185
Chewong people of Malaysia, 185
Child abuse, 28, 108–14, 128, 134, 158–9, 162, 164–5, 233–48
Cocaine, 86, 89
Cognitive causal chains, 20–22
Cognitive denial, 12–13
Cognitive dualism, 131
Cognitive judgments: anxiety and, 72
Cognitive reductionism, 19
Cognitive socialization, 58, 60
Cognitive theory, 213–32
Cognitive therapy, 10–12, 73–75, 194–95; eating disorders and, 95–96, 102–103; limitations of, 10, 63–64; trauma and, 129–30, 134
Cognitive vulnerability: depression and, 60–63
Collectivism, 109, 111–12, 227; society and, 254, 259; trauma and, 124–29
Communication: symbolic, 10–11
Community psychology, 13
Comorbidity: in anxiety, 71–72
Competition: society and, 251, 254–7
Compulsive disorders, 145
Conduct disorder, 260
Conformity, 127
Conscientization, 262
Consciousness, 41–43; consumer society and, 62
Consumer culture, 61–62, 251, 256–8
Core beliefs, 55, 96, 242, 247
Crime, 152, 245
Critical psychology, 263
Crosscultural psychology, 8–9, 26, 32–33, 35, 56, 69, 74, 95, 98, 120, 146–9, 171–2, 181–2, 193, 215, 221, 224, 228
Cultural accommodation: psychotherapy and, 194–5, 198
Cultural anthropology, 18–19, 35, 41, 216
Cultural assumptions, 251–4, 256–8, 260–3
Cultural attachment, 163–5
Cultural beliefs, 159, 165
Cultural cleansing: depression and, 54–55
Cultural cognition, 7–12, 17, 32–33, 215, 219; anxiety and, 67–79, 219–25;

consciousness and, 41; depression and, 54–66; dissociative disorders and, 157–69; eating disorders and, 95–105; implicit theories and, 233–46; motivation and, 41–44; personality disorders and, 145–56; postnatal type, 56–57; psychoanalysis and, 42; psychological immunity and, 58; psychotherapy and, 193–208; schizophrenia and, 171–89; sexual abuse and, 107–119; social justice and, 251–65; substance abuse and, 81–94; symptom formation and, 233–50; theoretical perspectives on, 213–27; theories of, 20–22; trauma and, 119–143
Cultural disintegration, 87, 91
Cultural diversity, 218–19, 228
Cultural images, 42
Cultural insights, 13, 227
Cultural pathology, 63–64, 73, 253–63
Cultural relativism, 32
Cultural schemas, 20–21, 24, 43, 157, 160
Cultural selfways, 100
Cultural suggestion, 55
Cultural transmission, 17, 21, 26, 218–19, 237
Culturally informed assessment interview, 198–204
Culture: as pathogen, 73; as preventive agent, 73; biology and, 214–16, 218–19, 223, 225, 227; cognitive theory and, 213–32; discursive self–positioning and, 11–12; dissociation and, 157–66; evolutionary theory and, 217–18; individualistic, 256–7; inoculating effects of, 163–5; knowledge and, 41–42; models of, 22–23; modularity of mind and, 217; personality and, 145–47; psychotherapy and, 193–208; sanctioned dissociation and, 73; theory and, 41
Culture-bound disorders, 69, 201, 222, 227

Death, 43, 59, 76, 124, 128, 162, 186, 201
Delusions, 68, 158, 171, 177, 183
Dementia, 227
Demonological therapies, 131

Dependent personality disorder, 44–45
Depression, 44, 68, 71–72, 76, 100, 214, 234; cognitive models of, 55; cultural cognition and, 53–66; increasing prevalence of, 53; internalization and, 56; non-Western expressions, 54–55; predisposing cultural factors and, 60–63, 260
Depression-resistance, 55–60
Desensitization theory, 77
Despair, 63, 100
Desymbolization, 11–12
Determinism, 9–10, 131–3
Dhat syndrome, 222
Diet industry, 256–7
Dietary customs, 127
Discursive possibilities, 11
Disempowerment, 12–13
Dissociation, 73, 77
Dissociative capacity, 161–2
Dissociative disorders: cultural cognition and, 157–69
Dissociative identity disorder, 157–69; as response to trauma, 159, 162–3; crosscultural variations in, 159–60, 218–19; cultural beliefs and, 159; cultural determinants of, 161–65; cultural inoculation against, 163–5; dissociative capacity and, 161–2; family dynamics and, 165; interpersonal aspects of, 159; maltreatment of children and, 159, 162; neurological variations and, 166; religion and, 157–8; sociocognitive model of, 165–6; trauma-ladenedness and, 163
Distributive justice, 254–5, 258; mental health and, 255
Divorce, 71
Domain specificity, 183–5
Dreams, 76
Dysphoria, 58

Eating disorders, 59; asceticism and, 102; attributional theory and, 101; causal attributions and, 98; cognitive theories of, 97–98; cultural cognition and, 95–105; cultural schemas and, 99–102; negative self-beliefs and, 97; sexual liberation and, 99; vulnerability to, 98, 101; women and, 98–99;
Economic exploitation, 12
Ego, 127
Electroconvulsive therapy, 135
Emotion, 61, 72, 109, 147, 151, 176, 184, 186, 227, 241, 255–6, 259–60; culture theory and, 213; dissociation and, 157; dysfunction and, 44–45; externalization of, 55–56; language and, 68; overregulation of, 63; pathological, 10; schizophrenia and, 171, 178; social support and, 164; suffering and, 13; trauma and, 121, 124, 129–31
Empiricism, 3
Enmeshment: ego and, 44
Entitlement: sexual offending and, 240–1, 247
Ethnic conflict, 13
Ethnocentrism, 13
Ethnocultural cognitions, 165
Ethnography, 19
Ethnomusicology, 22–23
Evolutionary psychology, 181–3, 187, 217–8, 220, 222, 225
Existential disorders, 131–2
Existential-humanistic theory, 5
Exorcism, 59

False needs: depression and, 62
Families, role of, 70, 122–3, 126–7, 147, 149–52, 165, 195, 199, 204, 259
Family pathology, 152
Fang people of Cameroon, 186
Fantasies, 9
Fatalism, 112, 132
Fatigue, 57
Fear, 12, 71, 138, 164, 183, 201, 221–3
Fertility rites, 24
Free will, 131–2
Fugue, 162
Functional analysis, 193–208
Funeral rites, 122–4, 130

Gang-warfare, 162
Genetic factors, 26
Gestalts, experiential, 41
Ghost-induced illness, 74, 134, 186

Goal-directed systems, 41
Goddesses, 42–43, 128
Grandiosity, 45
Greed, 262
Grief, 77, 124
Guilt, 100, 222

Hallucinations, 171, 173, 184, 186
Havik Brahmins, 58–59
Healing rites, 85–86, 90
Hedonism, 60–61, 256–7
Hermeneutics, 12
Heroin, 86
Hinduism, 43, 121–24, 137
Histrionic personality, 44
Hmong refugees, 71
Homicidal behavior, 27
Hopi Indians, 39
Hunter-gatherer societies, 26–27
Hysteria, 69

Identity, 38, 63
Illusion tests, 33–34
Image management, 63
Immunizing cognitions, 57, 92
Implicit theories: sexual abuse and,
    233–46
Impulsivity, 145, 147, 149, 176
Incest, 241
Indigenous psychotherapy, 195–6
Individualism, 3–16, 59–61, 108, 195,
    217, 256–62; actuarial, 6; depression
    and, 55–56; decline of, 216; hege-
    monic, 7; mental health and, 258–9;
    methodological, 5–6; psychological
    theory and, 13; sexual offending and,
    234, 241; social justice and, 253–4,
    261; theoretical, 5; trauma and,
    124–29; Western, 5–6
Inductive fallacy trap, 123
Initiation rites, 28
Injustice, social, 13
Inquiry, domains of, 32
Installation ceremonies, 24
Intellectual universe, 36
Interactionism, 20
Interdisciplinary approaches, 10–11
Internet, 8

Interpersonal processes, 10–11
Intersubjective processes, 12–13
Intrapsychic processes, 10–11
Inuit Indians of Canada, 152

Jealousy, 12

Kaluli people of New Guinea, 34, 55–56
Karma, 132
Kava, 88
Kayak angst, 222
Kipsigis people of Kenya, 56–57
Koro, 222

Language, 7, 10, 22–23, 34–41, 180,
    182–3, 197, 199; anxiety expression
    and, 68, 77; culture theory and, 215;
    psychotherapy and, 195; social jus-
    tice and, 258
Latah, 69
Life-history approaches, 11, 22
Life satisfaction: materialism and, 61–62
Linguistic theories, 10
Linguistics, 38–41, 127
Logic: temporal understanding and, 41
Loneliness, 204
Love, 12

Machismo, 112
Mania, 44
Marriage, 9, 11–12, 58–59, 130, 150
Materialism, 3, 124, 133, 136; mental
    health and, 61–62; social justice and,
    251, 257
Meaning: cognition and, 8–9, 19, 194
Media: society and, 257–8
Medical model, 84
Meditation, 206
Memory, 7, 18, 22, 24, 28, 107, 176–7,
    179
Mental illness: cultural psychology and,
    44–46, 260
Metaphorical structures, 41
Mnemonic triggers, 18
Modernity: depression and, 60–63
Modularity of mind, 217
Monocultural societies, 90
Morality, 83, 121, 124, 132

Morita therapy, 195
Mormon religion, 86
Motivation: cultural cognition and, 41–44, 108

Narcissism, 44–45
Narrative constructions, 6–7
Navajo Indians, 203
Neurasthenia, 69, 199–200
Normlessness, 150

Obsessive-compulsive disorder, 11, 67, 70
Ontological questions, 40
Opium, 86, 89
Oppression, 12; society, 254, 258

Panic disorder, 67, 69, 72, 222
Paranoia, 44, 68, 145, 171, 182–4, 186
Passivity, 45
Pathoplasticity: anxiety disorders and, 68–69
Peer influence, 146, 205
Penobscot Indians, 101
Perceptual mechanisms, 22, 33–35, 38, 63, 120, 220
Personality disorders, 26–28, 44, 258; crosscultural variations in, 147–9, 153; cultural cognition and, 145–56; family and, 150–1; interpersonal relationships and, 148; modernity and, 151–2; overprotective parenting and, 151; social disintegration and, 151–2; social roles and, 149–50; social structures and, 149–50, 258
Personality judgments, 36
Personality theories, 145–47
Personality traits, 27, 120, 128, 145–6
Phenomenological perspectives, 8–9
Phobias, 67–70, 77, 151, 220–1, 223
Political activism, 13
Pornography, 110, 238
Positivism, 133–4
Possession states, 59, 73, 158, 160
Postmodernism, 13, 150–2
Postnatal depression, 56–57
Poststructuralism, 7–8, 17
Posttraumatic stress disorder, 67, 72, 126, 131–2, 166

Poverty, society and, 13, 251, 259
Prevention strategies, 109
Processing mechanisms, 20
Prostitution, 122–23, 134
Psychoactive substances, 260; perceptions of, 85–87, 89–90, 92
Psychoanalysis, 5, 32, 41–43
Psychodynamic therapies, 10–11, 75
Psychological Anthropology, 11–12
Psychosensory capacities, 73
Psychotherapy, 63, 73–77, 160, 191–212, 254, 260; Buddhist approach to, 206; client's perceptions and, 199; cultural accommodation in, 194–5; cultural considerations in, 196–7; cultural observations and, 191–212; eating disorders and, 102–103; emic and etic aspects of, 195–6; ethnic minorities and, 194, 199; functional analytic approach to, 196–8, 202–4; sexual offending and, 246–8; substance abuse and, 90–92; trauma and, 129, 134–8
Psychotic disorders, 127–8
Psychotropic drugs, 135

Rape victims, 69, 108
Rational-emotive therapy, 129
Rationalism, 3
Reasoning, 7–8
Refugee children, 164
Reinforcement contingencies, 120
Relatedness needs: depression and, 62
Relativism, 215
Religion, 23–26, 62–63, 77, 121–22, 124, 126–27, 130–32, 146, 242; cultural cognition and, 62; depression and, 58–59; dissociation and, 158, 160; eating disorders and, 102; fundamentalistic, 12; psychotherapy and, 136–7, 195, 206; ritual and, 25; schizophrenia and, 184; substance abuse and, 86–87; trauma and, 120–37
Repression, 56
Ritual, 57, 128, 195–6
Ritualized terrorism, 28

Schemas, 8, 12, 20, 25, 35–36, 41–46, 60, 62, 99–102, 107, 157, 160, 220–1

Schizophrenia, 46, 53, 68, 158, 205, 214;
    biological basis of, 171, 174–5, 187;
    classification of, 172–4; crosscultural
    variations in, 174–5, 181–2; cultural
    cognition and, 171–89; domain
    specificity and, 183–5, 187; evolu-
    tionary perspectives on, 180, 182–3;
    executive functioning and, 176–7;
    intellectual impairment and, 177;
    interpersonal difficulties and, 183;
    memory and, 176–7; premorbid fac-
    tors in, 176; representational thinking
    and, 178–9; role of attention in,
    175–6; role of language in, 177–8,
    180; theory of mind and, 185–6; uni-
    versality of, 174, 184
Self, 11, 108–109, 111, 223, 228, 234;
    cognitive theory and, 225–7; post-
    modern, 13
Self-construal strategies, 60–61, 111
Self-esteem, 59, 61, 99–101, 129, 200,
    204, 223–4
Self-serving biases, 101
Self-understandings, 12
Selfways: eating disorders and, 100–101
Semantic relations, 21
Sensory perception, 31–33
Sexual abuse, 107–15; as societal prob-
    lem, 107, 260; child sexual education
    and, 111; collectivism and, 108–112;
    cultural cognition and, 107–118; cul-
    tural differences and, 107–114, 240;
    entitlement and, 240–1; ethnicity
    and, 108–109, 114; implicit theories
    and, 233–50; peer pressure and, 111;
    perception of victims and, 113–14;
    perception of women and, 112; pun-
    ishment of, 114; role of father and,
    112; treatment of, 115, 246–8; within
    cultural variability of, 112–115
Sexual aggression, 107–114, 233–37
Sexual liberation: eating disorders and, 99
Shinkeishitsu, 69, 73
Sleep deprivation, 24
Sleep disorders, 59, 71
Social anxiety, 145
Social buffering, 150
Social change, 13, 151–2, 260–263

Social disintegration, 151–2
Sociality: cooperation and, 27
Social justice: cultural assumptions and,
    251–4, 256–8, 260–2; individualism
    and, 251–61; materialism and, 251,
    257–8; media and, 257–8; mental
    health and, 251–63; needed improve-
    ments to, 260–3
Social learning, 145
Social orders, 13, 149–50, 251–63
Social phobia, 69–71, 77, 151, 223–4
Social reciprocity: depression and, 56
Social relations: commercialization of,
    61–62
Social support, 61–62, 129, 151, 163–5,
    204
Social taboos, 221
Social theory: cognition and, 17–19
Somatic symptoms, 58, 73
Spirit possession, 59, 73, 158, 160
Spiritualism, 133–4
Statistical psychology, 13
Stress, 54, 57, 61, 67, 77, 149–51, 204,
    239, 257; dissociation and, 161–2,
    166; trauma and, 128, 132
Subjectivity, 4
Substance abuse, 67–68, 72, 148; accul-
    turation and, 91; adolescence and,
    83; cultural cognition and, 81–94;
    cultural disintegration and, 87, 91;
    cultural identification and, 91; cul-
    tural norms and, 87–89; cultural vari-
    ations in, 83–89; ethnocultural
    differences and, 81–82; protective
    cognitions and, 92; theoretical mod-
    els of, 82–85
Suggestion process, 157
Suicide, 61, 100, 148–9, 152
Supernatural alters, 158
Syllogisms, 36–37
Symbolism, 35, 42, 197

Taijin Kyofusho, 222, 224, 227
Terrorism, 28, 162
Theory of mind: schizophrenia and, 185–6
Thought disorders, 258
Tic disorders, 207
Time, 130

Toraja people of Indonesia, 56
Trance, 73
Trauma, 13, 72–73, 247; actual versus
    perceived, 162–3; as neurological
    response, 159; child abuse and,
    128–9; cognitive appraisal and, 120;
    crosscultural variations in, 121,
    124–5, 130, 163; cultural attachment
    and, 163–5; cultural cognition and,
    119–43; culture specific, 121–4; dis-
    sociation and, 157, 161–3; emic–etic
    debate and, 123; emotionalism and,
    130–31; inductive fallacy and, 123;
    non-Western expressions of, 126;
    role of family in, 165; social support
    and, 163–5; socially sanctioned, 162;
    stress and, 128–9
Trauma cultures, 162
Tribal rituals, 24

Unconscious processes, 11, 42, 120, 129,
    161, 220
Universalism, 125, 166, 215, 224

Values, 9, 92, 111, 120–21, 138, 150,
    160–2, 164, 197, 214, 227–8, 234,
    236, 247, 263
Vedantic thought, 133
Victimization, 72–73, 107–109, 111, 114,
    242–5, 262
Violence: culture and, 27–28, 61, 110–11,
    114, 162, 201, 237
Volition: trauma and, 166

War: trauma and, 164

Yoga therapy, 136

About the Editors and Contributors

JOHN F. SCHUMAKER is Senior Lecturer in Clinical Psychology at the University of Canterbury in Christchurch, New Zealand.

TONY WARD is Associate Professor of Psychology and coordinator of the forensic doctoral program in the Department of Criminology at the University of Melbourne, Australia.

Myra Cooper, Research Tutor, Oxford Regional Training Course in Clinical Psychology, Warneford Hospital, Oxford, UK.

Eric Dieperink, Assistant Professor of Psychiatry, University of Minnesota; and Staff Psychiatrist, Minneapolis VA Medical Center, Minneapolis, Minnesota.

Martin J. Dorahy, Department of Psychology, University of New England, Armidale, NSW, Australia; and Cannon Institute, Belmont Private Hospital, Brisbane, Queensland, Australia.

Russil Durrant, Department of Psychology, University of Canterbury, Christchurch, New Zealand.

Gordon C. Nagayama Hall, Professor of Psychology, Department of Psychology, Pennsylvania State University, University Park, Pennsylvania.

Thomas Keenan, Senior Lecturer in Psychology, Department of Psychology, University of Canterbury, Christchurch, New Zealand.

Ka Nei Lam, Department of Psychology, Hofstra University, Hempstead, New York.

Pittu Laungani, Professor of Psychology, Department of Psychology, South Bank University, London, England.

Charles Nuckolls, Professor of Anthropology, and Director of the Blount Initiative, University of Alabama, Tuscaloosa, Alabama.

Joel Paris, Professor and Chair, Department of Psychiatry, McGill University; and Research Associate, Sir Mortimer B. Davis Jewish General Hospital, Montreal, Canada.

Amber H. Phung, Department of Psychology, Pennsylvania State University, University Park, Pennsylvania.

Isaac Prilleltensky, Professor of Psychology, Victoria University, Melbourne, Australia.

Douglas Y. Seiden, Department of Psychology, Hofstra University, Hempstead, New York.

Richard J. Siegert, Senior Lecturer and Head of Clinical Psychology, Department of Psychology, Victoria University, Wellington, New Zealand.

Tod Sloan, Professor and Chair of Psychology, Department of Psychology, University of Tulsa, Tulsa, Oklahoma.

Junko Tanaka-Matsumi, Professor of Psychology, Department of Psychology, Hofstra University, Hempstead, New York.

M. Dawn Terrell, Associate Professor of Psychology, San Francisco State University, San Francisco, California.

Jo Thakker, Department of Psychology, University of Canterbury, Christchurch, New Zealand.

Joseph Westermeyer, Professor of Psychiatry, University of Minnesota; and Chief of Psychiatry, Minneapolis VA Medical Center, Minneapolis, Minnesota.

Harvey Whitehouse, Reader of Anthropology, Department of Anthropology, Queen's University, Belfast, Northern Ireland.

DATE DUE

DEC 14 2012		
IDEC 03 2012		
GAYLORD		PRINTED IN U.S.A.